INDIA'S NORTH-EAST: DEVELOPMENTAL ISSUES IN A HISTORICAL PERSPECTIVE

Centre de Sciences Humaines (Centre for Social Sciences and Humanities): Created in New Delhi in 1989 the CSH, is part of network of research centres of the French Ministry of Foreign Affairs. The Centre's research work is primarily oriented towards the study of issues concerning the contemporary dynamics of development in India and South Asia. The activities of the Centre are focused on four main themes, namely: Economic transition and sustainable development, political dynamics, institutional set-up and social transformations, regional dynamics in South Asia and international relations International and regional relations, Institutional structures and political constructions of identity and urban dynamics.

Centre de Sciences Humaines, 2 Aurangzeb Road, New Delhi 110011, India, Tel: (91) 11 3041 00 70, Fax: (91) 11 3041 00 79
E-mail: public@csh-delhi.com
Website: http://www.csh-delhi.com

Institut Français de Pondichéry (French Institute of Pondicherry): Created in 1955, the IFP is a multidisciplinary research and advanced educational institute. Major research works are focusing on Sanskrit and Tamil Languages and literatures—in close collaboration with the Ecole Française d'Extrême-Orient—ecosystems, biodiversity and sustainability, dynamics of population and socio-economic development.

Institute Français de Pondichéry, 11 Saint Louis Street, PB 33, Pondicherry 605001, Tel: (91) 413 2334 168, Fax: (91) 413 2339 534
E-mail: ifpdir@ifpindia.org
Website: http://www.ifpindia.org

Disclaimer: The views expressed in this publication are those of the respective authors and are not necessarily endorsed by the Centre de Sciences Humaines or any other institution to which the authors may belong.

India's North-East Developmental Issues in a Historical Perspective

Edited by
ALOKESH BARUA

MANOHAR

CENTRE DE SCIENCES HUMAINES
2005

First published 2005

© Individual contributors, 2005

All rights reserved. No part of this publication may be reproduced or transmitted, in any form or by any means, without prior permission of the editor and the publisher

ISBN 81-7304-639-5

Published by
Ajay Kumar Jain for
Manohar Publishers & Distributors
4753/23 Ansari Road, Daryaganj
New Delhi 110 002

Typeset by
Kohli Print
Delhi 110 051

Printed at
Lordson Publishers Pvt. Ltd.
New Delhi 110 007

Distributed in South Asia by
FOUNDATION
BOOKS
4381/4, Ansari Rorad
Daryaganj, New Delhi 110 002
and its branches at Mumbai, Hyderabad,
Bangalore, Chennai, Kolkata

*In memory of
my parents*

Contents

Preface	11
1. Introduction Alokesh Barua	13

SECTION I: PRAGJYOTISHPUR TO THE END OF THE AHOM PERIOD, AD 1826

Past is Prologue	42
2. The Silk Route from North-East India to China and the Bay of Bengal: Some New Lights Harprasad Ray	43
3. The Tai Migration and its Impact on the Rice Economy of Medieval Assam Amalendu Guha	71
4. The Rise and Decline of the Ahom Dynastic Rule: A Suggestive Interpretation Alokesh Barua	93

SECTION II: THE COMPANY BAHADUR AND JOHN BULL, 1826–1947

Growth and Stagnation under the *Raj*	120
5. The Rise of an Enclave Economy Hiranya K. Nath	121
6. A Big Push without a Take-off: A Case Study of Assam 1871–1901 Amalendu Guha	141
7. A Nineteenth Century Puzzle Revisited: Clash of Land Use Regimes in Colonial Assam Sanjib Baruah	163

Section III: India after Independence: the North-East

The Hindu Rate of Growth — 180

8. Development and Decolonization
   Hiren Gohain — 181

9. Unwitting Accomplices: States as Agents of Inequality
   Dipankar Sengupta — 187

10. Development Strategy and Regional Inequality in India
    Manmohan Agarwal and *Sudip Ranjan Basu* — 213

11. Structural Change, Economic Growth and Regional Disparity in the North-East: Regional and National Perspectives
    Alokesh Barua and *Arindam Bandyopadhyay* — 239

Section IV: Resource Endowment and Development Policy in the North-East

Planning for Growth — 284

12. An Analysis of Resource Endowment and Economic Management (A Study of North-Eastern India)
    B.C. Barah and *A.K. Neog* — 285

13. North-Eastern Economy: New Policy Options
    Gulshan Sachdeva — 307

14. Convergence in the Consumption Behaviour: A North-East Perspective
    Sandwip Kumar Das and *Monica Das* — 331

Section V: Population and Migration

In a State of Permanent Flux — 354

15. The Migration Problem in Assam: An Analysis
    Jayanta Kumar Gogoi — 355

16. 'Why Do They Come?' Economic Incentives for Immigration to Assam
    Santanu Roy — 367

17. Growth of Tribal Population in Assam
    Jaishree Konwarh — 397

    SECTION VI: TRADE AND INDUSTRIALIZATION
    IN THE NORTH-EAST

    The Way Ahead — 410

18. Trade Policy in India, Growth and
    Regional Development
    Manmohan Agarwal and *Lodewijk Berlage* — 411

19. History, Trade and Development: An Exploration
    of the North-East Economy
    Alokesh Barua — 427

20. Trading Across China, Myanmar, Bangladesh
    and India: Impact on North-East India
    Homeswar Goswami and *Jayanta Kumar Gogoi* — 449

Maps — 467

Contributors — 473

Preface

This book from its conception to printed stage took a rather long time, which of course was not without sufficient reasons. My entry into the enterprise was partly due to my friends and well-wishers who often encouraged me for such a venture as they felt that the north-east was a much neglected region well worth exploring. Friendly compulsions alone perhaps could not have been so strong a motivating factor to take up the project unless I felt in myself a sense of purpose and also a cause. In fact, as a professional economist I always felt that to find an explanation of the long economic stagnation of the Ahom period (AD 1212 to 1826) was in itself a very fascinating and challenging subject of inquiry. What made things perhaps more challenging and interesting was the continuation of that stagnation throughout the entire British period (AD 1826 to 1947), down to the present day.

Economic compulsions made the north-east region more and more vulnerable to a rising ethnicity, insurgency, chaos and political instability and subjected it to frequent mass movements, violence and terrorism. In response to such social disturbances, the central government has systematically taken recourse to surgical rather than developmental solutions, which prompted the well-known political scientist Sanjib Baruah to dub the Central Government as the 'prime-mover' in the breaking up of Assam.

I realized the difficulty of my task once it became obvious to me that developmental constraints could not be studied in a vacuum. History has to be brought in an essential way since certain constraints have been historically posing as stumbling blocks against generating a development process. The region as a consequence has continued to exist for centuries on a low-level equilibrium trap. And the same constraints seem to continue on to the present times.

This realization compelled me to start the project from the beginning of the Ahom dynastic rule. It is necessary to understand the nature of the constraints that worked historically against development in order to suggest the ways to get out of the mess. I believe that an analysis of the stagnation during the Ahom period will provide us with the key to understand the fundamental constraints against development. It is beyond one's comprehension as to what prevented the monolithic dynasty that ruled unabatedly for six hundred years to follow a path of development if not for anything else but to become a more powerful country?

By making the canvas so large I made things somewhat problematic for myself. I had to search for scholars and researchers to contribute papers on developmental issues pertaining to different epochs of history of the region. It was not an easy task but I am happy that I received enthusiastic support and encouragement from many people with whom I communicated. It gives me immense pleasure to acknowledge my thanks and gratitude to all those who have responded to my request and written papers for the volume.

My professional debts are many. First of all, I wish to put on record my debt and appreciation for all those who have contributed papers in this volume. I take this opportunity to acknowledge that I have received much encouragement and support from Dr Hiren Gohain, Dr Amalendu Guha, Dr Jayanta Gogoi, Dr Hirnaya Nath, Dr Santanu Roy, Dr H.P. Ray, Dr Sanjib Baruah and my brother Shri Pulakesh Barua in taking up the task. I owe a lot to many others and in particular, I wish to thank my former student Dr Dipankar Sengupta for his many valuable suggestions on the organization of the papers in the volume as well as in editing the manuscript. I am also thankful to Mr K. Varghese for preparing the maps for this volume.

I take this opportunity to express my sincere gratitude to Dr Joël Ruet as well as to Dr Veronique Dupont, the present Director of the Centre de Sciences Humaines (CSH) for accepting the manuscript for publication and extending the necessary financial support. But for their generous support it would not have come to light today. I wish to thank Attreyee Roy Chowdhury, the current Publications in-Charge at the CSH, for often reminding me of my editorial obligations.

It is indeed a pleasure to acknowledge my thanks to Manohar Publishers for their very meticulous and professional editing of the manuscript and which they have accomplished with utmost care and efficiency.

Finally, a special word of appreciation for my wife Arati and son Imon who had to constantly bear with me for all those years while I was busy working on this manuscript.

Needless to say the editor bears the full responsibility for all the errors, which may remain.

ALOKESH BARUA

CHAPTER 1

Introduction

ALOKESH BARUA

THE NORTH-EAST: WHAT IT CONVEYS

Should a social scientist enjoy the luxury of waxing poetic? I suppose it has its inherent dangers. It could at times, make him look mischievous or at times, compel him to draw misleading conclusions. So, a poetic conceptualization of the north-east as, 'a rainbow country – extraordinarily diverse and colourful, mysterious when seen through parted clouds, a distant and troubled frontier for all too many'[1] is really empty in its value as an analytical concept to a social scientist. From the viewpoint of a social scientist, the notion of the north-east merely gives one a sense of geography and that is all. A geographical sense has, of course, its own merit; but its usefulness will be limited.

There is no need to emphasize the point that for any meaningful and logical analysis of an economic problem, we are primarily required to assume an entity or a unit of analysis in the sense that we use in economics textbooks. It could be a country, a firm, an individual or a region, which could independently take decisions relating to an economic problem. A geographical entity is not necessarily the relevant economic entity for analysing an economic problem; say appropriate policies for development, unless of course a geographical entity coincides with the relevant economic entity. The north-east as an entity does not satisfy this primary condition.[2] The condition however gets satisfied for any one state within the north-east as every state enjoys independent economic and political powers

*The author wishes to acknowledge his gratefulness to Dr Hiren Gohain, Dr Dipankar Sengupta and Dr Hiranya Nath for many useful and valuable comments on an earlier version of the paper. The author however is responsible for all errors and the views expressed.

to make such decisions. So, unless these states share a common policy of development or the markets are fully integrated both in terms of mobility of goods and factors, we cannot and should not talk about a common development strategy for the north-east. For, such a common strategy of economic development implies synchronization of policies across the states regarding production, investment and other decisions that affect economic outcomes. This would mean that there has to be certain limits to governmental control over the resources within the jurisdiction of each state and that the states observe such bindings. Since such synchronization is virtually absent, why then does one indulge in any discussion on the development potentials of the north-east? Does one talk about the development potentials of the southern, eastern or the western regions of India in the same way? What is therefore so peculiar about the north-east that one clubs all the states of the region under a single nomenclature? It simply reflects bureaucratic or intellectual arrogance or carelessness in the attitudinal approach towards the north-east, or mere ignorance about the history of the region at the pan-Indian level.

The term, north-east India may have been coined as an imagery to capture the varied and distinctive features of the life and people, the economy and polity, and the political geography of the various north-eastern states of India in contrast to the other regions of the country. But that is, again, not legitimate. The peculiarities that one focuses on, where one talks about the north-east regarding its languages, religions, dresses, customs and racial origins, exist, equally in other regions as well, or even within any state that one may think of. The extent of heterogeneity in the north-east is of subcontinental proportions and this is equally true for any region in India, southern, eastern or the western. Why should the north-east then, require a separate treatment?

THE MAIN ARGUMENTS FOR UNIFICATION

Such difficulties notwithstanding, one shall argue for the need of a concept like the north-east in this paper. What is being objected to, above, is the use of an idea or an image, which is actually, non-existent. Therefore, it has to be created if it is to serve any purpose. Despite manifold variations among the states that comprise the north-east, certain commonly-shared features are their history and geography, their economic structures and the structural changes, if any, that they have witnessed overtime, and their economic and psychological distances from mainstream India. These factors bind them all together. All the states of the north-east are basically agrarian and industrially backward. They have poor infrastructure and a very high rate of unemployment.[3] The consequence of non-development for more than half a century, has led to increasing poverty and destitution in the rural areas of the region. Yet, in the midst of abject poverty and destitution, they have been able to maintain high education and literacy rates,[4] thanks to the Christian missionaries for their abiding involvement in works of social welfare. Transport linkages within the region and with the Indian mainland are still very primitive in nature. Last but not the least, they all face a very high rate of population growth.[5] The stagnating economies of the region with agriculture and industry being technologically backward, and an everincreasing population, make it difficult for any democratic government to provide the basic minimum standard of living to the people. In such an economy a government cannot shy away from its responsibility of providing facilities for technological improvement in agriculture and productivity growth. A government however may not discharge its duty if its *time preference* to be in power is very short. In such a situation the society will be subject to violence, chaos, unrest and insurgency of the kind growing in the north-east. The rise of insurgency and various forms of separatist movements and the growth of sub-nationalisms in the nort-east can only be explained as the results of governmental failures. Contemporary Bihar is another example. As a consequence, the region has been witnessing various forms of social unrest and insurgency. It is now almost universally accepted among policy makers, that the only long-term solution to the pro-blems of the north-east is through the achievement of rapid and sustained economic development. The commonality of the nature and characteristics of the problems of this region shows that a basic pre-condition for the unification of its markets exists. The following are some reasons for unification.

Firstly, it is virtually impossible for any of the north-east states to industrialize and develop in isolation, due to the limitations posed by the size of the markets. As these states are land-locked and the peculiar topographical features do not allow them to easily expand the markets within, as well as between the states without heavy investment on roads and communication facilities, many modern industries cannot be set-up for want of a viable scale of production. One obvious way to overcome this difficulty is of course, through *trade*. By trade we mean (a) trade among the north-east states (b) between a state and the rest of India and (c) between a state and the outside world. Interestingly, it is impossible for many of the north-east states to jump to (b) and (c) without (a) because of their geographical interdependence. For instance, only Assam can access the metropolitan markets in Calcutta or Delhi. No other north-east state can do so, without bypassing Assam. Therefore, efficient and reliable transport connections among the north-east states will be a necessary precondition for the expansion of trade with the rest of India. Thus, the unification of the north-east markets will be the first step towards a successful trade-based process of industrialization.

Secondly, because of the above constraint, each of the north-east states must enjoy a sufficiently large home market, in order to be able to compete with their counterparts in the larger metropolitan markets in India and abroad. This is the standard home market hypothesis for exporting. The case for the unification of markets in the north-east is much more compelling towards achieving such a goal in comparison with the other regions of India.[6] This must be recognized as an important contrast *vis-à-vis* the other regions of India. For, big metropolitan markets unify the regions of the north, south, east and the west, but there are no such markets that unity the north-east.[7] Fundamental constraints to the development of such markets is, of course, the lack of development itself – but to be precise – development is constrained by the Smithian limitation of markets. Limitation of markets could be a result of history or the lack of transport linkages[8] and an absence of adequate political and economic relations among these states, will, as be discussed in the next few sections.

Thirdly, while the expansion of the size of the markets provides scope for the division of labour, size of the market alone is not sufficient to reap full advantages from scale economies where such economies may arise from a variety of externalities. In the presence of market failures, synchronization and integration of economic policies among the states, implying an integrated development programme, will be necessary to achieve the optimal allocation of resources. It saves duplication of investment and provides opportunities for vertical and horizontal specialization.

Fourthly, all the states border one or the other countries such as Bhutan, China, Burma and Bangladesh.[9] As a consequence, the north-east states face two main problems – one, of illegal immigration from neighbouring countries like Bangladesh and Nepal; and two, of the use of the border as an escape route by extremists who seek shelter in the neighbouring country. This is easy since the borders are porous at most points. In order to prevent illegal immigration and successfully control extremism, some degree of political unification among the states is necessary. After all, development cannot take off in an environment of political instability. Such political or administrative unification also implies an increase in the size of the government, which again, would give rise to certain economies in providing efficient governance, collection of revenues and tolls.

A fifth reason for such unification could be to acquire a better bargaining power *vis-à-vis* the Centre. This is particularly important while influencing the central budgetary allocation in a federal economy. For instance, the Assam Movement in the early 1980s had led to a significant increase in the budgetary allocation of development funds to the north-east.

Once that the logic of unification[10] is established, the next question would be, how to go about it. This is a much more difficult question to answer and therefore, what one intends to do in the next few sections, is to examine whether this need for unification has been historically felt or not. We can learn from history about the stumbling blocks in the way of such unification. However, before we address this issue, a brief idea about the anatomy of the north-east may perhaps be very rewarding to further our understanding.

THE ANATOMY OF THE NORTH-EAST

The north-east comprises of seven states, namely, Nagaland, Mizoram, Meghalaya, Arunachal Pradesh, Manipur, Tripura and Assam. Sikkim is also now included as the eighth state within the north-east. But, except for Sikkim, the other states are geographically contiguous and have enjoyed economic and political relationships with each other over centuries. However, we do not have any evidence of Sikkim being on such terms with the other north-eastern states. So, for obvious reasons, we exclude Sikkim from our purview as this book is primarily concerned with developmental issues pertaining to the north-east in a historical perspective. The political history of the region has undergone many changes from the pre-colonial to the colonial period and the post-colonial period, and as we see later, this makes the problems of the north-east, extremely difficult to comprehend, particularly if one is not quite familiar with the political history of the region. Let us, therefore, gain a preliminary knowledge about the political history of the various components of the north-east.

POLITICAL HISTORY OF THE REGION: A BRIEF BACKGROUND

ASSAM

Assam is in a sense, the fulcrum of the north-east, for which, continuous historical records are available for a fairly long period of time. For the remaining states, historical records are either scanty or are just not available, except for the British period. The availability of historical records for Assam from medieval times, often breeds confusion as to what we mean by Assam, as its very concept has changed historically. Therefore, apart from the definitional problems, conceptual problems arise in at least two important ways: firstly, while determining a historical benchmark in order to conceptualize Assam as a distinct political and economic entity; and secondly, while *identifying* some of Assam's cultural and linguistic affinities with other homogeneous groups. This problem arises because the Assamese language is used synonymously with the state of Assam. The second conceptual issue is relevant and important, in so far as it is binding on the first.

The first problem arises because the name *A-sam* (a Sanskrit word meaning 'unequalled') was originally applied to the Ahoms,[11] the Shan invaders from upper Burma but subsequently referred to the country conquered by them, that is, the region east of the present district of Kamrup. The term, however, was later expanded and it included the whole of the Brahmaputra valley as constituted by the British in 1874.[12] On the other hand, the *province* was also known as Pragjyotishpur or Kamrupa in earlier periods. It was known as the former in the *Ramayana* and the *Mahabharata*, and as the latter in classical literature.[13] The western boundary of Kamrupa was the river Karatoya in Bengal. Thus, it is important to recognize the sensitivity of the term Assam in its historical contexts, as the political boundary of the state has been historically changing. Therefore, an understanding of the politics and economics of the state will be incomplete without shedding light, specifically on its history.

The second conceptual problem arises because the state, Assam, is customarily associated with the language, Assamese. But the Ahoms,[14] from whom the name Assam originated, did not initially speak Assamese.[15] Many scholars at the pan-India level, do not know that the Ahoms spoke the Tai language, which was the official language in Assam for nearly two hundred years. They wrote their *Buranjis* (meaning historical chronicles) in Tai language[16] and even today, there are.Ahoms who speak the language. It was one thing that the Ahoms later became Hinduized and gave up their language in favour of the Assamese language, which developed and flourished in a region that lay outside the Ahom dominion.[17]

The important political formations in the region, apart from the Ahom Kingdom were the Kingdom of Kamrup[18] or Kamata,[19] the Koch kingdom[20] with its capital in Koch Bihar (now in Bengal), the Kachari Kingdom[21] and the Kingdoms of Jayantia.[22] There were other groups of people who may not have been politically formed in the sense of the above, but certainly had distinctive individualities. These were Chutia,[23] Naga,[24] Garo[25] and Lushai[26] along with many others. Thus, in the thirteenth century, two important kingdoms co-existed simultaneously, one, on the western front (the Koch kingdom) and the other on the eastern front (the Ahom kingdom). This was also the time when Assamese literature and culture had developed into a distinctive form through the assimilation of various sub-cultures. The centre of Assamese cultural renaissance was not in Assam, as it was known then but in the western front where the Koch King Naranarayan ruled. The great Vaishnava saint, Sankardeva lived in Koch Bihar,[27] where the foundation of modern Assamese literature in its many dimensions was built under his guidance and inspiration. His teachings had a remarkable impact on the assimilative process of different cultures and traditions in the region. This process had given rise to a certain degree of political unification within the north-east, but it had no impact on the unification of markets.[28] However, the emergence of a composite culture and political unification within the region had given rise to a somewhat egalitarian social structure in Assam, which as argued by Barua, played the role of a catalyst in the downfall of the Ahom dynasty (see Barua, 'The Rise and Decline of the Ahom Dynastic Rule' in this volume).

More importantly, the sixteenth-century Vaishnava cult in Assam had led to a cultural unification of Assam with the Indian mainstream in a significant way, so much so that even the Ahoms could not escape its influence. They abandoned their own language and culture and identified themselves with the Indian mainstream as its tributary. The Koch regime, however, could not survive for long and after the death of King Naranarayan, it broke up into two kingdoms and eventually fell into the hands of the Mohammedans. However, the Ahoms maintained their supremacy and successfully prevented Muslim penetration into the region. Their victory against the Mughals in the battle of Sarighat was decisive. With the rise of Ahom power and the decline of the Koch kingdom, the centre of literary importance during the later period, was shifted to eastern Assam.

Cultural unification, as mentioned above, was not followed by any political and economic unification of Assam with the Indian mainstream. There could perhaps be many reasons for that. However, no serious attempt so far has been made to examine this issue. Taking the evolutionary viewpoint of Ashok Guha (1981), an attempt has been made by Barua[29] to put forward a view that there was no compulsion of development during the Ahom rule which was solely responsible for lack of political and economic, unification of Assam with the rest of India. This is of course a contestable proposition and all the contributors in this volume may not agree with this idea.

The organization of the economy, Barua[30] argues, did not provide the necessary incentives for maximization of output and generation of surplus. Regions of different cultures, traditions, languages and religions co-existed together without much conflict. However, Assam had to pay a very heavy price for maintaining political independence for so long, as it helped sustain a highly inefficient economic system without the threat of change. The intrinsic desire of the Ahoms to remain in isolation and the easy maintenance of self-sufficiency were responsible for their lack of any outward-looking policies. Their economic interests were not guided by any motive to generate surplus beyond the basic minimum. Political independence insulated the economy from external influences. The effect of such insulation, in later centuries, prevented the region from enjoying the benefits of a better system of economic management, technology and trade with mainland India.

The above arguments that explain why market linkages did not develop with the more progressive areas outside Assam such as Bengal, does not explain what constrained the development of markets within Assam itself. Markets do not grow, on their own, unless there are primitive capital accumulation and expansion of demands. These forces do not exist in a self-sufficient economy without the intent to follow a military expansionist policy, a strong demonstration effect and population pressure (Guha, 1981). The insulation of the economy as described above, also prevented any demonstration effect from having an impact on the population. Assam, on the other hand, being very sparsely populated and the land being extremely fertile, could sustain itself easily in the milieu of a rural economy.

However, the spread effects of the Vaishnava cult were tremendous in terms of the unification of various regions, tribes and cultures, contributing to the rise of a homogeneous culture. As political segmentation broke certain forms of unification of markets took their place, giving rise to new conflicts of interests. With the incorporation of Kamrup into the Ahom empire towards the seventeenth century, economic conflicts became much more sharpened as Kamrup was, for a long-time, under the control of the Mughals. It was also exposed to the rich culture of Bengal much before upper Assam was. Certainly, it had led to certain forms of demonstration effect on consumption and production. As Kamrup was densely populated, migration of people from regions of higher density to those of lower density, also led to economic conflicts. Maintenance of self-sufficiency seemed no longer feasible. The forces of change contributed to the political unification of people and resulted in a mass uprising known as the Mayamoria Revolt, against the Ahom empire. It had such a devastating impact on the Ahom monarchy that the six hundred-year-old regime collapsed. The appearance of the Burmese and the British acted only as catalysts in the inevitable collapse of the glorified empire.

THE ADVENT OF THE BRITISH

The beginning of an entirely new historical process in which the East India Company played the prime role, followed the end of the monolithic rule of the Ahoms in 1826. The long civil war and the Burmese invasion had completely demoralized Assamese society. The impact of the wars on the population was so devastating, that it had been reduced to almost half of its original strength. People in general, therefore, welcomed with great respite the entry of the British into the political scenario of Assam, marked by complete anarchy, chaos and insecurity. By virtue of being the ruler, the British became the sole owner of large tract of wasteland (in some places) and other valuable natural resources. It was in the interest of the British to exploit these resources for profit, which resulted in the growth of a large tea plantation sector in Assam. The development of railways and waterways, and the establishment of other productive enterprises such as coal, petroleum and wood manufacturing, etc., were all guided by the sole objective of maximization of profit from the plantation economy. The local village economy and the plantation sector maintained their distance from one another and never converged, such that neither sector had any impact on the other. For instance, the labourers for the tea gardens were mostly drawn from places outside the region, and railways and waterways remained in the periphery of the village economy. The absence of trade between the two sectors did not help in the integration of markets and as a result, the large British investment did not give rise to any backward or forward linkages between the village and the plantation sectors.[31]

Like the Ahoms, the British were also not interested in the development of the village economy of Assam for of course, quite different reasons. The Ahoms could not perceive the need for development, as there were no strong compulsions for it. The British were not interested because they did not perceive any benefit from it. The growing market for tea was entirely outside Assam. The requirement of labourers for the plantation sector could be met by hiring them at a much cheaper price from outside the province. Since the marginal productivity of agricultural labourers was much above the wage paid to the contractual labourers brought from outside the region, it was, therefore, natural for the planters to hire labourers from abroad.[32] However, there was a significant difference. While Assam remained completely insulated from any outside influence during the long rule of the Ahoms, the annexation of Assam by the East India Company had broken down that insulation and with that, began the process of economic and political integration of Assam with the Indian mainstream. When the British rule ended in 1947, Assam became a full-fledged state of India and the process of cultural, political and economic integration with India was complete.

There was yet another important difference between the Ahom rule and that of the British. The advent of the British into the political scene of Assam, contributed to a much sharper political integration of the hill regions. The hill and other linguistic regions were incorporated within the domain of British rule and the hills were brought under the same administrative system. As a result, the geographic scope of the British Assam was very different from that of the Ahom Assam. In consequence of this integrative process, the earlier complementary relationship between the political and cultural affinity has been eventually broken down. With the successive divisions of Assam after Independence, what is left today, is in essence the *Ahom Assam*. Complementary relations have thus, become re-established. The Ahom kingdom, which Sanjib Barua has described as the cultural heartland of modern Assam,[33] roughly corresponds to the five districts of the *Brahmaputra Valley*,[34] namely, Kamrup, Darrang, Nowgong, Sibsagar and Lakhimpur, and portions of Sadiya Frontier Tract.[35] Could we then, following Sanjib Baruah, logically accuse the Central Government as being the prime mover of the break-up of Assam?

THE HILL DISTRICTS OF ASSAM IN 1947

Apart from the Brahmaputra valley, the hilly areas of the state of Assam, as defined immediately after Independence were the present states of Nagaland, Mizoram, Meghalaya and Arunachal Pradesh. Obviously, these states did not have their present identity of independent states at the dawn of India's Independence. These states were the integral parts of undivided Assam in 1947,[36] that was essentially the British province of Assam except for Sylhet,[37] which went to Pakistan (now in Bangladesh) after the Partition of India in 1947.[38] The British came to rule in this region in 1826 after the decline of the Ahom dynasty,[39] that had ruled in Assam for a period of over six hundred years. However, as discussed above, the pre-colonial Ahom Assam[40] was not the same as the British province of Assam. As mentioned above, the pre-colonial Ahom Assam was essentially the Brahmaputra valley. Only during the colonial period did the British expand the scope of Assam by annexing the surrounding hill regions. Yet, these hill areas being contiguous to the Brahmaputra Valley, they might have had certain forms of economic and political interaction with the Ahom kingdom. It is, therefore, important to understand the relation of the Ahoms and the British with these hill states.

THE NAGA AND THE PATKAI HILLS: NAGALAND

The Ahom rule was bounded on the north by a range of mountains inhabited by the Bhutanese, Akas, Duflas and Abors. On the east, there was another line of hills inhabited by the Mishmis and Singphos and on the south were the Garo, Khasi, Naga and Patkai hills. The Patkai range on the south-east has been the permanent abode of the aboriginal Nagas. They belong to a diversity of tribes, each speaking its own language[41] and calling itself by a distinctive name, but collectively known as the Nagas. Their habitat extends along a large portion of the Brahmaputra valley, from the Kapili river on the west to the Buri-Dihing on the east, bordering Nowgong, Sibsagar and Lakhimpur. The Ahoms had never subjugated the Nagas.[42] The general tribal policy of the Ahoms was in fact, not to subjugate them. So they paid no taxes to the Ahom King but they accept his sovereignty and obeyed some of his commands.[43] This policy of non-interference paid very high dividends to the Ahoms in the sense, that they were able to enjoy uninterrupted sovereignty for more than 600 years.

It was not the British policy either to absorb it,[44] perhaps. But the differential attitude in the policies towards the tribals between the Ahoms and the British, arise from the fact that while the Ahoms were no colonial power,[45] the British were. So, from a colonial perspective, the British saw their political interest in subjugating the Nagas and in 1866, they resolved to take the possession of the region and formed a new district with the headquarters located at Samaguting. Later, in 1878, this place was abandoned in favour of Kohima.[46]

THE GARO, KHASI AND JAINTIA HILLS: MEGHALAYA

THE GARO HILLS

The Garos live mainly in the region west of the Khasi hills. The Ahoms had really nothing to do with the Garos of the interior hills. They had some contact with the Garos who lived in the vassal states on the extremities of Assam in the south bank of the Brahmaputra.[47]

The British brought the Garo Hills under their administration and was it administered as a part of Goalpara from Rangpur. Goalpara was separated from Rangpur and made a new district in 1822.[48] The Garo hill was made a separate district in 1869,[49] with its headquarters at Tura.

THE KHASI AND JAINTIA HILLS

The Jaintia king ruled two entirely distinct tracts of regions, namely, the Khasi and Jaintia hills inhabited by the Khasi tribes, and the plains region, south of these hills, north of the Barak river, in Sylhet district.[50] The early history of the kingdom is obscure. Their interaction with other political formations in the region began around the middle of the sixteenth century when the Koch King Naranarayan defeated the king of Jaintia.[51] The Ahom King Rudra Singh attacked the Jaintia king during the early eighteenth century, but did not annex the kingdom.[52] In continuation with the Ahoms's general policy towards the hill people, King Rudra Singh returned the kingdom to the Jaintia king.[53]

On 15 March 1835, the British took possession of Jaintiapur.[54]

THE LUSHAI HILLS: MIZORAM

The present state of Mizoram was called by the British 'Lushai Hills' and the people lived there were called Lushai. By an Act of Parliament of India 'Lushai Hills' was renamed as Mizo district of Assam on 1 August 1954. People belonging to different ethnic groups live in Mizoram but all of them now identify themselves as Mizos. According to Lehman (1963) the Lushai are Northern Chin. Before they entered into the region, various tribes known as Kuki inhabited the region. The Ahom Kingdom had hardly come in contact with the tribes living in the Lushai hills.

The Lushais came to this frontier in 1840 and drove the Kukis into the plains of Cacher. The British brought the hills under their administration. The southern portion of the hills was first administered by the Bengal government and the northern by the Chief Commissioner of Assam. But on 1 April 1898, the two tracts were merged into one and placed under the Assam administration.[55]

THE AKAS, ABORS, DUFLAS, MIRIS MISHMIS AND SINGPHOS: ARUNACHAL PRADESH

The Akas live in the hills to the east of the Bharari river in Darrang district. The Duflas live in the hills situated between the Bharari river on the west and the upper course of Somdiri on the east. The Abors occupy the hill region between the Dihong and Dibong rivers. The Miris live in both the plains and hills. The Mishmis occupy the hills to the east of the Abor region. The Singphos are found in the upper Buri-Dihing and in Namrup.

The other Regions: Cacher, Manipur and Tripura

Cacher

On 14 August 1832, the British annexed Cacher[56] (excluding Karimganj subdivision) which included Cacher and the North Cacher districts of Assam, parts of Nowgong (Hojai-Davaka area) in Assam, Dayung-Dhansiri valley in Nagaland and the Jiri Frontier area in Manipur.[57] Silchar was made its headquarters. It was in charge of a superintendent, who was subordinate to the Commissioner of Assam. In 1836, it was transferred to the Dacca division.

The ruling tribe of the state was Dimasa,[58] which belonged to the Bodo[59] family of the Tibeto-Burman linguistic sub-family. There are legends that the Kacharis once ruled in Kamrupa, but in due course of time, they settled down in the Sadiya frontier. Thereafter, they shifted to Dimapur, now in Nagaland. There were frequent conflicts between the Kacharis and the Ahoms, and the Dimasa Raja, Khorapha, was defeated by the Ahoms in 1526. As a result, the Dimasa capital was shifted to Maibong in the North Cacher hills. The Ahoms were busy fighting the Mughals and so they avoided any confrontation with the Kacharis. The Ahom King Rudra Singha had forced Cacher and Jaintia to pay tribute to the Ahoms, but the Rajas of Cacher did not pay tribute for long. Of course, Cacher and Jaintia, both became partners in King Rudra Singha's confederacy against the Mughals. The clashes between the Ahoms and the Kacharis continued till they were both annexed by the British.

Manipur

Each of the seven states have had their own historical evolution, more or less in an isolated environment, ruled by their own inhabitants. They have, however, had diplomatic relations occasionally, with other neighbours of the north-east. A reliable and continuous historical account, is unfortunately, not available for many of these states. For instance, we know of Manipur since the times of the *Mahabharata*, but its long, independent existence remained in obscurity until a powerful kingdom, led by Gharib Nawaz[60] sprang up in its place in 1714.[61] The subsequent history of Manipur was essentially a history of its conflicts with the Burmese. Gharib Nawaz waged a series of successful wars against the Burmese and captured many of their towns. However, due to internal wars within the ruling elite, the dynasty eventually collapsed and as a consequence, the country was overrun by the Burmese in 1755, and again in 1758. The Burmese permanently annexed part of it. In 1762, the Manipuri King Jai Singh negotiated a treaty with the British Government for the recovery of the lost provinces, but the British could not do much for the King and the negotiations broke off. A fresh invasion by the Burmese took place in 1765 in which Jai Singh was defeated. But with the help of the Ahom King Rajesvar Singh, he was once more seated on the throne in 1768. Jai Singh died in 1799 and his sons succeeded him. However, the Burmese once again attacked Manipur, but this time the British intervened and expelled the Burmese from the land forever through the execution of a treaty known as the Yandabo Treaty on 24 February 1826. Gambhir Singh, the son of Jai Singh, was put on the throne of Manipur and the Treaty of Yandabo confirmed his position as Raja. Raja Gambhir Singh died in 1834 after which, continuous disorder prevailed in Manipur. In 1891, the British occupied Manipur, but decided that it would be ruled by the natives. Chura Chandra, a youthful scion of a collateral line, was placed upon the throne. During his rule, numerous reforms were executed. The land revenue administration was carefully revised, better judicial tribunals were introduced and the old system of forced labour was abolished. The boundaries of the state were defined and a cart road was opened from Imphal, the capital, to Kohima in Nagaland. The Raja was, however, only a formal head because the Resident of his *darbar* was a member of the ICS who was responsible for the administration of the hill tribes living within the state and for all matters of revenue and finance. The British Government, subsequently ruled Manipur from Assam.[62]

Tripura

As regards Tripura (also known as *Tipperah*), the Ahoms had no relation with them till the year 1710.[63] In 1710, the Ahom King Rudra Singha sent an embassy to the Raja Ratna Manikya, soliciting his aid to a confederacy of the rajas and zamindars of Bengal which the King of Assam was organizing at that time to overthrow the Mughals from their power. But King Rudra Singha died shortly after. So, this part of the region was never under the Ahom ruler. However, the King of Tripura accepted the Koch suzerainty in 1540.[64]

THE STATE REORGANIZATION COMMITTEE: 1955

The State Reorganization Commission in 1955 had initially recommended the merger of Manipur and Tripura with Assam,[65] but it did not happen. While recognizing the political independence of these states for long, the Committee had suggested the merger on the plea that such small units were not 'administratively viable'. Curiously, enough, the Committee also noted on the other hand, that 'its (Manipur's) economic development will be retarded if it is merged in Assam or in West Bengal or in the hill districts'. The State Reorganization Committee also had considered the possibility of creating a separate hill state, consisting of the Naga hill districts (now Nagaland), Garo, Khasi and Jaintia hills (now Meghalaya), Lushai hills (now Mizoram) and United Mikir and North Cacher hills (now a district in Assam). However, while the Naga National Council wanted independence from Assam and India, and sought to remain aloof from the proposed hill state, the United Mikir and North Cacher hills and the Mizo (Lushai) hills were not in favour of a separate hill state. The only hill district comprising the Garo, Khasi and Jaintia hills were in favour of a separate hill state. Considering these divergent views, the Commission concluded that the formation of a hill state is neither feasible, nor desirable in the interest of the tribal people themselves. It had thus recommended that the hill districts should continue to form part of Assam. Finally, the North-East Frontier Agency (NEFA, now Arunachal Pradesh) was constitutionally a part of Assam, but the Commission has suggested that the governance of this area be entrusted to the President of India, acting through the Governor of Assam.

Over the years, new states had been carved out of Assam by the Central Government, the prime mover, as described by Sanjib Baruah (1999), in the break up of Assam and consequently the creation of Nagaland, Mizoram, Meghalaya and Arunachal Pradesh as new states of the Indian Union.[66]

AN OVERVIEW: WHAT THIS VOLUME IS ALL ABOUT

The present volume is not intended to deal with the political and social history of the north-east. There are a fairly good number of books, both at the scholarly and popular levels on the subject.

But what is lacking, is a comprehensive, analytical research on the economic history of the north-east. Historians of repute, such as Amalendu Guha and H.K. Borpujari did pioneering research on the economic history of the north-east, particularly in the colonial period. However, serious research has hardly been attempted to examine post-colonial development in its relationship to the colonial and pre-colonial periods. In explaining today's underdevelopment, one has to strive to explain why the 600 years of monolithic rule by the Ahoms did not give rise to any process of development in the region. One of the major factors that help development is political stability and the Ahoms had very successfully provided that to the people of the region. Similarly, why could Assam not take off from a massive investment in the plantation economy by the British during the colonial period? Coming to the more recent period, we observe that the region has received a massive amount of central funds under a variety of projects but it yet did not trigger off any industrial growth worth mentioning. Perhaps, there historically existed certain key constraints to development, which may be sociological or economic. There is, however, no work that pertains to explaining the nature of these constraints and how to overcome these for the development of the north-east. This lacuna is often felt both at the regional and pan-Indian levels, when one is confronted with the attempt to resolve problems of rising extremism and political instability in the region through a set of economic policies that help induce the growth of employment and output in the region. We often hear people talk at the highest level of economic decision-making, that it can be done through a policy of pump priming and trade-oriented industrialization. We learn from history that paucity of fund is definitely not the key constraint to development in the north-east. We intend to bring this point into sharp focus in this book.

To the extent that economic development is a historical and an evolutionary process, we cannot ignore the historical past, since history appears in an essential way in any analysis of the evolutionary process of development. We also cannot ignore geography, since we need a reference point for giving a sense of continuity to the process of development. As we have seen above, the history of the north-east region has changed continuously overtime. Because of this lack of an invariant reference point, we are compelled to analyse the developmental problems of the region separately in three different epochs – the *Pre-colonial*, *Colonial* and the *Post-independence* periods. While we achieve a certain amount of geographical consistency by making this division, it obviously creates inconsistencies in terms of their comparability overtime, such as the geography of the region that had been changing under different epochs. Our answer to such criticism will be, that while the geography had been changing, there existed an internal unity among these states in the sense that Assam, as it stands today, had always been the 'core' or the 'hub' of the north-east. All other states are peripheral to Assam – the hub – in terms of trade, commerce and communication. The narrow neck on the western front of Assam, provides the only road and railway link for all the states of the region, with the rest of India. Even interlinkages between various states, including Manipur and Tripura are not possible without accessing Assam. As a result, independent developmental possibilities are severely limited for these states and therefore, the development of the peripheral states is intricately interwoven with the development of the 'hub'.

The lack of analytical research also results in a variety of inadequacies. From the viewpoint of the people from outside this region, there are inadequacies as regards the understanding of the problems of the region, the characteristics of the economy of the region, the people, their aspirations and their historical past. Similarly, from the viewpoint of the people from within the region, there are inadequacies in the understanding of the evolution of their economies over the years, the growing interdependence of their economies and the mainstream Indian economy, and the constraints of development that they have been facing. Such inadequacies of understanding act as serious handicaps in many ways, particularly in solving the problems of economic development of the region. As a result, attempts to close the gap between the region and mainstream India had failed to bring about too many positive results. Developmental policies designed to help the region achieve faster growth, actually ended up in a mere fiasco.

Ironically, a disintegrative process had started in the region soon after Independence. In the process, the hills have been endowed with political and economic independence. Various ethnic groups in Assam, such as the Bodos have also started demanding their separation from Assam. Economic regionalism in Assam began with the oil refinery movement in 1959, and subsequently the language movement in 1960. Interestingly, the Assamese fought for faster economic development and not for ethnic identity, like the others. They saw the possibility of industrialization through the installation of heavy industries such as the oil refineries. The language movement was essentially an attempt to make it easier for the local people of Assam to enter the job market. But, towards the early 1980s, frustration with stagnation, unemployment and economic backwardness, made certain groups of people within Assam raise slogans demanding political independence from India. Since then, the north-east has drawn much attention from various quarters at the pan-Indian level. The problem of the north-east is not entirely a creation of its own. The Central Government cannot shy away from its responsibility by taking pretext to an easy scapegoat that economic under-development of the region is the chief cause of the north-east syndrome.

These states are small enough to be viable units for the adoption of any independent path of development. However, there is enormous scope for a common strategy of development, with Assam as the core of the development programme. As the states are similarly endowed by nature and technology conflict among them is unlikely, in terms of the location of industry and the distribution of income as economic growth progresses. Further, they can enjoy a better bargaining power *vis-à-vis* the Centre, if they can stand together as a coherent group. The strategy of a joint development programme will put them on a better footing in terms of their ability to draw more resources from the Central Government for the development of infrastructure and industries in the region. In the same way, it will be easier for them to check extremism of various kinds that they suffer from, through a joint effort of the different state governments. Keeping extremism at its lowest level possible, will be the primary necessity for a development programme in the region to be successful.

The other important prerequisite for a successful implementation of economic reform is the political acceptability of the reform package by the larger mass of population in the region. It is, therefore, necessary to create consciousness amongst the people regarding the existing constraints of development, so that people respond positively to the reform measures. Our policy makers are often, unfortunate, victims of a widely-prevalent, but misconceived view that the mere transfer of financial resources to the state would be sufficient to achieve economic development. In the absence of the basic pre-conditions as outlined above, profitability in economic activities would be too low to motivate any inflow of private capital into the region. On top of it, if the political situation is also volatile, then profit-seeking private investment will not flow into the region. Such capital, in fact, will flow out of the economy. This has happened on a large scale in the recent past.

Therefore, as an integral part of any reform package, it would also be necessary to educate the vocal and articulate educated middle class, that there are no other solutions, but only rapid economic growth that could enable them to solve their problems in the long run. Of course, it requires a visionary local leadership to be able to translate the aspirations of the people to reality. But political stability and a friendly attitude towards others, are the basic minimum necessities for the successful implementation of a reform strategy to achieve economic development.

Our federal structure is such that it is not based on the economically sound concept of a unit of the federation, say, a state. The arbitrary re-organizatoin of the states based on language, has caused several irreparable distortions in the system. Smaller linguistic groups, for example, express their feelings of insecurity and consequently make their demands for a separate state. Behind such demands for separate states, is an implicit argument that political autonomy helps economic development. It is high time people were educated that such a view is false. For instance, the extent of political divisions that Assam has witnessed since the Independence of India, has no parallel in this country. Did that help economic transformation in the newly-created states? Yet, there exists even today, a strong urge for further division on any conceivable ethnic, cultural and linguistic basis. It needs to be emphasized, therefore, that political autonomy can provide neither peace nor economic development. The fact is that increasing regionalism growing all over the country today, is largely conditioned by the co-existence of big state hegemonies and the absence of a proper re-distributive mechanism to equalize inter-state income levels.

An increasing urge for political autonomy in any ethnic group has, of course, some valid reasons. There is indeed a rationale for greater political autonomy in a system where the dominant elite has certain distinctive advantages in terms of their command over social resources. So, the reasonably articulate elite belonging to any ethnic group, being unable to find for itself a position of strength within a bigger political unit, can therefore, find a rationale in the demand for a smaller, independent political unit where it can exercise its dominance. In an economically backward region, such a demand for autonomy can easily get mass political support within a narrow political base. The argument that the root cause of backwardness is lack of political independence seems to be quite persuasive. Such an argument easily wins mass political support. So much so, that a very strong sense of neglect prevails even today, in the minds of the people of this region that their interests are not taken seriously in our highly centralized democracy. This sense of neglect comes mainly from the lack of social, political and economic integration of the region with the rest of India. To a lesser extent, it is due to the demonstration effect based on relative income disparities. People from the northeast feel, that their agonies and sufferings are ignored and that their voices are not heard. They believe that in spite of being so rich in economic resources, they are economically poor because of exploitation by the Centre and therefore, the solution lies either in political autonomy or in disintegration from the Centre. Fallacious and misplaced though this view is, it is nonetheless a fact that such a view widely prevails. It is fallacious, because political autonomy within a smaller horizon does not guarantee economic viability and it is misplaced, because such a theory of underdevelopment based on Centre's neglect is undoubtedly an over-simplification and is highly far-fetched.

This book is an attempt to understand the nature, characteristics and structure of the north-east economy, in order to put forward a perspective for development strategies for the region. The volume consists of papers on economic and political history, as well as economic analytical research papers. The contributors constitute a cross-section of authors from various disciplines. They differ widely, not only in their subject areas, but also in terms of the methodological approaches they have adopted. They however, have at least one thing in common, and that is, they all have attempted to contribute towards an understanding of the complex phenomenon of the region's economic under-development, thereby seeking an explanation of the region's relative isolation from the rest of India.

The two main objectives of the study are: (a) to provide a brief background of the region to those readers who are not familiar with its history and economy; and (b) to examine the development alternatives for the region. In doing so, we adopt a framework in which the region is cast not in isolation, but as a part of the Indian mainstream.

NOTES

1. See, B.G. Verghese, *India's North-East Resurgent, Ethnicity, Insurgency, Governance, Development*, Konark Publishers, Delhi (1996), p. 1.
2. Therefore, it does not make any sense to have an organization or institute like the North-Eastern Council (NEC), since it cannot play a role of being more than a budgetary allocation body. It does not function like a state in a command system. The central budgetary allocation is sufficient for the purpose. So, why are so many resources being wanted on an institute like the NEC, which does not have any role in development?
3. See Barua and Bandyopadhyay, 'Structural Change, Economic Growth and Regional Disparity in the North-East: Regional and National Perspectives' in this volume.
4. The literacy rate among the north-east states, except for Arunachal Pradesh, is above the national average of 62 per cent in 1997. It is above 95 per cent for Mizoram.
5. See, Barua and Bandyopadhyay in this volume.
6. By unification of markets, one does not mean political unification, since that is neither necessary, nor sufficient for the enlargement of the size of the market. Better transport facilities and communication would do this job.
7. Commenting on an earlier version of this paper Dr Hiren Gohain observed that the absence of metropolitan centre in the north-east is not so surprising given the fact that these metropolitan centres were largely creation of the East India Company that functioned from seventeenth century onwards. True, but the relevant point for us is that the same East India Compamy that had entered into the north-east during the early nineteenth century had failed to play the same role in the north-east that it had played in other parts of India despite the fact that tea exports from the region was flourishing by leaps and bounds by the end of the century. Further, independent India also did not try to break the hegemony of the big metropolis.
8. The history of the development of transport in the north-east is a sad reflection of the Centre's total indifference to the region. Assam's trade with Bengal, Bihar and Orissa was mainly carried on by river transport in the early times. The colonial government in 1847, established the steamer service in the Brahmaputra between Calcutta and Gauhati (960 km.). In the year 1856, the steamer service was extended from Gauhati to Dibrugarh. In 1863, there was only one trip per month that connected Assam with Calcutta. S.B. Medhi, *Transport System and Economic Development in Assam*, Guwahati: Publication Board Assam, 1978, pp. 19–20.

    There were no reliable and convenient overland routes. Me Cosh, *Topography of Assam*, Calcutta, 1837, pp. 8–9.

The Assam Bengal Railway in 1895, connected Assam with the outside world for the first time. The total distance covered by the railway, during the British period was approximately 1,523 km. Independent India's contribution to the railway, up to 1970 was only about 400 km. As a result, even today there are no railway lines connecting the north-east states with each other and also with the Indian mainland.

The only bridge that connected upper Assam and other north-eastern states through railway with the rest of India, was available only after the Chinese aggression in 1962. Interestingly, it was the result of persistent political movements by the students of the north-east states. Air travel facilities are virtually non-existent in many north-east states and for those states which have an air connection, they are with the metropolis outside the region.

9. The north-east's share of the border with the mainland of the country is only 2 per cent and that with the international border, i.e. Bangladesh, China, Myanmar and Bhutan is 98 per cent. See Map 5.
10. On the question of unification of the states Hiren Gohain has questioned 'the feasibility of such a proposal' in his comments on an earlier version of the paper. He thinks that '... political will among the states will not be strong in support of such an idea'. This is indeed a legitimate point. But then our concern here is the 'logic' but not the 'feasibility' of unification although it is true that logic by itself is meaningless if the proposal is not feasible. Our answer would be that 'feasibility' is only a temporal problem. A strong logic may overrun political infeasibility as it happened in the Europe today.
11. See B.K. Kakati, *Assamese, its formation and Development*, published by the Govt. of Assam in the Department of Historical and Antiquarian Studies, N.H. Historical Institute, Guwahati, 1941, pp. 1–3.
12. See, op. cit., p. 3.
13. See, op. cit., p. 4.
14. A stream of immigrants from Burma invaded Assam in the early thirteenth century and established its kingdom in the north-eastern part of India. These immigrants called themselves *Tai* (meaning 'celestial origin') but were popularly known as the Ahoms. They belonged to the Shan dynasty. They ruled over Assam from the thirteenth century, till the British came to occupy the region in 1826. The name of the first Ahom King was *Sukapha* who had established the Ahom Kingdom in 1228. See Edward Gait (revised and enlarged by B.K. Barua and H.V.S. Murthy), *A History of Assam*, Calcutta: Thacker Spink and Co. Pvt. Ltd., 1933, pp. 77–8. The capital of the Ahom Kingdom was built at Charaideo in the thirteenth century, but it was later shifted to Garhgaon (in Sibsagar district) in the sixteenth century. Initially, they tried to consolidate their rule in Upper Assam by bringing various

tribes such as the Morans, Borahis, Kacharis and Chutias, etc., under their rule.

The boundary of the Ahom Kingdom or the Kingdom of Assam, 'embraced the whole of the north-east of the Indian subcontinent from the sources of the Brahmaputra to the river Karatoya and from the bottom of the Himalayas to the Hills of Surma and Subansiri valley. *They were so powerful that the kingdom they carved out for themselves came to be associated with their name as a nation.*' N.N. Acharya, *The History of Medieval Assam*, Guwahati: Dutta Baruah & Co., 1996, pp. 41–2. See Map 1.

15. In the words of the noted linguistic scholar B.K. Kakati, 'Though they [the Ahoms] constituted a ruling race for about six hundred years (1228–1824 A.D.), they gave up their language and religion in favour of Aryan habits and customs and their absorption was so complete that they contributed only a few words to Assamese vocabulary'.

16. As Kakati puts it, 'In the Ahom court, historical chronicles were at first composed in their original Tibeto-Chinese language, but when the Ahom rulers adopted Assamese as the court language, historical chronicles began to be written in Assamese'. See Kakati, p. 14.

17. Assamese literature grew and flourished in western Assam under the patronage of the kings of either Kamatapura or Koch Bihar. See Kakati, p. 14. See Map 1.

18. Before the invasion of the Ahoms, there was a powerful kingdom in the north-eastern part of the Indian subcontinent known as Kamarupa. It included roughly almost the whole region of the Brahmaputra valley, besides Rangpur, Bhutan, Coochbihar, Mymensingha and the Garo Hills. See S.K. Bhuyan, ed. *Kamrupar Buranji*, 2nd edn., Guwahati, 1958 p. 97; Gait, pp. 10–11.

During the times of the *Mahabharata*, it was known as Pragjyotishpur; but in the Puranas and the Tantras, it was referred to as Kamrupa. See Gait, p. 10.

By the beginning of the thirteenth century, the boundary between Kamrupa and the Muslim ruler of Bengal was the river Karatoya or Begmati. The eastern boundary was up to Nowgong. The subsequent history of Kamrup was the continued clash between various kings of Kamrup and the Muslims. N.N. Acharya, *The History of Medieval Assam*, p. 134.

19. The western part of the Brahmaputra valley, which was a part of the ancient Kamrupa, formed a single kingdom during the thirteenth century known as Kamata or Kamatapur. Hussain Shah overthrew the last representative of the Kamata dynasty, Nilambar, in 1498. See Gait, pp. 43–4.

20. The Koches are well spread out in Assam and Bengal. See Gait, pp. 47–70.

In the early sixteenth century, the Koches established a powerful kingdom on the ruins of the Kamata. Bisva Singh, the first Koch King, rose to power in 1515 and his kingdom was as far as to the river Karatoya in the west and the Bar Nadi in the east. However, towards the end of the century, the kingdom was broken into two – Koch Bihar and Koch Hajo. Koch Bihar became a vassal of the Mughal empire in 1596. Later, the Mughals also annexed Koch Hajo. See Gait, p. 67.

There were frequent wars between the Ahoms and the Muhammadans and in 1638, peace was negotiated between the Ahoms and the Mughals. The country, west of the Bar Nadi was given up to the Muhammadans and the Ahoms were given the rest of the eastern part of the Koch kingdom. See Map 1.

21. The Kacharis are the aboriginal people of the Brahmaputra valley. In the thirteenth century, the Kachari kingdom was extended along the south bank of the Brahmaputra, from the Dikhu to the Kallang, or beyond, and included also, the valley of the Dhansiri and the tract of the North Cachar subdivision. See Gait, p. 300.
22. The dominions of Jaintia included the Jaintia hills and the plains of Sylhet district. There was no difference between the inhabitants of the Khasi, and those of the Jaintia hills. See Gait, p. 311.
23. The Chutiyas are found chiefly in Lakhimpur and the adjacent part of Sibsagar.
24. The hilly tract inhabited by various tribes called collectively as Nagas had never been under the dominion of the Ahoms. See Gait, p. 366.

    However, by the end of the nineteenth century, the British brought certain parts of Nagaland under its control.
25. The Garo hill was a part of Goalpara during the first few years of the British rule. In 1869, a separate district was formed with its headquarters in Tura.
26. The term Lushai refers to the *Zomi* of the Lushai hills, which is situated to the south of the Surama velley. It was Mr Edger, the Deputy Commissioner of Cacher who first officially used the term 'Lushai' instead of 'Zomi' around the year 1897.

    The Lushais have changed their name to *Mizo* in 1946.
27. Sankardeva was born in Nowgong but could not live there because of the opposition of the Ahoms. He fled to Koch Bihar where he died at the age of 120 years.
28. What had constrained unification of markets needs more careful historical analysis. One view however is that (i) inefficeint Ahom economic institutions and (ii) the impact of the Vaishara teacher on social values were responsible for lack of developmental spirit and market formation in the region (see Barua, 'The Rise and Decline of the Ahom Dynastic Rule' in this volume.
29. See Barua, 'The Rise and Decline . . .', in this volume.

30. Ibid.
31. See for details A. Barua, 'History, Trade and Development: The Assamese Experience', in this volume.
32. Ibid., p. 438.
33. Sanjib Baruah, *India Against itself: Assam and the Politics & Nationality*: Oxford, New Delhi 1999. p. 21.
34. The Brahmaputra valley can be partitioned into two divisions – the Upper Assam and Lower Assam. The present districts of Goalpara, Dhubri, Kokrajhar, Bongaigaon, Barpeta, Guwahati, Nalbari and Darrang constitute Lower Assam. The rest of the valley is known as Upper Assam. See, A. Guha, *Medieval and Early Colonial Assam: Society, Polity and Economy*, Calcutta and New Delhi: K.P. Bagchi & Co., 1991, p. 28.
35. To quote S.K. Bhuyan, 'The kingdom of Assam, as it was constituted during the last 140 years of Ahom rule, was bounded on the north by a range of mountains inhabited by the Bhutanese, Akas, Duflas and Abors; on the east, by another line of hills peopled by the Mishmis and Singphos; on the south, by the Garo, Khasi, Naga and Patkai hills; and on the west, by the Manas or Manaha river on the north bank, and the Habraghat Perganah on the south in the Bengal district of Rungpore. The kingdom where it was entered from Bengal commenced from the Assam Choky on the north bank of the Brahmaputra, opposite Goalpara; while on the south bank it commenced from the Nagarbera hill at a distance of 21 miles to the east of Goalpara. The kingdom was about 500 miles in length with an average breadth of 60 miles.' See, S.K. Bhuyan, *Anglo-Assamese Relations*, 1974, p. 1. See Map 2.
36. See, Map 4, Assam, 1950.
37. Historically, Sylhet was a part of ancient Kamrupa. During the times of the Koch rule, Naranarayan annexed it. See, S.K. Bhuyan, p. 27.
   However, Sylhet was never been a part of Assam as it was known prior to 1874. It was made a part of the Assam province by the British in 1874. See Gait, p. 326.
38. See, Map 3, Assam under the jurisdiction of the Chief Commissioner, 1875, in Baruah, op. cit., p. 23.
39. By the Treaty of Yandabo, which was signed on 24 February 1826, the British forces expelled the Burmese from Assam for good and brought the entire region under the effective control of the East India Company. However, the Company Bahadur at the very initial phase was a bit indecisive about ruling and administering the entire region. Instead, the Company has decided to consolidate its power in a gradual and selective manner. For instance, Assam was divided into two divisions – Western Assam and Eastern Assam, which later on were called 'Lower Assam' and 'Upper Assam' respectively – and it took full possession of the Lower Assam on 7 March 1828. In July 1831, Lord William Bentinck

passed a formal order that Upper Assam should be restored to Purandar Singh, a Ahom prince and Sadiya must be maintained as a British post. In October 1838, the Upper Assam was brought under the full control of the British resulting in the final eclipse of the Ahom rule. See for detail *AHA*, pp. 341–70; *AAR*, pp. 551–77.

40. The phrase 'Ahom Assam' is often used to emphasize the association of the name Assam with the Ahoms. This view has however been contested by many. According to Gait, the name Assam was derived from the Sanskrit word *asama*. The Ahoms called themselves as Tai but the local tribes in admiration of their power called them as *asama* or 'unequalled' or 'peerless. In the course of time, the softening of the 's' to 'h', led to the change of Assam to Aham or Ahom. See, Gait, Appendix G.

    According to the noted linguistic Kakati, *Asama* may be a later Sanskritization of an earlier form like Acham, which originated from the Tai word Veham (meaning to be defeated) with the Assamese prefix 'A' (meaning undefeated).

    The important point to be noted here, is that there is some association between the terms Assam and Ahoms.

41. See Gait, p. 365.
42. Ibid., p. 366.
43. See S.K. Bhuyan, *Anglo-Assamese Relations (AAR)*, p. 47.
44. Gait, p. 366.
45. The Ahoms never tried to impose their culture on those they conquered, nor did they ever try to extend their racial interests through expansion. They, on the contrary, got themselves completely assimilated with the local culture. That is why, they were found concentrated only in Sibsagar and Dibrugarh districts of Assam. See, B.K. Kakati, p. 52.
46. See Gait, p. 367.
47. See *AAR*, p. 45.
48. Ibid., p. 570.
49. See Gait, p. 350.
50. See also, B. Pakem, 'State Formation in Pre-Colonial Jaintia'; and Hamlet Bareh, 'Khasi-Jaintia State Formation', in Surajit Sinha, ed., *'Tribal Politics and State Systems in Pre-Colonial Eastern and North Eastern India*, Calcutta: Centre for Studies in Social Sciences, K.P. Bagchi & Company, 1987.
51. Ibid., p. 314.
52. Ibid., pp. 182–3.
53. Ibid., p. 185.
54. Ibid., p. 358.
55. See F.K. Lehman, *The Structure of the Chin Society*, Urbana: University of Illinois Press, 1963, p. 35; J. Shakespeare, *Lushai Kuki Clans*, London: Macmillan and Co., 1912, B.B. Goswami, 'The Mizos in the Context of State Formation', in Surajit Sinha, ed., *Tribal Politics*

and *State Systems in Pre-Colonial Eastern and North Eastern India.* Also, *AAR*, p. 46.
56. See Gait, p. 356.
57. See J.B. Bhattacharjee, 'Dimasa State Formation in Cacher', in Surajit Sinha, ed., *Tribal Politics and State Systems in Pre-Colonial Eastern and North Eastern India.*
58. They were also called Kacharis.
59. The Bodos are also known as the original inhabitants of the Assam valley.
60. He was a Naga chief, who became a convert to Hinduism, taking the name Gharib Nawaz. E.A. Gait, *History of Assam*, p. 322.
61. Gait, pp. 321–5.
62. Ibid., pp. 400–2.
63. See *AAR*, p. 27.
64. Ibid., p. 260.
65. See, Sanjib Baruah, op. cit., p. 97.
66. The process of the break-up of Assam began in 1963, with the creation of Nagaland as an independent state. Meghalaya in 1970 and Mizoram in 1972, were separated from Assam. NEFA was initially brought under the direct control of the External Affairs Ministry, and was then transferred to the Home Ministry. In 1972, NEFA was renamed as a Union Territory and it was subsequently made a separate state in 1987. See Map 5, which represents the present Assam.

SECTION I

PRAGJYOTISHPUR TO THE END OF THE AHOM PERIOD, AD 1826

PAST IS PROLOGUE*

Surprising as it may sound, the extent of internationalization of the economy and society of ancient Assam, was far advanced than the rest of India, both ethnically as well as economically. Ancient Assam, in fact reveals itself as similar to what is being prescribed for the state today.

Indeed, as H.P. Ray points out, ancient Assam was linked by land routes to China and South-East Asia, and trade with these economies flourished. Additionally, even where ethnic diversity is concerned, Ray points out that the epics indicate that Assam, even during those days, was an exception to the general rule of ethnic homogeneity. However, trade was not overland in total, and there is evidence that ancient Pragjyotishpur also engaged in maritime commerce.

As to how Assam has gained from the continuous inflow of migrants/peoples is described by Amalendu Guha who shows how the Tai migration introduced wet rice cultivation, transforming the slash and burn cultivation of rice into a practice that was far more productive and sustainable. Guha also demonstrates that the contribution was not restricted to agricultural practices alone. The Tai also introduced participatory/communal infrastructure building on a grand scale, when it came to the construction of dykes and embankments. This gave rise to the distribution of water, necessary to support wet rice cultivation.

The decline of the Ahoms was inbuilt in their strategy of survival. Alokesh Barua points out that the Ahoms tried to keep their culturally-united subjects, divided by avoiding economic integration and growth. The lack of the 'will to grow' was reflected in the absence of a strong, standing army that could protect the Ahom State from internal disorder. Thus, opposition from a supposedly non-martial movement of the Vaishnavas in the form of the Moamaria revolt, the rebellion of the Prince of Darrang, the raids of the Burkendazes, self-assertations by local chiefs and raids by the frontier tribes were enough to bring down the six-century-old kingdom.

---

*These words are engraved on the pediment of the Archives Building in Washington.

CHAPTER 2

The Silk Route from North-East India to China and the Bay of Bengal: Some New Lights

HARPRASAD RAY

Assam is the product of the Brahmaputra valley civilization. In the wider context, Assam belongs to that great trans-Himalayan multinational habitat which is watered and nurtured by the Brahmaputra in India, the Chang jiang (Yangtse) in China and the Mekong river, which is the lifeline of South-East Asia. The Mekong river originates near the fountainhead of the Yangtse on the Tangle range (on Qinghai-Tibet border) with the name Langcangjiang and changes into Mekong, as soon as it flows out of the Yunnan province of south-west China. It then flows through Laos, Myanmar, Thailand, Kampuchea; and enters the Pacific ocean from Vietnam.

The Brahmaputra is another international river of this trinity, travelling along the Himalayan heights as the Tsangpo, it reincarnates in India as the son of Brahma (or mountain if we take Brahma as a variant of the Thai Kampuchean word *phram* = *phnam*, i.e. mountain), and flows into the Bay of Bengal through Bangladesh as the Jamuna.

There is yet another international river called Nujiang which also originates from the Tangle mountain. It flows from Yunnan into the Bay of Bengal through Myanmar as the Salveen river.

As we cut across these rivers from the Himalayas, it is difficult, not to conceive the entire valleys of the five rivers (include also the Ganga) as an integral trans-Himalayan region. This is a marvellous land, gifted to man by nature. This is a region which is one of the centres of the world, a region that is occupied by nearly one-half of the world's population. In ancient times, this was the largest natural zoo and botanical garden on the earth, with nearly half its flora and fauna originating in this area. Most parts of this region today, is one of the poorest and most backward areas on the globe. But, given a chance, nearly two billion minds here will transform their homelands into a paradise on earth. And the chance will surely come! Assam is a vital link between the east and the west, between the north and south of this trans-Himalayan world.

Scholars are increasingly inclined to believe that the foothills of the Himalayas and its surrounding areas is one of the cradles of the birth of humankind. The presence of the fossils of both the Rama Ape and Austro Ape in China (and in the Punjab), that too, so close to the Himalayan range suggests that this area is one of the earliest homes of species resembling humankind.[1] The discovery of the Yuanmou Human has provided us with a Himalayan species, that who was as old as, if not older than the Lantian Human discovered in Shaanxi (Shensi) province in the Yellow River valley of China.[2] This virtually extended the cradle of Chinese civilization from the Yellow River valley, further down south to the Himalayan foothills. Scholars believe that it is only a matter of time that early species of human apes would be discovered in areas of this region that are a part of India.[3]

The entire Gangetic belt is well-documented as an international and domestic trading centre in local archeological finds and in various literary sources dating earlier than 400 BC. The discovery of pre-Christian instances of Roman coins and other evidences, including the recently-studied Kharoshti and Kharoshti-Brahmi script inscriptions dated AD 100 to AD 500 found in lower Bengal, provide ample proof regarding trade, a substantial part of which might have gone via the sea route, simultaneously with the land route. Early Kushana coinage from Bengal and the Indo-China peninsula and the prevalence of Mahayana Buddhism in the ancient kingdom of Funan (Indo-China) as early as the fifth century when the entire South-East Asian insular as well as the peninsular region was under the sway of Hinayana Buddhism, show traffic through the overland route from eastern and north-eastern India to the Indo-Chinese peninsula, reinforcing the prevailing view that the early Mahayana monks like Dharmabodhi and others entered China through north-east India.[4] During the construction of the Farakka barrage, numerous materials and artifacts of daily use and structural remains found on both the banks of the river Ganga, attest the site as having flourished as early as the fourth century BC onwards.[5] The textile trade of Bengal, which included Chinese silks, must have contributed to the prosperity of the area. The areas find mention in Xuan Zang's travel account (Da Tang Xiyu Ji, j. X.) under the name *Ga-chu-wen-qi-luo* (Kajangala)[6] such strong and flourishing hinterland prove the link of other parts of India with Assam, Arunachal, Nagaland, Meghalaya and Manipur in north-east India.

RICE CULTIVATION AND SERICULTURE

Only in Asia, has wild rice been cultivated and the earliest homes of rice cultivation must be either in India, China or South-East Asia. One of the rice species has been found in the neolithic cultures discovered in Yunnan, Jiangxi, Zhejiang and Jiangsu provinces of China. Jiangxi has recently been confirmed as one of the earlist homes of rice cultivation.[7] This latest research may supplement the earlier findings of the Rice Research Institute in Manila that the earliest home of rice lies in north-east India.[8] It is possible that rice cultivation spread to other parts of India from Assam and other north-east regions.

Assam's trans-Himalayan linkage can be ascertained through its linguistic and racial connection. The great Indian joint family is made up of four major members:[9] Aryan, Dravidian, Austric and Mongoloid. All the four elements have merged into one stream in north-east India. The Mongoloid Indo Mongoloid was *Kirata* or *Cina kirata*. All, except the Aryan element, can be treated as trans-Himalayan elements. It is amply clear that a cultural confluence between the Indo-European and trans-Himalayan currents have given birth to the Indian civilization and its rich varieties which we see today, and throughout eastern India, one can recognize the contributions made by the trans-Himalayan Indo-Mongoloids such as the Newars, the Koch, the Kachari, the Tipra and other Bodo peoples, the Ahoms, the Jaintias and the Manipuris.[10]

Tantricism is another factor, which forms a bond between the north-eastern region, Tibet, Nepal and south China.[11] The Kamakhya hill and Umananda in Guwahati on the southern bank of the Brahmaputra are important centres of the Tantra cult. The famous story regarding friendship between the King of Kamrup, Kumar Bhaskara Varma (about AD 600–50) and the Chinese pilgrim Xuanzang shows traces of the historical development of this cult. Xuanzang was surprised that Bhaskara Varma had already had some knowledge about the heroic Tang Prime Li Shimin who is known as Emperor Taizong (AD 626–49). Some scholars believe that Xuanzang has translated *Laozi* or *Daode Jing* (Tao Te-Ching) into Sanskrit at the request of King Bhaskara Varma.[12] If this was true, it would establish the connection between the later Tantra cult in India. This is further strengthened by the fact that at least two of the eighteen *Sakta siddhas* of south India who propagated tourism and medicine in eastern India[13] were associated with the Indian tantric followers.

The close proximity of the locales in the trans-Himalayan region, has created cultural affinities in the entire area throughout history. This cultural nearness is surely the result of frequent economic contacts among various peoples in the region. We have indelible marks of cultural affinity, but trade and other economic activities among them, have evaded the notice of modern historians. Thus, cultural affinity helps us restore economic contacts in a concrete manner and put things in the right perspective for future programmes.

We know that China is the motherland of sericulture. But the fact is that Assam was the second country that developed this industry, side-by-side with China. This fact remains largely unknown. If Assam acquired the know-how from China, then it was surely through southwest China. However, one believes that Assamese silk is a native product, developed quite early from the wild variety grown in this region. This is evident from several facts. When Kautilya, one of the earliest to mention Chinese silk, spoke of *cinapatta*, he definitely meant silk produced in China. This means that *patta* a variety of Indian silk was already known to our ancestors. This is verified by the fact that silk is still today known as *pat* in Assam, although in Bengal it means hemp, jute, flaxen (corrupted as *patua* in Bihar). It is possible that silk came to Bengal and other parts of eastern India much later by which time, they had already started growing hemp, the name *pat* was given to hemp, because it has the look and partially the quality of Assamese silk (*pat*). By the third or the fourth century AD, we had various names for cultivated silk. It was known as *angsuka*, *kauseya*, etc. The name *cinapatta* disappears completely and is replaced by *cinangsuka*. The Assamese, however, preferred to cling to the original name, patta = pata = pata.[14] One may like to presume that a part of the consignment that was sent out from the Indian ports in the past contained Assamese silk also. Since, 'patta' silk originated in Assam, the name remained unchanged in Assamese language whereas we do not find this name in this sense in other Indian languages except in Tamil (called) Pattu or Patta. On the other hand, Assam did not adopt any of the other words for silk current in Sanskrit in its colloquial expression.

By AD 700, Assam's silk industry had reached its pinnacle of perfection. Banabhatta, the author of *Harsa Caritam* (the Biography of

Harsa) informs us that the King of Kamrup, Bhaskara Varma, presented to Harsavardhana silken towels which were described as 'silken towels as pure as the autumn moon's night . . . soft loin cloths smooth as birch barks, . . . bundles contained in sacks of woven silk and consisting of black aloe dark as pounded collyrium (Krisnagurutaila)'.[15] We have enough proof to substantiate that direct trade existed between north-east India, and south and south-west China. Historical records from China tell us how the Chinese Emperor Wu, attempted to open up the trade route from the capital to north-east India, through the hostile independent local rulers of Yunnan and the adjoining areas but failed.[16] If trade did not exist in the region, then these rulers would probably not have resisted the Han traders – they would have rather welcomed the prospect of commercial transaction with them. The ruler of Yunnan's jealousy on the establishment of direct trade between China and India at the cost of his own profit that he would have earned, as the middleman, prevented the Chinese from gaining access to India;[17] but the trade in *cinapatta* (otherwise known to the Chinese as the cloth of Sichuan province of China) and the Yunnan square bamboo continued unabated.

The Chinese Emperor was so keen to open up the route to northeast India, that he embanked upon conquering Yunnan, but failed.[18] Yunnan was annexed by China during the reign of the Han Emperor Ming (AD 58 till AD 75). After the Chinese administrators took over the country, they discovered foreign settlers of many countries at Yunnan, including Indians (*Shendu*, which means Sindhu or Juandu Janbudvipa) and the Garos of Meghalaya.[19] This means that the Indians, both from the plains and the hills, visited this area for the purpose of trade.

Cowries have been used in east India as currency from very early times. The Tang annals, *Jiu Tangshu*, has alluded to this, showing that the Chinese had known it before AD 900.[20] This was also the case in south China. Scholars have studied and compared its history with those of Assam and Yunnan.[21] There is a record in a Chinese text that mentions cowries as products of Xiao Poluomenguo (Brahmana desa Minor) which could be referring to the source of the import of cowries into China.[22] The name suggests that it was not 'India proper', a likely reference to eastern India, east of the Ganga which was considered to be outside the pale of Vedic influence. It is a well-known fact that cowries were an important import of Yunnan from India during the older days.[23] Both Yunnan and Sichuan provinces have been good markets for Indian precious and semi-precious stones – the fact being frequently testified till this day because of archaeological discoveries made in recent years.[24]

Excavations carried out at Ambari near Guwahati in Assam yielded some precious celadon ceramic wares (of later days) and pottery made out of *kaolin* (Chinese clay from early times). Guwahati was a flourishing river port along with Pandu, near Kamakhya, in the past. These two Assamese river ports must have attracted a large number of commodities from China, in exchange of native products.[25]

The accepted theory among international scholars on the advent of Buddism in China is that it was first introduced to China not through Central Asia, but through Burma (Myanmar) and Yunnan in an era before Christ. Also, it is rumoured that it was Ashoka's son Mahendra, who first introduced Buddhism into south-west China. He is supposed to have carried the ash urn with him. Recently, a Buddhist ash urn (*sarira*) was discovered in a casket, from under the base of a broken pagoda that scholars believe to be the *sarira* (*sali* in Chinese) brought into China by Mahendra or the earliest carrier of Buddhism. This view was expressed by authentic Chinese experts including the Director of the Famen Si Monastery Museum during the International Symposium on Xuanzang Studies, held from 16 to 22 April 1994 in Luoyang and Xian, the birthplace of Xuanzang and capital the erstwhile Chinese capitals respectively.[26]

It is even speculated that the two legendary Indian monks, Kasyapa Matanga and Dharmaratna entered China through the Yunnan Sichuan route to Luoyang.[27] Such views need to be supported by documentary or archaeological evidence to become historical facts. But, there is no denying that Yunnan was being under the influence of Buddhism at a very early date, which could be prior to the advent of Buddhism in north China through Central Asia. This also provides an indirect evidence of the ongoing trade and cultural contacts between Assam and its surrounding areas.[28]

Scholars have been debating on the possible existence of a historical highway between the ancient Pragjyotisha Kamrup and China through Burma. Some scholars, however, think that the evidences are too fragmented to draw firm conclusions about a well-established trade route.[29]

This opposite view is based on secondary references and seem to be prejudiced against the rich, cultural heritage of north-east India. In our opinion, a well-established trade link in history, may not be always recorded or written down. Recorded history mainly reveals what is amenable to the powers-that-be. Other borderline events, or events that do not directly favour the great emperors, are generally ignored. These linkages can be verified today, through what is now known as subaltern studies. While in China, we have to rely on unofficial histories and private accounts. It is in this context that we have to accept the fact that many great historical events are reconstructed today with the help of fragmented information, and in case of the Assam-Myanmar-Yunnan highway, we are gradually confronted with discoveries that are difficult to deny.[30] It is true that this route is difficult to be trodden today, with modern means of transport shying away from this path? However, during ancient times, people depended on destiny and yet hazarded the dangers of trade routes in water and land in the East. Ironically today, there exists a golden triangle of drug trafficking and other smuggling activities, despite hard conditions of journey.[31] The Nagas and other illegal elements continue to journey to Myanmar, China and further north. This is no longer a secret. If much of what is happening on the ground escapes documentation in this age of electronics and photoelectric cables, we must take the historical highway for granted in the absence of well-preserved historical documentation.[32]

Those who doubt the existence of a north-eastern route to China, are ignorant about the history of ethnic migration from different areas of China and South-East Asia to north-east India. Ethnic contacts and movements have continued since the dawn of human civilization throughout the ancient trans-Himalayan interface.[33]

THE SAGA OF THE AHOMS

The Ahoms of Assam, known as the Tai Shans (the Burmese called the Yunnanese Tais on the northern Burmese border as Shans) followed the old route through the Patkai Range from Maulung in the Hukong valley in Upper Burma and arrived at Tipam near the coal town of Mergherita in the eastern Brahmaputra valley around AD 1252.[34] A branch of it had even migrated to Assam, Cacher, Tripura and Manipur, as early as AD 800.[35] The Tai people were distributed all over from Yunnan to the southernmost extremity of Thailand.

For various reasons, both topographical and political, this route had to be supplemented or replaced by an alternative route passing through Tibet into India. It is even presumed by some scholars that the *shubu* (Sichuan fabric) and quing-bamboo (from Yunnan) that Zhang Qian found in Bactria in the 200 BC, may have been traded through the shorter and easier way, via Tibet.[36] We cannot say with certainty if this route was used in this particular instance, but we have definite proof of the route being used during the Tang and later periods. During the region of the Qing dynasty (the British period in India) both the Tibetan and the Bhutanese trade routes were used by people from both sides, for the exchange, buying and selling of goods. Apart from the Nathula pass which led into India directly from Lhasa, Shigatse, Gyangtse, Yadung and Phari, there were three other routes, two via Bhutan, the first from Tashi Lumpo (Tibet) through Paro Pilo (Bhutan) to the Buxa near present-day Alipur Duar in North Bengal from where Rangpur town in Bangladesh was approached; the second by the valley of the Monas river via Tassgong and Dewangiri and Hajo, north of Guwahati in the foothills; the third took the eastern course of the Tsangpo (Brahmaputra as known in Tibet) and passed through Zedang, Tawang and further on to Hajo.[37]

Trade and communication was (and still is) entirely carried on by the Tibetans only and a few of the Bhutanese (known as the Bhutias). They brought down principally red and partly-coloured blankets, gold dust and silver, rock salt, cowries (mostly Yak tail), musk, and Chinese silks, munjeet and bee-wax; these they exchanged in northeast India for rice lac, raw and manufactured silks of Assam, iron, cotton, dried fish and tobacco. Arriving here during winter, they took care to go back between February and March, before the return of the hot weather or rains.[38]

The road north of Guwahati near Hajo, was an important passage to Tibet via Tawang (India), Cuona (Tsona) on the Tibet border, reaching Zedang, south of the Tsangpo and thence on to Lhasa from where the route spread eastward to Chamdo, the all-weather route to China through Chengdu, the capital of Sichuan. The importance of this road is confirmed by the fact that the Muslim conqueror of Bengal, Muhammad-i-Bakhtiyar chose this route to Tibet in his wild dream of conquering the roof of the world around AD 1202.[39] The second invasion by Sultan Ghiyasuddin I, probably took place during the last month of AD 1226.[40] These incidents corroborate the fact that the invaders chose this route through north Assam, evidently due to the fact that this was the prevalent route negotiated by traders both from Tibet and China on the north, and other parts of India in the south.

According to Taranath (author of *Rising of Indian Dharma*) who lived in early thirteenth-century Tibet, painters, priests and scholars of Bihar and Bengal fled to Assam, Arakan and even to such far away places as Cambodia in South-East Asia, after the massive invasion of Bakhtiar Khilji.[41] This account shows that the routes to the sea through Arakan, and to Cambodia, etc., along the shores of the Pacific ocean and the south China sea, were still being used by people of various descriptions.[42]

The Ahom migration to Assam is another convincing proof of constant use of the north-eastern route to China. Sukapha, the leader of the Ahoms was not the first adventurer to follow the Patkai route. It is learnt from Assamese sources that some Mao-Shans (some time in the sixth century AD) crossed the Sri Lohit (Irrawaddy) and entered the country called Prophangpau (Puphangpom), which might be somewhere in the northern foothill of the Patkai and subduing the native people, consolidated the power of the Mao-Shans there.[43] The Khunlungs (AD 568–638) one of the two ancestors of the Tai-Ahoms, ruled over a vast empire extending from Chiong Mai in northern Siam in the east to the vicinity of the Lohit (Brahmaputra) in the west.[44] It is possible that during this period, some Tais and non-Tais like the Mons and the Chinese migrated to north-east India through the Patkai pass. These immigrants possibly took the shortest and the easiest route to the Patkai. But the Ahoms led by Sukapha, having mainly followed the river courses, the route of their migration was possibly not exactly the same with the one followed by these people.

It appears that a few years before Sukapha's advent in the Brahmaputra valley, Sam-long-pha, the brother and general of the Mao-Shan monarch Su-kan-pha, conquered Manipur, Cacher and Upper Assam. According to Ney Elias, Sam-long-pha led his first expedition to Manipur,[45] advancing probably from the Lushai Hills (Mizo Hills) and Tripura from northern Arakan, and as pointed out by Robinson, he first captured the capital of Cacher and 'returning thence he descended into the Manipur valley'.[46] During his Assam expedition, he marched by the way of the Mali valley into Khamti-Long on the east of the Chindwin river. He occupied Khamti-Long and established there, the rule of the Mao-Shans. From Khamti-Long he entered Upper Assam, then ruled by the Chutiyas, defeated and compelled them to pay him annual tribute.[47] According to Pemberton[48] and Phayre,[49] Sam-long-pha conquered Cacher and Tripura in addition to Manipur. Pemberton is of the opinion that having conquered Tripura, he marched back across the hills and descended into the

Manipur valley near Moirrang, on the western bank of the Logtak lake.⁵⁰ The chronicles of Manipur also make mention of Sam-long-pha's expedition.⁵¹ This makes it clear that besides the Assam-Burma route via Manipur, which was better known, there were also routes connecting north-east India with Burma and China through the Lushai Hills and Tripura. Whether Sam-long-pha crossed the Patkai hills through the Panchou pass or the Bissa pass, is not exactly known but his march to Upper Assam a few years ahead of Sukapha, inspired the latter to undertake the adventure.⁵²

The hazardous journey from Upper Burma to Upper Assam via the Patkai hills is, however, learnt in detail from a later source. Chang Ang, a chieftain of the village Mung Yang, who accompanied the Burmese contingent on its first invasion of Assam in AD 1817, has left a comprehensive account of the advance of the army from Mung Kwang till its arrival at Jorhat, then capital of the Ahoms, via the Patkai pass. The chronicle is written in Tai-Ahom and is entitled *Weissali* (Assam) *Hukong*.⁵³ According to sources, it took two weeks to reach Mung Khong (Mung-Kham) from Mung Yang via Mung-Kong. The army had to pass through dense forests and marshes and cross many stream and rivers. The area was inhabited by the Singphos, who were friendly to the Burmese invaders. Advancing from Mung Khong, the army reached the Tanai river and after crossing it, arrived at the territory of Bisanong, the chief of the Singphos of the area. Halting there for nine days, the army resumed its march and crossed the river Talung (Turung) which was a very difficult task. Then, moving towards the west, they reached the bank of the river Jalip. Meanwhile, the soldiers suffered from painful water sores, having had to march through the terrain hills, muddy swamps and cross rivers with strong currents. At last, they reached the bank of the river Nam-Tawa and then the Jaga hills, which were known in Burmese as Khong Tong or the western hills. Along these hills, the army made its way westward to Weissali or Assam. Thereafter, crossing the rivers Khojong and Loklai, they reached the Patkai hills. The Loklai River had such strong and swift currents and split rocks hidden under its surface, that many soldiers fell into them and lost their lives.

Crossing the Patkai ridges with the horses was very risky and difficult. In order to reach the top, one had to climb as many as eighteen ridges, nine small and nine big tones. From the summit, one could clearly see five roads girdling the mountain and passing through numerous rocks. The army had to continuously scale its way for

THE SILK ROUTE FROM NORTH-EAST INDIA TO CHINA 53

twelve days, at the end of which, it arrived on the banks of the Burhi Dihing in the valley of the Brahmaputra. Unable to withstand the hardships of the journey, many soldiers lost their lives. Six hundred years before this Burmese (Man) invasion, the Tai-Shans (Ahoms) while migrating to Assam, also followed almost the same route and were subjected to the same odds and hazards. It was again along this route that the Burmese army invaded Assam in AD 1819 and 1821, and were finally driven out of the Brahmaputra valley by the British troops in March 1823.[54]

During their long reign spanning six centuries, the Ahoms maintained their contact with their homeland through this route. Towards the later part of their rule, they even established friendly relations with the Burmese. Marriage alliances were also made between the royal families of Assam and Mung-Kawng, and later, several Assamese princesses and maidens were married to the Burmese emperors and generals. In such alliances, there was an interchange of valuable gifts of choicest products of the respective countries which included silk, gold embroidered head-dresses, cross-bows, ivory products, horses and elephants. The royal brides from Assam were accompanied by hundreds of soldiers with their families, besides slaves and attendants to Ava.[55] Such events promoted cultural assimilation. Francis Hamilton informs us that slaves were sent from Assam to Mung-Kawng from where they were probably exported to Ava.[56]

Initially, the Patkai route was under the surveillance of the Ahom government, route, but in AD 1401, by the terms of a formal treaty, the Patkai hill was fixed as the boundary between Assam and Mung-Kawng.[57] Thenceforth, this responsibility fell on the latter government which used to set up village or military settlements at every 12 or 15 miles along the route to ensure its safety.[58]

Subsequently, numerous routes were opened up, connecting northeast India with China via Burma, Bhutan and Tibet. M'Cosh in his *Topography of Assam*, makes mention of five routes, of which three, namely, the one through the pass of the Dihing, the other through the Mishmi hills and the third through the Phungan pass to Manchee and China, were most notable.[59] The accounts of British officers like Mitchell[60] and Butler[61] describe several routes connecting Assam with Burma and thence with China via the Naga hills, Manipur and the Lushai hills, some of which are being followed by present-day insurgents in the north-east to maintain cooperation with the Kachin Independence Army.[62]

There were also numerous passes through the northern mountains of Assam leading to China, Afghanistan and the West, through Bhutan and Tibet. According to the *Tabaquat-i-Nasiri*, a Persian work of the late thirteenth century, there were as many as 35 passes between Assam and Tibet which led to China and through which horses were brought to Lakhnauti, the capital of Gauda in Bengal.[63] Of all these passes, the safest and the most convenient was the one which connected the two important marts, Chuona (Tsona) within the border of Tibet and Gegunshur, 6.4 km. away from Chuona within the border of Assam. Tibetan merchants carried silver bullion to the tune of Rs. 1 lakh, besides a considerable quantity of rock salt for sale to merchants in Assam and purchased from the latter, articles like rice, Assam silk, iron, lac, otterskins, buffalo horns and pearls.[64] Though this information is in regard to the eighteenth century, the nature and articles of trade were possibly the same in earlier times as well. The Singphos, on the other hand, followed the Assam-Burma route to China and managed to procure copper, silver, tin and other articles from that country and exchanged them with Assam silk, ivory, musk, manjit, madder, etc., at the frontier market at Sadiya.[65] To this mart, the Mishmis, the hill-Miris and the Abors (Nishis) brought gold, iron implements and woollen cloth from China.[66] These tribes maintained their contact with China through the Mishmi hill route. Along the route through Bhutan, horses and Chinese silk were imported to Assam from China and Tibet.[67]

ASSAM-BHUTAN TRADE ROUTE[68]

If we turn the pages of the history of Assam, we find proof of the Assam-Bhutan intercourse right from the period of the Salastambha rulers of Assam from the middle of AD 700 to the first quarter of AD 1000. With its capital at Tezpur (Hadappesvara), and its massive sculptural and architectural achievements, it must have exercised political authority and exerted cultural influence on its neighbour, Bhutan. The *Darrang Rajavanshavali*, and even a later work by Ashley Eden in his *Political Mission to Bhutan* confirm genealogical connections between the Koch kings and Bhutanese royalty.

Tradition associates many religious places of Assam with those of Bhutan. The Trivenighat Thaan, about 7 km. north of Kokrajhar in north-west Assam, perpetuates, the memory of the great Assamese Vaishnava preacher Madhava Deva, who was believed to have been patronized by the Bhutanese king, which facilitated the conversion of a member of the Bhutanese royal family into Vaisnavism.

The *melas* and the fairs associated with religious festivals, also marked the social occasions where goods were exchanged between people assembled from various places in the surrounding areas of Assam. The present town of Udalguri in the Darrang district happened to be the venue of annual *mela* for Butanese trade, normally held between the dry season of January and mid-February each year, when the people combined socio-religious functions with trade. They came to this fair, via a road linking Bhairav Kunda in the north and Udalgiri, which was popularly known as the Bhutiya Road. The Bhutanese brought to the fair ponies, dogs, blankets, chillies, oranges, whisky, musk, *hing* (asafoetida), *jabrang*, etc., for sale and presumably purchased textiles and silks to wear, salt, perfumes and incenses. All the three districts of Goalpara, Kamrup and Darrang are associated with Bhutan. Their visits even today, during winter to the Gupteswara Siva temple on the north bank of Brahmaputra, about 50 km. south-east of Udalguri, include the shaving of heads at a fixed point atop the hill nearby, and performing the *shradha* ceremony to their ancestors. They make their pilgrimage to Hindu temples in and around Guwahati, such as Asva-Kranta, Umananda (the seat of Siva), Kamakhya (the seat of the Mother Goddess), Siddheswar (at Sualkuchi), and also to the Buddhist temple of Hayagriva Madhava, considered the seat of Tathagata (Buddha). They understand the *Hayagriva* (horse-faced) Madhava to be a Buddhist image.[69]

EXPORTS AND IMPORTS THROUGH THE AGES

Chinese sources give us an idea about the exchange of goods between north-east India and China during the ancient period.

Among the goods transported from Sichuan (south-west China) to India were, Sichuan cloth (silk or grass cloth known as huangrun in Chinese), square bamboo sticks (for use of mountain-dwellers), salt, iron, copper, iron, lead, tin, gold and silver and probably jade and agate.[70] Besides, north-eastern India also learnt to cultivate rice, sesame and tea bushes since very early times.[71]

The list of exports from India is interesting.[72] India exported cotton or flax cloth (known as *bodie* in China), myrobalan, pineapple, jackfruit, *cowries*, coloured glaze, precious stones, pearls, peacocks, halcyons, elephants, and even orangutans to Sichman. Some of the last few items, like pearls and precious stones were presumably from west and south India. The techniques of processing tea by rubbing with the hand and baking over the slow fire of a roaster emerged in China and were passed on to north-east India. It is quite possible, that a certain amount of tea bushes grew in India too, and that the local people used them as intoxicants or as an energizer by processing the leaves by hand before consuming them. The improved technique of processing tea, was learnt from the neighbouring parts of China.[73]

The *Arthashastra* of Kautilya contains references to the silk of Assam. It mentions a place, Suvarnakudya, where excellent silk fabrics were produced.[74] Suvarnakudya has been almost correctly identified with Sonkudiha in the Kamrup district of Assam, 9 km. from Hajo, that remained an important mart for Tibeto-Indian and Bhutan-Indian trade till recent times.[75] The same area also produced a kind of perfume called *tailaparnika*,[76] *aguru* (agallochum, resin of aloe) sandalwood[77] and malabathrum (*tejpat*), all transported down the streams of the Brahmaputra and the Ganga for export to south India, Sri Lanka and western countries.[78]

It seems that traditional trade during the entire medieval period has mainly been conducted through Tibet and the old items continued to be traded right up to the British period. Both the Bhutanese and the Tibetans carried their merchandise to northern Bengal at Rangpur and Hajo in Northern Assam.

The goods, imported from Bhutan were[79] debang (China silk), crow tails, hill ponies, wax, walnuts, musk, lac, madder or *munjeet*, blankets and silver. Goods exported to Bhutan were[80] indigo, cloves, nutmeg, cardamom, camphor, sugar, copper, broadcloth, goat skins, Endy cloth, coarse Endy cloth, googul (aguru), sandalwood, country gun powder, dried fish and tobacco.

The Khampas of eastern Tibet, exported the following goods to north-east India, via Hajo:[81] red and partly-coloured blankets, gold dust, silver, rock salt, *cowries*, musks, few coarse Chinese silks, *munjeet* (madder) and bee-wax.

Goods exported to Tibet (and probably to China via Tibet) were:[82] lac, raw and manufactured silks of Assam, cotton, dried fish and tobacco.

We may compare the above-mentioned articles with some of the items which are allowed to be traded on the borders of India and

China's Tibet region today. Even the trade agreements today, signed between India and China do not exceed the limits of traditional exports and imports; for instance, coffee, tobacco, iron ore and concentrates, chrome ore, finished leather and leather products, iron and steel bars, chemical dyes and dye intermediaries, sandalwood, myrobalan, wax, and such other natural products and minerals are invariably present in the inventory for export from India. From China, India normally imports beans, sulpher, borax, gypsum, silk and silk piece goods, wool, paper, nutmeg, musk, vermicelli, porcelain, resin, glassware, etc. Added to this in modern times, is machinery and other scientific products.[83]

Assam's and for that matter, north-east India's prosperity was closely related to the high level of development of its local handicrafts, natural products, silks and other textile products, forest products, etc., as well as its easy access to the different parts of India in the west, to Myanmar and south-west China in the east, to the north through the tribal intermediaries, and to the south through a direct sea route.

THE LUIT FLOWS HOME TO THE SEA

The combined waters of the Brahmaputra and the Meghna fell into the sea. There were navigable rivers connecting the Brahmaputra with the Ganga. Later (as per Rennel's map of 1783) the Jenni (Jamuna) which issued from the Brahmaputra near Sherpur (in Bangladesh) joined the Ganga near Jaffargunj below Pabna and Ruttongunj.[84] This facilitated direct navigation from the farthest point in Assam to the mouth of the Ganga (near Tamratipti and Ganga) on the sea.

The *Periplus* of the Erythraean Sea, in describing a cruise along the coast of Bengal from the west to the east, mentions that near the sea where the river Ganga meets it, there exists an island in the ocean called 'Chryse', meaning 'golden', which has wrongly been located in Burma or Java or the Malay peninsula. The text clearly indicates a place nearby, which could only be Sondip (a corruption of Suvarnadvipa) at the mouth of the united waters of the Ganga and the Brahmaputra, and no other place.[85]

There are many facts in history which remain obscure or neglected as a result of oversight or misinterpretation by historians who have scarce knowledge about the topography and ancient history of north-east India. The capital of Assam today, is located at Dispur. The word 'Dis' and 'pur', is a corruption of Pragjyotishpur. In ancient times, the place and the country was known as Pragjyotish [as in *Raghuvamsa cakampe tirna-Lauhtye tasmin Pragiyotiseswara* which means, the King of Pragjyotisa trembled when he (Raghu) crossed the river Lauhitye (Brahmaputra)] (IV.81). In ancient times too, the tribes around the country, as well as the foreigners called the country Pragjyotishpur. This is as evidenced in the *Periplus*. This valuable truth has been discoursed upon by a great historian of this region, the late N.K. Bhattasali. As the source material is not readily available today, it may be worthwhile to quote extensively from his paper.[86]

Periplus's description of the country of This follows immediately after Chryse:

After this region under the very north, the sea outside ending in a land called This, there is a very great inland city called Thinae, from which raw silk and silk yarn and silk cloth are brought on foot through Bactria to Barygaza and are also exported to Daminica by way of the river Ganges. But the land to This is to easy of access; few men come from there and seldom. The country lies under the Lesser Bear and is said to border on the farthest part of Pontus and the Caspian Sea, next to which lies Lake Maeotis, all of which empty into the ocean.

It will be remembered that the mouth of the Ganga and the Island of Gold, i.e. present Sondvip being talked of, immediately after which the above passage occurs. Unfortunately, translation from the original Greek by Mr Schoff has left some passages rather obscure. In the first sentence, we are told parenthetically that 'the sea outside ends in a land called This'. As the passage begins with a direction to the north, to any man of common sense, the passage would mean that at the end of the gulf to the arctic zones, the Black Sea (Pontus) and the Caspian Sea, stood the city called Thinae. Mr Schoff, in his notes (p. 261) has recognized in Thinae, the country of China and its great western state Ts'in, but has confused it with This which began according to the *Periplus*, at the end of the head-waters of the gulf of the Ganga. It appears to me clear that two different countries are being spoken of; one This beginning from the head-waters of the gulf of the Ganga and extending northwards to inaccessible places; and the other Thinae still further north extending to the arctic regions and to the Black Sea and the Caspian Sea. When we remember that Bhagadatta is described in the *Mahabharata* (Sabha: Ch. 34, Bhandarkar Institute edition, Ch. 31—*shloks* 9 and 10) as present in the Rajasuya sacrifice of Yudhisthira with his hosts of mlecchas and dwellers of the sea-coast, and when we take note of the fact that in historical times the kingdom of Pragjyotisa included Sylhet, Tippera and Noakhali districts and thus extended up to the sea-coast at the head-waters of the Gulf of the Ganga, we at once realize that the author of the *Periplus*, in talking of This, is really meaning Pragjyotisa. He calls the kingdom, 'This' the last part of the actual name, Pragjyotisa, the first portion of the long name having proved too much for him.[87] The other name Thinae, as recognized by Schoff and other scholars really refers to China, the land of silk after which the stuff became known Cinamsuka, as the fabric of China.

I have shown above that the hitherto unidentified country of This is none else than Pragjyotisa. The manner in which the well-known malabathrum or tejpat trade of the country of This is referred to in the next paragraph will this make clear:

Every year on the borders of the land of This there comes together a tribe of men with short bodies and broad flat faces and by nature peaceable; they are called Besatae, and are almost entirely uncivilised. They come with their wives and children carrying great packs and plaited baskets of what looks like green grape leaves. They meet in a place between their own country and the land of This. There they hold a feast for several days, spreading out the baskets under themselves as mats, and then return to their own places in the interior.

The Besatae appear to me to be none else than the Bhutiyas who carry on the overland trade with the northern districts of Assam, Darjeeling and Jalpaiguri of Bengal through the various *duars* or passes. The annual fairs on the borderland which attract them are well-known and I can just call to mind the great fair at the temple of galpes in Jalpaiguri district during the Shivaratri festival. Several more fairs are likely to exist all along the borderland of Bhutan and Assam, and *Periplus's* description of the custom shows that they have been held in this region from time immemorial.

And then the natives watching them come into that place and gather up their mats; and they pick out from the braids, the fibres which they call *petri*. They lay the leaves close together in several layers and make them into balls which they pierce with the fibres from the mats. And there are three sorts; those made of the largest leave are called the large-ball malabathrum; those of the smaller, the medium ball; and those of the smallest, the small ball. Thus there exist three sorts of malabathrum, and it is brought into India by those who prepare it.

The above is a rather confused account of the procurement, packing and marketing of the tejpat. Tejpat in Sanskrit is called simply *patra*, and *Periplus* actually calls the commodity by this Sanskrit name. The Bhutiyas who came to the border fairs of Pragjyotisa with this commodity are easily recognized by their short bodies, broad flat faces and peaceable nature. The packing of the leaves in wicker work baskets and their gradation in classes are followed even up to the present time. In Shillong, in the Jaiaw quarter of the town, by the bank of the hill stream Umkhra, I found Tejpat trees growing wild and Mr Hunter also, in his statistical account of Assam notes the fact in describing the produce of the Khasi hills. Mr Gordon in his monograph on the Khasis, on p. 47, gives an account of the extensive tejpat gardens in the Khasi and This states. This commodity of everyday use among the Indians, which now grows wild in the hill districts of Assam and is exported so largely to outside markets, appears in the first century AD, to have been obtained from the Bhutiyas with some trouble.

One point worthy of note that emerges, if we accept the proposed identification of This with Pragjyotisa, is that the kingdom, even in the first century AD, a period for which we have no political record, extended up to the Gulf of the Meghna, probably up to the Noakhali and Chittagong coasts.[88]

ASSAM'S OPENING TO THE SEA

It is now a well-known fact that the low-lying and waterlogged parts, to the south of the Assam range was perhaps connected with the Bay of Bengal by the estuary of the Brahmaputra and was known as the 'eastern sea' (*purba samudra*). Geologists have established that there was a time when sea-waves swept over the land forming the present Mymensing and Sylhet districts of Bangladesh lying south of the Garo, Khasi and Jaintia hills. Even in modern times, some parts of the Mymensing and Dhaka districts were marked as 'sea'. The low-lying parts of Sylhet, parts of Comilla, Noakhali, Mymensing (in Bangladesh) and Cacher, Karimganj and Hailakandi (in Assam) are still called *haor*, a corruption of the colloquial form of *sagar*.[89] It is interesting to note that Xuanzang (Yuan Chwang) says the same thing when he says that the kingdoms of Si-li-cha-da-lo (Sri Ksetra, meaning Srihatta) and other areas of Samatata (the shore or level country which denote that the country abuts the sea) bordered on the great sea.[90] Alberuni, in the eleventh century, has also referred to the area as being under the sea or near it.[91]

Our purpose of such detailed analysis of the geographical position of Assam *vis-à-vis* China is to underline the factors responsible for the prosperity on one hand and the adversity of north-east India, particularly after the ill-fated partition of the country for which the then leaders of Assam are also responsible. The importance of the route to the sea through Chittagong had been emphasized upon, for instance, in an editorial of *The Statesman*, dated 7 November 1893, subsequent to the transfer of the administration, of the Mizo (Lushai) hills to Assam. The editorial runs as:[92]

In common with the public generally, we have all along been led to believe that, on the transfer of the Lushai Hills to the Assam Chief Commissionership, the Chittagong division would also be made over, but, according to a contemporary, that consummation is not to have effect until the completion of the Chittagong-Assam Railway, or such portion of it as will run from the port to Silchar. Unless Chittagong, Tipperah, and Noakhally are incorporated, the Imperial Government must finance Assam for some years to come, for the latter will find it quite impossible to meet, unaided, the expenses entailed by the defence of her frontiers and possible (though not very probable) punitive expeditions. The severance of Assam from Bengal was dictated by motives of purely Imperial policy, and it becomes the bounden duty, therefore, of the Supreme Government to see that the newly-constituted Province does not suffer in any way.

This sounds as pathetic in the context of what happened during the century that followed.

RESUME

The traditional trade route came into being first as a track, then as a road that developed into a overland trade route with the expansion of commercial activities. It also brought about socio-economic development in the entire region.

Most sections of this route have the monsoon type of climate. The route receives the north-east wind in winter and the south-west monsoon in summer. The direction of course, varies with the season. There are roughly three seasons: the cool season (from November to February), the hot season (from March to May) and the rainy season (from June to October). During the rainy season, heavy rain accompanied by thunder, brings down torrents of water rushing down the mountains. Rivers are in spate – even small streams or brooks become turbulent rivers, very difficult to cross.

In the dry season, the atmospheric temperature rises to as high as 40 degrees centigrade, thus, communicable sub-tropical diseases are prevalent in the entire region. The cool season is the best time for trading activities. Every year, since November onwards, the strong north-east monsoon winds, blowing in from the Yunnan-Guizhou plateau of China, steadily dispel the damp and hot airflow from the Indian ocean. The days are sunny, the climate arid with rare rainfall. The river courses dry up, making it convenient for one to pass through. However, this 'dry' duration is short, whereas the journey is a long one – it is possible to make only one trip to and fro in a year, which to a large degree, places restrictions on the development of trade and commerce.

Also, the areas through which the overland trade route passes, are inhabited by many ethnic minorities whose political, economic and social organizations are more than primitive and backward. They are constantly at loggerheads with each other, which is extremely harmful to the advance of trade and safety of the route.

THE FUTURE

Assam is almost a land-locked state with hilly regions all around it. One of the solutions to its problems will be to open the southern gate to the sea by entering into friendly trade links with Bangladesh. As it is, even normal trade with Bangladesh (formerly East Pakistan) which existed till 1965, is at a standstill due to apathy from both sides, and under these circumstances, it will be a case of building castles in the air if we presume a breakthrough of any kind in this regard in the near future.

Ever since the first illegal Naga mission was rumoured to have reached the Tengcheng area of north-west Yunnan in China (on the trail of the ancient north-east India-China route via Burma) after a trek through the Kachin state in northern Myanmar (Burma) as early as 1967,[93] the existence of a regular route to south China has started arousing the interest of the historians of this Silk Route on the one hand, and has created tension in the minds of various security agencies of India on the other. Moreover, the illicit drug traffic involving this part of India and the Golden Triangle, comprising northern Thailand, Shan and Kachin states in eastern Myanmar, and western Laos has forced the governments concerned to strengthen their vigil in the area.[94] One of the steps would be to open the different border posts adjoining Myanmar to regular trade. A step in that direction has already been taken by opening the border towns of Moreh (110 km. from the capital town of Manipur) in India and Tamu (in Kabaw valley) in Myanmar to regularize border trade. Both these places were the hubs of smugglers.[95] More such border towns should be opened for trade.

Trade continued on the Tibetan border, till it was disrupted after strict Chinese control was enforced in the entire region of Tibet. Trade in this area had been going on since ancient times, and it is quite possible that it was more in use because of its easy accessibility to India in the south and inland China in the north. This is clear from our discussion in the earlier pages. After a long closure, some townships like Taklakot Puran, etc., on the northern border of India have been opened to trade. This is, however, an extremely inadequate step. The most viable route has emerged from the well-known textile manufacturing town of Hajo and leads to Tibet via Tsuona (Chuona) and thence to Chengdu, the capital of Sichuan through the all-weather road to China's heartland. This link should be re-opened for the mutual benefit of traders from both sides.

North-east India's trade with Tibet was disrupted whenever the Chinese asserted their role in the latter. Since their permanent occupation of Lhasa, they closed Tibet to the inhabitants of India, and the inhabitants of the neighbouring countries like Bhutan could pass the boundary only under the sanction of a passport.[96] Such restrictions were enforced not only in this part of the border, they enforced similar restrictions in relation to coastal trade with the other Asian countries and the West too.[97] Such sanctions undermined border trade. Gradual expansion of the Muslim rule to the north-eastern part of India in the medieval period did the same damage to trade.

British rule in India caused untold misery to the common people. The colonizers adopted systematic measures to disrupt our village economy and enforced subversive economic measures to destroy it so that the foundations of our textile industry and trade was jeopardized.

The apathy of the ruling politicians towards the importance of a comprehensive system of production and distribution which entails the opening of our doors to our neighbours for mutual give-and-take, is stalling our development. Mutual suspicion, mistrust, and mud-slinging have to be got rid of. Political stability is a *sine qua non* for economic progress. This and the determination to stand on one's own feet will smoothen the way for the progress of the north-east. All the factors that go into the making of such an atmosphere already exist. The British economy flourished at our cost. Textiles and other indigenous products which brought prosperity to us were banned for the benefit of our rulers. The benefits of scientific discoveries reaped by the industrial revolution were all monopolized by the Western countries and denied to us.

Much has been done after Independence. It is now high time, that other border posts, especially the one joining Hajo and Guwahati with the Tibetan area of Zedang be opened to trade. This will facilitate trade with the Tibetan as well as the Bhutia traders.

In our development programme, which includes an array of productive activities and trade, we have not paid attention to indigenous products and the traditional items of trade based on them. No serious attempts have been made to identify and study native products scientifically, classify them according to their value as commodities, apply modern scientific experiments to develop their uses to suit modern diversified requirements and put them up to compete in foreign markets. Ginger, catechu, putchuk, myryobalan, asafoetida, emblica officinalis (*amla*), etc., should be chemically analysed and their medicinal and food value should be assessed to meet our needs. Modern sophisticated technology should be used by local entrepreneurs to improve quality and increase varieties in the production of tea, silk, endy, muga, forest products, paper and sugar that are produced in abundance in Assam.

We have already mentioned the opening up of the road to the Bay of Bengal via Chittagong. But this is well-nigh impossible today. The most convenient outlet for Assam is through West Bengal. The airport at Rupsi in Dhubri district is the doorway to Assam and one of the best airports in the north-east, but it lies abandoned. As a result, traders and other citizens of the neighbouring area have to rush to Koch Bihar (now Coochbehar in north Bengal, to avail both the air service and road transport, thus causing a loss of revenue to Assam. Rather than vying with others in order to set-up heavy industries, Assamese entrepreneurs should brace up to the development of traditional items of production with the help of the latest technology.

Some who have the breadth of vision at home and abroad, advocate the building of an Asian-European railway or rail-cum-roadways, starting from Shanghai in the east and passing through Zhejiang, Jiangxi, Hunan, Guizhou and Yunnan (all in China), entering northern Myanmar, and going on to reach the north-eastern part of India to join the Indian railway network. Then, one can then go southwestward to the Bay of Bengal (at Chittagong port) and further west to the Indian Ocean. Proceeding westward, one can travel to Brest and France, through Pakistan and Central Asia. At present, there are two big gaps in this project – the railway lines in Yunnan (in China) and Myanmar have not been constructed as yet, nor has the line that would link Myanmar with the north-eastern part of India been laid. This magnificent plan will come true only after the efforts of all concerned are pulled up together. When this international railway link project is completed, it will play a very significant role in the social and economic life of north-east India, Myanmar and south-west China. It will then be extremely advantageous for India to develop eco-cultural contacts with its neighbours, reduce transport expenditure and improve the competitive capability of Indian products in the international market.[98]

NOTES

1. Tan Chung and Haraprasad Ray, 'Trans-Himalayan Multi-national Habitat', in Tan Chung, ed., *Indian Horizons* (special issue 'India and China'), vol. 43, nos. 1–2, 1994, p. 296.
2. Ibid., p. 297.
3. Ibid. pp. 297–8.
4. B.N. Mukherjee, 'Kharoshti and Kharoshti-Brahmi Inscriptions in West Bengal (India)', *Indian Museum Bulletin*, no. 25, 1990, pp. 23–39; K.K. Sarkar, 'Mahayana Buddhism in Funan', *Sino-Indian Studies*, vol. V, no. 1, 1995, pp. 73–4.
5. K. Chakravarty, 'On the Identification of Ka-Chu-Won-k'i-o (Kajangala) of Hiuen Tsang', *Journal of Indian History*, vol. VI, no. 1, 1978.
6. Ji Xianlin et al., eds., *Da Tang Xiyu Ji Jiaozhu (Journey to the Western Region During the Tang Dynasty*, annotated), Beijing, 1985, pp. 788–90.
7. Tan Chung and Ray, op. cit., p. 298.
8. T.T. Chang, 'The Rice Culture', in *The Early History of Agriculture*, pp. 143–55, Philosophical Transactions of the Royal Society of London, ser. B., p. 275.

9. Tan Chung and Ray, op. cit., p. 303.
10. Suniti Kumar Chatterji, *Karata-Jana-Kriti: The Indo-Mongoloids: Their Contribution to the History and Culture of India*, revd. 2nd edn., Calcutta, 1974, p. 184.
11. Tan Chung and Ray, op. cit., pp. 304–5.
12. Ibid., p. 305.
13. Huang Xinchuan, 'Hinduism and China', paper presented at the Assembly of World's Religion, San Francisco, 15–21 August 1990, p. 5.
14. Harprasad Ray, 'The Southern Silk Route from China to India—An approach from India', paper presented at the 34th International Congress of Asian and North African Studies (ICANAS), Hong Kong, 22–28 August 1993, p. 18. Our point gets support from R.L. Turner, *A Comparative Dictionary of the Indo-Aryan Languages*, London: OUP, 1966, rpt. 1973, p. 434.
15. P.V. Kane, ed., *The Harsacarita of Banabhatta*, Delhi-Varanasi-Patna, rpt. 1973, Ch. VII, p. 61; for English translation see, E.B. Cowell and F.W. Thomas, Delhi-Varanasi-Patna, 1961, p. 214.
16. Shiji by Sima Qian, j. 123, Zhonghua Shuju, 1965 edn., pp. 3158–60, 3166.
17. Ibid., also j. 116, pp. 2995–6.
18. Ibid.
19. Chang Qu (Jin Dynasty), Huayangguo Zhi, Nanzhong zhi (Chronicles of the Hua Yang Countries, Records of the Nanzhong Areas), quoted in the *Draft History of the Va Nationality*, Nationalities Institute, Chinese Academy of Sciences, 1963, pp. 24–5.
20. Tan Chung and Ray, op. cit., p. 307.
21. *Yunnan Wenwu (Cultural Relics in Yunnan)*, 22, 1987, p. 42; T.C. Sharma, 'Sources of the History of Assam–Ancient Period', in N.R. Ray, ed., *Sources of the History of India*, vol. 3, Calcutta, 1980, p. 51.
22. Jiang Yuxiang, 'Gudai Zhongguo Xinan Sichou Jianlun' (A Brief Discussion of the Ancient South-West Silk Route of China), paper presented at the 34th International Congress of Asia and North African Studies, Hong Kong, 22–28 August 1993.
23. *Yunnan Wenwu*, 20, 1986, p. 26.
24. *Sichuan Wenwu (Cultural Relics of Sichuan)* 5, 1988, p. 30; also *Yunnan Wenwu*, 22, 1987, p. 42.
25. Sharma, op. cit., p. 82; Haraprasad Ray, 'Southern Silk Route', op. cit., p. 38.
26. This point has been discussed in an international conference and published in *Renwen Zazhi (Journal of Humanities)*, additional issue, Xian, 1993, brief summary is given on pp. 1–2.
27. Jiang Yuxiang supports this theory after a lengthy discussion in his paper cited in n. 22.
28. Tan Chung and Ray, op. cit., pp. 307–8.

29. Ibid., p. 308.
30. Ray, 'Southern Silk Route,' op. cit., pp. 33–43.
31. Pradip Srivastava, 'India and South-East Asia: The Drug Connection', paper presented at the 1st Conference of the Indian Congress of Asian and Pacific Studies, 7–29 January 1995.
32. Tan Chung and Ray, op. cit., p. 308.
33. D.P. Sharma, 'Neolithic Industries of India and South-East Asia', paper presented at the 12th Conference of the International Association of the Historians of Asia, Hong Kong, 24–28 June 1991; Ray, 'The Southern Silk Route', op. cit., pp. 30–3.
34. S.K. Bhuyan, ed., *Deodhai Buranji*, Gauhati, 1932, 1962, p. 9; P. Gogoi, *The Tai and the Tai Kingdoms*, Guwahati, 1968, p. 265.
35. W.W. Hunter, *A Statistical Account of Assam*, vol. 1, London, 1879, p. 309.
36. W. Liebenthal, 'Sanskrit Inscriptions from Yunnan', II, *Sino-Indian Studies*, vol. 1, 1955, p. 62, f.n. 3.
37. R.B. Pemberton, *Report on Bootan*, Calcutta, 1839, rpt., 1961, p. 78.
38. Ibid., p. 79; also, idem, *The Eastern Frontier of British India*, Calcutta, 1835, rpt., Guwahati, 1966, p. 83.
39. N.K. Bhattasali, 'Muhammad-i-Bakhtiyar's Expedition to Tibet', in *Indian Historical Quarterly*, IX, 1933, pp. 49–62.
40. Ibid., 'New Lights on the History of Assam', *Indian Historical Quarterly*, XXII, 1946, pp. 1–14.
41. J. Filliozat, 'Emigration of Indian Buddhists to Indo-China, *c*. AD 1200', *Studies in Asian History*, Proceedings of Asian History Congress, 1961; ICCR, 1969, pp. 46–7.
42. Ibid., pp. 45–8.
43. P. Gogoi, op. cit., pp. 133f.
44. N. Elias, 'Introductory Sketch of the History of the Shans in Upper Burma and West Yunnan', Calcutta, 1876, p. 18.
45. W. Robinson, *A Descriptive Account of Assam*, Calcutta, 1809, p. 160.
46. N. Elias, op. cit., pp. 61f.
47. R.B. Pemberton, 'The Eastern Frontier', op. cit., pp. 113f.
48. A. Phayre, *History of Burma*, London, 1883, p. 15.
49. Pemberton, op. cit., p. 114.
50. Ibid.
51. English translation of the chronicle is by B. Barua and published along with another chronicle entitled *Weissali Mung-dun-Suri-Khan* with the title *Weissalisa*, Dibrugarh University (Assam), 1977.
52. S.L. Barua, 'The Indian Historical Evidence on the Southern Silk Route: The Route of Ahom Migration to Assam', paper presented at the 34th Session of the ICANAS, 22–28 August 1993, p. 8. I am indebted to this author for much of the information on Ahom migration.

53. *Weissalisa*, ibid., pp. 7f.
54. S.L. Barua, op. cit., p. 10.
55. Ibid., fn. 42. The *Deodhai Assam Buranji, Assam Buranji* and *Ahomar Din* cited in the footnote state that Hemo alias Bhamo Aideo, daughter of the Ahom prince Baga Konwar offered to the Burmese king Badawpaya (AD 1781–1819) in 1817, was accompanied by 500 soldiers along with their families. They were settled at a place which subsequently came to be known as Bhamo after the name of the princess; quoted in S.L. Barua, loc. cit.
56. Francis Hamilton, *An Account of Assam* (ed. S.K. Bhuyan), Guwahati, 1964, p. 64.
57. K.N. Tamuli Phukan, *Asam Buranji Sar* (in Assamese), ed. P.C. Choudhury, Guwahati, 1964, p. 14.
58. Barua, *A Cultural History of Assam*, Guwahiti, 1951, 1969, p. 101.
59. *Topography of Assam*, Calcutta, 1837, p. 10.
60. Mitchell, *The North-East Frontier of India*, Calcutta, 1883, Delhi, 1973, pp. 152f.
61. John Butler, *Travels and Adventures in the Province of Assam*, Calcutta, 1855, Delhi, 1978, pp. 45f.
62. B. Lintner, 'Burma and Its Neighbours', *China Report: A Journal of East Asian Studies*, 28, 3, 1992, pp. 255–9.
63. Elliot and Dowson, tr., vol. 1, *The History of India as Told by its Own Historians*, London, 1867, pp. 31f.
64. Pemberton, op. cit., p. 83.
65. Robinson, op. cit., p. 244.
66. Ibid., pp. 242f, Pemberton, op. cit., pp. 78 f.
67. Pemberton, op. cit., p. 83.
68. The details here are from, Pradip Sharma, 'Cultural Intercourse between Assam and Bhutan', *Bulletin of the Assam State Museum* (Golden Jubilee Issue), 12, 1991, pp. 27–33.
69. Ibid.
70. Tong Enzheng, *Gudai Bashu (The Ancient Bashu)*, Sichuan Renmin Chubanshe (Sichuan People's Publishing House), 1979, p. 112.
71. *Nanya Yanjiu (South Asian Studies)*, 2, 1983, p. 88, quoted in Zhu Changli, 'Nanfang sichou zhilu yu Zhong, Yin, Mian jingji wenhua jiaoliu' ('The Southern Silk Route: Eco-cultural exchange between China, India and Burma), in *Dongnanya (Southeast Asia)*, 32, 1991, p. 12.
72. See nn. 23 and 24; also see, Xiang Da, Manshu Jiaozhu (collation and notes on *A Book of Savage Tribes*), Zhonghua Shuju (Zhonghua Book Company), 1962, pp. 171–2, 191–2, 194, 195.
73. Zhu Changli, loc. cit.
74. R.P. Kangle, *The Arthashastra of Kautilya*, I (text); 2, 11, 113, p. 55; for English tr. see. R. Shamasastry, tr., *Kautilya's Arthashastra*, 5th edn., Mysore, 1956, p. 80.

75. N.K. Bhattasali, 'New lights on the History of Assam', *Indian Historical Quarterly*, 22, December 1946, pp. 248–9.
76. Kangle, op. cit., 2, 11, 57, p. 53; Shamasastry, loc. cit.
77. Kangle, loc. cit., Shamasastry, op. cit., p. 79.
78. A.L. Basham, *The Wonder that was India*, London, 1969; p. 230.
79. Pemberton, *Report on Bootan*, op. cit., p. 77.
80. Ibid., p. 77.
81. Ibid., p. 79.
82. Ibid.
83. As reported in the *Times of India*, 16 June 1994, and *Navabharat Times*, 29 September 1992.
84. K.L. Barua, *Early History of Kamrup*, 2nd edn., Guwahati, 1966, p. 57.
85. Bhattasali, op. cit., 249.
86. Ibid., pp. 250–2.
87. This view is confirmed by its present name, Dispur, the capital of Assam. It is the local name prevalent from time immemorial. The first part of its name, 'Dis' being a corrupt form of Jyotish, just as this was during the time of the Periplus about two millennium ago. See also B.K. Kakati's view that the name Pragjyotish was a Sanskritization of an earlier non-Aryan name Pagar-juhtic, meaning a region of extensive high hills; B.K. Kakati, *Mother Goddess Kamakhya*, Guwahati, 1948, p. 6.
88. Nagendra Nath Vasu, *The Social History of Kamrupa*, Calcutta, 1922, pp. 19–20.
89. K.L. Barua, op. cit., p. 59.
90. Samuel Beal, Hsi-yu-ki, *Buddhist Record of the Western World*, translated from the Chinese of Hiuen Tsiang, AD 629, 1384, rpt., Delhi, 1969, pp. 199–200; Ji Xianlin, et al., eds., op. cit., pp. 801–3.
91. K.L. Barma, op. cit., p. 6.
92. '100 Years Ago', *Statesman*, 7 November 1993.
93. B. Lintner, loc. cit.
94. Pradip Srivastava, op. cit., pp. 2–9.
95. J.B. Lama, 'A Tale of two Border Towns', *Impressions* (supplement), *Statesman*, 28 May 1995, p. 3.
96. Pemberton, op. cit., p. 78.
97. See for example Yuanshi, j. 104, p. 5a, Nanjian edn., quoted in W.W. Rockhill, 'Notes on the Relations and trade of China with the Eastern Archipelago and the coast of the Indian Ocean during the fourteenth century', Toung Poo, 15, 1914, p. 426; for King Dynasty ban, see King Taizu Shihlu, j. 70 (AD 1372), Academia Sinica, Taipei edn. (1966), p. 3; for a detailed discussion, see Stephen Chang Tsenghsin, *Maritime Activities on the South-East Coast of China in the Latter Part of the Ming Dynasty* (in Chinese), vol. 1, Taipei, 1988, pp. 3–11.
98. For example, let us take the distance from Kunming (capital of Yunnan

in South China) to Calcutta. The present railway route from Kunming to Guangzhou (Canton) is more than 2,000 km. and it is approximately 5926.4 km. from Guangzhou to Calcutta by sea. If we travel by land, it is less than 2,200 km. from Kunming via northern Myanmar to the frontier town Ledo in north-eastern India. From Ledo to Calcutta it is more than 1,600 km., which comes to a total of about 3,800 km. as against more than 7,926 km. by the sea route.

CHAPTER 3

The Tai Migration and its Impact on the Rice Economy of Medieval Assam*

AMALENDU GUHA

The economy of the Brahmaputra valley of Assam, in many ways a typical case of isolation, exhibits certain special features deriving from its history, physical configuration and social structure. The low-lying valley is shut in by hills on all sides, except the west. From time immemorial, its agriculture has been dominated by various tribes, mainly of the Tibeto-Burman stock. On conversion to Hinduism in course of time, many of them became altogether new castes, as such unknown elsewhere in the rest of India. Archaeological ruins, extant epigraphic records and the predominance of the age-old Assamese language undoubtedly prove the early existence of a process of Aryanization in this valley. But it was never very deep. In the medieval times, Mughal administration or Islam could touch only a fringe of its heterogeneous society. In fact, many tribes did manage to continue with their somewhat fossilized ways of life down to the present century. The agrarian history of the valley is particularly influenced by this isolation. Here, we propose to examine the impact of the thirteenth-century Tai immigration on the valley's medieval agriculture. It is then that a section of the northern Su Tai or Shan tribe (also called Thai) of Upper Burma led by their chief Sukapha in AD 1228 entered this valley and came to be known as the Ahoms. Numbering a few thousands or maybe, a few hundreds in the beginning, they rapidly swelled in number on their own and through assimilation of the local population. They also received fresh groups of Shan mi-

---

*An earlier version of this paper was first published is *Arthavinjnana* (Pune), vol. 9, June 1967, under a slightly different title.

grants from upper Burma from time to time. Within three centuries, they built a strong state and by 1682, they held almost the whole of the Brahmaputra valley up to the left bank of the Manas under their rule till the early nineteenth century. Their contribution to Assam's agriculture is interesting, in more than one aspect.

During the period between the thirteenth and the fifteenth centuries, Assam had no centralized government. On the north bank of the Brahmaputra, in the easternmost part of the valley, the Chutiya tribe reigned. They were an agricultural community who had come down from the hills and had settled along the banks of the tributaries of the Brahmaputra. They were already exposed to Hindu influence and were ruled over by a Hinduized dynasty. South of the Brahmaputra, in the same eastern most part of the valley, the non-Hindu Moran and Borahi tribes led a precarious existence. To their south, was the powerful kingdom of the Bodo-Kachari tribe in the central part of the valley.[1] West of the Kacharis as well as of the Chutiyas, there were a number of petty Hindu chiefs, together as a group called *Bara-Bhuyan*. In the western most part of the valley, the former districts of Kamrup and Goalpara, there still continued the waning influence of Kamata, a successor state to the ancient Kamrup empire. Kamata was overthrown by a short-lived Turko-Afghan invasion around 1498. By the early sixteenth century, the Koch tribe of lower Assam and adjoining north Bengal rose into prominence and established their kingdom upon the ruins of Kamata. They were at the height of their power around 1562, when the Ahom capital at Garhgaon was sacked by the Koch army. Thereafter, their domain was gradually encroached upon from the west by the Mughals and from the east by the Ahoms. From the last quarter of the seventeenth century, the Ahoms were the masters of almost the whole valley.

These political conditions and diverse culture-contacts must have had their imprint on the agricultural practices of the valley. Copperplate inscriptions or early literary sources, throw little light on the pattern of pre-Ahom agriculture. What is known is that, there were broadly, three kinds of land in the valley – *kshetra* (arable land), *khila* or *apakrsta bhumi* (wastelands) and *vastu* (building sites). *Kshetra* lands were generally paddy fields, criss-crossed with dykes. Ratnapala's Bargaon copper-plate inscription (AD 1035) however, also mentions *labukutikshetra*,[2] meaning fields of bottle gourds along with paddy fields. Rice was undoubtedly the dominant crop, since land measurements were often expressed in terms of paddy yield. But as to the relative importance of *Sali* and *Ahu* varieties of rice, or of permanent and shifting cultivation in pre-Ahom Brahmaputra valley, nothing is definitely known.

THE ETHNIC BACKGROUND OF THE AHOMS AND THEIR RICE-CULTURE

The Ahoms had their original home somewhere in south-western China. At the beginning of the Christian era, these early Tais were described in Chinese annals as living on hot, well-watered plains, growing wet rice through irrigation and terracing, using buffaloes and oxen, and living in pilehouses with verandahs.[3] It was from here, that they spread out in all directions, to upper Burma, Thailand, Cambodia, Laos and Vietnam. The fact that many words pertaining to rice cultivation, domestic animals and metals are common to the Shan, Thai and Ahom languages, reflects their common past.[4]

The legendary account of the origin of the Tai people in Ahom chronicles, hints at the agricultural superiority that these people had, over their backward neighbours. According to recorded legend, a council of gods decided after due deliberations, to send a group of heavenly people, the forefathers of the Ahoms, to earth, because, 'Large fields are lying fallow. These may be well-cultivated'. The people of the up and down countries are constantly at war with each other, and whosoever may be victorious, rules the countries for the time.[5]

Thus, the migrant Ahoms believed that they had a mission to fulfil, in introducing better cultivation in a territory where large fields were 'lying fallow'. The Ahoms had a developed technique of growing transplanted rice on wet, permanent fields, whereas, their tribal neighbours practised wasteful, shifting cultivation. The latter practice required in the long run, as it still requires, ten to fifteen times more land, than what cultivation on permanent fields required to maintain a family. It appears that at the time of the Ahom immigration, shifting cultivation, involving a large-scale following, dominated the agriculture of upper Assam and Burma. Divested of its myth, the chronicler's account suggests only this plain fact.

Shifting cultivation to this day, dominates the hills of Assam and was widely practised even in the Brahmaputra valley itself, particularly in its western and central parts and in Lakhimpur, as late as the nineteenth century. A description of this form of agriculture in the plains by Capt. J. Butler (1847) is worth reproducing here:

In January, February, March and April, the whole country adjoining Burpetah presents a spectacle seldom seen elsewhere; the natives set fire to the jungle to clear the land for cultivation and to open the thoroughfares between the different villages. The awful roar and rapidity with which the flames spread cannot be conceived. A space of many miles of grass jungle, twenty feet high is cleared in a few hours. . . . The jungle is burnt down and for three successive years two crops are annually realised from it. In February mustard seed is gathered in . . . and in June the spring rice, *sown broadcast*, is reaped. After the land has been thus impoverished it *is allowed to remain fallow for three years and fresh jungle land is burnt and prepared* in the *same primitive way* and with most simple implements of husbandry.[6]

The district gazetteers reveal that 50 per cent, 39 per cent and 9 per cent of the settled areas in the then Barpeta, North Lakhimpur and Guwahati subdivisions respectively, were under shifting cultivation of this form or some other, at the close of the nineteenth century.

A digression, at this stage, on the types of rice grown in Assam, will be useful to the understanding of the argument that follows. The variety of rice suited to shifting cultivation on undulating or sloping lands in submontane and riverine tracts is variously called 'upland', 'dry' or 'early' rice. Its local name is *Ahu,* and it is generally sown broadcast The other and more important variety of rice suited to permanent cultivation on low-lying flat and wet lands is *Sali.* It is generally transplanted in August and harvested in winter. *Sali* takes a long time, at least five months, to mature. Therefore, *Sali* fields rarely allow double-cropping. But as *Ahu* matures early, it is sometimes followed by another crop, pulses or mustard. However, after about three years, the *Ahu* fields become totally exhausted and have to be left fallow for several years. The *Sali* fields, on the other hand, are enriched by annual floods and they thus retain their natural fertility. *Sali* cultivation is highly labour-intensive at the stage of transplantation. But, for the subsequent period, there is not much work for farmers to do, until the time of harvesting. This is because weeds do not grow at all on waterlogged fields. *Ahu* cultivation, on the other hand, requires continuous weeding until harvesting. As *Ahu* fields are situated mostly in forested, submontane and riverline belts, the crops are exposed to wild animals, or to untimely floods. They are hence, very uncertain. Moreover, the yield of *Ahu* rice is small and its quality is inferior, as compared to *Sali.* Again, experiments have shown that if *Sali* is sown broadcast, its yield decreases by about 11 per cent or so.

The third variety of rice, known as *Bao*, is suited to natural marshes and sometimes, does not require any ploughing at all before sowing. *Bao* rice is generally sown broadcast. It matures late and its harvesting time coincides with that of *Sali*. *Bao* also gives a lesser yield per unit of land than *Sali*. Moreover, in the case of sowing broadcast, the practice associated with *Ahu* and *Bao*, the seed requirement is at least twice as high as that for transplanted *Sali*. Under the circumstances, the spread of *Sali* cultivation, at the cost of the two other varieties of rice, may be taken as a progressive trend in agriculture. It involves the crystallization of a large amount of labour into fixed capital. This point will be taken up and elaborated later. What now follows, is an account of the Ahom colonization of upper Assam and how it encouraged this trend.

AHOM COLONIZATION OF UPPER ASSAM

The Ahoms contained themselves in the tract east of the Namdang river and south of the Dihing for about 300 years to avoid any serious clash with the Chutiya and Kachari kingdoms. The Moran and Borahi tribes, however, were subdued and progressively assimilated during this period. The Borahis became altogether extinct as a separate tribe, but a section of the Morans managed to survive in remote jungles of the present district of Dibrugarh, as late as the census of 1891. By far, the greatest portion of this habitat that the Ahoms ruled over, was more or less, liable to heavy inundation. Hence, arose the need to guard the rivers by building embankments.

'The valley Shans', says Leach while discussing the cultural contacts between Shans and Kachins in Burma, 'have everywhere for centuries past, been assimilating their hill neighbours'.[7] The same process took place in upper Assam through the Ahomization of the Moran and Borahi tribes and later, even of sections of the Chutiyas. This went on until the Ahoms themselves, along with those Ahomized, were converted to Hinduism during the period from the sixteenth to the seventeenth century. In Ahom as well as the Northern Shan language, *kha* is a contemptuous term meaning 'slave', 'savage' or 'foreigner'. Autochthons of upper Assam were described as *kha*. For example, the Borahi and the Miri (Mishing) tribes were respectively known as *kha-lang* and *kha-kanglai*. But the chronicles provide ample instances of a *kha* becoming an Ahom. Thereby, a non-Ahom adopted the Shan (Tai) culture, the very essence of which in the words of anthropologist Von Eickstedt, was 'association with wet rice cultivation'.[8]

The closely-allied Moran and Borahi tribes practised shifting cultivation in the thirteenth century. No specific mention of this fact is made in early chronicles. But, if all the scant information available from early and late sources are pieced together, it cannot, but lead to this conclusion. They lived in a sparsely-populated wild territory. Their number was estimated by Sukapha's (1228–68) men at about four thousand in the area explored by them. The initial tributes offered to the Ahom conquerors as a token of their submission, indicated the backward state of their economy. Their tribute consisted of firewood, a kind of edible tuber, edible arum roots and an edible fern known as *dhenkia* which are mostly gathered, and not cultivated, to this day. An Ahom chronicle makes a mention of even the supply of brinjals from a Moran (Matak) family to Sukapha. But the chronicles are uniformly silent about any tribute from them in the form of rice or paddy. This, however, suggests only the existence of a deficient and inferior rice-economy, and not its total absence amongst the said tribes. For, described as they are by the chroniclers as consumers of rice-beer, they must have produced some rice. According to an old chronicle, they were dressed in scant cotton dhotis and it is therefore, likely that they produced cotton as well.[9]

The above reconstructed picture of the primitive agriculture of the Moran and Borahi tribes is corroborated by the evidence of an early nineteenth-century British administrator. In 1839, Hannay found a section of the Morans of the wild interior still practising shifting cultivation. He observed:

Their lands are high, and their cultivation is 'ahoo' crop of rice, once a year, and large crops of cotton and sugar cane but on account of scantiness of the population, compared to the extent of land capable of cultivation, their villages are scattered and *the inhabitants are constantly emigrating to new sites, for the sake of richer and newer lands.* There is comparatively little tree jungle in consequence of *this system having existed for ages*, the jungle being grass and hollow barnboos.[10]

The mode of agriculture that survived amongst only a section of the Morans, appears to have been the general feature of their economy from the thirteenth to the fifteenth century. With progressive Ahomization and later, Hinduization under the teachings of Aniruddha Dev, the area of shifting cultivation amongst them shrank constantly. At the close of the nineteenth century, only 1.5 per cent of the settled areas in the then Dibrugarh subdivision were reported to be under shifting cultivation. But, meanwhile, the ethnic composition of the population had also changed substantially.

It is likely, therefore, that the early Morans and Borahis, were producers of *Ahu* rice with slash-and-burn methods. They could hardly cultivate surplus rice over and above their own subsistence. As better rice farmers, the Ahom conquerors devoted themselves to wet rice (*Sali*) cultivation and depended on the conquered for other kinds of tributes and services. Chroniclers credit Sukapha with the establishment of three royal *khats* (farm or estate) through reclamation with the labour of the Moran servivors. One of these farms, the *Gachikala Khat*, supplied provisions for the worship of deities; the second, the *Bara-Khowa Khat* for ancestral rites of the king; and the third, the *Engera Khat*, for the royal houschold.[11] On the farms of the Ahom King and his nobles, the autochthons were soon engaged to work as serfs. Such Assarnese words as *bahatia* and *khatowal* stand for serfs attached to farms. Upper Assam abounds with such place-names as Madarkhat, Tengakhat, Khatowalgaon, Bahatiyagaon, etc., which are reminiscent of medieval serfdom. 'Every portion south and north of the Dibroo, with the exception of the Moran tract', reported Hannay in 1839, 'was occupied by the khatowals of the Rajahs of Assam'.[12] By 'Moran tract', Hannay obviously meant the interior-most region inhabited by the surviving Morans where the Ahom administration could hardly penetrate.

In Sukapha's times, some of the Moran and Borahi families had to supply fuelwood to the royal household, or look after the royal gardens. Others were engaged as hewers of wood, cooks, potters, medicine-men, valets, store-keepers and poultry-keepers. The Morans were later organized into several functional groups. One such group supplied the Ahom state with elephants and ivory; another with wild vegetable dyes; a third, with honey. Their very functions suggested that these sections were forest-dwellers. A section of the Morans (*Kapahia*) dwelling outside forests was entrusted with growing cotton for supply to the ladies of the royal household for being spun into yarn.[13]

It may be assumed that the bulk of the Morans and Borahis, gradually adopted the wet-rice culture of the migrant Ahoms and merged with the latter, in course of a few generations. Only a small section stubbornly clung to their old practise at least till 1839.

SOCIOLOGY OF CULTURAL PRACTICES

A scrutiny of the 1881 census of Assam suggests that almost half the indigenous population of the valley consisted of non-Hindus and erstwhile tribes who had been converted only in the course of the preceding two centuries or so. The Bodo-Kachari ethnic group alone accounted for some 40 per cent of the total indigenous population of the Brahmaputra valley in 1881. This ethnic element then, in all likelihood, must have been even more prominent in medieval times.

The Bodo-Kacharis of today are mostly found on submontane plains tracts and low hills of north-east India. During medieval times also, this distribution pattern of the population was not much different The Bodo-Kacharis preferred to remain at a safe distance from the periodically inundated area near the Brahmaputra and kept close to the hill-streams. Because of their early initiation into artificial gravitational irrigation, they were more independent of the rainfall than others. The narrow valleys of the Kopili, Jamuna and Dhansiri rivers, where the annual rainfall is poorest in Assam (only about 45 to 60 inches) formed the core of the Kachari kingdom during the late Ahom period. But they were also living in areas that had heavy rainfall. It appears that at the time of the Ahom immigration, the bulk of the Bodo-Kachari and allied tribes were shifting cultivators and farmers of *Ahu* rice. Nonetheless, their farming techniques were superior to those of the Moran and Borahi tribes who were ignorant of artificial irrigation.

At the time of Sukapha's exploration of the valley, 'the country round Dihing', the sparsely-populated habitat of the Morans and Borahis, 'was uncultivated and wild'.[14] But it was not so with the Namdang valley, then inhabited by the Kacharis. The impressive sight of 3,300 *ghats* on the river gave Sukapha an idea of the large Kachari population in the neighbourhood.[15] Their settlement in the upper valley of the Paimali river alone, was said to have 1,200,016 people.[16] These figures may not be taken at their face value, but they undoubtedly suggest that the early Ahoms were impressed by the numerical strength of their Kachari neighbours. How was this population fed, if they were not possessed of an agricultural practice superior to that of the less numerous Borahis and Morans?

By the thirteenth century, some Kachari communities appear to have already developed their peculiar form of cultivation of irrigated rice in the submontane regions. There is an oblique reference in an old Assamese chronicle to the damming of a hill-stream by a cattle-owning Kachari tribe in the thirteenth century. The chief of the Borahi tribe is recorded to have complained to Sukapha as follows: 'The Paimali river has emerged out of the mountain. It does not flow since the Kacharis began to wash their cattle and pigs (there).'[17] The complaint appears to have been against the same Kachari practise, as is found today, of damming a hill-stream several miles above the point at which the water supply is required for the rice fields. Even today, in areas inhabited by the Bodo-Kachari tribes, several villages often combine to construct *dongs* (irrigation channels) up to several miles long. A *dong* is constructed to lead water from above the dam to a particular area where rice fields are situated.

It was the irrigated rice cultivation of the Kachari tribe, which laid down their basis of early state formation. But their knowledge of irrigation and of domestication of cattle did not necessarily mean that they were using ploughs, nor did it mean that a large number of the Kacharis had taken to settled agriculture. All evidence is to the contrary. Around 1809, for example, the Kacharis of Sidli and Bijni were still hoe cultivators. The Kachari communities constantly retreated in the early decades of their confrontation with the Ahom immigrants without much resistance. This fact is perfectly in line with the general migratory habit of all Bodo-Kachari tribes who have been seen to leave old settlements for new ones at the slightest disturbance, even in recent times. The thirteenth century Kachari community of Paimali valley also did not hesitate to leave their irrigated sites at the mere approach of the Ahoms.[18] They did not behave like a stable, settled population.

Hence, the Kacharis probably did not generally use the plough in the thirteenth century. Hoe cultivation, as well as shifting plough cultivation co-existed almost with equal force in the nineteenth century amongst various Bodo-Kachari tribes of the valley. This can be firmly said on account of the evidences provided by Buchanan-Hamilton (1807–14), Fisher (1833), Hodgson (1847), Dalton (1872) and others.[19] The current agricultural practises of the Apatanis of Arunachal and the Khasi tribes of Meghalaya, demonstrate that fairly efficient wet-rice cultivation, transplanted or sown, could be carried on even with hoes.[20] The Meches, a Bodo-Kachari tribe of Assam-Bengal border, were reported in 1875 as going in 'for artificial irrigation in a surprising manner' and yet finding 'the proximity of permanent cultivation not congenial to their own habits'. They were in that year, still undergoing the transition from hoe culture to the use of ploughs through contacts with their more advanced neighbours,[21] the Rajbansis (Koch) who were earlier converts to Hinduism from the same Bodo-Kachari stock.

So, in the early years of British administration in Assam, most of the various Bodo-Kachari communities of the valley either used hoes, or were passing through a transition from the hoe to the plough. They were carrying on shifting cultivation in some form or the other. The only exceptions to this were the well-settled sonowal Kachari villages of Upper Assam who had adopted the plough and *Sali* rice culture side by side with *Ahu* quite early. So, it will not be incorrect to say that the use of plough, if any, by the Bodo-Kachari people in the thirteenth century was insignificant. Even when the plough was adopted, it did not signal an end to the system of shifting cultivation. Their rice economy was dominated by *Ahu* crop, and *Ahu* lands were suited to shifting cultivation. On the other hand, the scope of cultivating wet-rice in their submontane habitat was extremely limited by topographical conditions. Most of the undulating lands in such regions – the *faringti* or dry crop land – required fallowing every three years or so, after being continuously cultivated. Hence, the habit of shifting cultivation stubbornly persisted under conditions where land was available in abundance.

This point may be further elaborated. The slope is an important factor in the cultivation of rice. Wet-rice grows on those lands which can either be artificially flooded from adjacent streams, or be reduced to a dead-level so that it can retain the rain water deposited. Under natural conditions, most of the lands in the submontane and the riverine belts of the valley are not suited to wet rice. It is *Ahu* rice which is grown on such lands. But much of the lands on which *Ahu* crop is raised, as observed by W. Robinson (1841), could be converted into *rupit* (i.e. transplanted *Sali*) land by careful husbandry and paying attention to levelling and draining.[22] In this respect, the Ahoms had a definite superiority over their neighbours. The Bodo-Kacharis, having a preference for the submontane tract, did not undertake the reclamation of low-lying flat lands in the innermost areas of the valley. Nor did they particularly labour to level up their undulating or sloping fields. But the Ahoms did both. They were better-organized and had better iron implements to do the job.[23] They had the habit of taking much care to level up farmsites. As an example, a casual mention in a chronicle of such levelling-up activity in the royal farm, *Jaykhamdang* in the early seventeenth century may be cited.[24] It was during the several centuries of Ahom rule that much of upper Assam was turned into flat, level land. 'In this country, they make the surface of field and gardens so level', wrote Shihabuddin Talish around 1663, 'that the eye cannot find the least elevation in it up to the extreme horizon'.[25] The Ahom administration had built hundreds of miles of embankments primarily with a view to increasing the extent of wet rice cultivation.

We may now conclude that in the thirteenth century, while wet rice culture was traditional with the Ahoms, the tribal population of the valley, including the Bodo-Kacharis, were associated with the *Ahu* crop. Under slash-and-burn methods, it could have been grown even without hoeing or ploughing, like the 'hill rice' in some hilly areas of today. But we have no exact knowledge in this respect. In later times, ploughs were extensively used on the *Ahu* fields, but under a shifting type of cultivation as described by Butler and mentioned above. This tribal tradition of shifting cultivation was continued for long, obviously also by those Hindu agricultural communities who were converts from the Bodo-Kachari tribes. Even their advanced neighbours did supplement their settled agriculture with this form of cultivation in lower Assam. This happened despite the age-old process of Hinduization which involved a gradual economic transformation of the tribes. The process of acculturation was in fact, not merely a one-way traffic.

Shifting cultivation goes with the *Ahu*, and not with the *Sali* variety of rice. *Sali* is transplanted, while *Ahu* and *Bao* are generally sown broadcast. Under conditions of *dong* irrigation of the Bodo-Kacharis, *Ahu* is also transplanted. However, transplanted *Ahu* or *Kharma-ahu* is cultivated to a limited extent. Ahu is sometimes sown broadcast even on wet lands. It is then called *Asra-ahu*. But both *Kharma-ahu* and *Asra-ahu* are less productive than *Dhulia-ahu*, which is sown in dry, pulverized fields. The cultivation of *Ahu*, however, is almost universal with all agricultural communities over a greater part of the valley under geographic compulsion. Only that, its extent varies from one area to another. But the geographic compulsions as such, are not insurmountable, as was pointed out by Robinson. All these details are given here to facilitate the understanding of the sociological background of the relevant cultural practises, even at the risk of repetition.

Table 3.1 suggests something interesting. As one moves from the district of Sibsagar, the cradle and core of the Ahom dominion in the eastern extremity of the valley, towards the west or towards the north, one finds that the importance of *Sali* in the total rice crop goes on decreasing. This is no doubt, largely a result of the given topographical conditions. But sociological factors, also apparently had a role. Topographically, the valley can be divided into three belts: (a) the submontane tracts, (b) the riverine tracts of the Brahmaputra, and (c) the low-lying fields dotted with elevated housing and garden sites in the flat core of the valley. These three belts pass through all the relevant districts. Yet, the percentages of the total rice lands under *Sali* are the highest in the Sibsagar and Lakhimpur districts being 92 per cent and 85 per cent respectively, as of 1901-2 (Table 3.1). It was in these districts, that about 94 per cent of the Ahom population of the valley was concentrated in the last century (Table 3.2). In Sibsagar subdivision alone, for which we have no break-up of data, and where the Ahoms formed an absolute majority, the percentage of *Sali* to all rice lands was still higher. It could may be almost 100 per cent. Of the two subdivisions of the then Lakhimpur district, Dibrugarh was adjacent to the subdivision of Sibsagar. Dibrugarh had 98.5 per cent of its settled areas under permanent cultivation, while North Lakhim-pur, situated on the other side of the Brahmaputra, had only

TABLE 3.1: RICE ECONOMY OF ASSAM: 1901-2

(area in 1,000 acres)

District	Total acreage under rice	Acreage under each variety of rice			Estimated normal returns in lb. per acre		
		Ahu⁺	Bao*	Sali	Ahu	Bao	Sali
Goalpara	n.a.	n.a.	n.a.	n.a.	850	n.a.	1000
Kamrupa	420	124(30)	85	211(50)	800	650	900
Darrang	195	36(18)	8	151(77)	850	n.a.	1000
Nowgong	144	42(29)	30	72(50)	800	700	1000
Sibsagar	308	23(7)	2	283(92)	750	n.a.	800
Lakhimpur	127	17(13)	2	108(85)	800	n.a.	1000

Notes: Figures within brackets denote percentages of total rice acreage of respective districts.

+ *Ahu* in Sibsagar district was largely cultivated by the Miri (Mishing) tribe on the Majuli island.

* 67 per cent of all *Bao* was sown in Kamrupa, and only 3 per cent in Lakhimpur and Sibsagar districts.

Source: *An Account of the Province of Assam 1901-2*, pp. 23 and 26.

TABLE 3.2: DISTRIBUTION OF INDIGENOUS POPULATION GROUPS IN ASSAM PROPER: 1901

Indigenous population groups	Sibsagar		Lakhimpur		Darrang**		Nowgong		Kamrup	
	No.	%	No.	%	No.	%	No.	%	No.	%
Bodo-Kachari tribes uninfluenced by Hinduism or in the process of conversion (Kachari, Mech, Lalung, Hojai, Garo, Rabha, Mahalia, etc.)	17,656	(5.3)	24,222	(15.7)	88,624	(36.7)	65,063	(20.9)	126,704	(23.2)
Miri and Mikir tribes	16,723	(5.0)	18,640	(12.1)	5,111	(2.5)	48,124	(16.0)	13,813	(2.5)
Moran	1,676	(0.5)	4,130	(2.7)	–		–		–	
Koch/Rajbangsi	25,808	(7.7)	6,243	(4.0)	54,338	(22.5)	49,907	(16.0)	99,973	(18.3)
Chutiya*	54,587	(16.4)	17,206	(11.2)	3,546	(1.5)	10,468	(3.4)	1,036	(0.2)
Ahom and other Shan elements	99,129	(29.7)	50,410	(32.7)	3,136	(1.3)	5,265	(1.7)	475	–
Kalita	34,475	(10.3)	4,694	(3.0)	19,470	(8.0)	24,034	(7.7)	129,939	(22.7)
Dom/Nadial	23,564		12,185		7,988		26,223		14,826	
Kaibarta	587		522		246		97		22,468	
Kewat/Mahisya)	20,615		2,457		14,239		20,553		37,239	
Kayastha	3,442		1,088		1,301		2,656		1,207	
Brahman	12,177	(25.1)	2,465	(18.6)	4,741	(27.5)	7,430	(34.3)	24,738	(33.1)
Ganak (Daivajna)	2,081		170		8,121		348		5,967	
Saha/Sunri	475		212		574		1,009		16,423	

(contd.)

TABLE 3.2 (contd.)

Indogenous population groups	Sibsagar		Lakhimpur		Darrang**		Nowgong		Kamrup	
	No.	%	No.	%	No.	%	No.	%	No.	%
Jugi/Katani	8,622		3,162		19,957		22,076		17,484	
Other indigenous tribes/castes	11,839		6,138		9,593		27,171		34,926	
Total indigenous population (1608,257)	333,456	(100)	153,944	(100)	240,985	(100)	310,424	(100)	545,218	(100)
Indigenous population as % of total district population (1891)	73.8%		60.5%		78.2%		90.2%		85.9%	

Notes: Figures within brackets denote the population of each group as percentages of the indigenous population of the respective districts.

 *The Chutiya community was so influenced by the Ahoms, that many of them described themselves as Ahom-Chutiya, thus creating a problem for the census enumerators.

 **Of the old Darrang district, Tezpur subdivision might be taken as part of upper Assam, and Mangaldai subdivision as part of lower Assam. The Bodo-Kacharis of the district were mainly concentrated in the latter subdivision.

Source: Estimate by B.C. Allen in Subsidiary Table 3, *Assan Census Report*, 1901, pp. 29–30 (Adapted).

61 per cent of its settled areas under such cultivation. North Lakhimpur, like Kamrup and Goalpara, had hardly any Ahom population till the census of 1881.[26]

In Darrang, 77 per cent and in Nowgong and Kamrup 50 per cent of all rice lands were under *Sali* (Table 3.1). This distributional pattern of the rice crop is significant from the point of view of economic history. The significance lies in the fact that the yield of *Sali* is 50 to 200 pounds higher than that of *Ahu or Bao* rice per acre of cultivated land (Table 3.1). Further, *Sali* cultivation involves more than 50 per cent economy in the seed-rate and even a greater economy in the use of land. It is no surprise that the *Sali*-oriented agriculture of the Ahoms in upper Assam, yielded a higher surplus than the largely *Ahu*-oriented cultivation of others. I have tried to establish, that in medieval times, the Kacharis and other tribals, by and large, practised shifting cultivation of *Ahu* and were more used to sowing broadcast then to transplanting. But *Sali* cultivation, with its technique of transplantation, gradually spread amongst them through their deepening contacts with the process of Sanskritization from the west and with the expanding Ahom administration from the east. As to the agrarian evolution of the Chutiya tribe, nothing can be firmly stated. The Chutiya kingdom was situated in a heavy-rainfall area (100 to 120 inches) criss-crossed with shallow hill-streams. They came under Hindu influence, even before they were conquered by the Ahoms. Most probably, like the allied Kachari tribe, they had also initially an *Ahu* rice culture. We have already mentioned that even as late as the close of the last century, 39 per cent of the settled areas of the then North Lakhimpur subdivision, part of their original habitat, accounted for shifting cultivation. There is no tangible evidence to suggest that the Chutiyas had any ingenuity to overcome the topographical compulsion in earlier times.[27] It may, therefore, be assumed that they were more or less in the same stage of agricultural development as that of the Kacharis at the time of Ahom migration. However, they reached the stage of state formation, earlier than the Kacharis.

AHOM CONTRIBUTION TO THE RICE CULTURE OF ASSAM

To say that wet rice (*Sali*) cultivation was the essence of Shan culture, does not mean that it did not already exist in Assam. The Brahmaputra valley was already a rich rice bowl, supporting the big

Kamrup empire of olden times. Such an empire could not have been possible without a substantial economic surplus from its rice fields. *Sali* cultivation in the plains of Assam was at least as old as the process of Sanskritization itself. There is ample evidence to show that. But, in contrast to upper Assam under the Ahoms, lower Assam had never such extensive community investments in the form of manmade embankments and dykes, as could have converted much of *Ahu* and *Bao* lands into *Sali* fields. In 1841, Robinson observed that much valuable land there, then covered by reeds or abandoned owing to periodic floods, might be recovered by adopting a general system of bunds. Nearly every stream in upper Assam, he wrote, 'was anciently bunded'.[28]

Wet rice culture in lower Assam was limited by the extent of the flat terrain. Growing Sanskritization did not prove to be a factor that encouraged either lift irrigation – it was not so necessary in rain-rich Assam – or water control by large-scale dyke-building. Fifty per cent of rice lands in 1901–2, were under *Ahu* or *Bao* crops (Table 3.1) and shifting cultivation survived in the district of Kamrup, the ancient seat of civilization.[29] Obviously, assimilated tribal elements within the Hindu society still clung obstinately to some of their traditional habits. The Ahom rule of about 200 years there (during the seventeenth and eighteenth centuries), frequently interrupted as it was, did not obviously have an impact on the local rice economy.

The story, however, in upper Assam was different. From the very beginning, the Ahom state treated all wet rice lands, but not other lands and house-sites, as a common national pool. From this pool, the King distributed tax-free, wet rice plots to all his able-bodied, adult, male subjects at the rate of 2.66 acres per head for their lifetime, and in turn, exacted periodic service from them. The State's obligation to furnish every adult male with a fixed amount of wet rice land necessitated, in a period of increasing population under a stable government, the continuous extension of wet rice lands. The Ahom State proved itself equal to this task.

This was done by peace-time utilization of the national militia in embankment building and reclamation activities. Partial embankments to guard against the inundations of particular streams at specific places were not uncommon even to pre-Ahom Assam. The Guwahati copper-plate grant of Indrapala makes a mention of such road-cum-embankment works (*brhat ali*). But the scale, extent and the underlying grand purpose of such works under the Ahoms were certainly unprecedented. The embankments in upper Assam, laboriously built in the course of centuries to guard almost all the rivers, served as bunds and at the same time, also as a road system. Robinson in 1841 wrote about them as follows:

> These river embankments were crossed by high raised path ways, which were again joined by smaller bunds graduating down, and, connecting the mauzas, villages and fields, at once formed the most commodious means of communications, and *afforded opportunities for retaining or keeping out the inundation.*[30]

Earlier, Capt. Jenkins in his report on Assam to the Government of India dated 22 July 1833, made a similar statement:

> ... the embankments are not confined to the main lines but branch off in all directions whenever roads or bunds seemed to have been convenient or necessary, and certainly in respect to good solid embankments and commodious roadways *no part of India I have visited appears to have been so well provided as* Assam.[31]

During the years of unrest from 1769 to 1824 and during the early period of the subsequent British rule, the whole system of embankments was thrown into disrepair and utter neglect. As a result, large tracts of excellent rice lands were destroyed by heavy and frequent inundations. Only since the 1860s, did the British administration become conscious of the utility of embankments to Assam's agriculture and many of them were partially restored. All important road-cum-embankments constructed during the sixteenth and subsequent centuries are duly recorded in the chronicles.[32] It is the positive policy of building up a network of embankments that helped transplanted wet rice predominate in the rice culture of upper Assam. The lack of such a policy in lower Assam, the 350-mile bund-road constructed in the mid-sixteenth century by a Koch king, served only military ends and inhibited the spread of wet rice cultivation beyond a certain point.

The Ahoms also showed remarkable wisdom in avoiding the heavily-flooded banks of the Brahmaputra while selecting the site for their settlements. Although the Brahmaputra contains a large quantity of matter in suspension, its floods deposit mostly the sand in Assam, while the rich silt is carried off by strong currents to the plains of Eastern Bengal. Sukapha made a wise choice, when he selected the banks of the river Santak to settle down in, because he 'found that an equal quantity of the river water weighed twice that of the Dikhou river'.³³ It is from there, that the Ahoms spread all over the low-lying flat plains of the district of Sibsagar and its adjacent areas. In the seventeenth century, even organized colonies of multi-caste population were planted at the initiative of the State at far ends of the dominion.³⁴

This is how the Ahoms' wet rice culture spread in new areas.

Finally, it may be noted that one of the dozens of *Sali* varieties in Assam today is known as *Ahom sali*. It is one of the most high-yielding varieties, and was developed recently as a select seed strain (Strain S.L. 70) with an yield of more than 3,000 lbs. per acre, in suitable conditions, by the Department of Agriculture, Assam. It might have originated amongst the Ahom cultivators, but the supporting evidence is yet inconclusive. Another glutinous variety of *Sali*, known as *Bara*, was produced in one of the three royal farms of Sukapha even as far back as the thirteenth century.³⁵ The Ahom word for this rice, *Khao-nung*, is almost the same as the Thai word, *Khao-nieo*, in Thailand.³⁶ This indicates the early association of this variety in Assam with the Ahoms.

Taking all facts and circumstances into consideration, one cannot but conclude that Ahom migration and their administration were primarily responsible for the spread of *Sali* cultivation in the eastern half of the Brahmaputra valley. The high yield of *Sali* crop enabled the initial 9,000 or so Ahoms to multiply rapidly by ensuring enough supply of food. By the middle of the eighteenth century, their numbers rose to about 2 lakh, i.e. to an estimated 9 per cent or so of the total population in their dominion. The existence of a substantial surplus, helped the Ahom state not only to subjugate the Chutiya, Kachari and Koch powers in the Brahmaputra valley, but also to successfully confront the Mughal invaders for a prolonged period during the seventeenth century. Their capacity to build a network of embankments in order to control the distribution of flood and rain water in a desirable way over a considerable area, was the key factor on which their rice economy thrived.

SUMMARY

Of the three varieties of rice, *Ahu*, *Bao* and *Sali*, grown in the Brahmaputra valley of Assam, *Sali* is the most productive. Its yield is the highest per unit of cultivated land as well as per unit of seed input. It is associated with the technique of transplantation and requires low-lying, level fields to hold rain or flood water. The production of *Sali*, therefore, is limited to the extent of such terrain. In contrast to the valley's relatively higher lands (*faringati*) suitable for dry crops, the low-lying, level lands are annually rejuvenated by silt-rich floods. Consequently, they require no fallowing. Any increase in the extent of such land for *Sali* cultivation is, therefore, an indicator of agricultural progress.

Wet rice culture has been the tradition of the Ahoms. Their migration to Assam from the east in the thirteenth century and subsequent expansion of their rule, encouraged the extension of *Sali* cultivation in upper Assam. They built with free community labour, contributed by the tax-exempted paik labour force, a system of massive dykes and embankments, unparalleled elsewhere in India. Through this device, the distribution of flood water was controlled in such a manner, that much of the existing *Ahu* and *Bao* lands now transformed into levelled fields could grow the *Sali* crop. In other words, the Ahom initiative and administrative measures progressively provided for huge public investments in land improvement.

As one moves from the cradle and core of the erstwhile Ahom dominion in its eastern extremity, towards the west or to the north, one finds that the importance of *Sali* in the rice crop pattern of the valley goes on diminishing. This suggests some correlation, though not measurable, between the influence of the Ahoms and the importance of *Sali* in the valley's crop-pattern. In lower Assam, where the Ahom influence had been the least, both politically and sociologically, there had never been any system of massive embankments and dykes as those found in upper Assam. This is certainly one of the reasons why *Sali* crop today, is more widespread in upper Assam than in the lower reaches. Had the topographical limitations of the rice lands in lower Assam been partially overcome, as in the Ahom sphere of influence, *Sali* cultivation would have been widespread there too.

NOTES

1. According to Reverend Endle, the Bodo Kachari, Mech, Rabha, Dimasa, Hojai Hajong, Lalung and Garo tribes have so much in common that they may be grouped together as the Bodo-Kacharis. The Chutiya, Moran and Borahi tribes are also supposed to bear close affinities to the group: Endle, *The Kacharis* (London, 1911), p. 5.
2. M.M. Sharma (ed.), *Inscriptions of Ancient Assam* (Gauhati University, 1978), p. 159.

3. Thomas Fitzsimmons, ed., *Thailand*, New Haven, 1956, pp. 59–60.
4. For a brief comparative vocabulary, G.A. Grierson, *Linguistic Survey of India*, vol. 2 (1904), pp. 127–40.
5. Quote from *Ahom-Buranji, From the Earliest Time to the end of Ahom Rule*, ed. and trans. G.C. Barua (Calcutta, 1930), p. 10. Emphasis ours.
6. Quote from John Butler. *Sketch of Assam, with some Account of the Hill Tribes by an Officer*, London, 1854, pp. 21–3 (emphasis ours). It was the use of the plough which distinguished this form of shifting cultivation from what is known as swidden or *jhum* cultivation. The latter is associated with such tools as the *dao*, hoe and digging stick.
7. E.P. Leach, *Political Systems of Highland Burma: A Study of Kachin Social Structure* (London, 1954), p. 41.
8. Von Eickstedt quoted ibid., p. 37.
9. Relevant data in this Paragraph are collated from Anonymous, *Asam Buranji*, S.K. Bhuyan, ed. (2nd edn., Gauhati 1960), p. 5; *Ahom-Buranji*, n. 5, p. 38; Holiram Dhekial-Phukkan, *Asam Buranji* (in Bengali, Calcutta, 1829, rpt., ed. J. Bhattacharya, Gauhati, 1962, p. 49, *Deodhai Asam Buranji* (compiled from old Assamese Chronicles), ed. S.K. Bhuyan, Gauhati, 1962, pp. 100–2.
10. Quote from S.O. Hannay to Jenkins, *Sadiya*, 4 April 1839, *Foreign Pol. Proc.,* 14 August 1839, no. 105 (NAI), emphasis ours.
11. Kasinath Tamuli-Phukan, *Asam Buranji Sar* (Sibsagar, 1844), P.C. Chaudhary, ed., rpt. Gauhati, 1964, p. 10. The mention of *Sali* cultivation by chronicles goes as far back as Sukapha's rule (1228–68). *Deodhai Asam Buranji*, n. 9.
12. Quote from Hannay to Jenkins, *Sadiya*, 4 April 1839, *Foreign Pol. Proc.,* n. 10.
13. Endle, n. 1, p. 87; Hannay, *JASB*, vol. 7, n. 10, p. 675.
14. Quotes from J.P. Wade, *An Account of Assam, AD 1800*, ed. Benudhar Sharma, 1927, rpt. Gauhati, 1972, p. 18.
15. *Ahom-Buranji*, n. 5, p. 46.
16. *Deodhai Asam Buranji*, n. 9, p. 101.
17. For quote, ibid., p. 100.
18. Ibid., p. 101.
19. Buchanan Hamilton, *An Account of Assam, First Compiled* in 1807–14, S.K. Bhuyan, ed., 2nd edn., DHAS, Gauhati, 1963, p. 73; extract from his account of Rangpur reproduced in the Census of 1951, *West Bengal District Handbooks, Jalpaiguri*, Calcutta, pp. cxxxvi–cxxxix. Fisher to Robertson on Dharampur, Cachar, 12 March 1833, *Foreign Pol. Proc.*, 6 June 1833, no. 107; B.H. Hodgson, *Essay the First on the Koech, Bodo and Dhimal Tribes* (Calcutta, 1847), pp. 146–7, 154–6 and 180; E.T. Dalton, *Descriptive Ethnology of Bengal*, Calcutta, 1872, rpt. 1960), p. 81; Ashley Eden's report dated 1864, *Political Missions to Bootam* (Cal., 1865), p. 61; B.H. Baden-Powell, *Land Systems of British India*, vol. 3 (London, NY, 1892), pp. 417–18.

20. C. Von Furer-Haimendorf, *The Apatanis and Their Neighbours* (London, 1962), p. 13; P.R.T. Gurdon, The *Khasis* (London, 1914), 39–40.
21. Col. Money, Deputy Commissioner of Jalpaiguri on the Mech, quoted in 'Census of 1951', *West Bengal District Handbooks, Jalpaiguri*, n. 19, Appendix IV.
22. Quote from William Robinson, A *Descriptive Account of Assam* (Calcutta, London, 1841), p. 88.
23. 'Land Rights and Social Classes', Amalendu Guha, *Medieval and early Colonial Assam: Society, Polity and Economic*, Calcutta and New Delhi, 1991.
24. *Asam Buranji Sar*, n. 11, p. 28. A sloping site might have been found all right for settlement by its former occupants, but not so by the newcomers, the Ahoms. This is suggested by the extant Tai place-name nazira (na = field ; zi = slanting ; ra = much). Sarbananda Rajkumar's note, *Lik Phan Tai*, Periodicals, vol. 1, Gauhati, 1965, p. 83.
25. Quote from Shihabuddin Talish, *Fathiya i'ibriyu*, Jadunath Sarkar, tr., 'Assam and the Ahoms in 1660 AD', *Journal of the Bihar and Orissa Research* Society (vol. 1, 1915), pp. 179–94.
26. 'Assam Census Report', Census of India, 1881, vol . VI, p. 65. For the extent of shifting and permanent cultivation B.C. Allen, *Assam Provincial District Gazetteers*, vol. VII, pp. 148 and 251.
27. Ibid., p. 251.
28. Robinson, op. cit., p. 222.
29. For example, in the then subdivision of Barpeta, 50 per cent of the settled areas were under shift plough cultivation. However, as a result of large-scale immigration from East Bengal, the subdivision later recorded a 700 per cent increase in permanent cultivation during 1911–30. *Report, Assam Prov. Banking Enquiry Committee, 1929–30*, vol. 1 (Govt. of India, 1930), p. 23. B.C. Allen, *Assam Prov. District Gazetteers*, vol. 4, p. 199.
30. Quote from Robinson, op. cit., p. 317. Emphasis ours.
31. Jenkins to *Secy., Pol, Dept.*, 22 July 1833, *Foreign Pol. Proc.*, 11 February 1835, no. 90, para 53. Emphasis ours.
32. For example, *Asam Buranji Sar*, op. cit., pp. 17, 23, 26–7, 32 and 41.
33. *Ahom-Buranji*, op.cit., p. 46.
34. *Deodhai Asam Buranji*, op. cit., pp. 70, 130–1; Shrinath Duara (Barbarua), *Tungkhungia Buranji, c. 1806*, ed. S.K. Bhuyan, 2nd edn., Guwahati, 1964, p. 23.
35. *Asam Buranji Sar*, op. cit., p. 10.
36. R.L. Pendleton, *Thailand*, American Geological Society, New York, 1962, p. 159.

CHAPTER 4

The Rise and Decline of the Ahom Dynastic Rule: A Suggestive Interpretation

ALOKESH BARUA

INTRODUCTION

The medieval period in the north-east had witnessed the rise of several independent political formations like the kingdoms of Ahom, Koch, Cacher, Jayintia, Manipur and Tripura, besides many other small vassal states.[1] The economic and political history of the period has been very intricately interwoven by the interrelationships between these kingdoms and also, their relations with the outside powers. There were other hill tribes too, such as the Dafalas, Miris, Nagas, Khamptis, Singphos and Mishmis who maintained distinct identities and political independence.[2] However, the major kingdoms, which enjoyed a continuous existence for a long period of time and which had also been able to influence the economic, political and cultural history of the region in a very significant manner over centuries, were the Ahom kingdom[3] in the east and the Koch kingdom[4] in the west. The former, however, was by far the most powerful kingdom in the region. They ruled continuously, not only for a much longer period than the latter but also maintained their political independence against repeated attacks by none other than the mighty Mughals until the East India Company appeared on the scene to-wards the early nineteenth century.

The Ahoms[5] ruled in Assam from AD 1228[6] to AD 1826,[7] for nearly

*The author is grateful to Hiren Gohain for many helpful comments and suggestions.

six hundred years, a long period for a dynasty to rule continuously in any region. Lord William Bentinck[8] referred to the long continuance of the Ahom rule in Assam as, 'almost without example in history'.[9] He argued that, 'there must have been something intrinsically good in the original constitution',[10] which contributed to the long domination of the Ahoms in Assam. Bentinck's point perhaps may be relevant in explaining the success of the Ahoms in making themselves acceptable to the local tribes as their ruler. But it certainly cannot be taken as a reasonable explanation for their long continuance as a monolithic dynasty. Throughout their dynastic rule, the Ahoms had to fight inexhaustibly not only against the mighty Mughal empire, but also against the sub-regional powers such as the Koch[11] as well as the ferocious hill and plains tribes.[12] A constitution that remained unchanged[13] for so long and also which enabled the Ahoms to play the role of a unifying force in diverse social, political and economic conditions, therefore, deserves an explanation.

Moreover, an analysis that seeks to explain the long continuance of the Ahom dynastic rule, should also be able to tell us the story of the eventual decline of the dynasty. Bentink's explanation is thus, an incomplete one. The present paper, therefore, seeks to explain what the other plausible factors were, which could provide us with a better explanation of the continuity of the Ahom monarchical rule for so a long period of time and its final eclipse. Obviously, an explanation that sweeps across six centuries, must necessarily, be based on factors which are dynamic or evolutionary. In this paper, we intend to focus on some of the major dynamic factors towards seeking an explanation of the long continuance of the Ahom rule and its decline. While economic factors do play a dominant role in our frame of analysis, it should not, however, be taken as an attempt to deny the importance of other factors. It is the complex interplay of economic, political and social forces that can explain the historical process of development. We, therefore, need an evolutionary theory of development that takes into consideration the dynamic interaction of the forces just mentioned.[14] But, before we consider the evolutionary viewpoint, we need some idea of the rise of the Ahoms and the process of gradual expansion of their rule, and the political, economic and institutional structure that they had established in that corner of India, to organize their basic political and economic activities.

THE RISE OF THE AHOMS

As mentioned above, the Ahoms were the offshoot of the great Tai or Shan race. They have several divisions like the Siamese, Laos, Shans Tai-mow or Tai-khi (Chinese Shans), Khampti and Ahom.[15] The first Ahom conqueror of Assam was a prince whose name was Sukapha. He wandered for thirteen years in the Patkai range, until he finally arrived in Khamjang[16] in 1228. The first capital of the Ahom kingdom was established at Charaideo in 1253.[17] Gait writes about the Ahoms as follows:

> The so-called Aryans, and many later invaders, such as the Greeks, the Huns, the Pathans, and the Mughals, entered India from the north-west, while from the north-east, through Assam, have come successive hordes of immigrants from the great hive of the Mongolian race in Western China. Many of these immigrants passed on into Bengal, but in that province they have, as a rule, merged in the earlier population. . . . In Assam, on the other hand, although in the plains large sections of the population, like that of Bengal, are of mixed origin, there are also numerous tribes who are almost pure Mongolians, and the examination of their affinities, in respect of physique, language, religion and social customs, with other branches of the same family forms one of the most interesting lines of enquiry open to Ethnologists.[18]

The Ahoms did not enter India through its north-east frontier with an expansionist design.[19] The history of the Ahoms reveals that they never wanted to be a colonial power.[20] Thus, all that we can say regarding the rise of the Ahom dynasty in thirteenth-century Assam, is that it was a mere historical accident. They were a self-contented, self-sufficient oligarchy. If it were so, then there is very little historical interest in knowing about the rise of the Ahom dynasty in Assam. Yet, their long survival as a monolithic dynasty cannot be brushed aside as a mere accident. Indeed, it was a glorious period of medieval Indian history, which, however, had been completely ignored by the writers of colonial history. To quote the noted historian E.A. Gait:

> . . . there is, probably, no part of India of whose past, less is generally known. In the histories of India as a whole, Assam is barely mentioned, and only ten lines are devoted to its annals in the historical portion of Hunter's Indian Empire. The only attempt at a connected history in English is the brief account given by Robinson—some 43 pages in all—in his Descriptive Account of Assam, published in 1841.[21]

This neglect is much more glaring than what it appears to be at first sight, if one considers the contributions of the Ahoms to history writings in India. In the words of Gait again:

Prior to the advent of the Muhammadans the inhabitants of other parts of India had no idea of history; and our knowledge of them is limited to what can be laboriously pieced together from old inscriptions, the accounts of foreign invaders or travelers, and incidental references in religious writings. On the other hand, the Ahom conquerors of Assam had a keen historical sense; and they have given us a full and detailed account of their rule, which dates from the early part of the thirteenth century.[22]

Despite this, however, the fact is that we hardly find any reference of the Ahoms and their contribution to the development of Indian society and culture in our standard Indian history books. This is a lapse that may partly be responsible for the prevailing sense of neglect among the people of the region. True, Assam remained politically independent till 1826, when the East India Company appeared on the scene but one should not forget that the Ahom period also witnessed a remarkable cultural unification of the region with the mainstream Indian ethos. During the rule of the Ahoms, the great epics of India and other mythological books had been written in Assamese[23] in which Sri Sankardeva[24] and other Vaishnava leaders took the pioneering role. The Ahoms initially patronized the Vaishnava movement, but at a later stage they looked upon the Vaishnavas as a possible threat to their hegemony.[25] Koch Bihar eventually became the centre of Assamese creativity and the development of Assamese culture and literature had reached its zenith during this period under the leadership of Sankardeva. It may be true that there was very little trade in material goods between Assam and the rest of India, but there was a lot of intellectual give-and-take.

CHARAIDEO TO KARATOYA

The establishment of the Ahom rule by a migrant class from Upper Burma at Charaideo (see Map 1) and the subsequent consolidation and expansion of its power up to the river Karatoya[26] was a very exciting and eventful chapter in the annals of Assamese history. In their attempt to be assimilated into the local culture, the Ahoms abandoned their own culture and religion in favour of the latter, and by considering the river Karatoya as the limit of their territory,[27] they assumed upon themselves the role of the progenitor of the early Kamrup kings. What was the secret behind their success?

There could be many reasons for their phenomenal success. As a warring clan, the Ahoms perhaps, possessed a superior technology of warfare than the one that the local tribes possessed.[28] They were confronted with these tribes as they entered Assam through the eastern front. The Ahoms' technological advantage, coupled with the novelty of war strategies that they adopted, might have given them an edge over the indigenous tribes to ascend to power in an alien environment. However, such immediate advantage over some Naga tribes may not entirely explain, their success in the gradual expansion of their rule.

An alternative explanation could, however, be construed in terms of the prevailing social and political conditions of the valley. The valley in the thirteenth century could be conceived of consisting of several disjointed regions, where each region was ruled by a village chief or the head of a tribe. An evidence of this is the lack of a unified kingdom till the advent of the Ahoms and the existence of many petty rulers. The economic and political cost of expanding the domain of one's rule must have been prohibitively high. In such a situation, where the valley was highly stratified and also sparsely populated, there were very little, if any, linkages between the various regions in terms of movement of goods and people. Apart from the high cost of territorial expansion, the disjointedness was partly influenced by social, cultural and religious heterogeneity and partly by communication bottlenecks. As villages were self-sufficient, with primitive structures of production and consumption, there did not exist any strong economic market force to break the tightly-knit nature of the regions. There was, therefore, very little scope or necessity for trade. Inaccessible, dense forests in many parts perfected the closeness of the regions. Shihabuddin who accompanied Mir Jumlah described the valley as 'wild and dreadful, abounding in danger'.[29]

The political implications of negligible trade and commerce was that it was virtually impossible for any political unification of the regions under a single ruler and to erect a combined, protective regime that could thwart any external threats. The Ahoms exploited this advantage to enter into the region by subduing the neighbouring Naga tribes and then, gradually, expanding their rule by defeating the Morans[30] and Borahis, and later the Kacharis and Chutiyas in the east before they looked westwards. The difficulties posed by geography and other factors for expansion were so strong that the Ahoms took more than 200 years to consolidate their rule even in the domain of upper Assam.

But that is again, not enough to explain their success in gradually expanding westward to the Karatoya and in maintaining the stability and supremacy of their rule against repeated external threats posed by the mighty Mughal empire. Verily, to maintain their dominance within Assam against many powers such as the Nagas, Kacharis, Bodos, Chutiyas and the powers of Kamrup and Darrang was no ordinary achievement. The organizational structure of the Ahom kingdom must have had a unique character, which made it possible for the Ahoms to maintain uninterrupted rule over their territory for such a long period of time. Undoubtedly, their constitution must have had some principle, which could hold so many heterogeneous, powerful and ferocious groups of people together.

THE NATION-BUILDING PROCESS

As mentioned earlier, the Ahoms never tried to impose their views, their religion and culture and their language on the tribes they ruled in Assam. Instead, they tried to merge completely with the local culture and traditions. This attitude was purely political and strategic, as it would not have been otherwise possible for the minority migrant class[31] to maintain their domination over a large number of people with such varied cultures. The development of a common *lingua franca* was also essential for the establishment of a steady political system. The Ahoms realized this extremely well and thus helped develop Assamese as a common *lingua franca* in the region. Their acceptance of Hinduism and the introduction of Assamese language to replace the Tai language in the Ahom Court cannot be explained by any other reasoning. Further, by treating the subdued tribes as equals and encouraging intermarriage,[32] the Ahoms significantly contributed to the formation of the nascent Assamese nation-state. The *Buranjis*[33] played a major role in the early development of Assamese literature.[34] Social stratification was gradually broken as non-Ahom families were admitted into the Ahom fold and were given the status and privileges bestowed on nobles. Even the Muslims did not suffer any disability on account of their religious faith. A large number of Muslims were appointed in several departments of the state.[35] The Ahoms did this consciously as they realized the importance of increasing their political support base in order to continue in power against continued external threats and also against the threats from within, posed by the ferocious hill and plains tribes. This deliberate policy, whereby the Ahoms assimilated themselves, was a major reason for the formation of an Assamese society, free from caste prejudices, which was further strengthened by the equalizing impact of the Vaishnava movement.

The friendly attitude towards the local tribes and the enshrinement of the right of joint conquest[36] as a principle of the Ahom administration, helped the process of assimilation of different communities into a single, unified one.[37] Indirectly, it also helped the Ahoms adopt a policy of decentralization of powers with a powerful central authority. All the small powers subordinated to the Ahom kingdom provided a unified front in times of emergency posed by an external threat.

THE SLOW-GROWING EMPIRE

Interestingly, the empire that lasted for so long a period actually growing at a snail's pace for centuries, eventually reach the highly glorified size that it had attained, just before its final eclipse. This slow growth can be attributed, partly to the economic and political costs of and geographical impediments to expansion as explained above. Also, it was partly a result of the lack of dynamism and of an expansionist drive. Perhaps there were no compulsive forces to propel the ruling oligarchy towards expansion. Thus, for nearly three centuries, the Ahom empire, remained within the smaller orbit in upper Assam, gradually expanding its size by consolidating power over the neighbouring tribes. Thus, after bringing some sections of the Nagas under them, they brought the Morans[38] and Borahis into their fold. They also brought under their domination, some tribes of the Tai race who had settled in upper Assam, long before Sukapha's invasion. But the real expansion of the empire began from the sixteenth century onwards, when the Ahom King Suhungmung Dihingia Raja annexed the kingdom of the Chutiyas centering on their capital at Sadiya.[39] The same king also drove the Kacharis from their stronghold at Dimapur. The Bhuyans[40] were brought under Ahom control and were made to settle down in Nowgong. During the reign of Suhungmung, a new kingdom sprang up on the ruins of Kamata. Biswa Singha founded the ruling dynasty of Cooch Behar about the year 1515.[41] In 1527, the first Muslim invasion of Ahom Assam took place. Suhungmung's rule also witnessed the Vaishnava revival in

Assam. The Ahom capital remained in the possession of Mir Jumla (the Mughal general) only for 10 months during 1662–3. Similarly, the Mughals possessed Kamrup, which was annexed to the Ahom kingdom in 1615, for a total period of 26 years, once from 1639 to 1658 and again from 1663 to 1667, and from 1679 to 1682.[42]

THE ORGANIZATIONAL STRUCTURE OF THE AHOM STATE

A. The System of Governance

The Ahom government was monarchical[43] and the king was the supreme head of the state. The fundamental duty of the king was the protection of the people and to give them security of life, property and belief.[44] Yet, the king's powers were limited insofar as he had to act according to the advice of the three hereditary councillors of state, the *Buragohain*, the *Bargohain* and the *Barpatra Gohain*.[45] In matters of governance, the Ahoms adopted something like a federal structure of governance where the powers were decentralized according to well-defined duties and responsibilities but there always was a strong, central authority. Thus, they had other officials such as the *Barbarua* who was the head of the executive and the judiciary but could not act independently of the three *Gohains*. The *Barphukan* lived at Guwahati as the king's deputy and administered the territory from Kaliabar to the western frontier of Assam. He conducted the political relations with Bengal and Bhutan and the chieftains on the Assam pass. Apart from the above-said there were other officers such as the *Sadiya-khowa Gohain*,[46] the *Marangi-khowa Gohain*,[47] the *Solal Gohain*,[48] the *Jagialia Gohain* and the *Kajalimukhia Gohain*,[49] who protected the frontiers of the kingdom from inroads made by the hill people. They were, moreover, always selected from the families of the three *Gohains* at the metropolis. The raja of Saring and the raja of Tipam ruled in Saring and Tipam respectively.[50] The states of Jaintia, Cacher, Khyrim and Manipur were in friendly alliance with the Ahom Government, though a degree of subordination was accepted by the first two as a result of definite agreements. The province of Darrang enjoyed complete autonomy in its internal administration.

There were other ruling chiefs too, who had submitted to the Ahoms. The Ahoms too, had given them the status of governors to act on behalf of the king. These vassal chiefs administered justice and collected revenue and they had to pay an annual tribute to the Ahom king. Such vassal states were, Rani, Beltola, Luki, Barduar, Bholagaon, Mairapur, Pantan, Bangoon, Bagaduar, Dimarua, Neli, Gobha, Sahari, Dandua, Barepujia, Topakuchia, Khaigharia, Panbari, Sora, Mayang, Dhing, Tetelia, Salmara, Garakhia, Baghargaon and Bhurbandha. A vassal chief was bound to furnish a stipulated number of *paiks* to work on the king's account, or pay the commutation money if exempted from personal service. In case of war, the vassal raja was expected to take the field at the head of his contingent of *paiks* by the side of his liege lord.

There was an in-built defence mechanism within the system, which the Ahoms could exploit to their advantage. The chance of internal threats destabilizing the government were virtually absent because of the disjointed nature of the valley and the absence of a unity among them, that compelled each of the smaller vassal states to accept the sovereignty of the Ahom king, unquestionably. As there was very little political and economic interaction among the vassals and trade was virtually absent among them, each of the vassals lived in near-perfect isolation. The powerful central authority provided them with the necessary political security from outside threats and threats from within – from the other vassals. While the vassals were economically self-sufficient, yet some critical items which were not produced in the valley, such as salt, had to be imported from abroad. Salt was thus imported in large quantities from Bengal. As a result, the defence arrangement of the kingdom was absolutely at its minimum. This explains why the Ahoms never maintained an army for their defence and why the standing army at the capital was actually a very poor one. In the year 1809, it consisted merely of 300 up-country sepoys and 800 native troops.[51]

The Ahom Government always maintained vigil against the possible attacks from the tribes contiguous to their immediate frontier and they succeeded in containing these tribes by maintaining relations with them, though the relations with them were casual and sporadic. However, with the Muslim powers in Bengal and with Koch Bihar, their relations were systematic and consistent. The basis of Assam's foreign relations was the remembrance of the limits of the ancient Hindu kingdom of Kamrup, bounded on the west by the Karatoya river, including 'roughly, the Brahmaputra valley, Bhutan, Rangpur and Behar'.[52] The ultimate territorial ambition of the Ahoms, therefore, was to restore the old limit up to the Karatoya river, and they succeeded at times to bring parts of the ancient territories under their domination or under their political influence.

B. THE *PAIKS* AND THE *KHEL* SYSTEM

For an understanding of the dynamics of the political and economic strategy of the Ahoms, it may be necessary to have some idea about the basic economic and political organizational form of the Ahom state. While the Ahoms accepted joint conquest as a principle of state administration, in matters of land and other resources such as wood, forests, ferries and mines, etc., the Ahom kings claimed that all such resources belonged to the Crown.[53] Thus, the enjoyment of the soil was vested in the leader Sukapha and the principal nobles who accompanied him from Maulung. Yet, the king could alienate only those lands for the legal tenure of which, the occupier had no documentary evidence. However, all uncultivated lands were at his disposal. The distribution of land to the people was governed by what is known as the *paik* and *khel* system. Let us, therefore, turn to a discussion of the fundamentals of the *paik* and *khel* system, which was the backbone of the Ahom economic and political system.

The major administrative and organizational reforms in the political and economic sphere of the Ahom state were introduced only in the early seventeenth century, when the Ahoms were constantly facing threats of invasion from the Mughals. The chief architect of the *paik* and the *khel* system was Momai-Tamuli Barbarua, who initiated it in 1609 under the reign of Pratap Singha.[54] The sole objective of the system was to organize the economic, political and defence system of the state, by organizing the people into some kind of a hierarchical form. To be precise, the entire male population was divided into *khels* or guilds, according to their respective occupation. The *khels* were supposed to render specific services to the state, such as arrow-making, boat-building, boat-plying, house-building, provision-supplying, fighting, writing, revenue collecting, road-building, catching and training of elephants, superintendence of horses, training of hawks, and the supervision of forests. Each *khel* was allotted lands for cultivation by its constituent members, free of rent in return for the service they rendered to the State. The strength of a *khel* varied from 3,000 to 100. Each *khel* was placed in charge of a *Phukan* if it was an important one, and of a *Rajkhowa* or a *Barua* if it was of less importance. A gradation of officers, *Hazarikas* or commanders of 1,000, *Saikias* or commanders of 100, assisted the head of the *khel*. An adult male, whose name was registered for state service was called a *paik* and four *paiks* constituted a unit called a *got*. Every *paik* was bound to serve the state, either as a private or a public servant for one-fourth of the year, or was to supply a certain quantity of his produce in lieu of such services. He was entitled in return, to keep two *puras* (one *pura* is equivalent to a little over an acre) of *rupit* (arable) land, apart from land for his house and garden. At the end of his term, a second man from the same *got* had to serve the State and so forth. The remaining three *paiks*, therefore, looked after the cultivation and other domestic concerns of their absent comrades. In the case of an emergency, two men or even three men were recruited for state service from each *got*. The Ahom *khel* system was very similar to the Mughal *mansabdari* system.

The *Borahs, Saikias* and *Hazarikas* supervised the *paiks* under the command of higher officials, civil and military, the *Baruas, Rajkhowas* and *Phukans*. These officials were remunerated with *paiks* apart from rent-free grants. They could also occupy rent-free *khats* or wastelands, where they employed their attendants and slaves. Vast areas of arable land were also assigned rent-free or *lakhiraj* for the maintenance of temples and priests and the *satras* (the Vaishnava monasteries). Thus, the revenue of the state was realized in personal service and produce. As we shall argue later, this highly inefficient system of resource management was one of the major reasons for the eventual decline of the Ahom empire.

C. The Defence and Military System

The fact that the Ahoms carved out a place for themselves in an alien environment and that they had brought under their rule the entire region of the north-east and a part of modern Bengal, speaks volumes about their organizing skills and military efficiency. The infantry and cavalry under the command of the Ahoms while they were involved with the war against the Mughals in 1669–71 were about 1 lakh.[55] Although they did not maintain a standing army, steps however, were taken to form a standing army after the *Moamoria*[56] assault towards the end of the eighteenth century on the pattern maintained by the East India Company.[57] The Ahom army mostly consisted of infantry and elephants. As regards arms and weapons, they used matchlocks and guns. Although they did not maintain a huge reservoir of army, the non-serving *paiks* constituted the standing militia, which could be mobilized at short notice by the *Kheldar*. The organization of the militia was highly decentralized and therefore, it did not cost the exchequer a large amount for its maintenance. They also constructed highly ingenious and impregnable fortresses, which even the Mughals profusely admired. The defence arrangement at Guwahati, made by the Ahom General Lachit Borphukan explains the master war strategists that the Ahoms were. They were the best in guerrilla warfare and had attained a very high degree perfection in naval warfare. Diplomacy often played a major part in their war strategy.

D. POPULATION, FINANCE, TRADE AND THE ECONOMY

The first census on modern lines, was commenced in the seventeenth century, under the reign of Pratap Singha. The population of the kingdom, before the commencement of the Moamaria revolt in 1769–70 was estimated by Gunabhiran Barua to be about 25 lakh.[58] The Burmese war reduced the population by 50 per cent[59] during 1817–25, similar reduction occurred during the Moamaria civil wars.[60] There were about 80,000 *paiks* incorporated in the several official guilds (*khels*), both civil and military. The infantry and cavalry under the command of the Ahoms were reported to have totalled about 1 lakh.[61]

The main sources of revenue were the commutation money realized from those who were exempted from personal service and rent paid by *paiks* when they cultivated lands in excess of those allotted to them free of charge. Other sources were the house-tax for houses and gardens, hearth-tax and hoe-tax, royalties on elephants and timbers, and rent paid by farmers of mines and frontier traders. According to Sahabuddin, a Muslim chronicler, the revenue collected should have been around Rs 40 to 45 lakh. The value of the gold washed from the sands of the Brahmaputra would come to Rs 80,000 to 100,000. The currency of Assam consisted of gold and silver coins and conch-shells. Copper coins were not used in Assam. The revenue figures aptly describe the limited nature of state activities.

Although the Ahoms were not against trade, there was very little internal trade and commerce. Internal trade was of a very limited nature, because every village was self-sufficient[62] in satisfying the basic needs of the people.[63] But self-sufficiency is not enough to explain the non-existence of trade or the scope for division of labour, if differences in productivity existed across regions. Thus, the other possible reasons for lack of trade might have been the absence of trade opportunities or markets. Communication and the disjointed nature of the parts of the region mentioned earlier, were perhaps responsible for the lack of market opportunities.

Yet, there was a significant amount of external trade with the frontier tribes as well as with Bengal within India and with Tibet, China, Burma and even Afghanistan outside India.[64] While the Ahoms encouraged trade, they always put political consideration above trade.[65] Absolute availability as well as absolute non-availability of products within the state determined the pattern of trade. Thus, while the major export items were silk, elephants' tusks and forest products such as stick lac and *munjit*, major import items were salt and woollens. The Ahom's non-serious attitude towards trade and commerce, particularly in relation to the outside world was the result of their isolationist policy.[66] They did not encourage foreign merchants to enter and trade within Assam, nor did they encourage local people to openly trade with the people from outside. The isolationist policy of the Ahoms insulated the economy completely from any external influence.

The state machinery, therefore, monopolized the entire business of trade. The *Duaria Barua* acted as the principal agent of the Assam government at the Assam *Chokey*, situated at the mouth of the Manas river. He enjoyed the exclusive privilege of trade with Bengal for which he paid the Assam government, an annual rent. Occasionally, the privilege was granted to two men at the same time.[67] There were several trade routes which connected trade with China, Burma, Tibet and Bhutan. Trade with the neighbouring, inland provinces was carried on by river transport.

THE DECLINE AND THE FALL OF THE DYNASTY

The dynasty that can take pride in ruling over many centuries in the midst of repeated attacks by the Mughal empire and which was often thought to be inviolable, eventually collapsed due to internal disorder. Why did the Ahoms fail to contain such disorder while they had been so successful in protecting themselves against external attacks of all kinds in the past? We do not find any satisfactory explanation to this question. Gait sought an explanation in terms of 'physical and moral deterioration' of the Ahoms due to the 'damp' and 'relaxing' climate of the valley. He thus writes that, 'the history of the Ahoms shows how a brave and vigorous race may decay in the "sleepy hollow" of the Brahmaputra valley; and it was only the intervention of the British that prevented them from being blotted out by fresh hordes of invaders, first the Burmese, and then the Singphos and Khamtis, and also, possibly, the Daflas, Abors and Bhutias.'[68] Amalendu Guha suggests that the collapse was due to the endemic 'peasant revolt' and 'growing contradictions within' the dynasty.[69]

Both these explanations are unsatisfactory for obvious reasons. If Sir Gait is to be believed, then one has to answer why the same climate did not have any impact on the Ahom race during the first 500 years? Similarly, Guha's explanation is incomplete because if the collapse was due to 'peasant revolt', then one had to show that conditions for such a revolt actually existed during the end of eighteenth century when the Moamaria insurrection broke out. There were several causes of the Moamaria insurrection as discussed extensively by both Gait[70] and Bhuyan[71] and the prime cause according to both of them, was essentially religious. Available historical records show that the valley was fairly prosperous under the Ahom rule. There was neither too much prosperity, nor distressing starvation. In local Assamese language, they describe it like a situation where *akalo nai, bharalo nai*. So, where did the condition for peasant revolt arise? Of course, there may have been causes for mass discontentment, such as the fact that the Ahom penal law was extremely severe. But it existed since the inception of the Ahom dynastic rule. While our objective here, is not to find other explanations of the Moamaria insurrection, we are chiefly interested in explaining why the defence mechanism of the Ahoms, which played such a wonderful job for so long, suddenly became incapable of defending itself against the uprising of the Moamarias.

The incapability of the monarchy to defend itself against the Moamaria onslaught must, therefore, be sought in other economic factors. We shall argue in this paper that the absence of surplus maximization as an economic principle in the institutional framework of the Ahoms, was the sole cause of the downfall of the dynasty. While the Ahom economy was never faced with any economic crisis worth mentioning, it was nevertheless, always in a low-level equilibrium, which was determined by the lack of an accumulative process in the system. So we observe, that there were very few towns and the people had similar standards of living. Gait writes about this as follows:

Almost every house was built of mats and bamboos. There was, however, not much difference between the life of the towns and villages except that the people lived in the former in compact and concentrated form and in the latter in a diffused manner.[72]

The simplicity of life and standards of the people explains that Assamese society had yet to develop an accumulative process for growth and development. The absence of the will or desire to grow was partly due to a lack of population pressure on resources as Assam was very sparsely populated during those days and partly due to the absence of the demonstration effect. The latter effect could mainly be a result of the isolationist policies of the state. Such a policy insulated the economy totally from any outside effect. This limited the scope for trade and investment. The other important reason for disincentives for development, was the impact of Vaishnava teachings on the psyche of the people at large.

But what explains the lack of will to grow on the part of the state? In describing the prime movers of growth for an economy that fails to benefit from a large export market or substantial capital flows, Professor Ashok Guha writes:

Economies which lack such assets (such as large export markets or capital inflows) would either not develop rapidly or depend massively for development on government demand or intervention in the market. Government, of course, is no deus ex machina, stepping in whenever needed for the salvation of development process. On the contrary, it must be driven to act by powerful forces within the society: and I suggest that the three forces, which could do this, are population growth, demonstration effect, and military pressure. The responsiveness of states to these forces varies; it is a matter of the relative rigidity of different political structures – which, in turn, are legacies from the past and reflect, therefore, the political, military and economic conditions of an earlier era.[73]

The same forces of development that guide on individual or a family, also guide the state. The survival of a ruling dynasty, therefore, depends on its ability to provide the basic minimum necessities to the subjects it rules. Population pressure and demonstration effect put constant demand on the government to look for innovation and development opportunities because of the operation of the law of diminishing returns and an increase in needs through exposure and learning. The lack of growth, then creates the problems of satisfying the basic minimum needs of the people. Such failure would then cause social instability, that might eventually lead to the overthrow of one dynasty by another. But throughout history, the Ahoms did not face any problem of this kind, as there was always an abundance of resources to meet the basic demands of the people. However, the Ahoms had to confront constant attacks from the Muhammadans in the Western front of the region since 1527[74] and from the Koches in 1562.[75] Of course, there were such pressures within the region too, from Chutiyas and the hill tribes as well, but they were not so formidable because of the 'disjointed factor that we discussed earlier. The security threat, therefore, posed as the chief motivating factor for the Ahoms to develop, and indeed, the Ahoms made a number of innovations in state organization, military management, weaponry development and construction of roads and fortresses since the beginning of the attacks by the Muhammadans and the Koches. However, after the final defeat of the Mughals in 1682,[76] the Ahoms lived for nearly a century in peace and enjoyed uninterrupted hegemonic rule over the entire region. Thus, the motive force for development, i.e. military pressure, gradually faded away.

But apart from security considerations, there must have been other reasons for development. For instance, the desire to expand one's own territory could in itself, be a prime motive force for the development for any government. However, as explained above, the Ahoms were just not interested in colonial expansion. They never showed any great desire to expand beyond the old limits of Kamrup. The only exception was the King Rudra Singha, who had the ambition to invade Bengal.[77] His death in 1714 brought that ambition to an end, for good. The long continuance of undisturbed rule, made the dynasty quite complacent and the process of dynastic degeneration had started. After the death of the King Rudra Singha, the Ahom rulers came under the increasing influence of Brahminism and Saktism, which had far-reaching impact on the future course of the Ahom empire.[78]

I shall argue in what follows, that the lack of will to grow that was reflected in the complete absence of a strong, standing army of the Ahoms, that could protect the kingdom from any possible internal threat. In fact, the major cause of the breakdown of the empire was disintegration of military arrangement or the *paik* system, making the central authority very weak and vulnerable. The major factors responsible for the collapse of the dynasty are all internal to the system. These were (1) the insurrection of the Moamorias[79] (2) the rebellion of the Darrang Prince (3) the depredations of the Burkendazes (4) local chieftains raising their heads and assuming virtual independence and (5) frontier tribes carrying on with the plunder of Assamese villages.[80]

Thus, as the first Moamaria insurrection broke out in 1769, the Ahom empire lost its authority completely. The Morans took possession of the capital for five months. It appeared that the monarchy was not inviolable, as it was generally assumed and that anyone who had a determined and organized force at his disposal could place himself on the throne and reward his supporters by grant of rank and position. The only places, which had for a long time, remained immune from the Moamaria uprising, were Darrang and Kamrup. But eventually, they also joined the bandwagon and the state was incomplete disarray. It proved that the Ahom system of governance and military strategy was absolutely vulnerable to any form of internal dissent. The *paik* system was successful when the Ahoms fought against a common enemy like the Mughals, but there was generally treachery and collusion, when they were dispatched against their own countrymen. The proliferation of Vaishnava teachings to many areas and democratization of the institutions such as the *Satras* broke the 'disjointed' character of the Ahom state and helped in the mobilization of the people on a larger scale against the ruling authority. The transformation of the Moamarias from a religious sect into a fighting and ruling body was not merely an accident or the successful enterprise of anyone individual. It was the unified resistance of the common people against the Ahom rule.

The Moamaria insurrection destroyed the village economy completely, as chaos prevailed everywhere, since there was no order and governance in the state. As a result, the Ahom government sought the assistance of sepoys from Bengal. Despite the devastation caused by the Moamaria insurrection, the Ahom rule could have survived little longer. But the Burmese attack brought the British on the scene. The British integrated the valley with the Indian mainland and thus came the end to the long-lasting Ahom rule in Assam.

CONCLUSION

Cultural unification was not followed up with political and economic unification of any kind, of Assam with the Indian mainland during the Ahom rule. There were many reasons for the same. Despite repeated attempts[81] by the Mughals to conquer Assam, the Ahoms could not be subjugated. As a result, the Ahoms not only maintained their political independence, but also lived in near-perfect isolation without being influenced by the political and economic forces of the outside world. Their technology of warfare was far superior to that of the Mughals in the topography of Assam. Though they had embraced Hinduism towards the latter part of their rule, they were very suspicious of foreigners. Except for the King Rudrasingha, no Ahom ruler had ever shown any expansionist drive, precisely because of the fact that by temperament, they were no colonial power. This lack of interest in the augmentation of power made them virtually complacent in their self-sufficient economy in a low-level equilibrium. There was neither any necessity in the system, nor was there any ambition in the Ahoms to maintain any economic and political interaction with the outside world. It is therefore, important to explain as to how the Ahoms could prevent the Mughals from penetrating into Assam. As suggested by a historian, it was mainly because of their militaristic cult, that they successfully pursued, coupled with Assam's natural advantages and 'the organization and intrepidity of the Assamese generals'.[82] The key to the Ahoms' military rule was based on the principle of the 'right of joint conquest' to all, who helped the king establish Ahom domination in Assam.[83] The entire valley could be thought of as consisting of several disjointed regions, where each region was ruled over by a vassal chief of its own, enjoying autonomy and freedom, and accepting the supremacy of the king in all matters. In return for such freedom, the vassal chief had to furnish a stipulated number of *paiks* to work for the king, or pay the commutation money if exempted. In case of war, the vassal raja was expected to act as the head of his contingent of *paiks* under his command. This system of military organization essentially served two purposes, first, the king did not have to keep a large standing army and second, the administrative set-up was maintained at a bare minimum. As a result, the revenue requirement of managing such a system was also very limited. This system worked efficiently because of the disjointed nature of the organizations whereby the king could easily subjugate a region by using the others and the survival of each region depended on the survival of the kingdom. In the given circumstances, no vassal chief could successfully challenge the king. Each region lived in isolation in a self-sufficient, low-level equilibrium. Since there was no market integration with the outside world, there were, therefore, no demonstration and trade effects, which could usher in the forces of change within the region. The only possible force worth mentioning, could be population pressure, but the system responded to population pressure through the migration of people to areas of new settlements. As the land: man ratio was very favourable and virgin soil was abundant, migration did not lead to any conflicts.

The organization of the economy as described above, did not provide the necessary incentives to the maximization of output and the generation of surplus. Regions that had different cultures, traditions, languages and religions, co-existed together, without much conflict. However, Assam had to pay a very high cost in order to maintain its political independence for so long as it helped sustain a highly inefficient economic system, without the threat of change. The intrinsic desire of the Ahoms to remain in isolation and their easy maintenance of self-sufficiency were responsible for their lack of any outward-looking policies. Their economic interests were not guided by any motive to generate surplus beyond the basic minimum. Political independence insulated the economy from any outside effect. The effect of such insulation was, to prevent the region from enjoying the benefits of a better system of economic management, technology and trade with the Indian mainstream.

The above arguments that explain why market linkages did not develop with the more progressive areas outside Assam such as Bengal, does not explain, as to what factors constrained the development of markets within Assam itself. The market does not grow by itself, unless there is primitive capital accumulation and expansion of demands. These forces do not exist in a self-sufficient economy, without the desire to follow a military expansionary policy, a strong demonstration effect and population pressure. The insulation of the economy, as described above, also prevented any demonstration effect from having an impact on the population. On the other hand, Assam, being very sparsely populated and the land being very fertile, the rural economy could sustain itself without any difficulty.

However, the spread effects of the Vaishnava cult were tremendous, in terms of the unification of various regions, tribes and cultures, contributing to the rise of a homogeneous culture. As political segmentation broke down, certain forms of unification of markets took places, giving rise to new conflicts of interests. With the incorporation of Kamrup into the Ahom empire towards the seventeenth century, economic conflicts became much more sharpened as Kamrup was, for a long time, under the control of the Mughal administration. It was also exposed to the rich culture of Bengal much before upper Assam was. Certainly, it had led to certain forms of demonstration effect on consumption and production. As Kamrup was densely populated, the migration of people from regions of higher density, to that of regions having lower density, also led to economic conflicts. The maintenance of self-sufficiency seemed no more feasible. These forces of change contributed to the political unification of the people and resulted in a mass uprising against the Ahom empire, known as the Moamoria uprising. It had such devastating impact on the Ahom monarchy, that the 600-year-old regime, collapsed. The appearance of the Burmese and the British on the scene, acted merely as catalysts in the inevitable process of degeneration of the glorified empire.

NOTES

1. See for details Surajit Sinha, *Tribal Politics and State System in Pre-Colonial Eastern and North-Eastern India*, Calcutta: Centre for Studies in Social Science, 1987.
2. Although some of these tribes at times came under the control of the Ahoms or the Koches, they enjoyed near absolute freedom till the advent of the British. For further information on this see 'Introduction' by A. Barua in this volume.
3. Sukapha in AD 1218 laid the foundation of the Ahom kingdom in the easternmost part of India. Sukapha, a prince, left his native Shan state of Maulung in Upper Burma in 1215 as a result of some quarrel with his kinsmen. He came with 8 nobles and 9,000 men, women and children. He had with him two elephants and 300 horses. See *A History of Assam* (*AHA*, from now onwards) by E. Gait, p. 78.

    The Ahom kingdom of Assam during the last 140 years of Ahom rule corresponds to the following districts of the post-Independent Assam: Kamrup (now, Kamrup, Nalbari and Barpeta), Darrang (now, Sonitpur and Darrang), Nowgong (now, Nowgong and Marigaon), Sibasagar (now Sibsagar, Jorhat and Golaghat) and Lakhimpur (now Lakhimpur, Dibrugarh, Tinsukia and Dhemaji). A portion of the Arunachal (Sadiya frontier tract) was also included within Assam. See *Anglo-Assamese Relations* (*AAR*, from now onwards) by S.K. Bhuyan, p. 1.
4. See Chapter IV in *AHA*, on the Koch kings. According to Gait the ancestor of the Koch kings was a resident of the Goalpara district of present Assam. The Koch kingdom in the course of time expanded up to the river Karatoya in the west and the Bar Nadi near Mangaldoi district of present Assam in the east (see Map 2).

5. The Ahoms were the offshoot of the great Tai or Shan race. The Shan race spreads from the gulf of Siam northwards into Yunnan and westwards to Assam. It is still not known how they came to be known as Ahoms. According to *AHA*, the word Ahom was derived from the Sanskrit word *Asama*, meaning unequalled. The local tribes at the time of Sukapha's invasion of Assam called them as Ahom—*Asama*—in admiration of the way the Ahom king conquered and then conciliated them. Gait gives an interesting account about why Sukapha left his native land and invaded Assam. There are other stories in *Ahom Buranjis, Buranji* meaning history. See, *AHA*, 78; *AAR*, p. 17.
6. See *AHA*, p. 78.
7. By the Treaty of the Yandaboo enacted in February 1826, Assam passed into the hands of the East India Company. See *AAR*, p. 6.
8. Bentinck was the Governor General of India from 1828 to 1832.
9. See, *AAR*, p. 6.
10. Ibid., p. 7.
11. See *AHA*, pp. 99–100.
12. Ibid., pp. 90–7.
13. Changes in the constitution did take place according to the requirement of time and situation but the basic political and economic order of the Ahom system remained unaltered throughout the Ahom history.
14. In this paper we shall apply the basic evolutionary model of development suggested by Ashok Guha, *An Evolutionary Viewpoint of Economic Growth*, Oxford (1981) in explaining the long survival and decline of the Ahom empire.
15. *AAR*, p. 2.
16. See *AHA*, p. 78.
17. Ibid., p. 79; *AAR*, p. 17. It is located in the present Sibsagar district of Assam.
18. See *AHA*, p. ix.
19. As Gait writes, 'Early in the thirteenth century a band of hardy hill men wandered into the eastern extremity of the Brahmaputra valley, led by chance rather than by any deep-seated design.' See *AHA*, p. 71.
20. Discussing the contribution of Ahoms to the development of modern Assamese language, B.K. Kakati wrote, 'Unlike the Bodos, the Ahoms do not seem to have been a colonizing people spreading in groups of villages over different parts of the province. Neither does it appear that they were ever given to trade and commerce, which bring varied dialect speakers together and make linguistic borrowing possible. As it is even now the Ahoms live in concentrated mass in the Sibsagar sub-division of the same district. . . . The exigencies of the Ahom state in favour of a common lingua franca combined with the social habits of the Ahoms themselves may explain why their contribution to Assamese vocabulary is so small' (p. 52).

21. See *AHA*, p. x.
22. Ibid.
23. See the chapter on literature in *AHA*, p. 278.
24. Sankardeva was a great religious and social reformer who was born in 1449 and died in 1569. The Ahoms subjected him to so much persecution that he eventually had to take shelter in the Koch kingdom. See *AHA*, p. 59–60.
25. The first Ahom monarch to accept Hinduism was Jayadhawaj Singha (1648–63). Jayadhawaj and his successors up to Lora Raja (1679–81) took their initiation into Vaisnavism, which was the predominant faith in Assam at that time. But Gadadhar Singha (1681–95) had decided leanings towards Saktaism, as he considered Vaishnavism to be too passive and mild to be suitable for a ruling class. Further, he viewed the large accumulation of wealth and the grandeur and influence of the Vaishnava pontiffs as potential danger spots capable of diverting the loyalty of the subjects to themselves and thereby reducing the monarch to comparative non-entities. Gadadhar Singha, therefore, inaugurated a campaign of pillaging the Vaishnava monasteries and killing and expelling their heads. See *AAR*, p. 18.

    Gait, however, has given a different explanation of the persecution of the Vaishnavas. The religious teachings of Sankardeva became very popular and there were many followers who claimed exemption from the universal liability to fight and to assist in the construction of roads and tanks and other public works. This caused serious inconveniences and King Gadadhar Singha feared that Vaishnava teachings may cause great harm to the strength of the Ahom army. See *AHA*, p. 173.
26. The region through which the river Karatoya was flowing is now in modern Bengal. See Map 1.
27. The Ahoms after consolidating their power in the east gradually expanded their rule towards the west. Though they were a ruling race with a distinct religion and language, they gave up those identities in favour of Aryan habits and customs. Their absorption was so complete that they tended to believe they were the successors of the traditional kings of the Kamrup. As a result, their territorial ambition if at all any was to maintain their dominance up to the old limits of the Kamrup kingdom. See *AAR*, p. 21.

    They succeeded at times in bringing parts of the ancient territories under their domination or under their political influence. But for strategic reasons they retracted their limits of the western boundary further eastward near the river Manaha, which remained as such till the occupation of Assam by the British in 1824. See *AAR*, p. 24.
28. Sukapha first confronted the Nagas and defeated them. The ghastly barbarity he had shown to them created such widespread terror that the Nagas submitted to him. See *AHA*, p. 79.

29. *AHA*, p. 144.
30. The Morans played the major role in the downfall of the Ahom dynasty towards the end of the eighteenth century.
31. Sukapha brought with him a following of 8 nobles and 9,000 men, women and children. See *AHA*, p. 78.
32. Since majority of the people who followed Sukapha from Maulung were adult males, this intermingling was also necessary for the expansion of their population. See *AHA*, p. 79.
33. *Buranji* in Assamese means history. The Ahom Buranjis are essentially the chronicles of Ahom court. They contain a careful, reliable and continuous narrative of the Ahom rule. At first they were written in Ahom language but later they came to be compiled in Assamese as well. See *AHA*, pp. 282–3.
34. Gait writes that 'Buranjis constitute an unprecendented golden chapter in Assamese literature'. See *AHA*, p. 283.
35. See *AAR*, pp. 14–15.
36. See *AHA*, p. 270.
37. The impact of the assimilative philosophy of the Ahoms on Assamese society was overwhelming. Even today we observe the large-scale assimilation of Muslims from Bangladesh and also people from other states into the Assamese society. It only demonstrates the impact of the Ahom philosophy on Assamese society.
38. The Morans were also the people who were instrumental in the collapse of the Ahom dynasty six centuries later.
39. See Map 1.
40. Bhuyans were the pre-Ahom rulers of a part of eastern Assam. See *AAR*, pp. 117–18.
41. See 'Introduction' by A. Barua in this volume.
42. See *AAR*, p. 7.
43. See *AHA*, p. 239.
44. Ibid., p. 242.
45. The role of the three *Gohains* was so important that even the selection of a monarch depended upon the joint decisions of the *Gohains*. See *AHA*, p. 239.
46. The Sadiya-Khowa Gohain ruled in Sadiya. See *AHA*, p. 247.
47. He was the governor of the Naga marches west of Dhansiri. See *AHA*, p. 247.
48. He was the governor in most parts of Nowgong. See *AHA*, p. 247.
49. They were in-charge of the Jayantias. See *AAR*, p. 47.
50. See *AHA*, p. 247.
51. See *AAR*, p. 11.
52. *AHA*, p. 10.
53. See *AHA*, p. 270.
54. See *AAR*, p. 11.

55. Ibid., p. 2.
56. The Moamarias belong to a Vaishnava sect funded by Anirudha Dev, a follower of Sankardeva. *AHA*, p. 60.
57. See *AHA*, p. 219.
58. See, Gunabhiram Barua, *Assam Bandhu Journal*, vol. 1, no. 1, 1885, p. 3.
59. *Cambridge History of India*, vol. V, p. 558.
60. See fn. 2, p. 1, *AAR*. Population was estimated to be around 8 lakh in 1835. *AHA*, p. 351.
61. *AAR*, p. 2.
62. Gait writes: 'Each villege was self-sufficient in the sense that it contained men of different castes and professions such as Brahmanas, ganaks, black-smiths, mat-makers, potters, dhobis, chamars, etc.', p. 269.
63. Shihabuddin, a writer who accompanied Mir Jumlah on his invasion to Assam wrote about the state of market in this way: 'Near the Raja's palace, on both banks of the Dikhu river, the houses are numerous and there is a narrow bazaar-road. The only traders who sit in the bazaar, are betel-leaf sellers. It is not their practice to buy and sell articles of food in the marketplace. The inhabitants store in their houses one year's supply of food of all kinds, and are under no necessity to buy or sell any eatable.' See *AHA*, p. 153.
64. See *AAR*, pp. 4–55; *AHA*, pp. 273–6.
65. Ibid., p. 50.
66. See *AHA*, p. 274; *AAR*, p. 50.
67. *AAR*, p. 50; *AHA*, p. 274.
68. *AHA*, p. 8.
69. See Amalendu Guha, 'The Ahom Political System: An Enquiry into State Formation in Medieval Assam: 1228–1800' in Surajit Sinha, ed., *Tribal Politics and State System in Pre-Colonial Eastern and North-Eastern India*, Calcutta: Centre for Studies in Social Science, 1987, p. 172.
70. See *AHA*, pp. 195–227.
71. See *AAR*, pp. 188–271.
72. See *AHA*, p. 269.
73. See Ashok Guha, *An Evolutionary View of Economic Growth*, p. 49.
74. See *AHA*, p. 91.
75. Ibid., p. 101.
76. Ibid., p. 172.
77. Ibid., p. 185.
78. Ibid., p. 188.
79. The Moamorias belong to a Vaishnava sect founded by Anirudha Dev, a Kalita by caste, in Upper Assam. The Moamorias were mainly persons of low social rank, such as Doms, Morans, Kacharis, Haris, and Chutias

and they played an important role in the downfall of the Ahom rule.'
See *AHA*, p. 60.
80. See *AAR*, p. 188.
81. It was mainly because of Mughal's general policy not to allow any independent state to exist. However, they also had economic interest in Assam's forests for elephants, agar wood and other precious articles. See, *AAR*, p. 26.
82. See *AAR*, p. 26.
83. Ibid., pp. 7–8.

SECTION II

THE COMPANY BAHADUR AND JOHN BULL, 1826–1947

GROWTH AND STAGNATION UNDER THE *RAJ*

Like in Argentina of the late nineteenth century, Assam too, was the recepient of a large volume of investment, both infrastructural as well as entrepreneurial. Like Argentina, Assam belied expectations; it experienced, in the words of Amalendu Guha, 'A Big Push Without a Takeoff'. Why was this so?

Hiranya Nath holds that the economy so created, was an enclave economy where investment was received only by one sector, i.e. tea. On the basis of statistical and anecdotal evidence, Nath contends that this sector had no links with Assam's traditional sector through any of the following: capital, labour or the commodity markets. This gave rise to a dual economy with little prospect for growth.

In the same vein, Guha points out that although considerable investments were made in the tea industry as well as in infrastructure, especially railways, Assam did not embark on a trajectory of growth. He points out to examples of the predatory procurement of land of some of the planters and the manner in which local peasants were forced to offer labour at very low wages. Thus, the linkage effects of such employment could hardly be great. Indeed, wages in plantations were generally lower than what peasants could earn working on their own fields, which led to the import of labour from the rest of the country. Rising demand in food from plantations, stoked local inflation rather than growth, as increasing immigration into Assam had made it a food deficit state. More pertinently, he points out that even when profits were reinvested, they were reinvested in these sectors alone, leading to over-production (as in 1901).

Sanjib Baruah offers an explanation for the nineteenth-century puzzle—the total disinterest exhibited by the Assamese peasantry in acquiring long-term titles to land that they tilled despite its obvious advantages. Baruah points out that in a regime where a peasant could cultivate any previously uncultivated land, he would be irrational to claim a 10-year right to a piece of land and pay taxes on the same. It was only with the rise in migration, coupled with the Assamese version of the enclosure movement, which made the earlier practice increasingly difficult, that the Assamese farmer finally 'learnt'.

Thus, the nature of investment and in-migration in the British period (in contrast to the previous era) laid the foundation for a stagnant, dual economy.

CHAPTER 5

The Rise of an Enclave Economy[1]

HIRANYA K. NATH

I. INTRODUCTION

The economy of Assam,[2] on the eve of the British colonization was characterized by acute shortages of labour and capital. A series of civil wars during the last three decades of the eighteenth century and Burmese invasions in the beginning of the nineteenth century, 'brought in depopulation, disorder and all-round decadence' and left the economy in a state of mess. Persistent chaos and anarchy led to the Burmese occupation of the plains of Assam from the year 1817 to 1824. Then came the British, who rescued the people from the dissolute State and the Burmese were forced to surrender their claim over Assam under the Treaty of Yandabo in 1826. With this, came historic changes in the polity and, most importantly, in the economy of this region. The next few decades witnessed a gradual dilapidation of feudal institutions and the rise of capitalist economic entities. The discovery of tea in the Brahmaputra valley in the very beginning of the British administration was a prelude to the presence of the British capital in the following years and the subsequent evolution of a modern sector, which crucially hinged on the growth of the tea plantations. However, the growth of the modern sector did not bring a high standard of living to the people of this region. By the end of the nineteenth century 'the economy of Assam had developed all the characteristics of a dual economy',[3] with huge investments pouring into the modern sector and the traditional sector having been left out of this development process. Notwithstanding the role of imperialist designs, there were deeper economic reasons as to why there were no spillovers in the traditional sector. The peculiar socio-economic conditions of the region at that time, came in the way of a process of dynamic interaction between the two sectors. Consequently, the traditional sector remained an enclave in the years to come. It is in this context, that the present paper tries to analyse the economic factors behind the rise of this economic enclave.

The rest of the paper is organized as follows: Section II briefly describes the economy on the eve of the British rule, emphasizing the distinctive features of the region. In Section III, we discuss the growth and expansion of a modern sector in the nineteenth century. Section IV looks into the linkages between the traditional sector and the modern sector. Section V summarizes and concludes the discussion.

II. THE ECONOMY ON THE EVE OF BRITISH COLONIZATION

Assam, with its difficult terrain and a tribal population that lived on perpetually underdeveloped agrarian practices, had been a sparsely-populated region throughout ancient and medieval times. Shifting cultivation having been the mainstay of agricultural practices among the tribals, theirs was a nomadic lifestyle. Under such practices, land was held as communal territory. However, even before the Ahoms established their rule over the Assam plains in the thirteenth century, efforts had been made by the rulers of the land[4] to encourage settled agriculture by granting lands to Brahmins and religious institutions. Such grants usually came with a right over the people living on those lands, which empowered the grantees with political authority. For example, during the fourteenth and fifteenth centuries, the *Bhuyans* and the *Bara-bhuyans* held royal land grants and wielded considerable political power by providing protection to the subjects of the kings from whom they received land grants. This kind of devolution of power led to the feudal organization of land to a certain degree.

The existence of smaller kingdoms in the region, led to a situation in which there was no strong central governance. As the Ahoms consolidated their territories in the Brahmaputra valley, a slack political system gave way to a system that had centralized political authority. Economic institutions and production relations that evolved under their rule, however, had the distinct traits of feudalism. The entire male population, excepting those who were disabled or engaged in non-agricultural activities, was divided into *khel*s or guilds. The *khel*s were sub-divided into *got*s or units, each of which consisted of four and later, of three *paik*s or individuals. Every *paik* had to serve the state either as a private or public servant for one-third of the year, or to supply a certain quantity of his produce, in lieu thereof. In return, he was entitled to two *pura*s of *rupit* or arable land (*ga-mati*)[5] apart from homestead and garden (*bari* and *bori*) land. He could, however, acquire additional plots of land (*katanimati*) but had to pay rent in cash[6] for holding such lands. In this *khel* system, the land assigned to a *paik* for cultivation, did not go to his offsprings upon his death. In other words, there was no right of private property over cultivable lands.

The *paik*s were supervised by the *Borah*s, *Saikia*s and *Hazarika*s. In a hierarchy of officials, civil and military, they were under the command of the *Barua*s, *Rajkhowa*s and *Phukan*s. These officials were remunerated with *paik*s and rent-free grants, known as *nankar* and *manmati*. In addition, they could occupy rent-free *khat*s or wastelands where they employed their attendants and slaves. For the maintenance of temples and Vaishnava monasteries known as *Satra*s, huge areas of land were assigned rent-free or *lakhiraj*.

Thus, at the time of the British take-over of Assam, hereditary, private proprietary rights existed only in the case of homestead and garden lands, but not in the case of cultivable lands with exceptions in case of copper-plate grants. These lands were essentially, communal lands. This system of property rights over cultivable lands is one reason why there was apparently no incentive for the cultivators to innovate and to upgrade technology with an objective of increasing productivity.[7] In most cases, production was just sufficient for the household.

Another interesting feature of the Ahom system of governance was that, there was no regular army and during war, the *paik*s were pressed into fighting for the king. This had two important implications for the economy. First, the state exchequer didn't have to incur the expenditure of maintaining an army, which is one of the major expenditure items of a modern state. Secondly, the *paik*s were expected to acquire skills as varied as working in the field and fighting. Consequently, there was hardly any scope for specialization, which is a characteristic of an economically advanced society.

The economy, in medieval times, was essentially a barter economy. Only in the sixteenth century, were local coins were used in limited quantities. As we have already seen, land revenue was paid in terms of labour and produce. Non-cultivators or artisans, viz., braziers, gold washers, fishermen (who constituted a relatively small fraction of the population), ryots who had surplus lands and those failing to attend to their assigned duties or supply the requirement of produce, had to pay the revenue in coins. Officials received a portion of the contributed labour in lieu of salaries. Thus, state expenditure did not require the use of coins. The absence of a common medium of exchange and a standard of value was one factor that limited trade, and thus in a way, the scope for specialization, according to its comparative advantages. However, by the end of the Ahom rule, the use of coins had increased. Repeated Mughal invasions necessitated the establishment of a regular army which implied a heavy burden on the treasury. On the other hand, during the Mughal occupation of Kamrup (for a few years) money tax in lieu of personal services was introduced.[8]

Also, the geographic environment and the size and composition of the population, kept the economic activities in this region to their bare minimum. Agriculture was the major occupation. Handicrafts and weaving were practised mainly to cater to local needs. In the hills surrounding the Brahmaputra valley, rice was produced in a limited quantity. Among other things, cotton, long pepper, chillies, millets, vegetables and, in some areas oranges and pineapples were produced. *Jhum* or shifting cultivation was predominant. Barring a few exceptions, the hoe, instead of the plough had generally been used in the hill regions. The people of the hills were also involved in food gathering in the jungles, in hunting and fishing. In some parts, they took to horticulture and bee-keeping. The breeding of livestock as a source of meat supply and for ritual purposes was common in the hills. Crafts, like weaving, pottery and basketry were practised among some tribes. Technology was, however, backward.

In the plains of the Brahmaputra valley, more than half of the arable lands was under paddy cultivation. Among other crops, mustard, pulses, sugar cane, arecanuts, pepper, cotton, tobacco and som trees for rearing silk-worms were grown. The cultivation of indigo on a limited scale, can be traced back to the eighteenth century. However, agriculture in Assam remained for a long time in its primitive stage. The implements used were archaic. 'Population scarcity' and 'land abundance slow(ed) down the transition from shifting hoe cultivation to permanent plough cultivation not only in the hills but also in the plains'.[9] Heavy ploughs drawn by several bullocks or seed drills were never used in Assam.

Weaving and spinning were common to the womenfolk of the plains, irrespective of their caste and status. The extraction of mustard oil and *gur* was carried on in individual households. For reasons discussed above, there was virtually no market and the prevalence of these practices is a pointer to this fact which, in its turn, significantly reduced the scope for specialization. There was, however, specialization to some degree in the making of bell-metal and brass utensils, earthenware, ornaments and a few other articles.

The consumption basket of the valley people included rice, a wide variety of edible greens, milk, fish and meat. Salt was an expensive item, as it was locally not available. Needs however, were limited and people could afford their basic needs easily. There was hardly any inequality in terms of economic conditions among the common people.

A difficult topography and the relative ease with which the basic minimum needs were locally satisfied – mainly due to the abundant supply of land and a relatively small population – contributed to the stagnation of the economy by restricting movement and hence, trade. There was limited trade between the plains and the hills. Raw cotton, forest products, oranges, rock salt and iron from the hills were bartered for rice, dried fish, silk and cotton cloth from the plains in a chain of foothill marts and fairs. Trade between the plains of Assam and the rest of India was limited by difficult navigation on the Brahmaputra. The difficulty in using wheeled carts for carriages, the limited carrying capacity of canoes on rivers and of pack animals and human carriers on land, restricted the volume of trade. Assam's exports to Bengal during the eighteenth and the early nineteenth centuries, included raw cotton, lac, mustard seeds, *muga* silk cloth, *muga* silk thread, elephant tusks, slaves, bell metal utensils, iron hoes, pepper and miscellaneous forest products. Imports from Bengal included mainly salt and muslin. The figures recorded for the year 1808–9, show that the total exports from Assam were valued at Sicca Rs 130,900 against the imports of the value of Sicca Rs 228,300. Thus, Assam had a balance of trade deficit with the rest of India. During the first three decades of the nineteenth century, trade increased in volume and value and in the 1830s, trade deficit turned into trade surplus as shown in Table 5.1.

The difficulties faced in exporting goods and the absence of a local market for limited production (though the abundant land of the Brahmaputra valley had the potential for producing considerable surplus) made Assam, in other words, a demand-constrained economy on the eve of the British rule.

TABLE 5.1: ASSAM'S TRADE STATISTICS, 1808–35

Year	Exports Total Value in Rs (Sicca)	Imports Total Value in Rs (Sicca)	Trade Balance Total Value in Rs (Sicca)
1808–9	130,900	228,300	–97,400
1832–3	146,772	59,007	–87,765
1833–4	249,367	244,055	5,312
1834–5	304,186	247,393	56,793

Source: Tables 7.1 and 7.2 in A. Guha, 1991.

At the time of the takeover by the British, Assam didn't have huge, urban centres. The most important towns had no more than a few thousand inhabitants in medieval times. As market-oriented activities were almost non-existent, none of these centres had grown into a business hub. Villages were mostly the hamlet type of settlements, scattered over agricultural fields in an elongated, linear fashion, along the banks of tributaries of the Brahmaputra.

The most important change that took place immediately after the British had taken over, was the monetization of the economy. A polltax of Rs 3 per *paik* was introduced in place of the liability of personal service without changing the existing *khel* system. However, this was gradually replaced by a proprietory system under which, regular assessment of land, based on actual measurement was held. Lands were assessed according to their uses and the crops grown on them.[10] Also, the already money-starved, barter economy had to bear the brunt of transition from the use of local currencies to that of the British-Indian currency. The scope for currency flow was limited. A substantial portion of trade surplus, generated in the early 1830s, either accrued to traders of non-indigenous origin or represented the value of the goods received by the government in lieu of revenue. The administrative machinery was manned by people from outside the state and 'of the public money that has gone to defray the establishments, civil and military, at least half has been remitted out of the province, whilst all surplus revenue, above these expenses has been withdrawn to the treasuries of the government'.[11] Thus, there was an acute shortage of money during the transitional period which, in a way, debarred the indigenous people from taking advantage of the opportunities offered in the subsequent periods.

From the above discussion, one can draw the following conclusions about the state of the economy, on the eve of British colonization. Firstly, Assam was a labour-short, barter economy, having limited trade links with the rest of the world. Secondly, a system of governance that devolved no private property rights over cultivable lands, the small size of population and the absence of 'money'[12] severely restricted the evolution of a market. The topography of this region, aggravated the situation by restricting trade. Thus, the potential for producing substantial surplus was never realized and the economy stagnated. Moreover, after the British take-over of Assam, the monetization of the economy brought in a number of transitional crises that affected the local economy in an adverse way.

III. GROWTH OF A MODERN SECTOR

In the early 1820s, tea was discovered growing wild at many places in the Brahmaputra valley. Since the East India Company monopolized the import of Chinese tea to Europe, it didn't pay attention to growing tea in Assam which had recently come under their control. The Charter of 1833, which stripped the Company of its monopoly over the British trade to China, expedited its initiatives to take up tea plantation in the newly-conquered region. In 1839, the Assam Company was launched in London with an initial capital of 200,000 pound sterling.[13] In the early stages of plantation, 'experiments with tea plants were being carried on by officials, army officers, medical men and others. Most were technically successful, but for those who undertook tea growing as a commercial venture, hard times lay ahead. The Assam Company had virtual monopoly of tea production during the first decade.'[14] But soon, it ran into rough weather mainly due to ineffective management and incurred heavy losses. However, from the early 1850s, onwards, it started making profits. The glimpse of its newly-found success led to speculation and the expansion of tea plantation on a large scale, first in upper Assam, and then extending up to Sylhet and Cacher. This process received government patronage in the form of extremely favourable regulations for the reclamation of wastelands for tea plantation. Under these regulations the planters had to pay virtually nothing for lands cleared for tea cultivation. As a result, there was a mad rush for started new tea gardens. 'Clearances were made wholesale, often with the sole object of selling them to companies at a large profit; land was taken up irrespective of its suitability for the object in view, or of the supply of labour available, and was planted out with a wholly insufficient number of tea bushes.'[15] The result was an inevitable depression which, however, didn't last for long. Table 5.2 shows an increase in the area under tea cultivation and the output of tea plantations in Assam during the period 1850–1901.

This table shows that the area under tea plantation and the output of plantations, increased by leaps and bounds in the first three decades, beginning in 1850. During 1850–9 the annual average growth in acreage under tea cultivation was about 34 per cent. In the next two decades, it hovered around 23–5 per cent and in the last two decades of the nineteenth century, it dropped down to 4–6 per cent. It may be noted that liberal terms for holding lands for tea cultivation, led to a situation in which the planters held lands in excess of the areas they actually planted. For example, in 1858–9, the planters held 54,860 acres of land, of which 7,599 acres were actually brought under tea plantation. In the year 1900, the total area held by the planters was 1,059,624 acres.[16] An increase in output followed a pattern similar to that of acreage: from an annual average growth rate of as high as 51 per cent during 1850–9, it plummeted to 7 per cent by the end of the century. The differences in growth rates were

TABLE 5.2: GROWTH OF TEA PLANTATION IN ASSAM, 1850–1901

Year	No. of Estates	Area in Acres	Output in Pounds
1850	1	1,876	216,00
1853	10	2,425	366,700
1859	48	7,599	1,205,689
1869	260	25,174	4,714,769
1871	295	31,303	6,251,143
1875–6	–	59,864	12,602,098
1879–80	–	88,210	19,625,634
1880	–	89,475	21,465,551
1885	–	107,492	32,530,061
1887	–	115,578	39,081,121
1892	–	139,582	48,916,479
1895	–	154,389	56,497,593
1900	–	204,285	75,125,176
1901	–	204,682	72,381,251

Sources: D.H. Buchanan, 1966.
Statistical Tables for British India, 5th issue, *Agricultural Statistics of British India*, vol. I and subsequent volumes.

accounted for, by a steady growth in per acre productivity. During this half century, the average yield per acre, more than doubled, from an estimated 115 lbs per acre to 354 lbs in 1901. The reasons are rather obvious: firstly the period of experimentation was but a few years' time. After a few trials and errors, the cultivation and processing techniques were perfected. Secondly, in the beginning, there was a scarcity of labour. Before the migrant workers flocked into this region from the 1860s onwards, tea cultivation often fell short of the ideal ratio of 1.5 workers per acre.

As we have mentioned, the regulations enacted by the British administration for reclamation of the wastelands for tea plantation were extremely favourable to the European planters. At first, the government leased out land for long terms and with liberal postponements of the beginning of rentals and taxes. In 1861, regulations were introduced to facilitate the holding of wastelands in 'fee simple'. By 1873, nearly all tea lands were held in one of three ways – on a clearance lease for 99 years, in 'fee simple', or on cultivation lease. The clearing and improvement of wasteland for tea plantation was difficult. According to an estimate, 'in the early days . . . an estate could be cleared, planted and brought to the bearing stage for about 40 to 50 pound sterling per acre. In 1887, . . . the investment was nearly 70 pound sterling for each acre planted in tea.'[17] However, since the estates included vast areas partly reclaimed or totally untouched, the expenses could in fact, be much higher.

The average size of the tea gardens in Assam in 1871, was a little more than 100 acres.[18] Gradually, the gardens became larger, partly through the reclamation of more wasteland and partly through the consolidation of smaller gardens into large-scale enterprises. The financial stresses of the 1860s, forced individual planters to hand over the gardens to the managing agencies that operated in the form of companies. These companies were mostly British, and were registered in England.

The price of Assam tea steadily declined from as high as 8 shillings a pound in the 1840s to a low of 8.5d by the turn of the century. As a result of the massive expansion of tea plantations during the last quarter of the nineteenth century, supply outgrew demand and the industry was on the verge of making losses. There were concerted efforts to venture into new markets and to halt further expansion, and these efforts bore fruits: the price rose and touched new heights by the 1920s.

The growth and expansion of a modern industry, that was almost entirely dependent on the external market, necessitated a reasonably well-developed infrastructure. The basic minimum prerequisites for the expansion of tea plantations in Assam, included the construction of roads and bridges, and the establishment of a regular link route with Bengal. In the beginning, the Assam Company on its own, and later the government on its insistence, took up road and bridge construction on limited scale. The Public Works Department started constructing roads from the late 1860s onwards. The government started a steamer service on the Brahmaputra from 1847. But it became more regular, only from 1861, under a British private company. The construction of railways in Assam was started in 1881, but their importance in communication was greatly enhanced only in 1901 when the Assam-Bengal Railways was started. During the 1880s and the 1890s, a number of small railways were built. Prominent among them, were the Sadiya-Dibru Railways and the Tezpur-Balipara Railways. These railways linked the remote tea gardens with the transit points to the steamer service. Often, they passed through places without human habitation. There was hardly any concern for providing better communication to the traditional agricultural sector.

Coal-mining was first begun in Assam in the year 1828. Regular and consistent exploitation of the coal mines started in 1847, when there arose a steady demand for coal from the government steamers and the Assam Company's tea factory. According to the data provided in the Mills' *Report on the Province of Assam*, an amount of 2,500 maunds of coal valued at Rs 625 was exported to Bengal in 1852.

Oil was first discovered in the bed of the river Burhi Dihing in the mid-1820s of the nineteenth century. Historical evidence[19] suggests that first systematic drilling of a well for oil was undertaken in upper Assam by one Mr Goodenough, who was reported to have invested about Rs 50,000 around 1866–7. He was successful, to some extent, though he could never turned it into a commercially viable industry mainly due to the lack of infrastructure. However, after a few abortive attempts by Messrs Balmer Lawrie and Co., the Assam Oil Syndicate and the Assam Railways and Trading Company, the later was successful in extracting oil, though in small quantities, at Digboi by the end of the nineteenth century. At this point, the Assam Oil Company was floated in London with a capital of 310,000 pound sterling. The company set-up a refinery at Digboi and started producing lubricants and illuminating oils, candles and wax. In 1911, the production of petroleum amounted to 3,565,163 gallons.[20]

There were attempts by European investors to develop other industries based on the available resources. For example, in the early 1840s a Mr Becher set-up a Shellac factory and one Dr Scott, a 600-acre farm with patches of sugar cane, coffee and tea both at Guwahati. Dr Scott also set-up a sugar factory. In the early 1850s, the export of rubber looked promising. A European set-up a rubber press at Tezpur for processing the juice collected from wild rubber trees.

As it appears from the above discussion, the growth of a modern sector in Assam in the nineteenth century, revolved around the growth of the tea industry, which was triggered by immediate mercantile interests of the East India Company. Gradually, the profit motives of private entrepreneurs ensured its expansion under the liberal patronage of the government. As we will see in forthcoming pages, this industry did not attract as many investments from outside the country, as it did from within. Given the infrastructural bottlenecks and the topsy-turvy market condition, particularly in the later half of the nineteenth century, the British capital did not find it worthwhile to travel all the way to the north-east region of India. However, with extremely favourable government concessions, those who were already in business, found it highly lucrative to reinvest their profits and savings in tea plantation and a few other resource-based industries. The government contributed to the rise of this modern sector by extracting revenue from the agricultural sector. Thus, in a sense, the modern sector thrived at the cost of agriculture. This cost to the agricultural sector was multiplied by other linkage effects or by the absence of them.

IV. LINKAGES BETWEEN THE MODERN AND THE TRADITIONAL SECTORS

By the early 1870s, tea plantations were established as an industry that held tremendous potential for growth. By 1871, as Guha has estimated, a total investment of Rs 18.6 million had gone into tea plantations. In the next decade ending 1881, the total investment in tea had gone up by an estimated amount of Rs 63.8 million. As we have already discussed, the growth of a few other industries and infrastructure lent shape to a modern sector in the late nineteenth century.

According to an estimate,[21] 'total investments in the organized economic sector' of Assam during the period 1881–1901 were to the tune of Rs 200 million. There had also been an average annual investment of Rs 10 million. As shown in Table 5.3, tea accounted for more than half of these investments; railways took the second place with Rs 62.4 million or 31 per cent. Investments in other sectors were rather insignificant. From this pattern of investments, it is clear that the British interest lay in promoting tea plantation and the diversification that took place was to serve the interests of the plantation industry.

As far as the sources of capital are concerned, two distinct phases are discernible. In the beginning, there was an inflow of British capital that originated in London. Later, capital investment that took place in the tea industry, mostly originated from within India. According to an estimate,[22] Rs 5 million worth of British capital was invested in Assam until 1859. However, this amount did not originate entirely in the UK. In fact, the inflow of capital into the Assam Company, that originated in Britain, stopped in 1845. From the 1850s, 'the surplus extracted from plantations as well as savings from the personal earnings of the British officers on Indian Services, which were available for investment, were large enough for financing the rapid expansion of the tea acreage'.[23] The planters accumulated huge surpluses, mainly because of the following reasons: workers were paid low wages,[24] and the planters hardly paid anything to the government for the land that they had occupied.

The government at all levels, bore the expenditure of constructing railways in Assam. The funds were usually made available from

TABLE 5.3: DISTRIBUTION OF INVESTMENTS DURING 1881–1901

Industry	Investments (in million of Rs)
Tea	110.9 (55.5)
Railways	62.4 (31.0)
Coal	5.4 (3.0)
Petroleum	4.6 (2.0)
Saw Mills	1.0 (0.5)
Others	–

Note: Figures in brackets represent approximate shares of the respective industries in total investments.
Source: A. Guha, p. 189.

increased taxation and were invested in the railways to mainly serve the interests of the plantation industry.

Since domestic capital formation has a crucial role to play in the process of industrialization, a few comments are in order. At the beginning of the British rule, the indigenous people's per capita income was low and as such, they didn't have the capacity to save. Throughout the century, the lot of these people who were mainly engaged in agriculture, had hardly improved. Towards the end of the century, the peasants earned some cash by selling rice, mustard, pulses, poultry, vegetables, bamboo, thatching grass, etc., to the tea gardens. However, a portion of this income was appropriated by non-indigenous traders and middlemen. The remaining cash income was mostly used up by increased land revenue, leaving virtually nothing in savings to contribute to capital formation. On the other hand, those who came from outside to work as wage earners in plantations, as traders and as skilled professionals, had no particular interest in saving and investing within the state. One possible explanation is that they were risk-averse in the sense, that they didn't want to venture into relatively new industries in an unfamiliar land. They remitted a significant proportion of their income to their families and relatives living outside the state.

There was no organized banking to elicit savings from the commoners. The Keyas or the Marwaris who carried on limited banking services were mainly engaged in usury. Since the 1870s, the government introduced savings banks on an experimental basis at a few places. The depositors were mostly government servants. The interests paid on deposits were low, and hence these banks failed to invite deposits in sufficient quantities.

The investments in the modern sector, financed mainly through the re-investment of the undistributed surplus, were not sufficiently diversified, so as to facilitate a wholesome development of the economy. There was virtually no movement of capital from the modern sector to the traditional sector and vice-versa.

On the other hand, the environment was not at all conducive for the development of local entrepreneurship. As we have mentioned earlier, there was a dearth of local capital at the advent of the British rule. Domestic capital formation was non-existent. The regulations enacted by the British administration for reclamation of wastelands for tea cultivation, stipulated too high a limit for land to be reclaimed in order to be able to get the concessions. Also, the financial requirements of the entrepreneurs were exorbitant even for the local aristocrats. Nevertheless, by the end of the century, there emerged a class of local entrepreneurs who tried their hand in a few business ventures. Prominent among them were Manik Chandra Baruah who 'was both a timber-merchant and a tea-planter', Bholanath Baruah who, 'carried on extensive timber-trade in Orissa', and tea planters Jagannath Baruah, Kali Prasad Chaliha, Bishnuram Baruah, Ghanashyam Barua, Radhakanta Handique, Sheikh Sahanur Ali and Munshi Muhammad Ali.

The area under cultivation of each estate was limited to a few hundred acres with exception of Jagannath Baruah whose two gardens, Raraiah and Letekujan, reached 2,811 acres. Financial constraints prevented most indigenous planters from the extension of cultivation, and in fact, the majority of them had no factory of their own; they had to send their green leaves for manufacture to nearby European gardens.[25]

The shortage of labour posed formidable problems to the tea plantation industry in Assam, in the early years of its expansion. Moreover, the disinclination of the indigenous population to take continuous employment in the tea estates aggravated the situation. One explanation for this aversion is the low wage rates in plantations. Nevertheless, in the beginning, the tribal population of Darrang district provided an important source of labour. As a result, internal migration took place mostly from Darrang to the tea districts of upper Assam and thus, there was a demographic redistribution. However, various statistical and anecdotal evidences show that there was a high rate of labour turnover and a high proportion of casual labour. The British seemed to make deliberate attempts to draw labour from agriculture to work in plantations. For example, the policy to enhance land revenue can be seen as a measure to dissuade people from continuing with agricultural operations. Similarly, the planters wanted the British government to ban poppy cultivation to prevent people from being indolent, and to exhort them to join the workforce in plantation. These policies failed to attract people from the agricultural sector. This happened despite manifold increase in land revenue, mainly due to low plantation wages. The wages in other sectors, on the other hand, were rising.[26] Consequently, the proportion of indigenous workers in the plantation workforce in Assam, declined from about 46 per cent in the late 1860s to about 7 per cent in 1901, which represents a marginal increase of about 1,200 workers in absolute numbers during this period. During the same time, the total number of plantation workers rose from an estimated 40,450 to 307,000 or by seven times.[27]

The process of recruiting indentured labourers from outside, started in the early 1860s. 'The aboriginal tribes and people from the western parts of what was then Bengal, and the eastern parts of the United Provinces and the Central Province,'[28] were imported. The magnitude of outside recruitment during the last quarter of the nineteenth century was so high, that it changed the demographic composition of the state.

As we see from the Table 5.4 in about 10 years' time between 1891 and 1901, the proportion of non-indigenous people in the total population rose from about one-fifth to one-third. This non-indigenous population consisted not only of tea garden labourers, but also of traders, skilled professionals, etc., who flocked into the region to take advantage of the new opportunities. The indigenous population during this period had, in fact, declined in absolute numbers. Widespread epidemics reduced the population by the turn of the century and the indigenous people were the worst hit. This demographic pattern had important bearing on the dynamics of the economy.

Firstly, unlike what the development theories would predict, the traditional sector did not provide a source of labour supply to the modern sector. And hence, the important link between the two sectors in the labour market was never established. In a dual economy, such a link has a crucial role to play for long-run growth. However, as we have already mentioned, there was some migration of the indigenous tribal population from the district of Darrang to the tea

TABLE 5.4: POPULATION OF ASSAM PROPER

Year	Total Population	No. of Indigenous People*
1826	7–8 lakh	–
1853	10,59,513	–
1872	14,96,705	–
1891	20,23,708	15,84,027 (78.3)
1901	21,57,025	15,04,847 (67.8)

Notes: *Includes indigenous Hindu castes and tribes.
Figures in brackets indicate percentage shares in total.
Source: A. Guha, 1991, pp. 156–7.

districts. Also, there was the reverse movement of labourers from plantation to agriculture. Many tea garden workers, after their contract was over, started working in the agricultural fields. However, this limited interaction did not influence the growth of the traditional sector in a significant way.

Secondly, the income generated in the modern sector did not remain within the province. Apart from the profits being remitted in the form of dividends and transferred as savings outside the region, a substantial part of the wages earned in this sector was also remitted.[29] Moreover, the immigrants spent their incomes on items which were not locally supplied. Thus by the end of the century there was a huge drain of money from Assam.

Thirdly and most importantly, this had crucial implications for the commodity market, which potentially opened up new vistas for the two sectors to come together. The rapid growth of the workforce in the modern sector, raised the demand for agricultural products. This is reflected in the fact that by the end of the century the terms of trade was extremely favourable to the agricultural sector. The price of rice in particular, had gone up by 35 per cent during the last decade of the nineteenth century. On the other hand, the price of tea had gone down by about 22 per cent during the same period. There was a marginal increase in the supply of rice and bamboo to the gardens from the agricultural sector, but it had not been possible to keep pace with the demand. The reasons were manifold. First, the growth of the agricultural workforce was very slow. As we have already seen, the growth of the population was almost entirely accounted for by the influx of immigrants from outside the region and they were engaged in various activities in the modern sector. Second, in an economy, where labour was scarce, one would expect technological progress to take place so that agricultural productivity increased in order to fulfil the growing needs of the modern sector. That was what precisely happened in England during the time of the industrial revolution. But, there was virtually no technological innovation taking place in Assam. As we have already discussed, it was the system of property rights in the beginning and then the absence of capital formation in the traditional sector that thwarted any initiative to innovate in agriculture. Thirdly, there was a marginal increase in the acreage under cultivation. The government policy to increase land revenue for cultivated land, worked as a deterrent to increasing the acreage under cultivation. These factors combined to cause the domestic production of agricultural commodities to fall well short of the amount that was sufficient to feed the growing populace. In effect, imports of these commodities were on the rise. For example, 'during the eighties and early nineties the rice imports from Bengal into the Brahmaputra valley ranged from four to five lakh maunds per year. Thereafter the annual net import of rice exceeded seven lakh maunds'.[30] Traders and skilled professionals who landed in Assam with the advent of the modern sector, had a consumption basket that differed from the one of the local populace. The main items included wheat flour, edible oil, ghee, refined sugar, shoes and piece goods which were not locally available. Also, the local market was not large enough to induce people to take up a profitable venture of local production. The situation was aggravated by the government policy to purchase the bulk of the garden requirements of the stores in the UK and ship them to India.

On the other hand, there was no perceptible change in the consumption pattern of the indigenous people. A few items such as cheap cotton garments, shoes, umbrellas, etc.,[31] were used in limited quantities, but they had hardly any influence so as to effect a greater interaction between the modern and the traditional sectors in the commodity market. This absence of the demonstration effect is one factor that deterred the dynamics of a dual economy.

As the transportation facilities improved, trade with the rest of India, mainly with Bengal, increased in value and volume. As we see from the Table 5.5, exports in value increased by more than three times and imports by about six times between 1880–1 and 1904–5. The trade surplus increased from Rs 15.02 million in 1880–1 to Rs 376 million in 1899–1900 and then decreased to Rs 269 million.

TABLE 5.5: ASSAM'S TRADE STATISTICS, 1880–1 TO 1904–5

Year	Exports Rs lakh	Imports Rs lakh	Trade Balance
1880–1	229.7	79	150.2
1899–1900	699	323	376
1904–5	726	457	269

Source: H.K. Barpujari, 1993, vol. V, p. 127.

Among the export items, tea became one of the largest in quantity. Between 1880 and 1900, the amount of tea exported, rose from 288,754 maunds to 1,239,136 maunds or by more than four times. On the other hand, the export of oilseeds, the principal cash crop of the agriculture sector, increased only marginally from 689,103 to 718,311 maunds. By the end of the century, rice was exported in large quantities (1,393,257 maunds during 1899–1900) only to be imported back after it was cleaned.[32] This reflects the modern sector's lackadaisical attitude towards the agriculture-based economy. During this period, imports of European piece-goods increased from an estimated Rs 15,38,410 to 63,76,023[33] or by four times. Imports of sugar increased from 4,043 maunds to 2,779,981 maunds.

We have observed in this section, that the dual economy that emerged as a result of substantial investment in the modern sector, consisting mainly of tea plantations during the later half of the nineteenth century in Assam, did not have the crucial link between the modern sector and the traditional sector in any of the three important markets: the capital market, labour and the commodity markets. The modern sector thrived on alien interests; employed capital and labour from outside the region, and catered to the external market. There was a dearth of indigenous labour and capital, and the commodity market did not evolve within the region.

V. CONCLUSION

Thus, the prospect of a profitable venture in tea plantation brought British capital into Assam. A modern sector, consisting mainly of tea plantation, a few other resource-based industries and minimum infrastructure to support the growth of these industries, emerged by the end of the nineteenth century. The substantial investments that rolled in at the initiatives taken mainly by the Europeans, however, left the traditional agrarian sector untouched. The two sectors virtually, did not have any link through the linkage effects of these investments in labour, capital and commodity markets. The shortage of local labour and capital on the advent of the British colonizers and throughout the nineteenth century, coupled with the deliberate policies of the government, came in the way of dynamic interaction between these two sectors. As a result, the traditional sector that had hitherto been underdeveloped, remained an enclave untouched by the process of growth and development.

NOTES

1. I would like to thank Alokesh Barua for suggesting the topic and giving insights. I also thank Indro Dasgupta for his useful comments. However, I am alone responsible for the views expressed in this paper.
2. Over the years, the political boundary of and within Assam has changed. Geographically, this paper focuses on the Brahmaputra valley. In the early British administrative reports, the five districts of the Brahmaputra valley, namely Kamrup, Darrang, Nowgong, Sibsagar and Lakhimpur were known as Assam Proper.
3. A. Guha, 1991, p. 197.
4. At that time Assam was a cluster of small kingdoms.
5. Earlier there was no limit to the amount of *ga-mati* but later on as population increased and as the repeated confrontation with the Mughals put pressure on the treasury, the quota of tax-free land had to be fixed.
6. We follow Barpujari (1992) in using the term 'cash' which essentially refers to coins that were in vogue during those times.
7. However, there are other reasons including absence of market, which we will discuss later.
8. Guha, 1991, p. 47.
9. Ibid., p. 23.
10. A brief description of the revenue administration during the early years of the British rule can be found in E. Gait, 1984, pp. 294–6, 343–4.
11. Francis Jenkins as quoted in Guha, 1991, p. 143.
12. We here use the word money in the sense of a common medium of exchange.
13. D.H. Buchanan, 1966, p. 55.
14. Ibid.
15. Gait, 1984, p. 356.
16. Barpujari, 1993, p. 47.
17. Buchanan, 1966, p. 57.
18. Ibid.
19. Barpujari, 1993, p. 87.
20. Ibid., p. 91.
21. Guha, 1991, p. 189.
22. Ibid., p. 170.
23. Ibid., p. 190.
24. The wage rates were much lower than those prevalent in other sectors. For example, in 1864 while a free labourer was able to earn a wage of Rs 7 per month from the PWD, the going wage in the Assam Company's plantations was Rs 4 to 5 (A. Guha, 1991, p. 191). In a few instances, they were even lower than the minimum wage rates stipulated by the government.

25. Barpujari, 1993, pp. 367–8.
26. Scarcity of labour and gradual increase in demand due to expanded activities in the modern sector resulted in a steady rise in the wages of free labourers. However, the imported labourers who were mostly employed in plantations on contract were paid much lower wages and they were kept fixed for years. The PWD and the railways had to hire workers at competitive rates. The wage rate of agricultural labourers during the latter half of the nineteenth century reached as high as about Rs 10 per month while the wage rate for plantation workers hovered around Rs 3 to 6 per month.
27. It is difficult to get proper statistics for workers employed in plantations due to high rates of turnover and high proportion of casual workers.
28. Buchanan, 1966, p. 60.
29. Guha (1991) estimates that the income of people of small means that was remitted, grew from Rs 88,813 in 1880–1 to Rs 48,04,631 in 1904–5.
30. Guha, 1991, p. 193.
31. A detailed account of change in consumption habit can be found in Barpujari (1993), pp. 139–41.
32. Barpujari, 1993, p. 122.
33. Ibid., p. 128.

REFERENCES

Antrobus, H.A., *A History of the Assam Company 1839–1953*, Edinburgh, 1957.

Barpujari, H.K., *Assam in the Days of Company*, 2nd edn., Guwahati, 1980.

────── ed., *The Comprehensive History of Assam*, vols. 4 and 5, Guwahati: Publication Board, 1992.

Buchanan, D.H., *The Development of Capitalist Enterprise in India*, 2nd edn., London: Frank Cass, 1966.

Gait, Edward, *A History of Assam*, 3rd edn., Guwahati: LBS Publications, 1984.

Guha, Amalendu, *Planter-Raj to Swaraj—Freedom Struggle and Electoral Politics in Assam 1826–1947*, New Delhi: Indian Council of Historical Research, 1977.

──────, *Medieval and Early Colonial Assam: Society, Polity, Economy*, Calcutta: Centre for Studies in Social Sciences, 1991.

Mills, A.J.M., *Report on the Province of Assam*, rpt. Guwahati: Publication Board, 1989.

CHAPTER 6

A Big Push without a Take-off: A Case Study of Assam 1871-1901

AMALENDU GUHA

With Calcutta at its centre and with tea and jute as the main levers of change and population movements, eastern India presents an integrated pattern of historical development since the middle of the nineteenth century. An attempt is made here to bring out the basic character of this process and its impact on the agrarian society of the Brahmaputra valley. The main focus is on the five contiguous districts namely, Kamrup, Darrang, Nowgong, Lakhimpur and Sibsagar. In 1961 its area was 17,719 sq. miles. This area today, is the most developed core of Assam's economy.

AT THE THRESHOLD OF THE 1870s

The early period of British rule in Assam Proper, 1826 to 1870, was one of administrative and economic consolidation. The population increased from an estimated 7 or 8 lakh in 1826 to 11 lakh in 1853 and then to nearly 15 lakh by 1872. Slavery and serfdom, involving an estimated 5 to 9 per cent of the population and widespread poppy cultivation were suppressed in 1843 and 1860, respectively. But the unrestricted sale of *abkari* opium introduced in 1851–2 continued to be a menace to the Assamese society. Sales proceeds from opium, a government monopoly, accounted for almost half the total revenue

---

*An earlier version of this paper was published in the *Indian Economic and Social History Review* (Delhi), vol. V, Sept. 1968 and also reprinted in *Medieval and Early Colonial Assam: Society, Polity and Economy*, by Amalendu Guha (Calcutta and New Delhi, 1991).

collection in Assam Proper until the 1870s. In 1864–5, for example, the opium revenue amounted to Rs 1,083,642 while the land revenue yielded Rs 1,001,773 only. By the year 1872–3, the current land revenue demand was revamped to Rs 2,155,157. Opium revenue remained above Rs 1,100,000 lakh in 1873–4, even after a rise in its price. By the end of the century, it crossed the figure of Rs 1,800,000 lakh.

With the ascendancy of industrial capital over mercantile interests in Great Britain by 1833, the British, policy in Assam received a clear direction towards colonialization. By the year 1871, more than 3 lakh acres of wastelands had been settled with planters in Assam Proper alone. These settlements were fee-simple or charged at nominal rates, while, at the same time, the burden of land revenue on ordinary farmers was progressively and systematically enhanced in order to encourage their transfer from subsistence farming to plantation jobs. Although not high enough to serve the purpose, the average land revenue burden of Rs 1.47 per head of population in Assam Proper in 1872–3 was much heavier than what prevailed in permanently settled areas.[1] The actual burden was more than what was apparent as the inclusion of the negligible amount of land revenue paid by the planters for their tea lands and of the population thereupon, had the effect of largely deflating the average figure in the former case.

Introduced by 1839, tea was firmly established as a new crop by the 1870s. Assuming an investment of Rs 600 per planted acre (with a gestation period of four years) the total investment for 31,000 acres by 1871 may be estimated at Rs 18.6 million or Rs 12 per head of the total estimated population at that time.[2]

Steamer services began to ply up and down the Brahmaputra from 1847, but more regularly from 1861 under a British private company. The outgoing merchandise handled were mainly tea, rubber, gum and silk. Mustard-seeds were mostly transported in boats. The principal imports handled were rice, salt, various planters' stores, piece-goods and indentured labour. The Public Works Department started its road construction programme from the 1860s. But the building of railways did not start before, 1881; their importance in communications in Assam was not felt before 1901.

In 1874, Assam was separated from the Bengal Presidency and

was organized as a Chief Commissioner's Province, much to the satisfaction of the local public. The first English school had been established at Guwahati in 1835. In 1872 there were six such English Schools which sent forth candidates for the entrance examination of Calcutta University. Of the University's 938 successful matriculates that year, only four were from Assam Proper. Nevertheless, an enlightened West-oriented Assamese intelligentsia had already emerged by the 1870s. Anandaram Dhekial Phukan (1829–59), a product of the Hindu College, Calcutta, championed the cause of Assamese as a language, distinct from Bengali. After 36 years of suppression (since 1836) it was once again, recognized in 1872 for use in the schools and law-courts of Assam. In 1898 and 1899, 32 and 51 students from the Brahmaputra valley schools respectively, passed the entrance examination. During the twelve years ending 1900, 29 natives of the same area obtained their BA degree. The first printing press (1836) and the fast Assamese periodical, *Arunoday* (1846–83), introduced by the American Baptist Mission helped the dissemination of scientific outlook. By 1872, Assam Proper had altogether three local newspapers – two published from Sibsagar and one from Guwahati – the same number as Orissa had at the time.

What Assam meanwhile lacked, however, was a fair share in commerce. Despite new openings, the Assamese were found indifferent to trading as an occupation. Maniram Dewan, the first Indian tea planter, whose two tea gardens were confiscated on his martyrdom for alleged conspiracy during the 1857 revolts, was rather an exception. About a decade thereafter, Rosheswar Barua pioneered a few small gardens, but was ruined by the crisis of 1866-7.[3] Of the several hundred planters, hardly two to three dozens were natives of the Brahmaputra valley at the close of the century. Invariably, they were owners of very small tea gardens. Hence, the 1870s opened with an unrivalled British monopoly over the plantation sector, which continued to expand till the end of the British rule. Outside this sector, almost the entire internal trade – the export of lac, rubber, cotton, long pepper, silk, etc., and import of various manufactured consumer goods – was meanwhile in the hands of the Marwari trading community. The only exception to this was the trade in oilseeds. The indige-nous farmer traders of Kamrup were traditionally associated therewith from medieval times, but they were destined to lose their ground soon to Marwari traders.

THE MECHANISM OF ECONOMIC CHANGE: 1871–1901

THE BIG PUSH

The period was one of hectic investment activities on the part of British enterprise in its drive for the exploitation of colonial resources. A set of wasteland settlement rules were accordingly formulated and then repeatedly revised to facilitate British capital exports to northeast India. The total area of wastelands settled with planters in Assam Proper increased from slightly over 3 lakh acres in 1871 to 6.4 lakh acres by 1901. The total value of revenue concessions enjoyed by the planters over these lands till·1901, would have amounted to several crores of rupees if calculated at the ordinary rate paid by rice farmers.[4]

Tea-processing machinery was, increasingly used from the early 1870s onwards. The average investment per planted acre calculated at Rs 600 for an earlier period may therefore, be fairly revised at Rs 1,000 for the period 1872–1901.[5] In the decade ending 1881, the total acreage under tea in Assam Proper leaped by 63,800 acres. In other words, a sum of Rs 63.8 million was newly invested in that decade, as against an investment of Rs 13.2 million in the preceding 12 years. This tempo was maintained for the next two decades as well.

The acreage under tea increased from 93,802 acres in 1881 to 204,682 acres in 1901–2 (App. Table 6.1). This increase by about 111,000 acres, 118 per cent over the acreage in 1881, represents an investment of Rs 110.9 million. Railway investments amounted to Rs 62.4 million (total construction outlay on all Indian Railways as of 1900 amounted to Rs 3,295 million) calculated on the basis of construction outlay on the 400 miles of tracks in Assam Proper.[6] However, even as late as 1901, the railways still failed by a few miles to link up Assam Proper with the rest of India. British investments in coal (Rs 5.4 million approximately), petroleum (Rs 4.6 million approximately) and saw-mills (Rs 1 million approximately) were also newly made in these two decades. Some 100 or so new telegraph signalling offices and several hundred miles of telecommunications and pebbled roads were built by the government. So, total investments in the organized economic sector of Assam Proper during the period, 1881–1901, appears to have been around Rs 200 million, even at a conservative estimate.[7]

This gives us an approximate average investment of Rs 10 million or so annually, for a population rising from 1.8 million in 1881 to 2.2 million in 1901. This big push, although presumably equal in size to some 15 to 20 per cent of the region's then existing national income, did not however lead to any *commensurate* growth in the indigenous sector of the economy, either simultaneously or in the following decades.

Some Sources of Capital

Surplus: The huge investment was made possible no doubt by migrated British business leadership and capital. But the second factor should not be exaggerated. Only a small part of the total investments in tea appears to have originated from Britain's home savings – the major part represents undistributed surplus and ploughed – back dividends of the older companies already operating in Assam. Published histories of both the Assam Company for 1839–1953, and the Jorehaut Tea Company for 1850–1946 amply corroborate this view.

Between 1854 and 1901, the Assam Company did nothing to raise any additional capital or long-term loan to augment its initial capital of Rs 2 million. Yet, the acreage under tea had more than trebled from 3,313 acres in 1854 to 10,762 acres in 1901. Of this, an increase (5,562 acres) took place during the period 1872-1901, thus representing an estimated new investment of Rs 5.6 million. Even after providing for such a huge expansion out of the current earnings, the Company made a total dividend profit of Rs 9 million or 20 per cent of the gross earnings of these years. The founders of many companies, the second joint-stock concern in the field, the Jorehaut Tea Company (1859) for example, built up their initial capital by fraudulent use of the Assam Company's seeds, tools and manpower while planting their tea gardens. In this respect, the official history of the Assam Company may be quoted.[8]

... from the highest Administrative Officer in Calcutta and Assam to the newest joined Assistant, were, speaking generally, all in this racket of using the circumstances of their employment to open out land under tea in competition with their own employers....

They were blatant enough to have taken up their lands near the boundary or actually adjoining the Company's grants, and it would not be difficult to guess from whence they obtained their tea-seed and labour....

To put it plainly, their employment by the Assam Company as Assistants gave them the necessary subsistence on which to live in the province while they pursued the objects of their own enterprise.

Thus, what appeared as cost items in the accounts of the Assam Company became the initial capital of some new companies. This did not certainly represent fresh import of sterling capital, although the new company was floated in London apparently with sterling capital. The opening of new tea gardens by British district magistrates, police officers, civil surgeons, military officers, etc., after only a few years' service in India also does not represent home savings of Britain.[9] These facts induce us to believe that from 1854 onwards the surplus extracted from the plantations as well as savings from the personal earnings of British officers on Indian service, which were available for investment were large enough to finance the rapid expansion of tea acreage. Particularly so, since the industry had to pay practically nothing to the government either, as price or in the form of rent or taxes for the land in their occupation.

Labour Squeeze: To maximize the surplus, labourers were paid wages below the free market rate. Free market wages as recorded between 1875 and 1899, were at a 56 per cent increase in the Brahmaputra valley.[10] This was because of scarcity of labour and also because the price of rice was rising. With 1873 as the base year, the price of rice in the normal years showed, on the whole, an average upward trend during the period 1871–1901, as indicated below:

INDEX NO. OF RICE PRICES (187–100): SELECT YEARS

1864	1871	1875	1881	1885	1891	1895	1901
111.2	104.1	125.6	106.8	137.2	136.9	138.0	184.7

In 1864, while free labour was able to earn a wage of Rs 7 per month from the PWD, the going wage in the Assam Company's plantations was Rs 4 to 5. But the average rate earned in many gardens was Rs 3.50 only.[11] In the face of rising prices, the government attempted to set the norm of a minimum wage for contract labour in plantations at Rs 5, Rs 4 and Rs 3 for men, women and children, respectively. At the same time, there was the *proviso* that the planter would make rice available to them at the rate of Re 1 per maund. This was provided by the Act VI of 1865 under the shot title 'Transport of Native Labourers Act'. But for decades to come, the planters managed to pay a lower cash wage by manipulating the piece-rate task. They also brought down the real wages by raising the price of rice to Rs 2, then to Rs 2.50 and finally to Rs 3 by 1900.[12] Thus, throughout the period under review, contract labourers under the Emigration Act were receiving almost half the wage earned by the free agricultural labourers. The wage rate of able-bodied agricultural labourers in Lakhimpur, for example, was Rs 9.37 per month in 1873. Thereafter, it never decreased below Rs 6, except in 1875 and 1876. In most of the subsequent years till 1901, their monthly wage-rate ranged between Rs 8 and 11. As against this, only in rare cases, could a tea labourer earn a wage as high as Rs 6.50 (App. Table 6.3). In 1888–9, an Emigration Act labourer was receiving only about half the going wage. In the period of falling tea prices in the international market since 1881, the planters maximized their total profit by expanding the acreage, by increasing value yield per acre through the deepening of capital and freezing of wages.

Burden on Peasants

By the year 1901, the planters had already enclosed some one-fourth of the total settled area (or 5 per cent of the total area) of Assam Proper, under their exclusive proprietary rights.[13] Thereby, they limited to that extent, the facilities of fluctuating or shifting cultivation, as well as of grazing and collecting activities of the local population – particularly the tribals. Acreage under tea formed only 8 to 10 per cent of the occupied tea area in the early seventies and some 29 per cent even as late as 1947. Why did the tea gardens enclose excess lands or why did the government allow these to do so? Such a policy, like one of enhancing land revenue demand on peasant holdings, and that of increasing the monopoly price of opium, obviously aimed at forcing the local farmers into acceptance of plantation employment. This had only partial results. For, in 1868–9, there were as many as 18,783 local labourers on a monthly average as against 21,667 imported labourers on the plantations.[14] But thereafter, when thousands of additional hands were required every year, local labour supply did hardly respond to the low wages. This happened despite a 100 per cent increase in the total land revenue demand on Assam Proper between 1867–8 and 1872–3, and an increase in the opium price from Rs 14 per *seer* in 1860 to Rs 20 in 1862 and to Rs 23 by

1873. In 1893, the land revenue rates on peasant holdings were once more revamped, even in the face of a mass upsurge of protesting peasants in Kamrup and Darrang that was suppressed by police firings. The initial increase in the total land revenue demand in Assam Proper was 53 per cent, but it had to be reduced to 37 per cent.[15] The price of opium per *seer* was also gradually increased to Rs 37 by 1890, a 60 per cent increase during the period. But all these measures failed to attract Assamese labourers to wage employment. Of the 307,000 workers on the plantations of Assam Proper in 1901, only some 20,000 were reported to be local labourers of whom 14,000 were Kachari tribals.[16]

The planters, therefore, had to depend almost entirely on the famine-stricken tribal areas of the rest of India for steady labour supply. Between 1871 and 1901, more than 11 lakh recruits, men, women and children, entered Assam; mostly Assam Proper.[17] A considerable number were repatriated every year on the expiry of their contract period, but many settled down permanently in the tea districts voluntarily, or under duress. Throughout the period 1865 to 1908, the planters exercised the right of private arrest without warrant. Keeping wages in arrears occasionally, for as long as six months, appears to have been a common practice.[18]

Source of Railway Investments

Investments in the railways also did not wholly originate in the UK. For, under the Guarantee System, much of the guaranteed return on the capital outlay was financed by the government, even at the risk of loss on government revenue account. For example, the Government of India incurred a total loss of Rs 35.9 million towards supporting the Assam–Bengal Railways during the period 1895 to 1917–18, i.e. an average loss of nearly Rs 3 million annually. Similarly, a total subsidy of Rs 1.2 million was paid by the Assam Government to the Dibru-Sadiya Railways over the period 1884-1903. The Jorhat State Railways was a project of the Government of Assam, 'for the convenience of numerous tea gardens in the neighbourhood of Jorhat', involving public investment of nearly Rs 1 million and an accumulated loss of Rs 5 lakh up to 1901. Even Local Government funds were utilized for the railway construction. For example, in the case of the Tezpur-Balipara Light Railways, while tea gardens subscribed to 45 per cent of its paid-up capital of

A BIG PUSH WITHOUT A TAKE-OFF

Rs 4 lakh, the government supplied timber free of royalty, and the Local Board of Tezpur paid a total subsidy of Rs 1 lakh in 20 annual instalments.[19]

From these facts, it appears that the role of public funds realized from increased taxation was not inconsiderable in railway-building in Assam. But the plantation-oriented rate structure and the alignment of the railroads through thinly-populated submontane tracts did not benefit the farmers as much as they should have done under ordinary circumstances. Despite hectic development activities since the 1870s, Assam Proper had in 1901, only four townships with a population of above 5,000. In two of them – Guwahati and Barpeta – the population had actually declined since 1881; the former's from 11,695 to 11,561 and the latter's from 13,758 to 11,227. Thus, even the erstwhile centres of commerce were hardly helped by the forces of development in the field.

The Impact of Immigration

By the middle of the nineteenth century, Assam Proper had become a deficit area in food grains. The annual rice imports were estimated at no less than 3 lakh maunds in 1873. During the 1880s and early 1890s rice imports, from Bengal into the Brahmaputra valley ranged from 4 to 5 lakh maunds per year.[20] Thereafter, the annual net import of rice exceeded 7 lakh maunds. An increasing inflow of labour recruits to the plantation and railways construction sites led to rising prices of rice as against falling prices of tea and salt (App. Table 6.2). As shown above, the emigrant labourers of the tea industry were tied down to stationary or even falling real wages while food prices and the wages outside the plantations, were rising. On the expiry of contract, the labourers, therefore, preferred to settle down on wastelands as independent peasants. Many even escaped their contracts to find refuge in Assamese villages as agricultural labour. Thus, the competition of rice and tea for the scarce labourer, although greatly checked by the law of contract and labour recruitment, was nevertheless a force at play. That is why continued and heavy recruitment drives in other provinces became a permanent feature of the tea industry.

Until the beginning of a still bigger population movement from East Bengal to Assam in the early twentieth century, tea remained the biggest factor responsible for immigration. Large-scale labour recruitment from outside had started from the early 1860s. In 1872, imported labour on tea gardens alone was estimated at 40,000; and the total number of non-indigenous people, some 80,000 or so in a total population of 1,496,000. By 1881, the non-indigenous element appears to have increased to about 3 lakh in a population of 1,805,000.[21] Similar estimates for 1891 and 1901 were made in the Census Report of 1901, on the basis of a list of indigenous castes and tribes. These estimates, as given below, fairly reflect the increasing shares of non-indigenous elements in the population, since Muslims and Christians together formed a negligible fraction (6 per cent at the most) thereof.

Thus the non-indigenous population appears to have increased from less than 1 lakh in 1872 to anything between 5 and 6 lakh in 1901. But on the other hand, the indigenous Assamese population which had been growing fast during the years 1872–81, remained almost stationary for the next 20 years. In fact, it decreased by 6 per cent between 1891 and 1901, because of the black fever (*kalazar*) epidemic.

COMPOSITION OF POPULATION: ASSAM PROPER

	1891	(%)	1901	(%)
Total Population	2023,708	(100)	2157,025	(100)
Indigenous Hindu Castes and Tribals	1584,027	(78.3)	1504,847	(67.8)
The Rest	439.681	(21.7)	652, I78	(32.2)

Source: *Assam Census Report*, 1901, pp. 29–30.

This epidemic first appeared in the district of Goalpara in 1883, entered Assam Proper in 1888 and thereafter, spread throughout its length and breadth. During the decade, 1881–91, the population of Goalpara subdivision decreased by 18 per cent and that of Kamrup district by 1.6 per cent. During the next decade, the population of Kamrup decreased by 7.1 per cent, that of Mangaldai subdivision, by 9 per cent and that of Nowgong district by 24.8 per cent. It was the indigenous population, particularly the tribals, who were most hard-hit. As a result, despite an overall increase in the population of the district of Darrang due to immigration, its indigenous component was believed to have decreased by 8 per cent between 1891 and 1901. The districts of Lakhimpur and Sibsagar were, however, least affected, much to the relief of the planters. The population of Lakhimpur increased by 46.1 per cent during the decade – 16 per cent through natural growth and 30 per cent through immigration. The population of Sibsagar increased by 24.4 per cent, which was due in equal proportion to natural growth and immigration.[22]

Immigration from outside apart, there was also some migration of indigenous tribal populations from the district of Kamrup and Mangaldai to the tea districts. Thus, the pull of the plantation sector coupled with other factors, brought about two big demographic changes during the three decades ending 1901, firstly, in the ethnic composition of the population and secondly, in its spatial distribution over the districts. The proportion of indigenous Hindu castes and aboriginal, tribes in the total population came down from almost 100 per cent in the pre-annexation days to 78.3 per cent in 1881, and then to 67.8 per cent in 1901. Thus, non-indigenous elements constituted one-quarter to one-third of the population of Assam Proper in 1901. In that year, as well as in 1921, more than two-fifths of the population of Lakhimpur district was enumerated as born outside the province. At the same time, only 39 per cent of Lakhimpur's total population in 1901 returned Assamese as their mother tongue. People born outside the province constituted a quarter of the population of Darrang and Sibsagar districts in that year. The change in spatial distribution can be best seen in the density table (see App. Table 6.4). Until 1901, the density increased rapidly only in the tea districts. But thereafter and particularly from 1921, other factors contributed much more towards density.

The demographic changes of 1871–1901 were economically significant in more than one respect. Rapid increase in the number of immigrants, as against a stagnated indigenous population, almost all of whom were engaged in subsistence farming, could mean only two things. First, a continued imbalance between the fast growth of the modern sector composed of plantations, coal, petroleum and the associated infrastructure on the one hand and the slovenly growth, if any, of the traditional agricultural sector on the other. During the period under review, overall population increase kept pace with the increase in acreage under ordinary crops (see App. Table 6.5). The increased demand for rice, bamboo, etc., enhanced the farmers' cash incomes, no doubt. But they could not make the best use of the situation because of an acute labour shortage within the sector.

Secondly, the gap between the gross earnings of the economy and the locally disbursed income originating therefrom, increasingly widened. Not only that, the surplus was remitted abroad in the form of high dividends and transferred savings from high salaries, but a part of the poor wages was also remitted outside the geographic area. Such petty remittances by migrant workers were mostly carried on their persons at the time of return to their places of origin. Income-remitting people of small means also availed of the growing postal facilities, as is suggested by the available figures for the whole province of Assam:

Selected Year	Money orders issued within Assam, (no.)	Money orders issued within Assam (value) Rs	Money orders paid in Assam (no.)	Money orders paid in Assam (value) Rs	Money outflow through money orders (value) Rs
1880–1	43,680	134,613	11,738	45,800	88,813
1885–6	144,003	349,581	52,089	141,459	208,122
1897–8	394,577	926,704	124,413	405,581	521,123
1904–5	532,174	9787,328	204.010	4982,697	4804,631

Sources: Worked out from data in *Financial and Commercial Statistics of British India*, 6th Issue (1899), pp. 290–6; ibid. 13th Issue (1907), pp. 258 and 264.

Thus, the net remittance outside the province by money orders increased from less than Rs 90,000 in 1880–1 to more than Rs 5.2 lakh annually in 1897–8 and thereafter to nearly Rs 10 lakh by 1904–5. The bulk of this was presumably from Assam Proper.

Even that portion of surplus retained within the industries for self-financed, horizontal expansion was mostly spent on imported goods and services. Demand for trading, clerical, skilled and even unskilled services invited the migration of suitable personnel belonging to non-indigenous ethnic groups, such as the Marwari traders and Bengali professionals who had dependants at home to support. The variety of consumption goods required by these incoming people – wheat-flour, edible oil, *ghee,* refined sugar, shoes and piece goods – could not be readily produced locally because the small domestic market was not large enough to produce them profitably either with traditional or imported techniques. Hence, the spillover process of this colonial pattern of development was extremely limited. This problem was aggravated also, by a deliberate policy, as is stated by the official historian of the Assam Company:

It was the Company's normal policy to purchase the bulk of the gardens' requirement of stores in the United Kingdom and ship them to India.[23]

To sum up, the gross export earnings (tea alone accounting for 70 to 80 per cent thereof) of the economy were far in excess of the merchandise import bill. The excess represented a surplus which appears to have involved also an element of unrequited, unilateral transfer over and above what were legitimate payments for useful invisible imports. Throughout the period, both exports and imports were increasing rapidly, but the latter always remained at around 50 per cent of the former. Thus, the export surplus of the Brahmaputra valley, increased from nearly Rs 11 million in 1883–4 to an annual new average of Rs 18 million during the four years from 1892–3 to 1895–6. There was a return flow of net specie (treasures on government and private accounts) imports throughout this period, but the amount was less than Rs 2 million per year on the average. For example, in 1893–4, government treasures worth Rs 596,000 and public treasures worth Rs 1,457,282 moved into the Brahmaputra valley, while only public treasures valued at Rs 101,774 moved out of it.

The Bulk of the treasures was in the form of silver coins going into circulation under the pressure of increasing monetization of the economy. All this may be viewed against our estimated average annual investment of Rs 10 million and our assumed annual national income of Rs 50 million to 60 million for the area, during the period.

Thus, during the period 1871–1901, the economy of Assam Proper had developed all the characteristics of a dual economy with a cleavage between the traditional subsistence sector and a relatively capital-intensive, highly monetized modern sector. The main cash crop of the peasant sector was mustard seeds. It accounted at the most for 7 to 14 per cent of the total export earnings till 1895–6. But this share, along with the output in absolute terms, fluctuated violently from year to year, as is indicated below:

EXPORT OF MUSTARD SEEDS FROM THE BRAHMAPUTRA VALLEY

(in 1 lakh mds)				Average of three years ending
1880–1	1881–2	1882–3	1891–2	1901–2
8.55	6.89	4.63	12.75	4.50

Sources: *Assam Administrative Report*, 1882–3, p. vii; *An Account of the Province of Assam* 1901–2, p. 34.

Its share in export earnings declined heavily, particularly since the disastrous earthquake of June 1897. Increased cash sale of rice and bamboo to tea gardens, somewhat compensated the peasants. But the diffused increments in their cash incomes, cut to size by increased land revenue demand and an increase in the retail price of opium, could hardly encourage any capital formation on the farms. Doubly handicapped with shortage of labour as well as of capital, what the traditional sector could do, was to grow more rice by diverting family labour from the cultivation of other crops and from certain handicrafts to rice fields. Even so, and despite some additional rice production by ex-plantation labour, the rice acreage and output did not increase in tune with the demand. As a result, the price of rice was abnormally high, while that of tea was low in the 1890s. The index (1873 = 100: rice, 13.6 *seers* per rupee and tea, Rs 1–2 as per lb.) was as follows:

	1891	1893	1895	1897	1899	1901
Rice	136.9	174.8	138.0	225.2	127.6	184.7
Tea	65	62	71	54	52	51

Source: See App. Table 6.2.

The scarcity of rice and grain-riots were reported from Nowgong in October, 1896. The earthquake further worsened the situation for the next few years. Thus, the nineteenth century closed with an agrarian crisis. There was retardation or very slow growth in farm production on the one hand and over-production of tea as a result of continuous technological progress on the other. The planters had already founded the Indian Tea Association (ITA), the organ of their private monopoly power as early as 1881. Through this, they introduced fine plucking as a measure of crop restriction for the first time in 1901. Henceforward, the growing influence of the ITA was felt in every sphere of economic and political life in Assam, which persisted even after Independence.

THE TURNING POINT

The decade of 1901–11 provided a turning point in the pattern and mechanism of economic change. The growth in the tea acreage remarkably slowed down during the decade and thereafter. It was only

8.2 per cent (18,528 acres) representing an estimated investment of Rs 18.5 million during the decade. But the railway investments of the decade were as high as Rs 28 million for an additional 166 miles of tracks in Assam Proper. Another Rs 33.1 million was spent for 85 miles of tracks in the district of Goalpara and 100 miles in other parts of the province. Thus by 1911, transportation through railways became possible between Assam Proper and the rest of India along two routes. By now, Guwahati and Tinsukia were destined to soon become the province's leading commercial towns.

All this brought forward a qualitative change in the situation in two ways. First, the land-hungry jute-oriented peasants of East Bengal could now come by the thousands to colonize the riverine wastelands, on which the production potential of tea or wet rice was almost nil. Secondly, the usury and trading capital which had accumulated over the past decades in the hands of the Marwari *banias* could now be more productively used and speedily turned over as a result of increased commodity circulation. So long, their business had been limited to collecting forest produce and meagre farm surplus for the market as against the supply of imported manufactures. They also extended short-term finance to tea garden managers against *hundis* on Calcutta and maintained shops in the gardens. From now onwards, they began also to increasingly finance jute in addition to other cash crops, and to start mills for their processing. Better communications and the emergence of jute trade as a productive channel of rural finance were the two significant factors which, within years, gave a push to the agrarian economy through expanded commerce. For the first time, cultivation of jute became important in Assam Proper, the acreage increasing from less than 500 acres before 1901 to over 6,000 acres by 1911. (The total jute acreage exceeded 1 lakh acres by 1930–1 and 2 lakh acres by 1961.)

Meanwhile, the acreage under rice also recorded a 27 per cent increase during the decade, 1901–11, as against 5 per cent in the case of tea. The share of tea in the net cropped area decreased from 11.4 per cent to 9.4 per cent. Henceforth, jute and the associated cultivation of paddy and vegetables by immigrant jute-growers was to play an increasingly important role in the agrarian developments to follow. The East Bengal colonists formed one-fifth of the population of Goalpara by 1911, and thence began to move into Assam Proper.

CONCLUSION

There was undoubtedly, an impressive growth during the years 1871-1901 in terms of railway mileage, tea acreage and some extractive industries. The fast increase in tea exports (the output of tea increased from 6.3 million lbs. in 1871 to 72 million lbs. in 1901) was not different in magnitude from, say, that in the raw silk exports of Japan during the same period. But unlike in Japan, the benefits of external trade could not be widely absorbed into agrarian society, nor could they be used to back up expenditure on local resources. A part of the surplus was locally reinvested no doubt; but, it was in the same tea industry, leading to an over-production crisis by 1901, and in extractive industries. In both cases, almost all the inputs had to be imported. Consumer goods industries did not come up at all, mainly because the region's aggregate demand for new types of goods, was not enough to induce local production on a competitive basis. This was the basic problem till 1901 and remains so substantially, till today.

NOTES

1. *Arunoday*, vol. 12, January 1867; *Bengal Administration Report for 1872–73*, p. 85; *Bengal Adm. Rep. for 1871–2*, p. 155.
2. The investment per acre represents paid-out wage costs for 1.5 units of labour during the 4-year gestation period plus cost of seeds *plus pro rata* share of the overhead costs. My estimate is higher than that of the *Report of Commissioners Appointed to Enquire into the State and Prospects of Tea Cultivation in Assam, Cachar and Sylhet*, Calcutta, 1868, pp. 4–6. The total cost of bringing up an acre of tea plantation to crop-yielding stage was computed in the report at Rs 500 only.

    In 1872 and 1873—quite normal years – Assam Co. had 5,200 acres under tea, and the market price of its £20 (= Rs 200) shares ranged between £32 and £42 each. The value of its 10,000 shares at the average mean price divided by the given acreage will then roughly indicate the market value of per acre investment. This comes out to be as much as Rs 712. So our own estimate of Rs 600 for the period preceding mechanization of the tea processing may be considered fairly reasonable. Data used in our calculation are from H.A. Antrobus, *A History of the Assam Company, 1839–53* (Edinburgh, 1957), pp. 139–40, 409 and 416.
3. *Bengal Admn. Rep. for 1867–8*, p. 207 and *Bengal Admn. Rep. for 1868–9*, p. 191.

A BIG PUSH WITHOUT A TAKE-OFF 157

4. B.R. Medhi's Assam Budget speech of 1950–1 (Govt. of Assam, Shillong).
5. An investment of £70 was claimed for each planted acre in 1887, according to Buchanan, *The Development of Capitalist Enterprise in India*, N.Y., 1934, p. 57. Converted into rupees at the average exchange rate of the last two decades of the nineteenth century, the estimate roughly approximates Rs 1,000 per acre. This appears to be a fairly correct estimate, valid at least up to the early 1920s. In 1923, the book value of the Assam Co's properties, inclusive of 12,000 planted acres were revised at £754,070. This means that the Company's investment per planted acre was valued at £63, i.e. around Rs 900, having assumed zero value for company-held wastelands.
6. The estimates of railway investments have been worked out from available data on annual capital outlay and railway mileage for our relevant period in *Administrative Report on the Railways in India for the Calendar Year 1904*, London, 1905, pp. 22–3, 32–51, 179, 199–200, 231, 237–8 and 248; *History of Indian Railways Constructed and the Progress up to 31st March 1918* (Govt. of India, Simla, 1919), pp. 153–5 and 178–9. For the portion of Eastern Bengal Railway in Assam, the construction cost roughly averaged Rs 1.6 lakh per mile; for the portion of the Assam Bengal Railways, Rs 1.9 lakh per mile. For the minor railways, the average construction cost per mile varied from Rs 24,000 in the case of the Tezpur-Balipara Light Railway (narrow-gauge) to Rs 1.2 lakh in the case of the Dibru-Sadiya Railway. Tea acreage figures are culled from *Statistical Tables for British India*, 13th Issue and subsequent issues for other years. (GOI, Dept. of Statistics, Calcutta, 1889).
7. Investment figures for coal and petroleum are from *Imperial Gazetteer of India*, VI, pp. 70–1. For sawmills our estimate is based on relevant data in *Financial and Commercial Statistics of British India for the Year 1899* (GOI, Dept. of Statistics, Calcutta), 6th Issue. According to the latter source, the number of telegraph signalling offices increased from 10 during 1870–4 to 114 in 1897–8 in the then Assam Division.
8. Antrobus, n. 2, pp. 113–14. About the origins of the Jorehaut Tea Company, ibid., 110.
9. Among, such early planters may be mentioned J.B. Barrie, Civil Surgeon of Tezpur and S.O. Hannay, Commandant of the Light Infantry Battalion. Ibid., pp. 314–15 and 395.
10. *Assam Proc.*, Legis. Dept., Govt. of India, 1901, nos. 48–102. According to this source, unskilled average wage in Assam, outside the tea industry, slowly rose from Rs 4.28 during the period, 1875–6 to 1878–9, to Rs 6.50 during the period 1894–5 to 1898–9.
11. Antrobus, n. 2, p. 389; *Proc. of the Bengal Legis. Council, 1865–7*, p. 14.
12. Secy., Govt. of Bengal to Secy., Govt. of India, Home Dept., 3 Dec. 1866,

Assam, Proc., Legis. Dept., Govt. of Bengal. August 1867, no. 15; Assam Proc., Legis. Dept., Govt. of India, 1901, nos. 48–102, op. cit.
13. The total settled area in Assam Proper, as of 1903–4, was 2,562 thousand acres, according to *Imperial Gazetteer of India* (new edition, Oxford, 1908), Vl, p. 91. As of 1901, the total area in the occupation of tea gardens amounted to 642, 418 acres; of this 204,782 acres were planted and 437,636 acres remaining, unplanted.
14. *Bengal Adm. Report, 1868–9*, p. 191. These figures for Assam Proper are, however, stated to be incomplete.
15. *The Hinoo Patriot*, issues of 5 Feb. 1894, 30 March 1894 and 9 April 1894.
16. In 1901, the plantations of Assam Proper employed 289,676 permanent workers and an average of 17,743 temporary workers, totally 307,000 workers on a daily basis. The number of local recruits is from Allen, *Assam Prov. District Gazetteers*, vols. 1–10, Calcutta, 1905–6.
17. Wastage through high labour mortality and the desertions was considerable, *Report of the Assam Labour Enquiry Committee, 1906*, (Calcutta, 1906), Chs. 3–13. The total number of immigrant labour is estimated from annual immigration figures in the *Bengal Admn. Reports* up to 1873–4 and *Annual Reports on Inland Emigration*, 1978 to 1914–15.
18. Commissioner of Assam to Secy., Govt. of Bengal, 21 March 1867, *Assam Proc.*, Legis. Dept., Govt. of Bengal, August 1867, no. 15, and Antrobus, n. 2, p. 389.
19. *Administrative Report on the Railways*, n. 6, pp. 22–248; *History of Indian Railways*, n. 6, pp. 153–5 and 178–9; for quote, ibid., p. 248.
20. *Bengal Admn. Report, 1871–2*, p. 140, *Bengal Admn. Report, 1872–3*, p. 12, *Assam Proc.*, Revenue Agriculture and Commerce Dept., Dec. 1874, no. 11; *Assam Admn. Report, 1893–4*.
21. Estimated from data in Census of India, 1881, *Assam Admn. Report*, p. 29.
22. *An Account of the Province of Assam and its Administration* (reprint of *Report for 1901–2*, Shillong, 1903), pp. 20 and 129; *Report of the Administration of Eastern Bengal and Assam, 1905–6* (Shillong, 1907), p. 78; *Imperial Gazetteer of India*, n. 13, VI, pp. 40–1.
23. Quote from Antrobus, n. 2, p. 240.

APPENDIX

TABLE 6.1: TEA STATISTICS OF ASSAM PROPER 1875–6 TO 1901

	Total area under tea cultivation in acres (mature and not mature)	Total (aprox.) yield (in lbs.)	Average yield per acre of mature plants (in lbs.)	Acreage taken up but not planted
1875–6	59,864	12602,098	228.80	–
1876–7	67,337	15533,792	254.11	–
1877–8	78,495	18852,992	325.83	–
1878–9	89,423	18804,256	289.35	–
1879–80	88,210	19625,634	303.52	–
1880	89,475	21465,551	311.03	–
1881	93,802	23683,721	311.17	–
1882	108,673	28023,527	296.90	–
1883	111,012	34041,487	345.16	–
1884	106,162	32901,486	353.90	–
1885	107,492	32530,061	358.68	–
1886	113,016	37362,740	384.78	–
1887	115,578	39081,121	389.44	–
1892	139,582	48916,479	408.86	435,933
1893	145,134	56926,108	457.12	436,807
1894	153,874	56402,244	426.24	440,915
1895	154,389	56497,593	414.39	424,422
1897	178,720	58936,773	384.37	394,912
1898	191,203	63603,751	397.06	399,168
1900	204,285	75125,176	426.75	422,002
1901	204,682	72381,251	395.17	437,636

Sources: *Statistical Tables for British India*, 5th Issue, *Agricultural Statistics of British India*, vol. 1 and subsequent volumes.

TABLE 6.2: AVERAGE PRICE INDEX OF RICE, SALT AND TEA 1861 TO 1901 (BASE YEAR 1973: AVERAGE OF ALL PRICES =100)

4-year period	Average of prices: Kamrup, Nowgong, Lakhimpur, and Goalpara taken together)		Average of maximum price of Indian Pekoe tea quoted in Calcutta
	Rice	Salt	
1861–4	96.71	94.87	–
1865–8	116.52	104.82	–
1869–72	105.47	98.58	–
1874–7	136.87	97.65	113.50
1878–81	144.89	93.75	113.25
1882–5	124.20	68.35	92.25
1886–9	117.04	73.81	68.75
1890–3	153.08	78.72	63.25
1894–7	174.63	77.88	67.50
1898–1901	153.45	75.91	51.50

Note: In 1873, average price of rice was 18.60 *seers* per rupee and that of salt, 7.20 *seers* per rupee. The price of tea (Indian Pekoe) per pound, in the same year, was 1 Re 2 As.
Source: Processed from *Prices and Wages in India, 19th Issue*, pp. 2–3, 80–1 and 230.

TABLE 6.3: AVERAGE MONTHLY WAGE OF AGRICULTURAL AND PLANTATION LABOUR

Year	Wage of able-bodied agricultural labour in Lakhimpur (in Rs)	Index of the previous column (base year: 1873)	Year	Wage of Kachari labour at the Salonah Tea Plantation Nowgong district (in Rs)	Index of the previous column (base year: 1870)
1873	9.37	100	1870	5.83	100
1874–7	6 to 9	77	1880	6.50	111
1878–81	7 to 10	93	1890–2	6.50	111
1882–5	7 to 10	101	1893	5.90	102
1886–9	7 to 10	92	1894	5.90	102
1890–3	8 to 10	95	1900	4.80	82
1894–7	8 to 11	100	1901–2	4.80	82
1898–1901	8 to 12	104			

Note: Wage of Kachari labour includes all allowances. In hoeing, full wage was earned on completion of light hoeing work of 20 *nulls* a day.
Source: Processed from *Prices and Wages in India, 19th Issue*, pp. 264–82, 319.

TABLE 6.4: DENSITY OF POPULATION PER SQ. MILE

	1972	1881	1891	1901	1911	1921	1951
I. Districts							
Kamrupa	146	167	164	153	173	198	387
Darrang	69	80	90	99	110	170	326
Nowgong	68	82	90	69	79	108	409
Sibsagar	64	79	96	120	138	162	351
Lakhimpur	27	40	56	82	104	143	265
Goalpara	98	113	115	117	152	193	278
II. Subdivision of Darrang							
Tezpur		42	–	77	101	157	333
Mangaldoi		146	–	137	124	140	316

Sources: *Assam Census Reports* and *District Census Handbooks*. The density per sq. mile in Assam Proper in 1951 was 347.

TABLE 6.5: INDEX OF CROPPED ACREAGE UP TO 1901 FOR ASSAM PROPER (BASE 1884–5 = 100)

Year	Rice	Tea	Area cropped more than once	Net cropped area	Index of gross cropped area (less area under tea)	Index of population
1881	–	–	–	–	–	100
1884–5	100	100	100	100	100	
1885–6	105	101	110	105	106	
1886–7	145	106	130	112	114	
1887–8	117	109	123	113	114	
1888–9	118	110	129	114	116	
1889–90	115	117	129	114	115	
1890–1	120	123	130	118	119	112
1891–2	113	128	127	120	120	
1892–3	126	131	132	128	129	
1893–4	122	137	130	129	125	
1894–5	124	145	119	123	121	
1895–6	121	145	125	124	122	
1896–7	121	155	126	125	122	
1897–8	120	168	109	123	118	
1898–9	122	180	107	124	118	
1899–1900	120	186	94	123	116	
1900–1	116	192	90	122	113	119

Source: Worked out from government statistics.

TABLE 6.6: PERCENTAGE AREA UNDER DIFFERENT CROPS TO TOTAL CROPPED AREA FOR ASSAM PROPER: 1882–3 TO 1900–1

Year	Rice	Other food grains including pulses	Sugar cane	Fibres	Oil	Tea seeds	Mis.
1882–3	3.47	3.26	1.10	–	6.33	7.07	8.77
1884–5	67.30	3.11	1.17	0.05	9.13	7.04	12.19
1885–6	67.08	3.38	1.29	0.11	9.45	6.74	11.96
1886–7	68.29	3.04	1.19	0.12	8.75	6.60	12.02
1887–8	69.20	2.71	1.03	0.07	8.32	6.75	11.92
1888–9	68.72	3.42	1.10	0.06	6.37	8.70	11.92
1889–90	67.05	3.20	1.11	0.05	9.37	7.16	12.06
1890–1	67.82	3.10	1.05	0.05	8.65	7.27	12.07
1891–2	63.44	4.13	1.02	0.04	9.72	7.50	14.15
1892–3	66.08	3.68	1.01	0.02	9.08	7.18	12.95
1893–4	65.05	3.49	0.91	0.15	9.86	7.65	12.89
1894–5	67.74	3.31	0.97	0.13	7.12	8.31	12.42
1895–6	65.56	3.29	0.81	0.14	9.12	8.26	12.75
1896–7	65.21	3.96	1.00	0.21	9.45	8.75	11.42
1897–8	66.51	2.76	0.87	0.23	8.16	9.72	11.75
1898–9	67.10	3.56	0.81	0.20	6.55	10.35	11.43
1899–1900	66.79	3.88	0.91	0.24	5.86	10.88	11.44
1900–1	65.77	3.54	0.99	0.21	6.45	11.39	11.65

Source: Worked out from official statistics.

CHAPTER 7

A Nineteenth Century Puzzle Revisited: Clash of Land Use Regimes in Colonial Assam

SANJIB BARUAH

In the latter part of the nineteenth century, the British colonial government in Assam tried to change the land titles of Assamese peasants from annual leases to decennial leases.[1] The colonial government's efforts at regularizing the land rights of peasants to their land was also the time when the foundation of the tea industry in Assam was laid. Assam today is one of the world's leading tea-producing regions – and tea occupies much of Assam's best agricultural lands todays. In 1868 the Land Revenue Regulation sought to make it compulsory for government *ryots*, i.e. owner cultivators, to take 10-year renewable leases on their land. Annual titles were to be given only in the *firingoti* or *chapori mahals* close to the river or on land cultivated by tribal peasants on the northern edges of the valley. The goal was to get the Assamese peasantry 'accustomed' to the virtues of exclusively settled agriculture and to relieve officers from the 'useless labour' of writing hundreds and thousands of land titles every year.[2]

But the colonial authorities faced an unexpected hurdle. The Assamese peasants were not interested in long-term titles. They mostly abandoned their claim to their land after a single harvest. The process of converting annual land titles to decennial titles therefore, was painfully slow. The process began in 1868; but by 1875–6 only 8,000 acres were under annual titles, while 1.3 million acres of land remained under annual titles. The next year, the area under decennial titles went up slightly to 10,000 acres, but land under the annual title also went up.[3] The report of 1889–90 noted that even after 10 years, the Assamese peasant was yet to 'appreciate the advantages of the periodic lease, and makes no effort to obtain it in place of the annual lease'.[4] The situation did not change significantly for nearly three more decades.

Why did the Assamese peasants resist long-term titles to land, despite what would seem to us to be its obvious advantages? This puzzle provides an important clue to understanding the impact of colonial land settlement project on Assam and of the larger meaning of colonial rule in terms of the shifts in the global geography of resource use. These consequences are often lost in the discourses of economic development. The ostensible purpose of land settlement – probably the most important administrative enterprise of the colonial administration in Assam – was to record pre-existing land rights not only of peasants, but of others, including that of *Xatras* and other religious establishments. But the notion of protecting existing land rights was shaped by a whole host of ideas that the British brought with them. Among them were their ideas about 'civilization': a dense population and industry, for instance, were seen as markers of civilization and on a continuum between civilization and barbarism, settled agriculture belonged to a higher plane than shifting agriculture or hunting and gathering.

The other side of recording land rights was the colonial state's assertion of claims to the vast majority of land in which it assumed that no private rights existed. That was the land on which the colonial state made the most far-reaching of decisions. Among them were lands declared wastelands, enabling their allocation to tea plantations or surplus land in which to settle peasant immigrants from more crowded parts of the subcontinent. Even though large amounts of land were also set aside as reserve forests or grazing lands; most of them were later either reclassified as ordinary cultivable land or, in practice, the state – both in colonial and postcolonial times – was ineffective in preserving them as forests or as grazing lands for long.

WHAT WERE THE ASSAMESE PEASANTS UP TO?

Early colonial officials believed that the reason the Assamese peasants were not interested in land titles beyond a single harvest was because they practised land fallowing on a large scale. But even then, the lack of interest of Assamese peasants in acquiring long-term land titles still intrigued colonial officials. Why should a peasant give up his ownership rights to the land that he keeps fallow? The length of time that he left a land fallow also seemed inordinately long. Even more intriguing was the fact that when land left fallow was cultivated again, it was rarely reclaimed by its previous cultivators.

The *Land Revenue Administration Report for 1884–5* tried to solve the puzzle by making a distinction between two parts of an Assamese peasant's agricultural land: that which he cultivates every year and that which he cultivates occasionally. The Assamese peasant practised very little land fallow in the lands that he cultivated 'permanently' and he practices fallowing on 'an enormous scale' when it comes to his 'fluctuating cultivation', where he 'leaves the land to go into the jungle for years'.[5] Another official, however, expressed his doubts on whether fallowing practices had anything to do with the Assamese peasant's lack of interest in long-term land titles. After all, the cultivator rarely returns to the original land at the end of the so-called fallowing period. 'Fallowing in the ordinary sense of the term', he wrote:

is not ordinarily practised by the Assam cultivator; that is to say, the cultivator does not retain his holding, and, when the land ceases to yield abundantly, and without imposing on him the labour of eradicating the weeds which became prolific after the second or third year of cultivation, he throws up the land altogether and goes in search of fresh soil; in the majority of cases he never contemplates a return to what he has resigned, though others may doubtless take the land up again at some future day, the period after which such land is retaken being longer or shorter as there is or is not plenty of waste virgin so available in the neighbourhood.

In some areas such as Lakhimpur, he pointed out, land was not reclaimed for as long as 20 years, even though in other areas it was shorter. But in all these cases, he concluded, 'it is entirely misleading' to refer to land that is not cultivated for some period and to which a cultivator abandons his ownership claim as a 'period of fallow' or to say that in Lakhimpur the 'cultivator fallows on an enormous scale, as do most uncivilized (*sic*) tribes'.[6]

HABITS OF ABUNDANCE?
A DISSENTING COLONIAL MEMO

A dissenting administrative memo by Colonel Henry Hopkinson in 1872 was closer to figuring out why Assamese peasants were reluctant to accept long-term land titles. The key, he suggested, was the land abundance of Assam which made it possible for a peasant to find fresh soil with little difficulty. In such a situation, long-term land titles was little more than an encumbrance: an unnecessary commitment to pay taxes on land even when it is not being cultivated.

In most parts of the world, the first hurdle that a cultivator confronts is to find land. But in Assam, the difficulty is 'reduced to the minimum'. Here wrote Hopkinson, 'if land is not absolutely so free and common to all as air, still it has hardly any intrinsic value'. In such conditions, Hopkinson suggested, it is more appropriate to think of what an owner-cultivator pays the government in exchange for his land title as license fee and not as a tax or revenue on land.

It is a license 'to extract a certain quantity of produce' out of a plot of land. It is a 'license to labour, so that our land tax is really a tax on labour and the labourer's stock and implements required in cultivation'. It is not surprising, therefore, that a peasant would be disinclined to accept a decennial land title because that amounted to a 10-year commitment of his and his family's labour and capital. He would not want to make such a commitment because he cannot be sure as to how long he will be able to put in the necessary labour to cultivate that land. He knows that he can always get land when he wants. But what he is not sure of is, whether his family or his cattle will survive illnesses or in cases where he has debts, whether he can pay them back. In such circumstances, why would he 'entangle himself in a covenant which, while only confirming what he is already secure of, will add to his embarrassment if those conditions of his undertaking which are variable and uncertain turn out unfavourably'?

Hopkinson believed that the source of the confusion was the tendency of colonial administrators to think that what they saw in the rest of India is true of Assam as well. He made his point rather colourfully. 'Whether the Assamese of the Valley are Hindus in their manners, customs, and institutions,' he wrote, 'might furnish the subject of an agreeable essay.' Much could be said on both sides of the question. But even if they are, he said, he did 'not see why they should have accepted their agricultural polity from the Hindus also'. Referring to ideas popular at that time about Assamese Hindus being migrants from the Indian heartland he said, 'I have an idea that an emigrant from Surrey would not take his agricultural polity with him to town.'[7]

TRANSITION BETWEEN LAND USE REGIMES

Hopkinson was right. Assam's land abundance indeed provides a clue to the puzzle, but no more than a clue. The Assamese peasant could find and cultivate other lands, but that was only partly a function of the physical fact of land abundance. One also has to ask questions about the prevailing norms of land use. The fact that peasants did not have to pay for the new land – either in rent or in price – or even register his use of that land with anyone is a function of local rules and norms of land use. Obviously, there was no land market; nor was there private property in our sense of the term. It was generally accepted that the peasant was entitled to that particular land. If he took the trouble of clearing another plot of jungle land, no authority could stop him from doing so. While the colonial administrator concentrated on the agricultural use of these lands, far more important than clearing those lands for purposes of cultivation were their non-agricultural uses in ways that were central to Assam's rural economy. Among them were collecting materials like bamboo or wood used for constructing houses, boats, household implements, mats and baskets; raising silk worms – the foundation of the large indigenous silk industry – as well as collecting animal and vegetable products for household consumption and trade.

British colonial rule has been described as a 'crucial watershed' in the ecological history of India.[8] Colonial rule enabled the global expansion of the resource base of industrial societies as land and natural resources earlier controlled by gatherer and peasant societies came under the control of new rules of property that created the legal foundation for the industrial mode of resource use.[9] The effect of the colonial land settlement policy was to incorporate Assam into this new global resource use regime. One major consequence of the colonial land settlement project was to eliminate the access to these lands of the shifting cultivators and hunter-gatherers of the Brahmaputra Valley and the surrounding hills. The full effects of the denial of access, however, were experienced only gradually. The attitude of the Assamese peasant toward decennial leases – the initial rejection and subsequent acceptance – reflect the uncertainties of the transition between two regimes of resource use.

The new rules of property provided the legal foundation for the new projects – those that the early colonials thought will bring 'civilization' to Assam and in post-colonial times came to be seen as projects that would bring about development, modernization and progress. Whatever its contribution to 'progress', the colonial land settlement project resulted in significant dispossession of the Assamese peasantry and of the shifting cultivators and hunter-gatherers of the Brahmaputra Valley and the surrounding hills. The shift becomes clear when the new rules of property are contrasted with the old rules of access to resources.

BEFORE COLONIAL RULE: LAND USE UNDER THE AHOM POLITY

The foundation of the pre-colonial Ahom economy and polity was a system of corvee labour. Leaving aside a significant portion of the population that were servile – *bondi*, *beti*, etc., who worked in the fields and the households of the aristocracy and of the religious establishments – the entire non-servile population had to contribute labour to the state. The male population of this segment of the population was divided into groups of three or four persons, each called a *paik* and units called *got*. A *paik* from each *got* was obliged to serve the state for three or four months a year in times of peace. They were assigned to public works such as constructing roads, tanks, embankments or to the royal household or the households of the nobility.

The *gots* in turn were divided into *khels* that consisted of 1,000 to 5,000 *paiks*. A *khel* could be responsible for tasks such as catching and supplying elephants, supplying particular needs of the royal court such as hand-fans and umbrellas. The *khel* organization extended to some of the surrounding hills as well. Access to lands and forests – well beyond what colonial administrators saw as the family plot – was crucial for this political economy.

Each *paik* family got free of rent 2 *puras* (about 2.66 acres) of wetland and another piece of homestead and garden land. This was called their *ga-mati* – literally body-land.[10] In addition, *paiks* were free to reclaim uncultivated land. During a *paik's* time away from his home as contributor of corvee labour, other members of the *got* looked after the cultivation of his *ga-mati*. During times of war when all *paiks* of a *got* could be called to state service, cultivation became the responsibility of women and children.

Despite the change in the rules of access, the Assamese peasantry continued to utilize lands apart from their *ga-mati* well into the colonial period. This is apparent from historian Amalendu Guha's observation on late nineteenth-century Assam, based on British colonial documents. After distinguishing between the modes of cultivation of Assam in three belts: the flood plains, transplanted rice belt and the submontane belt, Guha describes how the transplanted rice cultivators – the bulk of *paiks* – also had an interest in the two other belts.

> They collected all sorts of materials for making their houses, boats, implements, mats and baskets, from these tracks. At selected spots on these tracts, often several miles away from settled villages, peasants would erect their temporary clusters of huts known as *pam basti* to carry on shifting cultivation of mustard, pulses and *ahu* rice.

There is a common perception that only 'tribal' peasants were shifting cultivators while what we would now call the ethnic Assamese – both Hindu and Muslim peasants – were settled cultivators. Such a distinction, based on the civilized-primitive dichotomy, however, had little foundation in reality. Most Assamese peasants did some amount of shifting cultivation, apart from using those lands for non-agricultural purposes.[11]

GOALS OF LAND SETTLEMENT

The goal of the British land settlement policy was ostensibly to recognize all traditional rights to land and create long-term hereditary and transferable rights in land. But even if one assumes that the colonial authorities had managed to recognize the property rights of all peasant families to their *ga-mati*, this would still have radically restricted the peasants' traditional access to other lands. In making his proposals on the new rules of land settlement, Moffatt Mills in 1853, for instance, had this to say on whether the Assamese cultivator had the right to dispose of his land by sale, gift, or by mortgage. He noted that it was 'generally understood' that the cultivator had that right and argued for its recognition. But he noted: 'I would restrict his rights to his paternal acres (i.e. his *ga-mati*) or to such lands he occupies in his or her own village. He cannot have, and has not, any hereditary rights of occupancy of lands in other villages, which he cultivates one year and throws up the next.'[12] The privileging of land in a peasant's 'native village' – his so-called 'paternal acres' – and his exclusion from lands supposedly outside his 'native village' was obviously a clever device to exclude the peasants from lands other than his *ga-mati*. The idea also anticipates the notion of the self-sufficient Indian village that later became a part of the repertoire of colonial scholarship on India.

But the *ga-mati*, as I have said before, was only a small part of the peasant household's entitlements. Peasants had access to surrounding lands, both for occasional cultivation, to collect fish, fruits and vegetables and for essential non-agricultural purposes such as collecting house-building material and raw material for basket-weaving, etc., and to raise silk-worms. His *ga-mati* was not the only 'property' from which a family had to make a living. Peasants in pre-colonial Assam were not agricultural specialists – a division of labour that was yet to be created. Even under the best of assumptions – of colonial authorities succeeding in recognizing and recording all rights to *ga-mati* – the new rules of property resulted in enormous dispossession of the Assamese peasantry.

The inability of the Assamese peasant to understand the value of long-term land titles can be understood only with reference to the norms of the old order. In a world where a peasant could cultivate any previously uncultivated land, it made perfect sense that he would not be interested in claiming 10-year rights to land and assume responsibility for paying taxes for its use.

WHY DID PEASANTS FINALLY 'LEARN?'

From the perspective of colonial officials, the Assamese peasant did eventually 'learn' the value of long-term land titles. It happened during the second and third decades of the twentieth century with the arrival of East Bengali settlers. Officials gave a scientific gloss to this process of what they saw as Assamese peasants 'learning' from their enterprising new neighbours. According to this view, Assamese peasants were uninterested in decennial titles because of their misperceptions about land fertility. They had the false perception that land fertility gets exhausted in three or four years. Indeed according to a colonial report, the 'backward people' in the submontane belt were so 'superstitious' that they even moved their homesteads 'on a mere suspicion that a site was getting unhealthy'.[13] By watching the enterprising East Bengali cultivator produce successive harvests in these lands, the Assamese peasant, according to this explanation, learnt the scientific truth that 'only adventitious fertility is exhausted, intrinsic fertility still determines yields'.

But this 'scientific' explanation is hardly convincing. While we don't know whether the indigenous system made a distinction analogous to adventitious fertility and intrinsic fertility, the assumption that people would simply give up their land just because they don't know about different kinds of fertility is unconvincing. A more plausible explanation is that the colonial policy of settling East Bengali cultivators in these so-called uncultivated lands changed the ground reality. Amalendu Guha notes that in Kamrup, shifting cultivation (which as I have said before was done by tribal as well as non-tribal peasants) begins to disappear in the early decades of the twentieth century. 'One misses the scene of burning grass jungles as described by Butler.' The new factor that was responsible for the change, he writes, was that immigrants from East Bengal were now settled in the *chapori* belt.[14] With the arrival of the East Bengali peasants and the policy to settle them in belts that the Assamese peasant had traditionally used for shifting cultivation, the most significant feature of the new land regime – the peasant's exclusion from land other than his *ga-mati* – became a *fait accompli*.

MAKING ROOM FOR TEA: ENCLOSURE A COLONIAL CONTEXT

The most dramatic aspect of the colonial land settlement project in nineteenth century Assam, was the allocation of vast tracts of land to tea plantations. When the viability of the commercial production of tea in Assam became established, according to Percival Griffiths, historian of the Indian tea industry, 'a madness comparable in intensity with that of the South Sea Bubble', hit the London stock exchange as 'normally level-headed financiers and speculators began to scramble wildly for tea shares and tea lands'.[15]

But even prior to that, Assam's land abundance next to the densely-populated Indian heartland – and especially the more populous Bengal – appeared striking to early European visitors to Assam. Indeed, the idea of settling Assam's 'wastelands' with Englishmen with capital was mooted as early as 1833 – seven years after the British conquest of Assam, and even before the prospects of tea production in Assam were established. To Francis Jenkins, one of the earliest colonial officials in charge of making a land policy in Assam, it appeared that a scheme of colonization 'offered a better prospect for the speedy realization of improvements than any measure that could be adopted in the present ignorant and demoralized state of native inhabitants'. He proposed that a class of European planters with capital be encouraged to settle in Assam and produce sugar cane, indigo and other plantation crops. 'To obtain the full advantage that could accrue from European settlers,' he proposed that lands should be 'absolutely unencumbered by tenants and sub-tenants.'[16]

The Waste Land Grant Rule of 1838 was the earlier law under which land was given to tea plantations. The conditions of the grants were very liberal. For instance, one-fourth of the area was perpetually revenue-free and no revenue had to be paid on the remaining land for 20 years if it was under forest and for fewer years if it was under reeds and high grass. The land revenue rates to be paid after the expiry of that period was very low, lower compared to even what Assam's impoverished peasant cultivators were paying.[17]

Moffatt Mills in his magisterial report on Assam in 1853, recommended even more liberal terms. 'When land is taken up by speculators, involving outlay and a distant return,' he said, 'the terms cannot be too liberal.' He noted that European speculators had not found the existing terms attractive enough and that 'nothing but the absolute rent-free tenure of the land will induce people to bring English capital largely into the market'. The goal of wasteland grants, he said, should not be immediate returns in terms of government revenue, 'the object is to clear those vast tracts of forest, and promote immigration'.[18] In 1854, new rules were introduced to give 99 years' lease and to raise the minimum area of a grant to 500 acres. The new rules stimulated a land rush, though the terms were further liberalized in subsequent years.[19] Some of the tea planters in Assam became not only 'the biggest landlords in the countryside they dominated, but they paid the lowest average rates per acre of holdings'.[20]

Only a small part of the land acquired by tea gardens, however, was actually used for growing tea. For instance, the Assam Company founded in 1839 and the first Indian tea company had the grant of an area of 33,665 acres under the Waste Land Grant Rules of 1838. In 1859, the Company had planted tea in only about 4,000 acres of land.[21] In the 1870s, the acreage under tea was only 8 to

10 per cent of the area occupied by tea gardens and the percentage was about 29 per cent when British rule ended in 1947.[22] Tea planters even settled some tenant cultivators on their lands to ensure temporary labour supply during peak seasons.[23]

WHOSE LAND WAS IT ANYWAY?

By 1901, tea gardens enclosed 'some one-fourth of the total settled area (or 5 per cent of the total area) of Assam proper under their exclusive property rights'.[24] The disruption that the land grab caused to the old order was anything but subtle. Even communication between villages was disrupted as parts of public roads were fenced off and villagers were denied access. This included ancient public roads like Rajgarh Ali, Lahdoi Garh, Kharikotia Road and Raja Ali. Even many weekly bazaars and *hats*, where the villagers brought their farm products for sale, came within the limits of tea gardens. Planters exercised exclusive control over these markets. Indeed, the right of way through tea plantations became a major issue during the anti-colonial struggle in the twentieth century. For in many parts of Assam, a villager had to walk many miles around tea gardens. The use of roads that went through the gardens was restricted. For instance, Indians could not go though a tea plantation on a bicycle or on horse-back, or with his umbrella open. When the automobile arrived on the scene there were cases when bullock carts were not allowed on these roads for they might damage the roads and make them unfit for the automobile. During the non-cooperation movement of the 1930s, tea planters sought to prohibit the Indian National Congress activists from the plantations.[25]

'As one mode of resource use comes into contact with another mode organized on very different social and ecological principles,' write ecological historians Guha and Gadgil, 'we expect the occurrence of substantial social strife. In fact, the clash of two modes has invariably resulted in massive bursts of violent and sometimes genocidal conflict.'[26] The violent encounter between the Nagas and the British – a process that colonial rulers described as the 'pacification' of the Naga 'savages' – can be best understood in these terms. There were 10 'punitive expeditions' between 1835 and 1851. After a period of relative quiet, there was an uprising by the Angami Nagas in 1879, when they seized the British military base in Kohima, leading to the last major military encounter.

Land grabbing by tea planters had profoundly disrupted the hunting and gathering economies of the Naga peoples who lived on the hills that border the Assamese plains where the first generation of tea plantations were established. The decision in 1873 to introduce the Inner Line, which, in some parts of the north-east, continues till this day, was partly a response to the reckless expansion of British entrepreneurs into new lands. This threatened British political relations with the hill tribes. Among the British adventurers, were tea planters as well as speculators in raw rubber, who tried to enclose as many tracts of new land as they could. The Bengal Eastern Frontier Regulation of 1873, therefore, empowered the colonial government to 'prescribe, and from time to time, alter by notification . . . , a line to be called the Inner Line'. The line was drawn along the foothills and the peoples living beyond this line were supposedly, 'left to manage their own affairs with only such interference on the part of the frontier officers in their political capacity as may be considered advisable with the view to establishing a personal influence for good among the chiefs and the tribes'.[27]

The colonial government laid down rules to bring, 'under more stringent control the commercial relations of our own subjects with the frontier tribes living on the borders of our jurisdiction'. These rules governed activities by British subjects beyond the Inner Line; no British subject or foreign citizen could cross the line without a licence, and trade or possession of land beyond the line was severely restricted.[28] The following account of the process of drawing the Inner Line illustrates the substantive role of the expansion of tea plantations in the conflicts between the Nagas and the British:

The question of laying down of the Inner Line for the Luckimpore [Lakhimpur] district generally was taken up by the Chief Commissioners of Assam in 1875. South of Jeipur it was found necessary to enclose within it a tract of country which had not up to that time been subject to the formal and plenary authority of the district officer. The object of enclosing the tract was to bring into the ordinary jurisdiction the tea gardens of Namsang, Taurack and Hukanjuri [Xukanjuri]. For the Taurack Garden compensation was paid to Mithonia Nagas. For the Hukanjuri and Namsang Gardens similar compensation was paid to the Namsang and Borduwaria Nagas. The sums thus paid are of course recovered as revenue from the occupiers of the gardens.[29]

The violence of the Naga-British encounter and the tensions in the relations between tea plantations and Assamese society during the anti-British struggle, however, were only some of the early consequences of the new property regime imposed by the colonial land settlement project. The fallout of this shift, continues to be a subtext in political instability in the area till this day; notably the insurgencies that blame the Indian Government for its economic underdevelopment and indeed, sometimes of treating the area as a colony, the perennial tensions between immigrants and the indigenous peoples and unrest among 'tribal' people such as the Bodos and Karbis, whose reliance on shifting cultivation had been more pronounced than that of the rest of the population. Indeed, one reason why the economic grievances of the Bodo people did not come to a head till the 1980s was that for nearly a century as shifting cultivators, many of them were able to move around cultivating lands formally designated as protected forests. The fact that these most indigenous of Assam's inhabitants came to be seen as encroachers by the Assam Government, became a source of consternation for many Bodo activists.

RESOURCE USE UNDER THE NEW OWNERS

Like their shifting cultivator predecessors, the tea planters too, found the extraordinary fertility of land cleared of forests very attractive. In a 'standard instruction' William Roberts of the Jorehaut Tea Company, for instance, recommended to new planters the superiority of forest lands. 'Forest lands,' he said are, 'to be preferred to grass lands, in consequence of the fine rich deposits of decayed vegetable matter which are found on the surface, and which stimulates the lush growth of the young tea plants, better than any other description of manure.' Given the large tracts of land available to them, many planters had a choice of the lands to use for growing tea. Even though the indentured labour recruited by the tea planters cannot be called expensive, the instruction made the case of forest lands on grounds of cost, swell. 'The cost of clearing forest land and preparing it for sowing', said the instruction, 'is about the same as that attending the preparation of grass land', since in order to remove the grass roots, those lands had to be deeply trenched or hoed. Roberts then proceeded to detail the 'standard practice' for clearing forest lands for tea. One can see why the new owners of these lands would be proud of their 'civilized' methods of cutting down forests, compared to the 'slash and burn' ways of their shifting cultivating predecessors.

> By cutting down and burning the small-sized trees and under-wood, the only 'ringing' the large trees about five feet from the ground, in order that a certain amount of shade may be afforded to the young plants; and in the course of about three years these large trees decay, beyond lying in inconvenient positions. . . . It is strongly recommended that the clearance should be thoroughly completed in the first instance, by felling all the forest trees, cutting the stems close to the ground, by means of either an American axe, or a cross-cut saw, having a rope attached to the upper part of the tree, in order to direct it in the falling.

Of course, unlike their shifting cultivating predecessors, who cleared only small amounts of land for cultivating for short periods before returning them to the jungle once again, deforestation by tea planters was much larger in scale and was permanent. Perhaps the first generation of tea planters even saw their ability to convert trees into charcoal as a marker of their 'civilized' ways. Indeed, the standard instruction was impressively precise on how to make use of the burnt trees as charcoal:

> The whole of the timber can be profitably utilized by cutting the large trees into lengths, and collecting and packing them properly into smaller branches, in large heaps, say thirty feet in width, and ten feet in height, covering the whole over the small branches, leaves and clay and then burning the mass and converting it to charcoal; which can be carted away and stored, either in a godown, or collected in heap and protected with covering in thatch; where it will remain in good condition for years, or until it is required for manufacturing operations.[30]

Perhaps this standard instruction illustrates the ultimate meaning of the project of land settlement in Assam: to shift large amounts of Assam's land and forest resources from the control of the peasantry – both settled and shifting cultivators – and hunter gatherers to the colonial state. The state then reallocated that land and the most significant private beneficiary of the largess were the tea planters. In light of the subsequent history of political upheavals and economic deprivation in the region, the promise of 'civilization' and 'progress' – in whose name the project of land settlement was taken up – would seem to be a cruel joke.

A NINETEENTH CENTURY PUZZLE REVISITED 177

NOTES

1. Most of Assam was under ryotwari and not zamindari settlement.
2. 'Resolution on the Land Revenue Report', *Land Revenue Report of the Assam Valley Districts, 1881–2*, Shillong: Assam Secretariat Press, 1882, p. 6.
3. *Report on the Administration of the Province of Assam, 1876–77*, Shillong: Assam Secretariat Press, 1878, p. 19.
4. *Annual Report on the Administration of Land Revenue in Assam, 1889–90*, Shillong: Assam Secretariat Press, 1890, p. 13.
5. *Land Revenue Administration Report of the Assam Valley Districts, 1884–85*, Shillong: Assam Secretariat Press, 1885, p. 28.
6. *Resolution on the Land Revenue Report*, in ibid., p. 4.
7. Henry Hopkinson to the Secretary, Government of Bengal, Revenue Department, 6 April 1872 (Assam Commissioner's File, 1867–73, file no. 219, 'Land Revenue Settlements and Land Question in Assam' of the Assam State Archives, Guwahati), pp. 7–8.
8. Madhav Gadgil and Ramchandra Guha, *This Fissured Land: An Ecological History of India*, Delhi: Oxford University Press, 1993, p. 5.
9. See 'Habitats in Human History', Ch. 1 of ibid.
10. One British official, Captain Brodie, believed that the right to *ga-mati* was vested in the *khel* and that on the death of a *paik* the land reverted to the *khel*. Moffatt Mills, however, found that Brodie's judgement was not shared by other British officials. Mills himself concluded that *ga-mati* was 'the property of the state and neither hereditary, nor transferable'. A.J. Moffatt Mills, *Report on the Province of Assam*, 1854, Guwahati: Publication Board, Assam, 1984. Moffatt Mills's report shaped colonial land policies.
11. Amalendu Guha, *Medieval and Early Colonial Assam: Society, Polity, Economy*, Calcutta: K.P. Bagchi and Company (on behalf of the Centre for Studies in the Social Sciences), 1991, p. 13.
12. Moffatt Mills, *Report on the Province of Assam*, p. 6.
13. S.P. Desai, *Report on the Land Revenue Settlement of the Kamrup District*, Shillong: Assam Government Printing Press, March 1928, p. 10.
14. Guha, *Medieval and Early Colonial Assam*, p. 13. The reference to Butler in Guha's account is John Butler, *Sketch of Assam with Some Account of the Hill Tribes by An Officer*, London, 1884, pp. 21–3.
15. Percival Griffiths, *The History of the Indian Tea Industry*, London: Weidenfeld and Nicholson, 1967, p. 96.
16. Report by Francis Jenkins to Secretary of the Government of Fort William, 2 July 1833. Cited in Guha, *Medieval and Early Colonial Assam*, p. 149.

17. D.K. Gangopadhyay, *Revenue Administration in Assam*, Dispur: Government of Assam, 1990, p. 134.
18. Moffatt Mills, *Report on the Province of Assam*, p. 17.
19. Guha, *Medieval and Early Colonial Assam*, p. 167.
20. Guha, *Planter Raj to Swaraj: Freedom Struggle and Electoral Politics in Assam 1826–1947*, New Delhi: People's Publishing House, 1977, p. 15.
21. Gangopadhyay, *Revenue Administration in Assam*, pp. 132–3.
22. Guha, *Medieval and Early Colonial Assam*, p. 191.
23. Ibid., *Planter Raj to Swaraj*, p. 15.
24. Ibid., *Medieval and Early Colonial Assam*, p. 191.
25. Ibid., *Planter Raj to Swaraj*, pp. 134–5.
26. Gadgil and Guha, *This Fissured Land*, p. 53.
27. Alexander Mackenzie, *The North-East Frontier of India*, Delhi: Mittal Publications, 1979 (originally published in 1884 as *History of the Relations of the Government with the Hill Tribes of the North-East Frontier of Bengal*), pp. 89–90.
28. Ibid., p. 55.
29. Ibid., p. 89.
30. William Roberts, 'Observations on the Cultivation of the Tea Plant and the Manufacture of Tea', Appendix in H.A. Antrobus, *A History of the Jorehaut Tea Company Ltd., 1859–1946*, pp. 345–6.

SECTION III

INDIA AFTER INDEPENDENCE: THE NORTH-EAST

THE HINDU RATE OF GROWTH

If the north-east had been the recipient of investment that converted it into a dual economy during the Raj, its experience under planning after Independence was hardly more encouraging.

Hiren Gohain examines if under-deveopment of the region is the consequence of 'lack of investment' or 'lack of enterprise and proverbial laziness of the Assamese people. He argues that these two explanations are actually not two distinct propositions but the two sides of the same coin. He has stressed upon a consistent policy of state intervention not only for development but also for the growth a self-sustained capitalist economy like South Korea, Taiwan or earlier Japan. The vicious circle can be broken only by a new kind of determined leadership of the enlightened middle class.

As Dipankar Sengupta points out, the dominant model as well as the means used to implement it left very little in the hands of the states, either by way of resources or authority to pursue economic development. Ironically, few state-level politicians if any, opposed this model of development and in this sense were accomplices to the economic stagnation that followed. To compound matters, states, instead of emphasizing agriculture, pushed heavy industry, further compounding the problem of growth and employment generation. As these public ventures failed, the states went in for populist measures which mired them further into a fiscal debt trap, severely affecting their manoeuverability when the Central Government finally liberalized. Thus, even when the licence-permit *raj* ended, states that were poor and had little industry to begin with or had not received requisite licences during the licence *raj*, lagged behind those states that were already industrialized at the time of independence because of the policies they themselves had followed and advocated.

Manmohan Agarwal and Sudip Ranjan Basu in some sense, bear out Sengupta's thesis by showing that inter-state had indeed increased. As this has happened in spite of central and state governments' concerns, it shows that the present policy network has not been adequate to stem this tendency, especially in the 1980s.

Alokesh Barua and Arindam Bandyopadhyay show that given the fact that growth in Indian states is strongly linked to the share of manufacturing, the nature of change in the structure of the economy of the north-eastern states, infrastructure and services gaining share at the expense of agriculture and manufacturing, has led to this region performing below the national average when it comes to growth, but above it when it comes to inequality. They call for policies aimed at market expansion, targeted capital spending through village panchayats, scale of investment proportionate to the respective factor proportions of the state and express doubts whether capital-intensive projects like petrochemicals will able to stoke growth or employment. They opine that inter-state inequalities may be reduced only if industrialization is labour absorbing.

CHAPTER 8

Development and Decolonization

HIREN GOHAIN*

Public discussion on Assam's economic backwardness may be broadly reduced to a polemic between two positions – the 'indigenists' speaking for 'sons of the soil' stress upon under-development as a consequence of lack of investment, and their critics, mainly from the more advanced regions of the country, dwell on the historic lack of enterprise and proverbial laziness of the Assamese. It does not seem to occur to either party that the two distinct positions are actually two sides of the same coin. This article proposes to bypass the either-or explanation of Central Neglect *vs.* Regional Plunder as the cause of under-development of the region. The two are shown as systematically related. But the system does work against the true interest of the autochthones.

Whatever the success or failure of the economies of the so-called 'Asian Tigers' like South Korea and Thailand, they have at least exploded the age-old myth that an inherited 'national character' accounts for a nation's economic success or failure. What is normally inherited, is a social system with an economic and a cultural component, and if either undergoes a major change, the other also follows suit. The people of the Hermit Kingdom and the proverbial easy-going, fun-loving Thais have now acquired qualities like enterprise and grit, thanks to the dynamism injected by foreign capital into the Thai economy.

Hence, there is little enlightenment to be gained by attributing

---

*Based on a talk given to Assamese students at University of Delhi in February 2000.

Assam's persistent backwardness to the Assamese 'national character'. Yet, it has also got to be admitted that certain cultural factors also contribute to the backwardness of Assam.

Actually, modern Assam is by and large a product of colonial rule and the colonial economic system. Colonization brought about certain major changes in the economy, laws and public administration, but also retained and encouraged certain elements of native society and culture. Leftist circles usually formulate the situation as 'colonial – semi-feudal'. For instance, it introduced modern industries like oil prospecting and drilling and modern means of transport and communication like railways and motorable roads. But the biggest colonial industry, tea, virtually retained feudal bondage instead of depending on free wage-labour. The inequities of the caste-system were kept undisturbed, so that as in feudal times, only people of 'noble ancestry and respectable families' were recruited for higher government posts. Indeed, quite a few brilliant candidates from tribes and lower castes were denied a place in the administration in spite of sound academic results and sterling performances in the tests.

The colonial system in Assam was a complex of several distinct sections (1) An 'enclave economy', dominated by the tea-industry; (2) Extractive enterprises that exploited the rich natural resources of the state, particularly timber; (3) Subsistence farming engaged in by the small and middle peasants, and absentee landlords under the *ryotwari* system, who depended on share-croppers or partially bonded labour, usually tribals and lower castes. These sections had minimum links with one another and none of them played a pivotal role in transforming the economy and social system. For instance, tea-plantations required a huge supply of various goods, from implements to building materials and provisions for labour, but local people were not encouraged to produce and provide them. Orders were placed outside Assam and Marwari merchants served as middlemen for bulk supplies. According to the *District Gazetteer* brought out at intervals by the colonial administration, the requirements of the tea industry did play a part in improving the lot of the farmer in upper Assam up to the first two decades of the twentieth century, but eventually, the growth levelled off and Marwari merchants began to supply provisions like rice, *dal*, and mustard oil, etc., purchased outside the state to the tea-gardens.

A consistent policy of state intervention is required not only for the development of a socialist economy but also for the growth of a self-sustained capitalist economy. South Korea, Taiwan, and earlier even Japan, are glaring examples to prove that point. But the colonial administration were primarily and overwhelmingly interested in colonial enterprise in the form of various 'managing agencies' running a variety of industries and business including tea-gardens, procurement and supply of timber, other extractive industries, etc. Development of the native population had a low priority in this scheme of things. They were to be subjected to both force and persuasion so that they did not rock the boat. Promising centres of native commercial enterprise like Barpeta, which thrived up to first decade of the twentieth century, ultimately declined, as there were few outlets for the capital accumulated there. In fact, colonial industry and commerce, deliberately restricted the channels where native entrepreneurs might have put to use their resources and skill. Land, as a source of semi-fedual rent was the only safe harbour for the savings of the 'respectable' Assamese. There were a few Assamese tea-gardens, but they were entirely in the shadow of the major British tea companies, which controlled marketing through monopoly distributing firms.

Enterprise was positively discouraged in such a socio-economic environment. There, leadership of native society passed during the British rule to the educated middle-class, composed of government servants, rent-sucking landlords, small traders and a few planters and minor tea-employees, not to speak of troops of ill-paid lawyers subsisting on land-disputes provoked by colonial land-law marginalizing community intervention. This entire middle class failed to develop a spirit of productive enterprise under these circumstances. From time to time, there were stirring clarion-calls to the educated Assamese from prophetic voices in the pages of middle class magazines like *Jonaki*, *Banhi* and *Awahon*, but alas! Those prophets spoke only of profiting from its limited spin-offs. Unfortunately, even there, the far more active, advanced and stronger merchant capital of Marwaris severely restricted the scope for Assamese achievement.

This is the economic framework that Assam inherited from colonial times at the dawn of Independence. Its inherent and fundamental weakness was felt by the people of Assam, but they had no clue to it theoretically (the economics of development itself had been in its infancy in the whole country. The first chief minister of Assam after Independence, had a passionate interest in development issues, as seen in records of his discussions during his prison-term in the 1940s.

But it does not suggest that he too had a properly worked-out strategy of development. When his life was cut short soon after Independence, there was none to don his mantle. The succeeding chief ministers, veteran freedom fighters and Gandhians were charismatic popular leaders, but they neither had a concrete, nor a far-sighted vision of the state's economic future, nor a team of capable experts whom they could rely on, to impart the momentum for self-sustained growth of the state's economy.

For decades after Independence too, such a vision did not materialize, to say nothing of concrete plans. The people, frustrated by mounting (educated) unemployment, demanded central intervention for industrialization through a number of unique movements (e.g. the 'Refinery movements' that demanded local industrial developments on the basis of local resources which used to be siphoned off). But again, there was no general perspective and integrated thinking for economic development of the state.

The educated middle class failed to provide leadership to a movement for overall industrial development of the state for various reasons. By virtue of its leading role in the freedom movement, the middle class inherited the administration of the state (earlier called 'province'). But the tea industry passed from British hands into the hands of big Indian business houses and Marwari merchants. In spite of the fact that many Assamese managers can claim extensive and acute knowledge and understanding of the production of tea, few or none get selected as superintendents and managing directors.

The tea industry is yet to play a pivotal role in the economic reconstruction of the state, more than a hundred years after its establishment.

Oil has been a little more help in the recent decades, offering help and patronage to local contractors and transporters, and providing jobs to technical hands, engineers, and fourth-grade staff. But its colonial role had not undergone any change, and its impact on the rest of the state's economy is still marginal. No one has built a theoretical model, where oil has a major role for economic development of the state.

The state has benefited marginally from numerous central (either centrally directed or administered by the state) schemes for small industries and crafts. But their success has been sporadic. Primarily because, in drawing up such schemes, local initiative is always discounted. Central schemes have no room for local conditions or active local participation. The people are regarded as passive vehicles, rather than active agents of change affecting their own lives. The set-up remains in a sense, colonial.

The State Government also formed scores of corporations with a view to fostering development. They now wallow in losses amounting to several thousand crores, with no hope of recovery. Significantly, their use has been mostly political, with discarded, yet dangerous politicians serving as chairmen, and employment overwhelming production as its primary end. Such corporations could thus, hardly free the people from the shackles of age old underdevelopment. They too, have succumbed to the colonial syndrome.

This is not to say that any hope of change in this dismal scenario must be ruled out. But that will require a change in the mindset of the educated middle class that still enjoys ideological and political supremacy in the state. There are large numbers of trained engineers and technicians in this dominant middle class. But few of them expect to be called upon to help build the economic future of the state. Most of them seem to have formed an unholy nexus with politicians and contractors to plunder the funds that are made available to the state government for development. They milk the corporations dry, leave the virgin forests denuded, and the finances of the state, burdened with debts. A parasite like attitude, rather than productive one, has become the principal of their existence and their historic mission. Enterprise, skills, the drive to achieve, are all casualties of this process.

This is a vicious circle, and even though it is possible to break it, a most determined effort by a new kind of leadership alone, can guide the middle class back from the path of plunder, waste and self-aggrandizement, and prevent the surge of frustration and extremist violence among the poor and the oppressed.

CHAPTER 9

Unwitting Accomplices: States as Agents of Inequality

DIPANKAR SENGUPTA

INTRODUCTION

For many observers, one of the most glaring failures of India's economic management, has been the widespread regional inequality that shows no signs of abating.[1] This is in stark contrast to what has been experienced in the USA, Europe and Japan.[2] From this undisputed fact, accusations of gross economic neglect, even charges of siphoning funds (especially from states with rich natural resources) to the benefit of the richer states, can never be far away. Indeed, the populations of poor states that wallow in poverty, suffer low self-esteem at the sight of states that increasingly become richer in these times of globalization and draw the attention of the likes of Bill Gates and Bill Clinton. Questions as to how this state of affairs has come about, therefore, become inevitable. The answers to all the variants, are without exception, disquieting.

There are various answers to this question. I too, have one. The aim of this paper is to establish that the model of development aimed at maximizing a long-term growth rate or alternatively minimizing the time required to acquire a certain industrial structure with the aid of industrialization inevitably meant that inequality, both personal and regional, would arise. The manner in which this strategy was sought to be implemented, i.e. through a system of licences and permits, meant that states not in the ambit of the Central Government's immediate attention could not do much to foster growth on their own, even by mobilizing their own savings. Ironically, no chief minister, or for that matter any politician of note (except the late C. Rajagopalachari) objected to this model of development or the subsequent legislation ensuring the huge concentration and arbitrary use of economic power in the hands of the Central Government. Indeed, these features of economic policy were considered socialist and with the exception of the Swatantra Party (and perhaps the Bharatiya Jana Sangh), all political formations (at least on paper) claimed socialism as their ideology.[3] The result was an increasingly uneven economic growth where palliatives like 'factoring in of regional inequality into the plan objectives' had little impact. One also argues that many states did not help themselves by their own policies. By neglecting agriculture and focusing on industry, as well as by following populist policies, they laid the foundations of their own stagnation, or indeed a low level equilibrium from which there seems to be no escape, far less take advantage of a liberalized economy which is opening up to the prospects of international trade.

The paper is organized as follows. In Section I, we discuss the strategy of development, specifically the Mahalanobis Model (MM), followed by the political leadership after Independence and discuss the reasons for adopting such a strategy. In Section II, we try to show how regional inequality was the inevitable consequence of the strategy of development pursued. In Section III, we discuss how the licence-permit *raj* (which was imposed to implement the strategy) also seriously inhibited the scope of autonomous action by the states. We discuss whether such a regime was necessary to implement the strategy decided upon. In Section IV, we discuss how the MM could have worked in a market economy rid of controls in the form of licences. We also discuss whether it is possible (or indeed necessary) to incorporate a regional inequality constraint in such a growth strategy and whether inequality could have been reduced, had such a constraint been built in. In Section V, we discuss the prospects of the poorer states in an era where the economic regime has been liberalized and the economy thrown open to competition, and the steps that they can take to avail of the advantages of the new regime.

I. THE MAHALANOBIS MODEL

The model of development followed by India's policy makers after Independence has been described with a certain degree of accuracy as an Import-Substituting Industrialization (ISI) development model. The theoretical underpinnings of this model, as laid down by the

MM[4] stressed on maximizing long-term growth and attaining a self-sustaining, economically independent industrial structure (in contrast to the myopic objective maximizing the present level of national income). This was to be achieved by heavy initial investments in basic industries (in contrast to developing light industries and agriculture, sectors where India's comparative advantage lay).

The economic logic behind such models (known in economic parlance as turnpike models) is the following. If an economy wants to *minimize* the *time* required to reach a certain level of income or capital stock[5] (as opposed to the objective of maximizing current national income) then the investment strategy calls for initial concentration of investment in the (capital intensive) capital goods industry. The concentration in (labour intensive) consumption goods industry is low initially and rises only in the later stages of planning. The initial output of the capital goods sector is by and large, even more capital goods for the capital goods sector. Only later, is the accumulated capacity in the capital goods sector diverted to produce capital goods for the consumer goods industry. This shift is delayed even more if the target income to be reached is more ambitious. Theoretically, such models exhibit slow initial growth that rise overtime and does so dramatically, in the terminal stages of the planning process. The initial, sluggish growth rates are the results of investment in a sector with high capital output ratios. However, as this entire sector slowly, but increasingly, starts to support the less capital-intensive consumer goods sector, growth rates start to rise.

Modern industry is characterized by the economies of scale. Therefore, for investments to be viable, they must be above a given scale. Thus, for a less developed country with scarce resources (such as India surely was at the time of Independence) it makes sense to concentrate only on a few sectors so that the plants and factories set up were of optimal size. India, given her goal of self-sufficiency decided instead, to develop and invest in all sectors of the economy. Given her scarce resources, this meant a whole lot of plants with inoptimal scales in all sectors of the economy. As a result of this spreading of scarce investment resources in an inoptimal manner, India became a high cost economy, one that could survive only behind high tariff walls. As tariffs were set up to protect industry, the Terms of Trade turned against agriculture. Exports either as an instrument to boost growth or as one to pay for your imports was not pursued vigorously.

As a result, India's share of exports in total World Trade fell from 2 per cent at the time of Independence to 0.4 per cent in the 1990s.

The MM was sought to be followed/implemented by a policy of direct state investment into the desired areas, combined with a complicated system of discretionary controls (which came to be dubbed the licence-permit *raj*).

The question that arises is, why did the national leadership turn to the MM as its model for development? Specifically, what prompted the Indian leadership to go into all industries ignoring the considerations of optimal scales? And lastly, why was the export sector largely ignored? Why was a policy of controls, rather than a tax-cum-subsidy policy, chosen to implement this plan?

There are a host of reasons for the above. At the time of Independence, almost all leaders felt that the existing economic and political order of the day was biased against the erstwhile colonized countries. The West (then just in the process of disbanding their empires) had reduced its colonies (some of them once proud manufacturing economies) into 'drawers of water and hewers of wood'. Now deindustrialized, their economies subsisted by supplying raw materials to the colonizing powers. In return for the exports of raw materials, they imported manufactures. As if this were not bad enough, the terms of trade against primary products, *vis-à-vis* manufactured goods, were thought to be in a process of secular decline.[6] So, with time, a given bundle of primary goods would buy less of manufactured goods, implying in effect that given their present structure, the erstwhile colonies could increase productivity and yet not enjoy the fruits of growth. At best, it implied that a Less Developed Economy that adopted an export-led growth strategy based on the export of primary products would never be able to catch up with the developed countries as even its growth rate would be lower.[7]

From this it followed, that if the erstwhile colonies had to grow, they had to change the structure of their economies. That is, from an economy that produced largely primary goods, they had to develop a manufacturing base as well. Given the declining economies of scale in agriculture, the only hope of sustained growth lay in transforming the economy into a manufacturing economy producing goods with high income elasticities of demand. Even agriculture would be helped by such a transformation as the prime ingredients for productivity growth in agriculture, were products of research of an industrial economy.

Lastly, economic independence in itself, was a value that the national leadership cherished. Economic independence would give India freedom from pressures from either bloc and enable her to take up positions internationally, that would have not been possible otherwise. It enabled India to aspire for leadership among third world countries by taking up issues dear to them (like de-colonization of Africa in the late 1950s and early 1960s, the Anglo-French seizure of the Suez, the movement against apartheid in the 1980s) against the erstwhile colonizers. Furthermore, an economically independent and self-sufficient India would be able to insulate itself from external shocks.

As we have stated earlier, India chose to eschew considerations of comparative advantage. She was not interested in the myopic objective of maximizing present levels of national income. She was more interested in minimizing the time to acquire a self-sustaining economically independent industrial structure. All this called for heavy initial investment in the capital goods sector. Moreover, the aim of economic independence (in the guise of self-sufficiency) ensured spreading of scarce investible resources in all sectors with its implications for costs. To enable such a high cost industry to survive, high tariffs had to be imposed on exports. And keeping in mind the objective of establishing a socialistic pattern of society that most political formations of the day swore by, it was the state which undertook most of the planned investment. The residual investment was to be controlled by a system of licences and permits, following the enactment of the Industries Development and Regulation Act (IDRA) of 1951. The aim of this regime was to ensure that while minimizing the time required to attain a particular economic structure, the growth of the domestic capitalist class was controlled, and as far as possible, progressively marginalized as the economy grew.[8]

This array of objectives which included long-term growth, a socialistic pattern of society, the fostering of national power and independence, could only be served by a theoretical model such as the MM that on paper had the potential to do all this. Considerations of regional inequality or any other inequality were never given serious thought. As profits from the state-owned enterprises were to be socialised anyway (for further investment) this was one aspect that did not apparently bother the planners, at least, not initially. In the long run, the rate of accumulation and its inevitable spread would ensure that all parts of the country would be enveloped in the process of economic growth.

II. THE REGIONAL IMPLICATIONS OF THE MAHALANOBIS MODEL

The adoption of the MM and the manner in which it was implemented, had its implications for economic inequality. The fact that a policy of heavy industrialization was chosen, meant that investment per worker in the concerned industries would be high. Thus, very few (well-paid) people would be employed, meaning that increases in income would accrue to very few. This meant a greater degree of inequality than what an investment, based on comparative advantage (in India's case – abundant labour) would have implied.

Secondly as this high-wage employment was more regionally concentrated than the results of the latter strategy would have been, regional inequality also rose. As the Central Government set up industries in those regions possessing raw materials required for heavy industry or those that already possessed an industrial base, other regions were at a disadvantage. Indeed, the adoption of the MM meant that it could not be otherwise. Investment in the steel industry meant that these industries had to be set up in areas that had access to minerals like coal, iron-ore, manganese, etc. Machine tool industries also, could not be set up in remote areas merely for the sake of regional equity. They had to be set up in areas well served by railroads and at distances not too great from their markets and sources of raw materials. Thus, in so far as the MM directed investment towards greenfield sites that had hitherto seen no industrial development during British rule, it was because of economic considerations, viz., the exploitation of plentiful mineral resources, not considerations, of regional redistribution.[9] Given the objectives of the model, this policy was a sensible one.

We have already said that the planners, instead of concentrating resources on a few sectors and taking advantage of the economies of scale, decided to spread resources at their disposal into several sectors with self-sufficiency as their objective. As a result of in-optimal scales, the costs of production rose, transforming Indian industry into a high-cost industry. To protect this industry, India had to impose high tariffs on industrial imports. As high tariffs were taken recourse to, agriculture was discriminated against, as the price farmers now paid for industrial goods became higher because of the terms of trade effect. Thus, apart from sectoral inequality, regional inequality would have also been adversely affected as some states are more dependent on agriculture than others.

Could the poorer states have expected growth to trickle down as a result of sustained growth? This is unlikely. First of all, given the MM's stress on initial heavy investment in capital goods and basic goods, it becomes clear that the industries that such sectors stimulate, did not exist in most poor states. Industries likely to receive increased orders as a consequence of state investment in capital goods industries as well as basic goods sector would be specialized engineering and construction. Such services are likely to have been imported, or were supplied by companies located in the industrial states to begin with.

It becomes clear that states that had no mineral wealth, did not generally receive significant Central Government investment. This is not to say that mineral wealth was the key to success. For one, mines and minerals being largely in the Central Government's domain, states which had only mineral wealth to begin with did not benefit (except for an increase in employment of the residents of the states in the mines). The rest of the state's economy (if it had no industry to begin with) was not greatly benefited by any sort of linkage.

The output of the basic and capital goods sector went to other industries which were by and large, located in those states which already had an industrial base even under British rule. Indeed, this was precisely what the MM was designed to do, i.e. supply the consumption goods sector (as well as the capital goods sector itself) with basic inputs for their continued growth.

Thus, the demand-creating effects of the MM, as well as its supply effects benefited a handful of industrial centres. Economic interaction and exchange, therefore, remained restricted to these centres. The periphery was left out of the growth process.

III. THE CONSEQUENCES OF THE LICENCE-PERMIT *RAJ*

Faced with Central Government neglect in the form of industrial investment, states that did not historically possess an industrial base, could have marshalled their meagre financial resources in exploiting their own natural resources. However, as the Central Government monopolized even the issue of licences (ironically to bring in socialism by marginalizing the domestic bourgeoisie), the possibility of fostering local entrepreneurship or individual action by entrepreneurs (in states which were not the beneficiaries of Central Government investment) leading to growth also became extremely difficult. Thus, apart from good governance, it seemed the *willingness* and *ability* to lobby on behalf of local businessmen to procure licences was also required for states to grow.

However, as things turned out, in line with Stigler's[10] contention, established industrialists invariably cornered most of the licences, in effect ending up controlling the very institution that was set up to control them and curb their monopoly. Thus, a state with an industrial base, where established business houses were most likely to be based was more likely to receive a licence to set up an industrial plant, than a non-industrialized state.

Did the Mahalanobis Model Imply a Licensing Raj?

Did the MM imply the licensing *raj*? Did the implementation of the required investment programme require physical controls over the volume and direction of overall investment activity? This question is easily answered. It was not. According to traditional economic theory, a tax-cum-subsidy policy can determine both the volume of investment as well as its direction. In fact, economic theory in general does not discuss physical controls other than quotas in Trade theory. Even then, the general result obtained is that tariffs (taxes) are better than quotas.

Could the centre have used the licence system to promote regional growth? Again, there is no reason as to why the use of conventional methods, as suggested by economic theories like tax-holidays and subsidies would not have done as well.

In fact, even those who subscribe to the MM will be hard put to support the use of licencing to implement the plan. Licencing as a tool, was used in order to make economic growth in India an exclusive process. Although nominally a democracy, the state ensured that economic growth (in so far as industry was concerned) remained non-participatory and was open to a few favoured businessmen.

It is interesting to note that when the licencing procedure was liberalized in the 1980s, one beneficiary was Nirma, that used labour-intensive techniques to make detergents that ate into niches hitherto occupied ironically, by Hindustan Lever, a Multi-National Corporation (MNC) long unchallenged, because of the license *raj*. The region that benefited was a rural and tribal area of Gujarat. It might have been a poorer state, had their attitudes not been conducive to enterprise.

It can be argued, however, that the above example represents a latter-day case when the MM for intents and purposes was on the verge of being aborted. Had the economic programme being followed still been the MM, delicensing would have done little to spread growth. We answer this question in the next section.

IV. THE MAHALANOBIS MODEL IN A MARKET ECONOMY

Would the MM have worked out differently in a market economy without the device of licencing? Would its implications for regional inequality been different? And lastly, was the MM, optimally designed to fulfil its own targets? The answers to these questions are interrelated and provide explanations to some basic issues on regional inequality, including the question of incorporating a regional inequality constraint in the MM.

Would the MM have worked differently in a regime that (as per conventional economic theory) utilized tax-cum-subsidies to direct investment in the direction of the plan, rather than use the devices of licences and permits? The answer is that it would.[11] This is because according to the original plan, whenever a sector under-performed, given that its output were necessary inputs for other industries, production had to be curtailed, or rationing had to be resorted to. In a market regime, prices of the commodity in short supply would have risen, attracting investment and inducing output responses. Indeed, in the 1980s, cement, once a commodity under rationing started to become readily available in the open market once the licences were readily dispersed. It may be questioned whether this increased demand for investment by this sector itself, would not deprive other industries of investible resources or put pressure on the balance of payments.

Here, the MM's inoptimal use of the resources available to the country becomes apparent. India's vast labour force (of which a significant portion is only partially employed) as well as her comparative advantages in agriculture and light industries such as textiles and jute were not sought to be utilized by the MM to supplement investment. Using these relatively under-utilized sectors with very little capital, the rest of the world might well have been a vent for surplus for India's products.[12] Thus, export revenues through the use of hitherto unutilized resources could have supplemented capital accumulation in the MM.

The 'vent for surplus' argument has its implications for economic inequality. Given the fact that India would have traded to take advantage of its differences with the rest of the world, this would have meant the exploitation of its abundant resources or resources peculiar to it. These were typically labour and geographical factors that conferred on her, a natural advantage in the production of labour-intensive goods and the cultivation of a wide variety of agricultural products. This meant that using labour and other factors to use the rest of the world as a vent for surplus (if only to supplement capital accumulation in the MM) would increase wages and incomes for labour. This would temper the heavily inequalising effects of the ISI. Secondly, those poor states that did not possess the required mineral wealth for industrial growth and were thus left to fend for themselves in the extremely inhibitive regime of ISI would also experience growth. To be sure, given the fact that sectors like textiles where India had an obvious comparative advantage, was also located by and large in the richer states, it may be argued that exports too, have benefited them more. However, there were also other sectors located in poorer states that had considerable export potential, e.g. tea. However, lack of investment in enhancing productivity and the inability of establishing Indian-owned brands of repute, ensured that this sector and the states growing tea stagnated. In any case, entrepreneurship aimed at utilizing whatever endowments India possessed was choked by the licence-*raj* that effectively ruled out even spontaneous developments which could have had demonstration effects throughout the economy.

Thus, even where regional inequality is concerned, a market economy would have done better even if the MM was being followed. What was required was a more positive approach to exports; not necessarily a programme of export-led growth. *Thus, it becomes clear, that there was no need to factor in regional-inequality considerations in the MM.*

An implementation approach that was tax-cum-subsidy based (instead of licences and permits) and was not averse to using exports to support the MM might have done as well.

Paths Not Taken

It is clear now, that in the absence of the licence *raj*, the poorer states would have not fared worse. What the regime *prevented* was a possibility whose demonstration effects could have been significant. Consider the following hypothetical development; a possible development of a successful horticultural sector based on exports of fruit to the rest of the world.[13] This is not a development that calls for massive investment or indeed an enormous leap in technological know-how. It does, however, call for the existence of roads and ports (which were not totally absent). In any case even the MM demanded some of these infrastructural facilities. What it *requires* mainly (and cannot be easily provided by local businessmen) is the availability of credit and facilities for collection of goods at certain nodal points and their subsequent air-shipment. What it *calls for* is organization and coordination, which should not be beyond the capability of a state government. If such a sector is built up largely by local business and entrepreneurs, the demonstration effect can be considerable and there is no reason why this cannot be repeated in other sectors. Indeed, given the establishment of a local business class of a critical minimum size, travelling up the technological ladder becomes easier, if not inevitable. For example, an owner of a cycle repair unit may graduate to actually assembling cycles and then building it. He could then diversify to mopeds, scooters, motorcycles and end up manufacturing cars. Similarly, in a state with forests, the timber merchant could diversify to plyboard and end up establishing a paper mill.

For poor states, industrialization itself was a mirage, forget about climbing the technological ladder. This is because our hypothetical trajectory of development assumes (among other things) the existence of a regime where restrictions are not in the form of licences and a state government is supportive of private enterprise. The former was not true, given the IDRA and the latter not true especially where the poorer states were concerned.

A Hypothetical Agriculture-led Growth Programme

Although states had considerable power to deal with agriculture, few of the poor states ever devoted substantial attention or resources to this sector. Indeed, the alternative policy of economic growth as suggested by Vakil and Brahmanand[14] that suggested the usage of under-utilized labour for capital formation was, and probably is ideal for all states with unemployed labour. This theory was based on the realistic assumption that much of the labour in rural India was idle, under-utilized or only seasonally unemployed. However, such labour did not starve because family members fed even those who were not gainfully employed. Employing such labour did not necessarily mean that that all the money in the form of wages paid to it would be spent on food, causing inflation. Indeed, as this investment was in the form of addition of physical capital like irrigation channels, dykes and small dams, etc., its impact on agriculture would likely to have been substantial. Thus, investment would have increased productivity in agriculture, liquidating the inflation it may have set into motion in the first place.[15]

Secondly, payment to labour need not have been in the form of cash. A promise/commitment to a piece of (what was formerly unimproved) land to which addition of physical capital will have increased productivity, could have also substituted (in part) for monetary payment. Indeed, such incentives could have dominated monetary payments.

It might be argued that land improvement schemes could have run into problems as this required coordinating very large numbers of small projects as large projects were being eschewed due to heavy expenditures that they would entail. Secondly, in those states where land was scarce, land improvement schemes would increase tensions over the ownership of hitherto unclaimed land and water rights.

One way of dealing with the problem is to have local self-governing units, given the powers as well as the resources to resolve such problems. Mobilizing labour teams, especially when the average size of such teams is not likely to be large is best done locally. Similarly, problems that crop up due to disputes arising out of claims of ownership of once fallow and unimproved land is also best resolved locally. However, this calls for effective local self-government, which is possible only when the state government devolves power and resources to the districts and the villages. Most states, especially poor ones have shown a marked reluctance to share power with other institutions. While insisting that the Centre embark on a decentralizing exercise, they insist that the downward/outward movement of power stop at the state capitals. Even regional parties are not different in this regard.

Along with the use of the indigenous resource to improve agriculture, specifically those sectors where the state had a natural advantage due to geographical reasons, investment in focused research and development aimed at improving these sectors was also called for. This hardly ever happened except in the Punjab, where Partap Singh Kairon, not particularly known for his intellectualism or socialist leanings was actively involved in the setting up of the Punjab Agricultural University, whose efforts at improving crop yields are well known.

From a vibrant agriculture catering to the domestic market, to one that also exports is a short and eminently manageable step. The state, after improving productivity, now takes advantage of better prices. Thus, the rise in incomes that take place are not just a result of capital-widening and productivity increases, but is also due to price rises. If exports are handled by local businessmen, then the states's economy gains on account of the increasing expertise of its businessmen, which is not just due to increased knowledge of export market conditions, but also because of the fact that they are now acquainted with how business is conducted in extremely competitive conditions which prevail abroad. This is an intangible but extremely essential quality/gain, without which a movement up the technological ladder becomes impossible when the growth potential of agriculture declines, as it inevitably must.

Unwitting Accomplices

As we have already stated, the ISI left the states with very little leeway to foster economic growth. The adoption of the MM implied that heavy industries (specifically capital goods) requiring large amounts of capital be set up. Given the preferred pattern of ownership (state-owned) this meant that a smaller proportion of the total resources that the Centre could raise would go to the states. And given the fact that the tools employed to direct investment according to the MM were licences and permits doled out by the Centre, the power of the states to attract investment was severely circumscribed. The states thus were at a disadvantage both financially as well as administratively.

The only sector that the states could develop largely unhindered, was agriculture. And indeed, it was also in this sector that India's comparative advantage lay. Thus, if the states (especially those with no industry) were to grow, it would have to be agriculture. This is a sector where employment created requires long hours of physical labour. However, the class that occupied office in the state governments in post-Independent India came from the middle-class. The influence of the middle-class on such politicians was out of proportion to their actual population. Jobs that called for long hours of physical labour was not the kind of employment the educated unemployed youth was looking for. They wanted white collar jobs.

The states invariably buckled in to middle-class pressure. Employment was artificially created by sanctioning extra positions in the government and state-owned corporations. Thus, from its revenues (already limited to begin with) even less would be left over for investment, after current expenses were met. As this process continued, the salary bill of many state governments outstripped their revenues, leaving nothing for investment in any sector. While industrial units were also created, they wasted no time in becoming white elephants.[16]

Electoral populism also took its toll when reckless promises to provide electricity free of cost were made and kept. As the State Electricity Boards (SEB) became increasingly constrained financially, investment in capacity addition and later even maintenance, declined. Power generation and efficiency of transmission suffered, which affected industry.[17] Thus, 1991 found the poorer states with inadequate infrastructure, an agriculture still served by traditional methods and without an entrepreneurial class. The blame for this state of affairs in all fairness, belonged to both the states as well as the Centre.

Lessons not Learnt: The Common Mindset

Most political formations did not accept the fact that the MM, by its very nature, called for increasing inequality, both regional and sectoral (at least in the initial stages). If they did, they considered it a short-term phenomenon curable by appropriate policies. Their outlook for the greater part was to look for large projects to pull them out of poverty.

They never looked at agriculture as a sector that could lead to or initiate growth. In keeping with the times, when agriculture was ignored and *small* invited derision, there was no attempt to foster growth in agriculture (where there was some administrative lee-way: no licences were required) by investing in technological upgradation and spreading of these skills by the poorer states. There was no attempt to utilize local idle labour that existed into building capital by way of minor irrigation projects like canal building. This no doubt required effective local government like panchayats and the states like the Central Government did not want devolution of power. This attitude did not change fundamentally even when regional parties came to power protesting against the central government's monopolization of political and economic power. All states, poorer ones included, thought big and relied on big projects to transform their states economically.

There was no attempt to foster local entrepreneurship by encouraging local people to go into business by opening small factories. This, while not to be condoned, was understandable. To encourage local businesses would mean wresting a large number of licences from Delhi for an aggregate sum of investment that would probably be less than one large project financed by an established business house. Given the complexity of the licencing procedure, wrestling with the bureaucrats in Delhi time and time again as atomistic businessmen in their numbers kept on applying, would be a thankless task. Secondly and most importantly, given the socialist outlook of political life in most of the poorer states, entrepreneurship of any kind was not explicitly encouraged in any case (making the first reason totally hypothetical).[18] Ironically, private investment when sought (because Central Government investment was not forthcoming and the state did not have sufficient resources to do the job) came from big business based outside the state. This contradiction between ideology and practice was ignored and did not draw comment from academia either.

At the end of the day, the Central Government's monopoly over the issue of industrial licences and permits remained unchallenged. This was primarily the result of a shared mindset. Development policy was seen to be an exclusive process where only the state would decide on who would participate and to what degree.

This was not to say that the poorer states were totally averse to dealing with private capital. Indeed, Indian corporate houses had a substantial stake in the few going concerns in the poorer states and their relations with the state governments in power was sufficiently cordial for them to maintain their presence in that state. This was generally true, regardless of which party came to power in the state. However, this attitude was singularly non-existent when it came to creating conditions where local businesses could grow and prosper.

It is ironic that the effect of ideology for most of these poor states fell not on big business domiciled elsewhere, but killed the possibility of a flourishing local business class. But this is hardly surprising. Big business has the money power to temper radicalism either through bribes or through threats to close down their factories with its implications for employment and revenues. A class that is nascent or non-existent, does not enjoy this luxury.

The mindset of regional politicians was not very different from that of the planners and the plan implementers of the Central Government. Even those who would later call for autonomy as a measure to deal with regional inequality or stagnation, shared the mindset. What they called for was a transfer of power, economic and political from Delhi to the state capitals. What was not on the cards was a subsequent transfer of authority to the districts and the villages. Nor was a curb on the state's authority to regulate business by issuing licences considered. Indeed, the record of the poor states in investing in education and other social services is abysmal. As to how states that could not implement the limited responsibilities given to them should be entrusted with greater powers is not a question that has been satisfactorily answered.

However, when states left behind in the development process started to protest their growing poverty and neglect, they did not question the MM *per se*. At most, what they spoke about was to incorporate programmes to temper the effects on the regional inequality that the MM necessarily had, or better still that the Central Government hand over a larger share of revenues to the states. The MM with its accent on heavy industry was still sacrosanct; the licence-permit *raj*, still a guarantor of the socialist path of development (except for C. Rajagopalachari and his Swatantra Party) and investment by the state, the only way out of poverty.

To be fair to regional politicians, even economists trained in neoclassical economics where licences have no rationale, did not question policy and hardly ever advanced rigorous arguments in favour of it. They issued nebulous statements in its defence only after it was in the process of being discarded.

The Crisis of the 1960s

In the mid-1960s, the economy ran into trouble due to severe Balance of Payments (BOP) problems and food shortages caused by droughts. In a manner of speaking, this crisis was written into the MM. The model, by design had laid stress on building up a capital goods sector. For a developing economy, such a sector could only be built by importing capital goods as given the sophisticated nature of the industry, the under-developed domestic industrial sector could hardly supply the bulk of the necessary inputs. In a regime which neglected exports (and in fact militated against it) this could only imply a growing and continued trade deficit that would manifest itself on a later date as a BOP crisis.

Similarly, the relative neglect of agriculture and irrigation (given its size in terms of share of output and especially employment) meant that successive droughts (an eminently possible contingency) would push the economy to the wall as food supply would be affected. This was more so as prior to the Green Revolution, India was not a notable food surplus nation. The plan did not provide for failure in a sector that it neglected to begin with but one whose consistent performance was a key to its success.[19] As it turned out, the plan had assumed too much. The droughts of the mid-1960s caused massive food shortages which implied that food had to be imported. This sudden rise in imports without a commensurate rise in exports ushered in the BOP crisis of 1966.

The initial steps to deal with the crisis were textbook measures. The rupee was devalued by a third, the logic being that such a step would promote exports and push down imports. However, this was a neo-classical medicine for an economy that was guided largely by policies rather than market signals. Moreover, to expect an economy that had an inward (if not an autarkic) orientation to increase exports dramatically just because of a large devaluation, was unrealistic. As was to be expected, such a policy did not work. It led instead, to high inflation and contributed in no small measure to the Congress' poor showing in the 1967 Lok Sabha and State Assembly elections.

Such price-led policies were soon abandoned and alternative steps taken to resolve the crisis. On the agricultural front, food production was sought to be boosted by the introduction of High Yield Variety (HYV) seeds developed by Norman Borlaug and his associates. This was a quick-fix solution to the problem of lack of agricultural surplus. The success of such seeds depended critically on the availability of certain complementary inputs like synthetic fertilizers and a regular supply of water. While the first set of inputs could be supplied anywhere, the second factor ensured that this policy be tried out in only those areas that were well-irrigated by a system of canals. Thus, almost by default the states of Punjab, Haryana, parts of western UP and parts of north Rajasthan were the beneficiaries of this new policy. What helped of course, was that the initial HYV seeds were that of wheat. However, when new strains were developed for rice, it was again these states that benefited, as the required complementary input of regular water supply, were met only by these regions. Thus, the poorer states that had been neglected by the MM were also bypassed by the Green Revolution. This would not have been the case had they concentrated on agriculture, especially irrigation. Indeed, as several studies have shown, tube well irrigation in West Bengal which rose rapidly after devolution of power to the Gram Panchayats, had a dramatic impact on agricultural growth[20] as it ensured regular water supply needed for the application of HYV seeds.

Even when exports were sought to be promoted, in so far as these exports were manufactures, they came from the industrialized states. Economic growth and development remained non-participatory as the licence-permit *raj* remained in place.

Thus, planning in India had a curious, if perverse effect on regional inequality. The implementation of the MM laid the foundations for increased inequality. When policies were enacted to deal with the problems of BOP deficits and food shortages that arose from the implementation of the MM, their effect was to push up incomes in sectors of the richer states even further. The poorer states were completely left out both in the making of the MM as well as in its unmaking.

The reforms of 1991 are, however, fundamentally different from the ones taken below. While previous reforms tinkered with the existing system, making them incrementally liberal, which implied that a few more businessmen were lucky with their requests for setting up an industry than previously, the reforms of 1991 overhauled the IDRA completely. Licencing was effectively abolished. The devaluations undertaken that year as well as the policy-shifts that commenced in 1991, irrevocably laid the foundations of a market-driven economy that viewed the rest of the world as a market as well as a source of investment. It soon became clear that as the opposition parties fell in line with the basic tenets of the liberalization programme that these reforms were irreversible, unlike the ones undertaken in 1966. The earlier skepticism about global markets was thrown to the winds while Indian industry was urged to be competitive, to export and to compete with imports.

V. REGIONAL INEQUALITY IN A GLOBALIZING ECONOMY

What does India's increasing openness hold for regional inequality, especially given the fact that India has done away with the licence permit system? Given our arguments, regional inequality should come down and the income of labour-abundant poor states as well as natural resource rich states should rise, as private agents rush in to take advantage of these factors. So far, this has not happened.[21] The aim of this section is to answer why this is so and whether economic stagnation can be brought to an end and foundations laid for sustainable growth.

It is our contention, that the poorer states have not been able to take advantage of the liberalized economic regime because of the following: inadequate infrastructure, a polity and a state government that does not know how to cohabit with businessmen and the lack of a local entrepreneurial class. In contrast, if we take a look at the states who have done especially well in the post-liberalization era, they generally turn out to be those with a more or less reasonable level of infrastructure, a state government and a polity that is comfortable with business and the presence of a local entrepreneurial class. They are also states who did well in the previous regime, i.e. Maharashtra. Of course, there are now other entrants in the list of performers.

The role of infrastructure in development is well known. States that did well before liberalization were obviously ones who at least maintained the infrastructure at reasonable standards. This is because without a minimum level of infrastructure, no industrial activity is possible. For the poorer states with little industry, there was no lobby interested in ensuring that infrastructure would be a minimum standard. Furthermore, an additional constraint operated on the states given their meagre resources. Secondly, in contrast to the governments in the richer states who had who had more experience in dealing with businessmen and investors, the poorer states knew very little about how to draw in investment. Their previous experiences were restricted to dealing with a handful of business houses concentrated in a few sectors. The richer states, as we have mentioned earlier, had lobbied alongside businessmen for licences and other benefits. The experience thus gained, placed them at an advantage vis-à-vis the poorer states. This existing working relationship made richer states look more attractive and safe for investors, while better infrastructural facilities added to this attraction. Unlike in the poorer states, radical slogans aimed at obtaining political support by targetting the business class was not common.

Thirdly, the existence of a local entrepreneurial class, who knew local conditions and knew exactly where local advantage and opportunities lay, *vis-à-vis* the rest of the world, ensured that there would be a section of investors with the means, ability and willingness to invest when the economy was liberalized. The poorer states had no corresponding counterpart to this class. The earlier regulatory regime and the attitude of the state governments to entrepreneurial activities had seen to it that such a class was stillborn.

It should be noted that the lack of capital in poor states has not been given pride of place in the list of factors explaining regional inequality. No doubt, capital is important. However, given the comparative advantage of the poorer states, it is not clear that massive investment is called for. Nor is it clear, that an infusion of massive amounts of capital would automatically translate into economic growth. What would be more useful, would be a number of small projects, each individually requiring small amounts of capital but backed by entrepreneurial skill, and state and infrastructural support. Capital can be borrowed on the basis of entrepreneurial reputation and project evaluation. The other qualities have to be developed and nurtured over decades. This is not something that has happened in the poorer states; partly because of the regulatory regime that existed prior to the economic reforms and partly because the state governments neglected to foster an indigenous entrepreneurial class in the narrow area of economic activity left out of the purview of the licencing regime. As a result, the poorer states find themselves singularly unable to take advantage of a liberalized economy as well as the communications revolution, to get onto a trajectory of growth.

A PLAN FOR GROWTH IN THE NEW ECONOMY

Given this baggage of poor infrastructure, lack of experience in attracting investment as well as the lack of a local entrepreneurial class, what can the poorer states do to take advantage of the new national as well as international economic regime?

It is clear that given the state of public finances of most Indian states, subsidies to attract investment, or investments in infrastructure, or investment in industrial units by the states is ruled out. The policies that are possible (and possibly even called for) are likely to be non-financial in nature.

Specifically, this implies that in the short run, policies should be aimed at:

(i) Developing those sectors of the economies whose demands on infrastructure are not high.
(ii) Encouraging the development of a class of local entrepreneurs who are active in such sectors.

The first policy calls for investments in those areas where production is possible with whatever resources are at hand. Such products are likely to be agricultural in nature. For example, floriculture could be one area that some of the poorer states could encourage. Existing infrastructure would most probably support such an endeavour. What the state could do is to organize the producers and help them to sort out transportation problems locally by setting up collection nodes, and internationally by organizing flights by cargo aircraft as and when required to ship away flowers. As we have said earlier, such problems are generally coordination and organization problems, whose financial implications (if properly handled) on the state government can be minimal. It could stand guarantor for businesses in this sector, thus helping them to borrow money. It arranges for the collection and dissemination of information, a task which has become cheap as well as easy in the aftermath of the telecommunications revolution. It can also, if the businessmen of the state so want, bargain on their behalf with international buyers and thus enable them to get a better price.

The state must make sure, that unlike the MM, its programme of intervention remains one that enables private agents to participate and does not exclude them from the growth process. An exclusive approach (that existed in India prior to 1991) serves no purpose and indeed does not allow the rest of the system to correct (at least in part) the shortcomings/errors of the State.

The second policy is somewhat more difficult and requires more imagination than the first. It is, none the less, essential. To depend exclusively on external entrepreneurial talent (who have little idea of local potential and difficulties) to bring in capital and set-up shop, can at best produce uncertain results. While investment from any source should almost always be welcomed, it is best to foster local talent. The question is, how to do it.

One of the first things that the government must do, is to send a signal to the residents of the state that the job of the government is not to provide employment to unemployed graduates. The state government must do everything possible to rid business as a profession of its perjorative connotations, especially regarding exploitation and dishonesty. Indeed, business as a viable career with potential for great rewards must be stressed by the state at the senior school and college levels, and appropriate training provided. As for problems of finance for these entrepreneurs, these may be significant, but not wholly insurmountable as the sectors being promoted are not likely to be capital-intensive.

In the longer run, the states must supplement these steps with public sector reforms aimed at bringing public finances back to the rails. This would imply bringing in line the size of the government with what is appropriate, with the services provided. Secondly, subsidies like free power must be done away with. Fortunately, it is now widely recognized that subsidies of this sort have a pernicious influence on the economy. Hopefully, the polity will find a way of doing away with this kind of populism in the near future and have enough money left over for education and infrastructure. Indeed, there is no better way of climbing up the technological ladder. The former supplies a work force capable of working in sectors that call for greater skills, the latter draws in investment from within and without the state.

On an administrative level, a strengthening of the local self-governments are called for. Much of the physical investment required, can be effected by mobilizing under-employed or seasonally employed labour and this is best done through institutions like the panchayats. Capital accumulation then becomes a faster and a less expensive process.

Given the fact that the MM has been effectively aborted, the states should ask for a bigger share of the revenue from the Centre. However, in so far as the investment once undertaken by the Centre is now being undertaken privately, the claims of the states will have to be adjusted accordingly. Administratively, the states have all the power required to carry out programmes aimed at bringing about economic development.

All this requires a mindset that is willing to devolve power and accepts that growth and development are best implemented by a participatory process. A regime that is deliberately exclusionary by design, is one that is by definition ruling out the possibility of the optimal utilization of all the skill that is available to the economy.

CONCLUSION

No serious observer of the Indian economy doubts that India is beset with grave, regional inequalities. The object of this paper was to show that the path of import-substituting industrialization, implemented with the help of quantitative measures like licences and permits dispensed by the Central Government was at least in part, responsible for it. The poorer states that were left behind in this dispensation, did not help themselves by neglecting sectors like agriculture which were in their purview. Nor did they show any interest in promoting a class of local entrepreneurs who could have exploited the admittedly narrow space unoccupied by the licence-permit *raj*. Their leaders, like the leaders at the Centre thought 'big' and set-up large industrial projects many of which became white elephants. They bowed to pressure from the middle class and created jobs by increasing government employment, in the process, diminishing their capacity to intervene effectively in the infrastructural and social sectors.

The result is that these states faced a new liberalized and open regime in 1991 without having the necessary factors to take advantage of the opportunities that were now available. It was again the rich states who took advantage of this new open economy. So ironically, the previous regulatory regime (helped in no small measure by the state governments of the poorer states) created certain grave shortcomings in the poorer states which inhibited growth even when the regulatory regime itself was overthrown.

Nonetheless, the liberalized open economy presents an opportunity to break with the past. It calls for a change in attitude and practices and the adoption of new values; specifically, it calls for giving entrepreneurship the respect it deserves and recognize that there is dignity in labour. It also calls for an end to self-defeating populism in the form of irrational subsidies and transfers.

However, this is an era where innovation in policy rather than financial muscle which will be the key player. Thus, what states do rather than how much they spend, will determine their future trajectories. Inequality like growth, will follow policy and not depend on Central Government handouts.

NOTES

1. See Sandwip Kumar Das and Alokesh Barua, 'Regional Inequalities, Economic Growth and Liberalization: A Study of the Indian Economy', *The Journal of Development Studies*, vol. 32, no. 3, 1996, pp. 364–90 and 'Structural Change, Economic Growth and Regional Disparity in the North-East: Regional and National Perspective', by Barua and Bandyopadhyay, Ch. 11.
2. See Robert Barro and Sala-i-Martin, *Economic Growth*, New York, McGraw-Hill, 1995, for a discussion of the experiences of these three regions.
3. Even well-known Right-wing members of the Congress like Morarjee Desai and S.K. Patil had to put up with the Congress's socialism such as it was. In fact, Desai was outmanoeuvered in 1969 when Mrs Gandhi played the economic radical card to the former's avowed conservatism on the Bank Nationalization issue.
4. See P.C. Mahalanobis, 'Some Observations on the Process of Growth of National Income', *Sankhya*, 12 (4), 1953.
5. Or, alternatively a specified vector of capital representing the desired level and composition of industries.
6. Following Raul Prebisch, *The Economic Development of Latin America and Its Principal Problems*, New York: Economic Commission for Latin America, UN Department for Economic Affairs, 1950, and Hans Singer, 'The Distribution of Gains between Investing and Borrowing Countries', *American Economic Review* (Papers and Proceedings), 1950, pp. 251–73.
7. See R. Dixon and A.P. Thirlwall, 'A Model of Regional Growth Differences on Kaldorian Lines', *Oxford Economic Papers*, July 1975.
8. We do not agree with the contention put forward by certain scholars that the MM as implemented by the Congress was actually a strategy aimed at helping the domestic capitalist class by increasing the profitability of their investment by investing in sectors such as heavy industries and infrastructure where profitability was low or called for heavy investment with long gestation periods. This is because investment in these sectors was expressedly reserved for the state and private sector *prohibited* from entering these sectors. Additionally, as we have already stated, private investment was also sought to be vigorously controlled in almost all sectors by the IDRA.
9. Although it is likely that such investments would cause regional inequality to fall temporarily before rising again as seen in A.K. Mathur, 'Regional Development and Income Disparities in India: A Sectoral Analysis', *Economic Development and Cultural Change*, vol. 31 (3), 1983, pp. 475–505. The analysis is carried out for the period 1950–75.
10. See George Stigler, *The Citizen and the State: Essays on Regulation*,

Chicago: University of Chicago Press, 1975. While they maintained their monopoly position in their respective fields, they were, however, generally prevented from competing with one another and limits were imposed on the quantum of investment made by them in any sector.
11. We assume that in a market economy, anybody, private agents as well as the State can set up industrial units. It must be noted that the MM does not make any assumptions regarding ownership of the means of production, i.e. the model is ownership neutral.
12. For a discussion on the Vent for Surplus Theory, see Adam Smith, *An Inquiry into the Nature and Causes of the Wealth of Nations, 1776*, London: Methuen, 1961, and Hla Myint, 'The Classical Theory' of International Trade and the Under-developed Countries', *Economic Journal*, June 1958.
13. Although the IDRA would have permitted the development of a horticultural sector, the logical subsequent step of value-addition in the form of food processing would have been severely circumscribed by legislation.
14. See C.N. Vakil and P.R. Brahmanand, *Planning for an Expanding Economy*, Bombay: Vora & Co., 1956. Also see Ragnar Nurkse, *Problems of Capital Formation in Underdeveloped Countries*, Oxford: Basil Blackwell, 1953.
15. For case studies on Ecuador and Mexico, see A. Bottomley, 'Keynesian Monetary Theory and Developing Countries', *Indian Economic Journal*, April–June 1965; and D. Jackson and H.A. Turner, 'How to Provide More Employment in a Labour-surplus Economy', *International Labour Review*, April 1973.
16. Ashok Paper Mills Co. Ltd. in Jogighopa, Goalpara district, Assam, is a case in point.
17. While richer states were also guilty of such populism, their larger resource base enabled them to add to infrastructure at regular intervals. Also, they were far more responsive to the needs of agriculture than the poorer states were.
18. Compare this to the role played by the political leadership of the states of Karnataka, Haryana and Punjab who actively encouraged local entrepreneurship and ensured that infrastructure needed for industrialization was in place. The result was a rapid growth of industry far above the national average. West Bengal, given the ruling coalition's attitude towards industry, experienced industrial stagnation. Similarly, Tamil Nadu, which was given to populist politics in the 1980s saw a marked fall in industrial growth after it did well in the 1970s. Maharashtra and Gujarat on account of their pro-business attitude maintained their positions although the textile industry, a very large component of industry in these states, became sick implying that industrial growth in other sectors had played a compensating role.

19. Agriculture was the 'bargain sector' from which unlimited food supplies could be had as large parts of this sector was untouched by modern technology. It was assumed that for this purpose relatively small investments would suffice *provided a certain minimum infrastructure* was in place. See S. Chakravarty, *Development Planning, The Indian Experience*, New Delhi: Oxford University Press, 1987.
20. L.K. Joshi, 'Irrigation and its Management in India, Need for a Parachigm Shift', http://www.iar.ube.ca/centres/cisan/joshi/j1.html.
21. See accompanying paper by Barua and Bandyopadhyay in this volume. Indeed, if China's experience is any indication, regional inequalities are likely to get much worse; see Fan Gang, Dwight Perkins and Lora Sabin, 'People's Republic of China: Economic Performance and Prospects', *Asian Development Report*, vol. 15, no. 2, 1997, pp. 43–85. However, China's inequality stems form the fact that the high performers (generally the coastal provinces) have grown very dramatically (approx. 8 per cent p.a.) since China opened up. The other provinces have experienced milder growth rates averaging over 4 per cent p.a. In India, the poorer provinces have not broken from the stagnation even after liberalization.

CHAPTER 10

Development Strategy and Regional Inequality in India

MANMOHAN AGARWAL AND
SUDIP RANJAN BASU

I. INTRODUCTION

The desire for equity has been one of the main motives driving Indian policy makers. Equity has been sought in many different dimensions, and one of these has been regional equity. Policy makers have sought to reduce regional inequality through the development strategy adopted, and the amount and criteria by which resources have been transferred from the centre to the states. But there could be serious gaps between what was sought to be achieved and what was actually achieved because of differences in the ability of the states to utilize the resources made available to them by the Centre.

One of the measures adopted was to provide various incentives for the establishment of industrial units in backward districts. At the time of Independence, Indian industry was almost entirely concentrated around three or four cities such as Calcutta, Bombay, Ahmedabad, Madras, etc. Today industry is much more widespread. Most states have an industrial base. Karnataka is famous for its software industry, Punjab for its small-scale industry in many sectors but particularly hosiery and small engineering, etc. Despite the spread of manufacturing to most states, the extent of differences in per capita incomes between the different states has not decreased, in fact it has increased. So the plans of the governments to reduce regional inequality have had very limited success.

---

*We are grateful to Prof. A.L. Nagar for his comments on the methodology and measurement issue of the Social Well-Being Index (SWBI).

The present paper attempts to study trends in state inequality over almost 40 years, from 1960–1 to 1996–7, both in terms of per capita state domestic product (Section II) and in terms of broader indicators of development, such as a Social Well-Being Index (SWBI) (Section III). The development strategies during the planning period, how these strategies sought to reduce regional inequality, how they evolved overtime and why the adopted strategies did not succeed are discussed in Section IV.

II. REGIONAL INEQUALITY: MAJOR INDIAN STATES

After 50 years of development, the richest states continue to be the richest and the poorest remain the poorest. Our data that covers nearly 40 years, shows that there has been little change in the ranking of the states in terms of the Per Capita State Domestic Product (PCSDP) over this period (Table 10.1). The richest states in 1960–1 – Punjab, Maharashtra, Gujarat, Tamil Nadu and West Bengal – continued to be the richest states in 1996–7 except for West Bengal that has slipped down the ladder. The poorest states in 1960–1 – Madhya Pradesh, Jammu & Kashmir, Uttar Pradesh, Orissa and Bihar continued to be the poorest in 1996–7.

The rank correlation of the states when they are ranked by per capita income is about 0.9 for any two consecutive plans and also 0.9 for the entire period (Table 10.2). Other indicators also point to a widening in regional income disparities. The Gini coefficient has shown a mild increase over the years, covered by the Third to the Eighth Plans (Table 10.3), though the increase is quite mild from 0.33 at the beginning of the Third Plan to 0.36 at the beginning of the Eighth Plan. There is also an increase in the coefficient of variation of per capita income among the states from 0.20 in 1960–1 to about 0.33 by the late seventies; after being stable during the 1980s, the coefficient increased strongly in the 1990s (Table 10.4). Furthermore, the ratio of per capita income in the richest states to that in the poorest states increased from 1.90 in 1960–1 to 4.75 in 1996–7. The increase was particularly rapid in the 1960s and 1970s. The ratio had reached 3.05 by 1978–9 (Table 10.5). The same pattern is followed by the ratio of income of the richest one-fifth to that of the second, third, and fourth poorest one-fifths. The ratio of the third and fourth-poorest, show some decline in the 1980s.[1]

TABLE 10.1: RANKING OF THE STATES BY PER CAPITA SDP

States/Year	1960–1	1967–8	1972–3	1978–9	1983–4	1990–1	1996–7
AP	8	9	10	10	8	7	7
AS	14	–	14	12	12	10	14
BI	13	15	16	16	16	16	16
GU	4	5	5	4	3	4	4
HR	–	2	2	2	4	2	3
HI	–	7	6	6	5	6	10
KA	6	6	8	7	6	9	6
KE	9	12	9	9	10	11	9
MP	10	13	15	14	14	13	12
MA	1	3	3	3	2	3	2
OR	12	14	13	15	13	15	15
PU	3	1	1	1	1	1	1
RA	7	8	11	8	11	12	11
TN	5	11	7	11	9	5	5
UP	11	10	12	13	15	14	13
WB	2	4	4	5	7	8	8

Notes: See Annex for Data Sources.
– data not available.

TABLE 10.2: RANK CORRELATION BETWEEN PCSDP AT DIFFERENT POINTS OF TIME

Year	1960–1	1967–8	1972–3	1978–9	1983–4	1990–1	1996–7
1960–1	1.000	–	–	–	–	–	–
1967–8	0.896	1.000	–	–	–	–	–
1972–3	0.930	0.916	1.000	–	–	–	–
1978–9	0.883	0.962	0.944	1.000	–	–	–
1983–4	0.867	0.892	0.932	0.944	1.000	–	–
1990–1	0.816	0.842	0.906	0.876	0.932	1.000	–
1996–7	0.896	0.835	0.903	0.868	0.909	0.926	1.000

TABLE 10.3: INEQUALITY OF PER CAPITA INCOME AND PLAN OUTLAY

Plan	Rank Correlation between Income and Plan Outlay	Gini Coefficients	
		PCSDP	Plan Outlay
Third	–0.31	0.33	0.23
Fourth	0.18	0.35	0.29
Fifth	0.20	0.34	0.31
Sixth	–0.18	0.34	0.31
Seventh	–0.44	0.34	0.33
Eighth	–0.48	0.36	0.26

TABLE 10.4: PER CAPITA STATE DOMESTIC PRODUCT (PCSDP)

Year	1960–1	1967–8	1972–3	1978–9	1983–4	1990–1	1996–7
CV(%)	0.20	0.22	0.26	0.33	0.29	0.32	0.41

III A. THE DEVELOPMENT/WELL-BEING ISSUES AND MEASUREMENT

The above analysis shows that there has been very little convergence in the level of per capita income between the rich and the poor states.[2] However, many analysts consider per capita income to be a poor measure of economic well-being. Many other indicators have been proposed to measure changes in welfare. States that are rated poorly by per capita income standards may be considerably higher if other indicators are used. The first attempt to use other indicators was made by Beckerman and Bacon (1966). In recent years, the search for additional indicators has been basically centred around the extent of availability of health and education services.[3]

Morris D. Morris (1979) proposed the Physical Quality of Life Index (PQLI) to focus on development as achieved well-being.[4] The social indicators used in the construction of the PQLI were: life expectancy at age one (LE), Infant Mortality Rate (IMR) and literacy rate (LIT). But the PQLI proved unpopular among researchers since it had a major technical problem, namely the correlation between the first two indicators.

The Human Development Index proposed by the UNDP in its Human Development Report (1990) found immediate acceptance and is used widely. The Report observes, 'human development is a process of enlarging choices. In principle, these choices can be infinite and change overtime. But at all levels of development, the three essential ones are for people to lead a long and healthy life, to acquire knowledge and to have access to resources needed for a decent standard of living. If these essential choices are not available, many other opportunities remain inaccessible.' The Report continues that, 'development therefore, be more than just the expansion of income and wealth. Its focus must be people.'[5] A method to compute the Human Development Index (HDI) was proposed.[6] This method has come under several criticisms over the years. Nagar and Basu (2000) noted that 'if a human development index could be measured quant-

TABLE 10.5: RATIO OF PCSDP IN THE RICHEST STATE TO THAT IN THE POOREST STATE

Year	1960-1	1967-8	1972-3	1978-9	1983-4	1990-1	1996-7	GR(1)	GR(2)	GR(3)
Richest and Poorest	1.90	2.13	2.60	3.05	2.88	3.13	4.75	2.57	2.65	0.22
Richest and 2nd Poorest	1.88	1.91	2.16	2.70	2.21	2.70	2.95	1.25	2.01	0.02
Richest and 3rd Poorest	1.62	1.86	2.16	2.64	2.10	2.32	2.84	1.57	2.73	-1.07
Richest and 4th Poorest	1.62	1.81	2.15	2.51	2.07	2.29	2.73	1.47	2.48	-0.76
Richest and 5th Poorest	1.58	1.78	2.06	2.38	2.06	2.05	2.71	1.51	2.31	-1.23

Notes: GR(1) Compound Growth Rate: 1960-1 to 1996-7; GR(2): 1960-1 to 1978-9; and GR(3) 1978-9 to 1990-1.

itatively, in the usual manner, we would simply postulate a regression of H on the causal variables (social indicators) and determine optimal estimates by a suitable statistical method.' However, human development is, in fact, an abstract conceptual variable, which cannot be directly measured, but is supposed to be determined by the interaction of a large number of socio-economic variables.[7]

III B. THE COMPUTATION OF SOCIAL WELL-BEING INDEX (SWBI)

To measure the level of development/well-being, we have considered 14 different indicators related to human resources, availability of health services, utilization of technology, availability of physical infrastructure, and the flow of financial services in the states. The well-being index combines these different indicators into one index which seeks to capture several facets of the environment in which the states could grow and prosper.

The 14 indicators proposed to compute the SWBI are the following: per capita SDP (Rs), Literacy Rate (per cent), Combined Enrolment Ratio (per cent), Infant Mortality Rate (per 1,000 live births), Life Expectancy at Birth (years), Population per Hospital Bed (no.), Per Capita Electricity Consumption (kWh), Post Offices (per lakh population), Bank Branches (per lakh population), Telephone Lines (per lakh population), Road Length (per 100 sq. km. area), Railway Route (per 100 sq. km. area), Intensity of Cropping (per cent), and Fertiliser Consumption (per cent) (see Annex 1 for the data sources and measurement of the Indicators).

These 14 indicators are expected to capture different aspects of the socio-economic condition. The SWBI is computed for the four time points (i.e. 1970s, 1980s, 1990s, and 1996–7 for 16 major Indian states on the basis of these indicators. We now discuss the computation of the SWBI (the 16 states for which the SWBI is calculated are listed in Annex 2).

We believe that these indicators are mutually interdependent. We take a closer look at this phenomenon, as we believe that this interdependence may not only provide a better indicator of the level of well-being, but also help in understanding the process of development. We use factor analysis to compute the SWBI.

The Factor Analysis (FA) technique is used to do the following:

- to reduce the number of influencing indicators,
- to detect structure in the relationships among indicators, that is to classify variables according to their effect on the variables of interest.

The technique reduces the set of observed indicators to a smaller number of unobserved factors, which have a common causation influence. The underlying assumptions of factor analysis are that there exist a number of unobserved 'factors' that account for the correlation among the observed indicators, and because of this relation, the unobserved factors can be inferred from the observed indicators.[8]

We estimate factor scores in the FA model as below: for a given factor f_j the ith extracted factor score, denoted by F_{ij}, is given by

$$\hat{F}_{ij} = \beta_1 X_{i1} + \cdots + \beta_p X_{ip}$$

where $\beta_1, \beta_2, \ldots \beta_p$ are referred to as regression coefficients and $X_{i1}, X_{i2}, \ldots X_{ip}$ are the p observed indicators, for the ith observations.

Now, we define the SWBI as a weighed average of the factor scores, where the weights λ's, are the eigenvalues of the correlation matrix R (the original observed indicators are standardized, by subtracting from means and dividing by their variance respectively, the basic FA model is the correlation matrix of R).

Thus:

$$SWBI^k = \frac{\sum F_j \lambda_j}{\sum \lambda_j}, \text{ where } k = 1, 2, \ldots 16 \text{ (states of India)}$$

➢ Finally, we normalize the SWBI value by the following procedure,

$$SWBI^k = \frac{SWBI^k - Minimum\ (SWBI^k)}{Maximum\ (SWBI^k) - Minimum\ (SWBI^k)}$$

where $k = 1, 2, \ldots 16$ (states of India)

and then re-scale the index value from 0 to 10, where 0 represents the worst performing state and 10, the best performing state in the sample of 16 major Indian states.

Before we proceed further, we must mention that the states are divided into three categories on the basis of their SWBI value: the high development state category if the SWBI value is greater than or equal to 7.00 (on a 0 to 10 scale), medium development category, if the index value is greater than or equal to 5.00, but less than 7.00

and low developed states, if the values are less than 5.00. Thus, on the basis of the SWBI value, we classify the state's status on the well-being level and could identify the extent of regional inequality in the level of development/well-being that still exists. We have divided the states on the basis of the SWBI so that we can analyse the trend of their well-being level over the period.

III. C. ANALYSIS OF THE SWBI RESULTS

Now, we discuss the results on the basis of the SWBI for all the states over these three decades.

1970s: THE STATUS OF THE STATES

The analysis of Table 10.6 indicates the classification of the states on the basis of the SWBI. We observe that PU tops the list, and is followed by KE, TN and MA. BI, MP, OR, UP, are the states, with the lowest well being level.

Table 10.7 shows the status of the states in the different categories. We notice that during this period, there are 5 states that are in the 'high development' category, 4 states are in the 'medium development' category, and 7 states are in the 'low development' category.

1980s: THE STATUS OF THE STATES

In the 1980s, the well-being level in general declined to a great extent, as only KE and PU are in the first category, with a ranking of 1 and 2 respectively. We also see that the number of states in the low development category increased to 10 among the 16 states given in the sample. In this period, MP recorded the lowest rank, and is followed by BI, AS, UP, whereas in the previous period, BI had recorded the lowest rank followed by MP, OR and UP.

1990s: THE STATUS OF THE STATES

The situation improved a bit, in this period: the number of states in the high development category is 3, PU, KE and MA. The states in the 'medium development' category, are TN, GU, HI and KA. The total number of states in the 'low development category in this period is 9. MP, BI, OR and UP are the worst-performing states.

TABLE 10.6: SOCIAL WELL-BEING INDEX (SWBI)
AND THE RANKINGS

States/Year	SWBI (normalized)				Rankings of the SWBI			
	1970s	1980s	1990s	1997s	1970s	1980s	1990s	1997s
AP	4.24	3.55	3.50	2.78	10	10	10	11
AS	2.21	0.72	1.12	3.46	12	14	12	10
BI	0.00	0.45	0.12	0.00	16	15	15	16
GU	7.16	5.99	6.85	6.15	5	4	5	5
HR	6.66	5.37	4.61	4.02	6	6	8	8
HI	5.98	4.77	5.29	6.56	9	8	6	3
KA	5.99	4.77	5.04	5.44	8	7	7	7
KE	9.03	7.60	9.42	10.00	2	2	2	1
MP	1.53	0.00	0.00	1.85	15	16	16	14
MA	7.85	6.33	7.81	7.63	4	3	3	2
OR	2.03	0.92	0.62	2.43	14	12	14	13
PU	10.00	10.00	10.00	6.27	1	1	1	4
RA	2.72	1.45	1.35	2.50	11	11	11	12
TN	8.01	5.81	7.23	6.04	3	5	4	6
UP	2.11	0.88	0.80	0.86	13	13	13	15
WB	6.15	3.81	4.37	4.02	7	9	9	9
Spearmans Rank Correlation*		0.968(1)	0.968(2)	0.882(3)	0.974(4)	0.897(5)	0.941(6)	

Notes: *All the coefficients are statistically significant at 1 per cent level.
Here (1) denotes rank correlation between 1970s and 1980s, (2) 1970s and 1990s, (3) 1970s and 1997s, (4) 1980s and 1990s, (5) 1980s and 1997s, and (6) 1990s and 1997s.

1996–1997: The Status of the States

The situation did not improve any further after liberalization, rather PU has slipped from the 'high development' category. In the latest period, only KE and MA are in the first category. Though there is some shuffling among the ranks of the worst state, BI, UP, MP, and OR remain the lowest-ranked states.

We calculate the rank correlation to see whether the ranking of the states by SWBI has changed. The rank correlation shows that the ranking of the states over the period has not changed much, and all the coefficients are statistically significant at the 1 per cent level (Table 10.6). The rank correlation between the 1970s and 1997 is 0.882, which is remarkably high. This, in turn, indicates that the states, which were on the top in the 1970s or at the bottom, have not changed their position much during the period.

States such as AP, AS, BI, MP, OR, RA, and UP have been throughout the period in the 'low development' category (Table 10.7). Our results suggest that only KE has maintained its position in the 'high development' category throughout the period. MA (except for the 1980s) and PU (except for 1997) have also been in the 'high development' category.

A closer look at the table shows some changes in the categorization of the states over the period. For instance, GU which was in the high development category in the 1970s, slipped into the 'middle development' category in the 1980s; but has remained in the group for the rest of the period. TN is in a similar category, slipping from the high development category in the 1970s to the middle category in the 1980s and remaining in that category for the rest of the period. Other examples of a decline in the level of category are HR, which was in the 'medium development' category in the 1970s, and 1980s, but later declined to the third category (low development), and WB, which was in the 'medium development' category in the 1970s, but fell to the 'low development' category in the later decades. But there are no states which have consistently improved their SWBI during the period.

Thus, on the basis of SWBI, which broadens the concept of development/well-being, the states which were ranked high in the 1970s, remain on the top in the latest period as well. The rank correlation coefficients are pretty high and statistically significant over any two periods (Table 10.6). This result also suggests that there has been very little change in the status of the major states over such a long period of time. Hence, SWBI also enables us to understand the fact that there has been a great amount of regional inequality in India.

We also examine whether the concept of the SWBI adds significantly to the notion of welfare as compared to using per capita income alone as the indicator of welfare. The rank correlation between per capita state domestic product and the SWBI is very high, though it has been declining. It has declined from 0.84 in the early 1970s to 0.70 in the late 1990s and there is increasing discrepancy between performance as measure by per capita income and as measured by SWBI in HI and HR (Table 10.8). Much of the decline has been in the 1990s. Kerala has always been noted at having a very high ranking

TABLE 10.7: STATUS OF THE 16 STATES ACCORDING TO SWBI

States/Period	1970s			1980s			1990s			1997s		
	HD	MD	LD	HD	MD	LD	HD	MD	LD	HD	MD	LD
AP			✓			✓			✓			✓
AS			✓			✓			✓			✓
BI			✓			✓			✓			✓
GU		✓			✓			✓			✓	
HR		✓			✓			✓			✓	
HI		✓			✓			✓			✓	
KA			✓			✓			✓			✓
KE	✓			✓			✓			✓		
MP	✓					✓			✓			✓
MA			✓		✓				✓			✓
OR			✓			✓			✓			✓
PU	✓			✓				✓			✓	
RA			✓			✓			✓			✓
TN		✓				✓		✓			✓	
UP			✓			✓			✓			✓
WB		✓				✓			✓			✓

Notes: The states are grouped into three different categories. These are, HD: High development category, MD: Medium development category, LD: Low development category. *Classification is based on Table 6.*

TABLE 10.8: RANK CORRELATION BETWEEN
PCSDP AND SWBI

Year	1970s	1980s	1990s	1996–7
Correlation Coeff	0.84	0.80	0.78	0.70

on the human development index though ranked considerably lower in per capita income. It has been joined in this category in the 1990s by HI. HI's ranking by per capita income dropped sharply in the 1990s from the earlier 5–6 to 10, while it continued to steadily improve its ranking by SWBI, reaching the third rank by 1996–7. On the other hand, HR's performance as ranked by SWBI declined, while its rank on the basis of per capita income continued to be high.

A glance at the overall trend in SWBI indicates that the average declined sharply from 5.10 in the 1970s to 3.90 in the 1980s; later the index increased to 4.26 in the 1990s and to 4.38 in 1996–7. But at the end of period, it remained lower than in the 1970s. There is also an increase in the coefficient variation of SWBI among the 16 major states from 0.59 in the 1970s to 0.75 in the 1980s and further to 0.79 in the 1990s; but it declined in the latest period to 0.61. So, overall during the 30 years, there is little change in the coefficient of variation of the SWBI, but there has been some decline in its average value.

The failure to achieve the desired goals of regional equity either on the basis of per capita income or the SWBI, can be explained by believing that the rhetoric of equity has not been matched by actual endeavour. Though for political reasons, politicians have had to champion the cause of equity, their heart has not been in it and the actual policies have tended to ignore equity considerations. The desire for growth has been stronger than the desire for equity.

Alternatively, politicians may have tried to reduce regional disparities but either they could not implement appropriate policies because of vested interests or they had not adopted appropriate policies, because of lack of knowledge or information. In particular, it can be argued that states differed in their capabilities in implementing the policies. The poorer states have lacked the capacity to utilise the resource made available by the Centre and so their growth rate has lagged behind that of the richer states. We examine below, some of these different explanations of the failure to reduce regional inequalities.

IV A. DEVELOPMENT STRATEGY

The policy makers adopted a development strategy designed to overcome the major constraints facing the economy – the low level of savings, that would limit the extent of increase in investment that could be planned, the lack of private entrepreneurship, the unbalanced industrial structure – unbalanced not only regionally but in terms of the industries that had been established, and the low agricultural production per capita.[9] The development strategy in the face of these constraints stressed the role of the public sector, and concentrated investment in heavy industries, which over a period of time, would enable higher levels of savings and investment. The strategic role of the public sector was attractive to the policy makers also, because it would prevent concentration of incomes and high levels of inequality.

The development strategy adopted in the Second and Third Plans, the Mahalanobis development strategy, was two-pronged.[10] For rapid growth, investment was concentrated in heavy industries in the public sector. These were capital-intensive and large industries. Their output was often demanded by other basic goods industries in the public sector. Their low employment effect was particularly unattractive in a country with high levels of unemployment and poverty. The policy makers shifted the burden of meeting the equity goals onto the consumer goods industries in general and on the small-scale sector and handicraft industries in particular. Consumer goods industries, which would use some of the output of these industries, were to be in the private sector, and would be more labour-intensive. It was expected that these labour-intensive industries would provide the bulk of the employment. Also, these consumer goods industries would be distributed throughout the country, contributing to regional development and equity. The small-scale and handicrafts sectors were particularly important for regional equity, as these would be widely dispersed.

The heavy industries had obviously to be located where the required raw materials were available. So, economic considerations dictated their location and this was quite concentrated. As it happened, many raw materials were located in the poorer states such as Bihar and Orissa. However, these industries did not provide many backward and forward linkages and so their location did not result in the overall development of these states. These industries were very capital-intensive and would not generate much employment. In addition, a considerable part of the labour employed in these industries was skilled, was recruited at the national level and provided little fillip to local employment.

Why were the industries using the outputs of these basic industries, not located close by, thereby providing a boost to local development? Local purchasing power was low so that any consumer units established locally by the private sector would have to cater to the demand from faraway markets. The choice was between establishing these industries where the required intermediate goods were and transporting the final goods or transporting the intermediate goods and producing the final goods elsewhere. For a number of reasons, including the freight equalization policy adopted by the governments, the latter strategy was adopted by entrepreneurs. The main reasons were the advantages of agglomeration and transport costs. Policies to encourage dispersion of industries and licencing policies designed to prevent concentration, also favoured the establishment of a number of companies, each close to a consumer market rather than one larger company near the source of intermediate goods.

The role accorded to the small-scale sector in meeting the equity goals of the planners may suggest that this was a mere afterthought. But it would be wrong to take this viewpoint. That policy makers placed considerable weight on equity, can be seen by the fact that in 1960, they established a commission to examine the trends in inequality in per capita income and to look at what was happening to the extent of poverty. The First Plan had really been a collection of ongoing projects, rather than a serious attempt to accelerate growth, and only the Second Plan had tried to do this. One would thus think that the time elapsed was too limited to get any definite trend on inequality or poverty. It must also be remembered that the operation of the Second Plan had been interrupted by a severe Balance of Payments (BOP) crisis that had disrupted its implementation.

The concern about the lack of reduction in poverty was, however, not reflected in any change in the development strategy for the Third Five Year Plan. The policy of import substitution in heavy industries under the aegis of the public sector continued. The only modification in polices was that greater importance was given to exports because of the BOP problems facing the economy. The substantial modifications in development strategy that occurred in the mid-1960s and the early 1970s, were not in response to equity considerations, but because of the changing constraints facing the economy. The droughts of the mid-1960s and US attempts to use its food aid as a lever for imposing policy changes on India brought into very sharp focus that the low agricultural output was posing a severe constraint to growth.[11] Similarly, the considerable increase in oil prices in the early 1970s and the ensuing BOP crisis forced the government to embark on a much expanded programme of oil exploration and production.

IV B. EFFECTS OF DEVELOPMENT STRATEGY ON REGIONAL INEQUALITY

These changes, however, actually worsened regional inequality. The greater emphasis on agricultural development manifested itself though the spread of the set of technological and policy choices which resulted in what has come to be known as the 'Green Revolution'. This resulted in increased government investment in the agricultural sector and its concentration in states that already had a relatively developed irrigation infrastructure. These tended to be the richer states. The increased agricultural investment, and even more significantly, the increased investment in oil was at the expense of investment in public sector manufacturing units and in infrastructure. The share of investment in manufacturing in plan outlay, declined from almost 25 per cent during the period 1956 to 1968 to about 20 per cent in the 1970s and further to under 15 per cent in the 1980s.

Concerns about regional equity do not seem to have substantially influenced the development strategy adopted. The shifts in strategy at different points were due to constraints in implementing the desired policy arising mainly from the BOP and not because of considerations of regional inequality. The shifts may have actually acted against the goal of regional equity. One of the main instruments available to the government to reduce inter-state inequality is to raise the growth rate in the poorer states, and growth rates can be raised by increasing investment in these states. The net effect of the shifts was reduced investment in manufacturing and increased concentration of agricultural investment. The Fourth Plan which covered the period 1969–74 showed a sharp increase in the coefficient of variation of plan outlay as a per cent of state domestic product (Chart 1). Also, the rank correlation between per capita income and per capita plan outlay is positive for the Fourth and Fifth Plans, whereas, for the other plans it is negative (Table 10.3). The Gini coefficient for per capita plan outlays shows a considerable increase between the Third

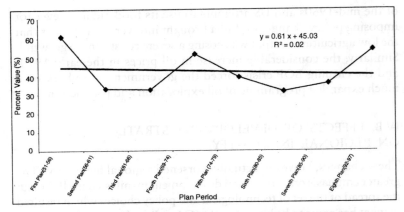

Chart 1: Coefficient of Variation (%): Plan Outlay to Per Capita State Domestic Product (PCSDP)

Plan and the Fourth Plan, and the Fourth Plan and the Fifth Plan. It is only with the Eighth Plan that there is a substantial decline in the Gini coefficient for the distribution of per capita plan outlays among the different states (Table 10.3).

The decline in the importance of public investment in manufacturing, limited the ability of the government to enhance public investment to address the problem of regional inequality. Greater dependence had, therefore, to be placed on private sector investments. Various tax concessions were given to companies set up in backward districts. However, these concessions could not compensate for the poor infrastructure and other facilities in these backward districts. The decline in infrastructure investment actually worsened the ability of these areas to attract private investment. A major concern in addressing the problem of slow growth in backward states appears to be the lack of state level analysis identifying state level strengths and weaknesses and then designing a state level plan based on such analysis.

Plan outlays can be used to raise the growth rates in lagging states and there is considerable lobbying by states for these outlays. We present the ranking of the 16 major states on the basis of the plan outlay (Table 10.9). The table shows that UP, MA, BI, MP are the states that have had maximum allocation of plan outlays among the states, whereas HI, KE, AS, HR are the states with lowest allocation

TABLE 10.9: THE STATEWISE TREND IN PLAN OUTLAY

States/Year	1966–9	1974–9	1985–90	1992–7	Rankings			
AP	3.53	3.43	2.89	2.42	4	4	6	8
AS	1.30	1.22	1.17	1.07	14	15	14	15
BI	3.25	3.34	2.83	2.99	5	5	7	3
GU	3.11	3.05	3.33	2.65	6	7	4	5
HR	1.27	1.55	1.61	1.31	15	12	12	13
HI	0.60	0.62	0.58	0.58	16	16	16	16
KA	2.87	2.57	1.94	2.83	7	10	9	4
KE	2.17	1.46	1.17	1.26	10	14	14	14
MP	2.50	3.55	3.89	2.56	8	3	3	7
MA	5.82	6.04	5.83	4.27	2	2	1	2
OR	1.84	1.51	1.50	2.30	12	13	13	10
PU	1.82	2.61	1.83	1.51	13	9	10	12
RA	2.05	1.82	1.67	2.65	11	11	11	5
TN	3.98	2.89	3.19	2.35	3	8	5	9
UP	6.74	6.30	5.80	4.84	1	1	2	1
WB	2.41	3.21	2.29	2.25	9	6	8	11

Rank Correlation Coefficient between the 1966–9 to the later periods
0.835 *(a)   0.876* (b)   0.806* (c)

Notes: * all the coefficients are statistically significant at 1 per cent level.
(a) denotes the coefficient between 1966–9 to 1974–97, (b) the coefficient between 1966–9 to 1985–90, and (c) the coefficient between 1966–9 to 1992–7.

of plan outlays in the selected periods. Now, the question is whether the states that have been given the larger share of the plan outlay, are the states that are the most developed ones or the least developed. The Spearman rank correlation coefficient between the SWBI and PLOU shows that throughout the period, the values are –0.038, –0.171, –0.088 and –0.392. This result indicates that the plan outlay has failed to induce development/well-being in most of the states, even though more plan outlays had gone to the poor states as the rank correlation between per capita state income and a states plan outlay has usually been negative (Table 10.3).

The decline in public investment in manufacturing has meant that the Central Government could not directly influence the rates of growth in the different states.[12] Increasingly, the states are merely providing the infrastructure for the private sector to respond to the opportunities created by investment in infrastructure. With the liberalization of trade and investment decisions in the beginning of the nineties and the adoption of market-oriented policies, the importance of private sector actions has increased further.

It cannot be claimed that the governments were uninterested in the issue of regional inequality and that this was not a consideration in the design of the plans. Except for the Fourth and Fifth Plans which were drawn up under exceptional circumstances, the other plans show a negative Spearman rank correlation coefficient between per capita income and per capita plan outlays (Table 10.3). But this attempt to reduce regional inequality was unsuccessful. The later attempt in the Eighth and Ninth Plans to increase plan allocation to the lagging states has been unsuccessful in tackling regional inequality, because this period also coincided with the withdrawal of the state from manufacturing production and concentration of public investment in the infrastructure sector. Larger allocations for infrastructure investment in the poorer states have not been successful in raising their growth rates. The lack of data on actual expenditure makes it difficult to examine whether the allocations were actually translated into projects and expenditures. This lack of data also makes it difficult to judge to what extent the states have diffused in their ability to design and implement a project.[13]

V. CONCLUSION

In brief, while the Central and state governments have been concerned about the issue of regional inequality, the policy framework has not been adequate to address this question. The lacuna has not been in the attempts to address this question. As we have seen, apart from the Fourth and Fifth Plans, there has generally been a negative correlation between per capita plan outlays and per capita state product, and this negative relation has been very strong since the mid-1980s. Moreover, correlation between the plan outlay and SWBI rankings are consistently negative, and have even increased in the recent period. We believe the extent of regional inequality has tended to increase because of lack of adequate attention to local realities in state plans to actually address the specific factors preventing faster growth or preventing the benefits of growth and social expenditures from reaching the poor. The lack of sufficient information on actual plan expenditures prevents a further analysis of this issue.

NOTES

1. For further analysis of inter-state inequality, see Das and Barua (1996); Cashin and Sahay (1996 a, b); Marjit and Mitra (1996); Ghosh, Marjit and Neogi (1997); Rao et al. 1999; Dasgupta et al. 2000; Kalirajan et al. 2000. Also see Barua and Bandyopadhyay in this volume.
2. In the literature on convergence of per capita income, two measures are widely used, one is CV (per cent), and another measure is to use a simple regression model of per capita income growth rates to test model is referred as 'beta convergence'. The model used to test for unconditional convergence takes the following linear form:

$$\frac{1}{T} \log \left(\frac{y_{it}}{y_{i, t-T}}\right) = \beta_0 + \beta_1 \log (y_{i,t-T}) + e_i$$

The left-hand side dependent variable represents the annual average growth rate in the per capita income of the state i over the periods. The logarithm of PCNSDP of each state in the initial year appears as the independent variable on the right-hand side of the model. A negative and statistically significant coefficient for β_1 implies the existence of unconditional 'beta convergence'. The result shows that the beta convergence tests (whether the poorer states have shown higher than the richer states) for PCSDP also indicates that there is no tendency of convergence among the states. The result below states that the coefficient of beta is positive and statstically significant. In conclusion, we can say that the states have not shown any tendency to converge over the study period.

Testing β-Convergence

	β_0	β_1	R^2	s.e. of regression
PCNSDP	−0.118983* (2.038693)	0.023773* (2.610248)	0.448409	0.006803

Notes: t-statistic in the parentheses
*coefficients are statistically significant at 1 per cent level

3. See Dasgupta, 1993.
4. In some seminal studies, the relationship between economic development and development in non-economic features was analysed. In a pioneering study, Adelman and Morris (1967) examined the interactions among the process of social, economic and political change with the level and pace of economic development. They inferred that the quality of life could be measured by looking at these, and stressed an intimate association between the pace of economic progress and the state of the non-economic forces.

They indicated that the importance of the non-economic determinants of economic dynamism tends to vary systematically with the stage of a country's socio-political development. In another study, McGranahan (1972) and associates examined the interaction of several development indicators – some relating to mortality and morbidity, others to social factors, such as urbanisation – to other economic factors.

5. See UNDP HDR 1990.
6. Although over the years, some changes have been made in the construction of HDIs, the methodology has remained the same. As stated in the HDR 2000, the HDI is based on three indicators:

   (i) *Longevity*: as measured by Life Expectancy (LE) at birth;
   (ii) *Educational attainment*: measured as a weighted average of (a) adult literacy rate with two-third weight, and (b) combined gross primary, secondary and tertiary enrolment ratio with one third weight; and
   (iii) *Standard of living*: as measured by real Gross Domestic Product (GDP) per capita (pppUS$). To construct the index, minimum and maximum values of each of these indicators are taken, and then the individual indices for any component of the HDI, are computed as:

   Index = (actual value – minimum value)/(maximum value – minimum value)
   The real GDP is transformed as

   $$\frac{\log_e Y_{actual} - \log_e Y_{min}}{\log_e Y_{max} - \log_e Y_{min}}$$

   HDI is obtained as a simple (unweighted) arithmetic mean of these indices.

7. See Nagar and Basu (2000) and also (2001a). The authors in their recent paper have discussed the statistical properties of the index (2001b).
8. For further theoretical details see, Beck (ed.); Anderson; Dillon and Goldstein.
9. For a further analysis of plan strategies, see Agarwal (1997); Chakravarty (1987).
10. For further analysis of the Mahalanobis development strategies, see Bhagwati and Chakravarty (1969); Chakravarty (1987).
11. For a detailed discussion of these factors on development strategy and the repercussions of the changed development strategy, see Lele and Agarwal (1991).
12. Nagar and Basu (2001a) propose a method to compute a composite measure of Infrastructure Development Index (IDI) by combining the

available services of physical services, viz., electricity consumption per capita, villages electrified per state, railway route, surfaced roads in total road length per state, and telephone lines. Then they determine the correlation between PCSDP with the IDI, and find a positive relationship between them. The states that have done well in providing the basic services, have done well in terms of per capita income also.

13. The lack of such data may lead one to suspect the sincerity of the entire planning process and not merely suspect the seriousness of the effects to reduce regional inequality.

REFERENCES

Adelman, I. and C.T. Morris, *Society, Politics and Economic Development: A Quantitative Approach*, 2nd edn., Baltimore: JHU Press, 1967.

Agarwal, M. and P. Desai, eds., *Going Global: Transition from Plan to Market in the World Economy*, Cambridge and London: MIT Press, 1997.

──── 'Economic Reforms and Policy', in S. Bhatt and U.S. Muni, eds., *Shape of Things to Come*, New Delhi: Lancers Books, 1999.

Anderson, T.W., *An Introduction to Multivariate Statistical Analysis*, New York: John Wiley and Sons, 1984.

Basu, Sudip Ranjan, 'The Development Process in Indian States', M.Phil. Dissertation, International Trade and Development Division, School of International Studies, Jawaharlal Nehru University, New Delhi, 2001.

Beckerman, W. and R. Bacon, 'International Comparisons of Real Incomes: A New Measure', *Economic Journal*, September 1969.

Bhagwati, J. and S. Chakravarty, 'Contribution to Indian Economic Analysis: A Survey', *American Economic Review*, 59, no. 4, 1969, pp. 1–73.

Cashin, P. and R. Sahay, *Internal Migration, Centre State Grants and Economic Growth in the States of India*, IMF staff papers, 43, 1996a, pp. 123–71.

────, *Regional Economic Growth and Convergence in India: Global Economic Prospects and the Developing Countries*, Finance and Development, 33, 1, 1996b, pp. 49–53.

Centre for Monitoring Indian Economy (CMIE), *Basic Statistics Relating to Indian Economy: India and States*, Mumbai: CMIE Pvt. Ltd. (various issues).

Chakravarty, S., 'On the question of Home Market and Prospects for Indian Growth', *Economic and Political Weekly*, 14, special no., 1987.

Das, S.K. and A. Barua, 'Regional Inequalities, Economic Growth and Liberalization: A Case Study of the Indian Economy', *Journal of Development Studies*, vol. 32, no. 3, 1996, pp. 364–91.

Dasgupta, D. et al., 'Growth and Interstate Disparities in India', *Economic and Political Weekly*, 1 July 2000.
Dasgupta, P., *An Inquiry into Well Being and Distribution*, Oxford: Clarendon Press, 1993.
Dillon, W.P. and M. Goldstein, *Multivariate Analysis: Methods and Applications*, New York: John Wiley and Sons, 1984.
Ghosh, B.S. Marjit and C. Neogi, 'Economic Growth and Regional Divergence in India 1960 to 1995', *Economic and Political Weekly*, 33, 27 June–3 July 1998, pp. 1623–3.
Hair, J.F. et al., *Multivariate Data Analysis*, 5th edn., New Jersey: Prentice Hall International, 1998.
India, Government of, Planning Commission, Five Year Plans (III–VIII).
Kalirajan, P., R.T. Shand and S. Bhide, 'Economic Reforms and Convergence of Incomes Across Indian States: Benefits for the Poor', in S. Gangopadhyay and W. Wadhwa, eds., *Economic Reforms for the Poor*, in association with RGICS, RGF and SERFA, New Delhi: Konark.
Lele, U. and M. Agarwal, 'Four Decades of Economic Development in India and the Role of External Assistance, in U. Lele and I. Nabi, eds., *Transitions in Development: The Role of Aid and Commercial Flows*, San Francisco: ICS Press, 1991.
Lewis-Beck, M.S., ed., 'Factor Analysis and Related Techniques', *International Handbook of Quantitative Applications in the Social Sciences*, vol. 5, UK: Sage Publications, 1994.
Marjit, S. and S. Mitra, 'Convergence in Regional Growth Rates: Indian Research Agenda', *Economic and Political Weekly*, 17 August 1996.
McGranahan, V.C. Richard, N.V. Sovani, and M. Subramanian, *Contrast and Measurement of Socio-economic Development*, United Nations Research Institute for Social Development (UNRISD), New York: Praeger Publishers, 1972.
Morris, D. Morris, *Measuring the Condition of the Words' Poor: The Physical Quality of Life Index*, New York: Pergamon, 1979.
Nagar, A.L. and Sudip Ranjan Basu, 'The Socio-Economic Indicators of Human Development: A Latent Variable Approach', working paper, National Institute of Public Finance and Policy, New Delhi, in A. Ullah, et al., eds., *Handbook of Applied Econometrics and Statistical Inference*, forthcoming.
——, 'Infrastructure Development Index: An Analysis for 17 Major Indian States (1990–1 to 1996–7), working paper, National Institute of Public Finance and Policy, New Delhi (under editorial consideration of the Journal of Policy Modeling /Eco-Models.com), 2001a.
——, 'Statistical Properties of a Composite Index as Estimator of a Single Latent Variable', working paper, National Institute of Public Finance and Policy, New Delhi.

Rao, M.G., R.T.S. Shand and K.P. Kalirajan, 'Convergence of Income Across Indian States, *Economic and Political Weekly*, 34, 13, 27 March–2 April 1999, pp. 769–78.

UNDP, *Human Development Report (1990–2001)*, New York: Oxford University Press, 2001b.

ANNEX 1: THE DATA SOURCES AND MEASUREMENTS OF INDICATORS

Indicators	Units	Code	Data Periods	Sources
Per Capita State Domestic Product	Rs	PCSDP	Table 1 and 1970–3, 1980–3, 1990–3, 1995–7	CSO (various issues), *EPW* Research Foundation, and Chandok Group
Literacy Rate	(per cent)	LIT	1971, 1981, 1991, 2001	Census of India, 1971, 1981, 1991, 2001
Combined Enrolment Ratio	(per cent)	CER	1971, 1981, 1991, 1997	Selected educational statistics (various years)
Infant Mortality Rate	(per 1000 live births)	IMR	1971, 1981, 1991, 1997	Census of India
Life Expectancy Rate of Birth	(years)	LEB	1971, 1981, 1991, 1995	Statistical Abstract of India CMIE (various issues)
Population per Hospital Beds	(number)	PHB	1972, 1980, 1989, 1995	Health Information of India and CMIE (various issues)
Per Capita Electricity Consumption	(kWh)	PCEC	1970–1, 1980–1, 1990–1 1997–8	Statistical Abstract of India and CMIE (various issues)
Post Office	(per lakh population)	PO	1971, 1980, 1990, 1997	Gupta et al. (1983) and CMIE (various issues)
Bank Branch	(per lakh population)	BB	1971, 1980, 1990, 1997	Do
Telephone Lines	(per lakh population)	TEL	1971, 1980, 1990, 1997	Do
Road Length	(per 100 sq. kms.)	ROD	1971, 1981, 1991, 1998	Do
Railway Route	(per 100 sq. kms.)	RR	1971, 1980, 1990, 1997	Do
Intensity of Irrigation	(per cent)	IR	1970–1, 1980–1 1990–1, 1995–6	Fertilizer Statistics of India and CMIE (various issues)
Fertilizer Consumption	(per cent)	FC	1970–1, 1980–1 1990–1, 1997–8	Fertilizer Statistics of India
Plan Outlay	(per cent)	PLOU	3rd to 8th Plan	Planning Commission, CMIE

ANNEX 2: THE INDIAN STATES AND UNION TERRITORIES

States (Sample)	Code	States (not in sample)	UTs (not in sample)
Andhra Pradesh (S)	AP	Arunachal Pradesh (NE)	Andaman & Nicobar Island (E)
Assam (NE)	AS	Goa (S)	Chandigarh (N)
Bihar (E)	BI	Jammu & Kashmir (N)	Dadra & Nagar Haveli (W)
Gujarat (W)	GU	Manipur (NE)	Daman & Diu (W)
Haryana (N)	HR	Meghalaya (NE)	Delhi (N)
Himachal Pradesh (N)	HI	Mizoram (NE)	Lakshadweep (S)
Karnataka (S)	KA	Nagaland (NE)	Pondichery (S)
Kerala (S)	KE	Sikkim (E)	
Madhya Pradesh (C)	MP	Tripura (NE)	
Maharashtra (W)	MA	Chhatishgarh (C)	
Orissa (E)	OR	Uttaranchal (C)	
Punjab (N)	PU	Jharkhand (C)	
Rajasthan (N)	RA		
Tamil Nadu (S)	TN		
Uttar Pradesh (C)	UP		
West Bengal (E)	WB		

Notes: Presently, there are 28 states and 7 UTs in India. In 1956 (States Reorganization Act), there were 14 states and 5 UTs only. Then, new states were created by the subdivision of older ones in 1960 and 1966, and some UTs have been converted into states. However, in this study, one only confines one's study to 16 states of India, since the 1970s.

States/UTs (.) where, S = Southern, N = Northern, W = Western, E = Eastern, NE = North Eastern, C = Central region of India.

CHAPTER 11

Structural Change, Economic Growth and Regional Disparity in the North-East: Regional and National Perspectives

ALOKESH BARUA AND
ARINDAM BANDYOPADHYAY

INTRODUCTION

A view commonly shared by many in the north-east is that the Indian development process has failed to integrate the economy of the north-east with the Indian mainstream and as a result, the region has been economically stagnating for long. Economic stagnation, it is argued, was solely responsible for rising poverty, unemployment and a fall in the general well-being of the people. The argument is stressed upon, one step further, in constructing an in-built reasoning that the lack of development and industrialization has resulted in growing relative economic disparity of the region *vis-à-vis* the national average. This rising disparity, it is further alleged, has led to the growing sense of alienation among the people and has manifested itself in various forms of separatist movements in the region. The basic foundation of these movements thus, is an increasingly saleable theory of under-development based on the assumption that the Central Government has been neglecting the region since Independence, causing much of its present-day economic woes. This paper seeks to critically examine these views.

In analysing the above issue, we proceed as follows. The first section of the paper examines the economic growth performance of the region during the last two decades. One compares the growth performance of all the individual states of the north-east, as well as the region on the whole, with the all-India performance. This would tell one, whether there is any truth in the view that the region and the individual states have been stagnating over the years. In the second section, one examines the nature of structural changes for India as well as for the north-east. One expects that in the process of economic development, the share of agriculture falls and the share of the manufacturing continuously rises. Structural changes will be development-oriented if it follows the above pattern. However, the structural change could as well be consumption-oriented, which might be detrimental to growth.

The third section deals with the relative income inequalities within the north-east, where one isolates the region from the rest of India. This is to examine whether disparities within the north-east have been rising or falling, as there is a feeling in the region that certain states have developed at the cost of the others. In one's attempt to examine the relative income disparities, one adopts the Theil measure, which was discussed at length by Das and Barua (1996). In the fourth section of the paper, one tries to cast the north-east as a part of India and examine in a broader framework, the relative income disparities among the various states of India. If economic development has been based on the concentration of economic activities in some regions while neglecting others, then this would be reflected in rising inter-regional inequalities. In other words, one shall examine the frequently held notion that the process of development in India has been at the cost of increasing regional disparities. In this context, we would also examine if income inequalities have adversely affected the overall growth prospects of the country.

REVIEW OF LITERATURE ON INEQUALITY AND GROWTH IN INDIA

There is a huge literature on the analysis of income disparities across Indian states which can be stratified according to two main lines of inquiries, namely (i) measures of income inequality and (ii) inequality and growth disparity. Taking *the first line of inquiry*, we have a large number of studies attempting to analyse income inequality by calculating either the Gini coefficient or the coefficient of variation or the Theil index of inequality in state-wise income or in consumption expenditure. In recent years however we have a few studies which had attempted to test the hypothesis of convergence in per capita income across regions overtime a la Barro and Sala-i-Martin (1995). Thus, if per capita income across states converges as time proceeds then it can be said that income inequality has been reduced. However, none of these approaches makes any attempt to explain the causalities of income inequality although various suggestive remarks were made as passing references. On the other hand, the *second line of inquiry* as mentioned above has been devoted to examining the issue of income inequality in relation to growth. That is, it has been of interest to find whether income inequality is good or bad for growth performance. Thus, if income inequality is inconsequential to growth in income and that the inter-state growth rates tend to converge overtime irrespective of the existence of income inequality, then income inequality *per se* need not concern us. If however the inequality in income affects the growth performance then the initial levels of income inequality not only may lead to disparities in growth rates but also may lead to further increase inequalities overtime.

The conclusions that can be drawn from various studies on income inequality in India can be broadly placed under two main viewpoints. The first viewpoint is that income inequality has not changed much but if anything at all has changed then what can perhaps be observed is a tendency for it to fall. As opposed to the above view there are also substantial numbers of studies which show widening of regional disparities. It is therefore important to examine representative samples belonging to each viewpoint to shed some lights on the reasons for such diametrically opposite findings which is intriguing because most of these studies use the same sources of data and also follow more or less the same methodologies in estimating inequality.

Some of the earlier studies on inter-state income inequality up to the 1970s such as by Nair (1971), Choudhury (1974) and Gupta (1973) had observed *no noticeable reduction in income differentials*. In contrast, Majumdar and Kapoor (1980) had found that over the period 1962–76 there has been a *steady increase in inter-state inequalities* of income in India.

Similarly, there were few other studies which examined inter-regional disparities in consumption expenditure [Vaidyanathan (1974) and Chatterjee and Bhattacharya (1974)]. Vaidyanathan observed that while inter-state consumption inequality remained more or less stable up to 1957–8, it has started declining since then however (p. 235). On the other hand, Chatterjee and Bhattacharyya (1974) observed a decline in rural inequality without however observing any noticeable change in urban inequality. The authors observed that the decline in rural inequality in consumption may be illusory due to relatively lower consumer price index in the relatively prosperous states. An interesting observation made by Bhatty (1974) using NCAER data on household incomes was that inequality in the distribution of per capita consumption expenditure is uniformly less than the inequality in the distribution of income in all states. For later period, 1961–87, it has been observed that for the rural sector the Lorenz ratio calculated on current prices data does not indicate any sustained trend either for India or for any state (Dev et al., 1991).

At this point it needs to be emphasized that inequality in income should not be taken as the same thing as inequality in consumption. The main reason for this can be given as the fact that inequality in consumption excludes savings which is a part of income. It is quite possible that 'a decrease in consumption inequality may accompany an increase in income inequality, in the short run' (Dev et al.). Therefore, income data while includes basic and consumption goods, the consumption expenditure data includes mainly the consumption goods only. Also, consumption data do not capture aspects of welfare like access to public goods. It can therefore be argued that while inequality in income may be interpreted as inequality in the *accumulative capacities* of regions to the extent that income determines savings and hence growth performance, inequality in consumption expenditure only reflect differences in the *levels of sustenance* only. And the fact mentioned above that consumption inequality lies uniformly below income inequality in a way supports this view.

Let us now look at the results of studies covering the period up to the early 1990s, that is, the pre-reform era. These studies are by Dholakia (1985), Mathur (1983), Choudhury (1992), Das, Barua and Ghosh (1993) and Das and Barua (1996). The main conclusion of these studies is that there has been increasing interregional inequalities in income. However, Das, Barua and Ghosh (1993) also examined inequality in consumption expenditure and they observed rising inequality in consumption as well. However, like the previous studies they also observed that inequality in consumption lies uniformly below the inequality in income.

The study by Das and Barua (1996) has been quite comprehensive in the sense that they included more number of states in their analysis and also that they decomposed the income data into its various components such as agriculture, manufacturing, infrastructure, primary products and services and examined the nature of inequality for each of the components of income. They observed that except for the primary sector all other sectors have shown increasing regional disparities during the period 1970-1 to 1991-2. However, a break-up of the period shows a significant increasing trend during the period 1970-80 and a significant decreasing trend during the period 1980-92. In essence, they observed non-linearity in the relationship between inequality measure and time.

There are also a few studies which have looked at the inter-regional variations in growth rates [Mathur (1987), Dholakia (1994)]. Interestingly, while Mathur had observed diverging growth performances, Dholakia had observed marked tendencies of convergence of long term economic growth rates for the period of 1960-1 to 1989-90 for 20 Indian states. Cashin and Sahay (1996) too claim absolute convergence on the basis of data relating to 20 Indian states for the period 1961-91 and at the same time that the dispersion of real per capita income increased during the period. On the other hand, Rao, Shand and Kaliranjan (1999) suggest that per capita SDP in the Indian states have tended to diverge rather than converge.

Nagraj (1997) considered the growth performance of Indian states during 1960-94 period and found evidence of conditional convergence, i.e. convergence relative to state specific steady states. Some studies that have discerned tendencies of divergence are Majumder and Kapoor (1980), Bajpai and Sachs (1996), Marjit and Mitra (1996), Raman (1996), Rao et al. (1999), Dasgupta et al. (2000) and Sachs et al. (2002).

Nagraj et al. (2000) provide an empirical analysis of conditional convergence across Indian states of which they assess the extent to which differences in core, social and economic infrastructure endowments give rise to differences in steady-state levels of output and therefore to differences in their long run growth performance. Dasgupta et al. (2000) used the per capita SDP up to 1995-6 and find a clear tendency for the Indian states to have diverged during the period in question as far as per capita SDP goes. Kurian (2000) finds widening regional disparities among the Indian States and a clear dichotomy between what he calls the forward and backward States. The former having higher levels of per capita income, better infrastructure, higher resource flows and private investment and better social and demographic indicators.

In this respect, the studies that covered the recent post-reform period are by Sachs et al. (2002), Ahluwalia (2001) and Shetty (2003). The study by Sachs et al. (2002) concludes that like other they also 'find a tendency towards divergence rather than convergence'. Using different measures of convergence, the authors find that India, like China, does not show any signs of uneven conditional convergence, let alone unconditional convergence. In the list of the studies cited by them is the one by Ahluwalia (2001) addresses the issues of differential economic performances of Indian States under the influence of the forces of globalization in the 1990s and finds in agreement with most others that no evidence of unconditional convergence. However, he claims that there is evidence of conditional convergence.

Nagraj (2002), examining the effects of economic reforms on output, investment and employment, singled out the distribution of Net State Domestic Product (NSDP) originating in the manufacturing sector across states. This is because economic reforms in India have essentially focused on the manufacturing sector. Nagraj's analysis shows no statistically significant improvement in the growth performance of states that have initiated market-oriented policies.

Singh and Srinivasan (2002) looking at the period 1990–1 to 1998–9 however found that the evidence does not permit one to reach very definite conclusions on convergence or divergence across Indian states.

In one of the most recent studies by Singh et al. (2003) it has been shown that India's record with respect to inequality in the post reform period is not bad with respect to potential problems of growing regional disparities which seem to be similar to our article.

DATA SOURCES

The National Accounts Statistics (NAS) brought out by the Central Statistical Organization (CSO) is the main source of data for various regional economic activities in India. The statistical department of the state prepares the regional data for each state and the CSO accepts them. One has procured the data directly from the CSO in computer tapes. The data are available both in current as well as in constant prices.

I. ECONOMIC GROWTH IN THE NORTH-EAST ECONOMY

Here, one will consider the growth performance of the north-east as a whole and also of the states within the north-east for the period of 1980–1 to 1997–8. Table 11.1 gives the growth rates of NSDP and its different components for the north-east as a whole in comparison to all-India performance for the period of 1980–1 to 1997–8 at constant 1980–1 prices. We have divided the NSDP into five major sectors such as agriculture, manufacturing, the primary sector, services and infrastructure. One defines agriculture as agriculture plus forestry, logging and fishing. The primary sector is defined as one that has mining and quarrying activities. Manufacture includes both registered and unregistered manufacturing activities. The infrastructure sector includes construction, electricity, gas and water supply, transport, storage and communication. Finally, the service sector is defined as that of trade, hotels and restaurants, banking and insurance, real estate, business services, public administration, and other services.

Table 11.1 clearly indicates that there is no basis to believe that the north-east has been stagnating. Rather, it has been growing, though its growth performance has been poor, relative to the all India levels. That is, while the NSDP for India has been growing at an average rate of 5.1 per cent per annum, the north-east has been growing at an annual average rate of 3.88 per cent. The scenario is nearly the same for the different components of NSDP, except for the primary sector

TABLE 11.1: COMPOUND GROWTH RATES OF DIFFERENT SECTORS OF GDP AT 1980–1 PRICE: A COMPARISON BETWEEN THE NORTH-EAST AND THE ALL INDIA PERFORMANCE, 1980–1 TO 1997–8

Sectors	Growth Rates for NE	R^2	Growth Rates for India	$\bar{R}^2$
Agriculture	2.34* (16.85)	0.94	2.9* (12.06)	0.90
Manufacturing	2.33* (7.22)	0.76	6.4* (43.57)	0.99
Primary Sector	2.80* (4.12)	0.51	2.3* (7.16)	0.76
Services	5.20* (44.16)	0.99	6.3* (58.39)	0.99
Infrastructure	5.79* (28.95)	0.98	5.8* (49.85)	0.99
NSDP	3.88* (32.49)	0.98	5.1* (43.27)	0.99

Note: The figures in the parenthesis are the *t* values and * denotes the significance at less than 5 per cent level.

whose growth rate is a little above the national average. This is quite understandable in view of the north-east's relative abundance in natural resources. In the case of infrastructure sector, the growth rate is very close to the all-India average. This indicates the impact of increasing Central investments in power, electricity, oil and gas. Strikingly indeed, it can be observed that the differences in the growth rates are much more pronounced in the case of manufactures. It shows that while India, as a whole, has been experiencing an annual average growth of 6.4 per cent, the north-east has been growing only at the rate of 2.33 per cent per annum. This, perhaps, can explain why the NSDP for the north-east has been growing at an annual rate, which is much below the all-India average rate. Indirectly, it implies that the people of the north-east could not improve their well-being as much as their all-India counterpart, due to such low growth in manufacturing. It becomes very obvious when we look at the per capita growth rates of NSDP for the various north-east states.

Table 11.2 shows the NSDP growth and also per capita growth rates for each of the north-east states individually. It can be seen that except for Assam, Manipur and Meghalaya, NSDP growth rates are above or close to the national average rate of 5.1 per cent. However, the NSDP growth rate for the major state of the region, Assam, is very dismal. Its growth rate, 3.3 per cent, is far behind the all-India average.

A growth rate by itself does not say enough about the impact of growth on the well-being of people. For this, we need to look at the per capita growth rates. Table 11.2 gives a contrasting view. The per capita growth rates of NSDP for four (Assam, Manipur, Meghalaya, Nagaland) out of seven states are much lower, relative to the all-India per capita growth rate. Only Arunachal Pradesh's performance is well above the national average and the performances of Mizoram and Tripura are very close to the all-India average. While the high levels of NSDP growth rates for some states such as Arunachal Pradesh, Mizoram, Nagaland and Meghalaya could perhaps be explained by low initial values of NSDP, the relatively lower levels in terms of per capita growth, could be explained by very rapid population growth in these states. As is obvious from the table, the population growth rates for all the states are much above the national average of 1.8 per cent. Nagaland and Mizoram, both have experienced phenomenal rates of population growth. This alarming rate of population growth has not only adversely affected the per capita growth, but has also

TABLE 11.2: COMPOUND GROWTH RATES OF NSDP AND PER CAPITA NSDP FOR DIFFERENT STATES OF THE NORTH-EAST AT 1980–81 PRICE, 1980-1 TO 1997-8

N-E States	NSDP Growth Rates	R^2	Per Capita Growth	R^2	Population Growth	$\bar{R}^2$
Arunachal Pradesh	8.12* (41.08)	0.99	5.20* (27.9)	0.98	2.9* (76.17)	0.99
Assam	3.31* (28.73)	0.98	1.13* (9.62)	0.85	2.2* (182.51)	0.99
Manipur	4.86* (70.96)	0.99	2.38* (32.03)	0.98	2.5* (153.32)	0.99
Meghalaya	4.97* (22.66)	0.97	2.11* (11.31)	0.88	2.8* (175.93)	0.99
Mizoram	8.31* (14.65)	0.93	5.74* (12.14)	0.90	3.3* (37.07)	0.98
Nagaland	7.28* (25.94)	0.98	3.04* (9.74)	0.88	4.2* (56.21)	0.99
Tripura	6.42* (21.93)	0.97	3.67* (11.75)	0.89	2.7* (76.87)	0.99
NE	3.88* (32.49)	0.98	3.33* (33.77)	0.98	2.4* (230.84)	0.99
India	5.1* (43.27)	0.99	3.30* (23.14)	0.97* (13.38)	1.8	0.91

Note: The figures in the parenthesis are the *t* values and * denotes the significance at less than 5 per cent level.

become an issue of intense political debate on the role of illegal immigration to population growth.

Sparsely-populated Arunachal Pradesh has been able to maintain very high per capita growth rates in NSDP, but being the third highest in terms of population growth, this advantage of Arunachal Pradesh will be lost very soon if it fails to progress rapidly on its economic front. Thus, we can conclude that economic growth could not improve the well-being of the people too much, due to rapid growth in population.

The above picture apparently lends some credence to the 'commonly held view' that the north-east has been neglected and that the fruits of development have not been evenly distributed across various regions of the country. However, one should take care and precautions in drawing such a conclusion. The above analysis of data does not ascribe any causality of low growth performance, that is, one can in no way, say that the centre is responsible for the poor performance of the north-east. To the extent that economic growth is endogenous to a system, the north-east itself may as well be responsible for its low growth performance. It could be due to a lack of economic dynamism in policy framing or just lack of will to grow. All that one can therefore say, is that without a detailed analysis, we cannot pinpoint anyone as being responsible for the poor economic performance of the northeast. Quite possibly, it might be true that there are other constraints to industrialization, such as a lack of markets and adequate infrastructures for which the Central Government may be held responsible for not doing enough over the last five decades.

However, how the actual growth is changing overtime, can't be seen from the linear model as shown above (Table 11.1). For this, we have to examine if there exists any non-linearity in the growth paths. Estimates of non-linear regressions for growth rates are given in Table 11.1A (see Appendix A). Our non-linear results show that except for the NSDP, all other growth paths show non-linear relationship. Agriculture and manufacture show that growth rates have indicated a downward trend by 1986, while the primary sector has shown an upward turn around 1994. The ever-increasing population growth rate has, however, shown a decreasing trend towards 1996. Similarly, Table 11.2A (see Appendix A) gives the non-linear relationships in per capita NSDP growth rates. It shows that except for Arunachal Pradesh, Meghalaya and Nagaland, the remaining four states show non-linear patterns.

II A. STRUCTURAL CHANGE: AN INDIAN PERSPECTIVE

Did economic growth change the structure of the economy? In our next step, we shall be examining whether the nature of growth has been growth-augmenting or growth-retarding. One of the main features of structural transformation is a rapid rise in the relative importance of manufacturing production accompanied by a relative decline in primary production.[1] We assume that an economic growth will be of the growth-augmenting type if in the initial process of economic growth, the shares of agriculture fall and the shares of manufactures rise. In contrast, the growth process will be of the growth-retarding type if the shares of manufactures fall and the shares of services rise. This is because, while the manufacturing sector provides the basic foundation of growth by providing various externalities and scale economies, and thereby continuous growth potentialities, a rise in the service sector at the initial phase of growth may only overheat an economy rather than causing growth. As hypothesized above, we expect that with growth, certain structural changes must have taken place within the north-east, such that the shares of agriculture declines and the shares of manufactures and services rise.

According to Chenery et al. (1988), the structural transformation of a developing economy is defined as the set of changes in the composition of demand, trade, production, and factor use that takes place as the per capita income rises. The main objective of his study was to understand how country differences in the sources and also in the rates of growth determine the process of transformation as a whole. Chenery et al. (1988) in their cross-country study, have identified three common features of industrialization and they are (i) shifts in domestic demand, (ii) the growing intermediate use of industrial products and (iii) the transformation of comparative advantage as factor proportions change. In their phenomenal study, they have compared nine economies: Colombia, Korea, Taiwan, Turkey, Mexico, Yugoslavia, Israel, Japan and Norway. In assessing the shifts in domestic demand, their study finds a substantial fall in the share of food demand and increases in the share of producer goods and social overhead with the rise in per capita income. The tendency for the share of intermediate use of commodities to increase with rising income is found in their empirical analysis. The third major source of industrialization, as pointed out by the Chenery et al. study, is the transformation of international trade. In our empirical study, we have ignored the role of trade as source of industrialization because in India, international trade doesn't contribute more than 10 per cent (up to 1995) of the national economy.[2] Hence, the main focus of our panel study for 28 Indian states over the years 1981–98 is to understand the role of demand and supply side factors in explaining the industrialization of states. Industrialization is commonly measured by the rise in the share of manufacturing in NSDP. Manufacturing output is determined by demand and supply side factors. The underlying logic of the model that we have estimated from state level panel data (28 states over the period 1981–98) is that it traces changes in the economic structure to the evolution of two main factors: the level of demand and population.[3] Our regression model traces changes in the economic structure through a rise in manufacturing output, dependent on three major factors:

purchasing power of the state captured by per capita NSDP (NSDPPERCAP), domestic demand measured by state population (POPL) and the composition of factor supply (infrastructure). We have incorporated 28 state dummies to take into account the state-specific characteristics. Similarly, the time dummies will take care of the periodic changes on manufacturing growth.

We have carried out Feasible Genarilsed Least Squares (GLS) to test our model:

$$MO_{it} = \alpha_o + \beta_1 NSDPPERCAP_{it} + \beta_2 POPL_{it} + \beta_1 INFRA_{it} + y_1 (STD_1\text{-}STD_{28})$$
$$+ y_2(YREND_1\text{-}YREND_{18}) + \varepsilon_{it} + v_i$$

The results are reported in Table 11.3

Our econometric results show that growth in manufacturing output is significantly and positively dependent on purchasing power (NSDP per capita), state's domestic market (state population) and infrastructure facilities available. We have dropped the twenty-seventh state dummy which is the UP. Thus, the dummy coefficients measure the state effects with respect to the dropped state. Tellingly, all state effects are significant, when compared to the twenty-seventh state. This tells that 'state characteristics' are significantly determining the levels of manufacturing output. What is also interesting is that the pre-liberalization periods are more significantly affecting manufacturing growth, compared to the post-liberalization period, which

TABLE 11.3: GLS REGRESSION, 1980–1 TO 1997–8

	MO
NSDPPERCAP	5084545*
	(8.515)
POPL	0.005187*
	(8.555)
INFRA	1.425986*
	(15.543)
Chi² (47)	10389.82
Prob> Chi²	0.0000
N	484

Notes: *denotes significance less than 5 per cent.
 The dependent variable in column (1) is manufacturing output. The regression includes 28 state dummies (not reported) and 18-year dummies (not reported). The numbers are the coefficients of the regression model. Figures inside brackets are the z-statistic.

is captured by the time dummies. This result is quite surprising, as one would expect that the opening up of the economy is likely to break the monopoly power of states by weakening the traditional forward and backward linkages and lead to a more even distribution of economic activities across regions, along with an expansion of foreign trade [Elizodo and Krugman (1992)]. But our econometric results show that overall significance for the post-liberalization periods have become weaker in explaining manufacturing growth. This is mostly because some states, which have traditionally developed infrastructure facilities, financial transactions and marketing, are doing better in terms of manufacturing output compared to other states, that is indicated by the significance of state effects.

The major finding of our regression result is that manufacturing output is significantly determining the growth prospect of the states. The higher the share of manufacturing to the NSDP, the higher is the income of the state. Hence, states which have a slow pace, have to rise to push the income level through the multiplier effect, as the manufacturing sector plays a crucial role in economic development (Chenery 1988).

It will be interesting to find out how 28 states and UTs have performed in certain selected years in respect of their income shares and manufacturing orientations. Chart 1 presents the state's manufacturing orientation ratio (m/p) and relative income position (y/p) for three years, 1980, 1990 and 1996; y, m and p are the state's share in total NSDP, total manufacturing output and total population respectively. The state reporting m/p > 1 has manufacturing orientation and the state reporting y/p > 1 is better placed in interstate income distribution. Thus, we expect that a manufacturing orientation may be associated with high-income positions. The graphic description of Chart 1, presented below, shows the relative position of 28 states in respect of income, as well as their manufacturing orientation.

The Chart 1 is based on the Table 11.4, presents certain interesting developments in the regional structure of the Indian economy.

(i) The states which have high manufacturing (m/p >1) orientations in all three years are Delhi, Goa, Gujarat, Haryana, Maharashtra, Pondicherry, Punjab, and Tamil Nadu. West Bengal and the Andaman and Nicobar Islands have both declined in their initial high status of manufacturing orientation by 1990 and they could not climb up to their initial position of high manufacturing orientation till 1996. All these states' NSDP shares exceed the respective population share

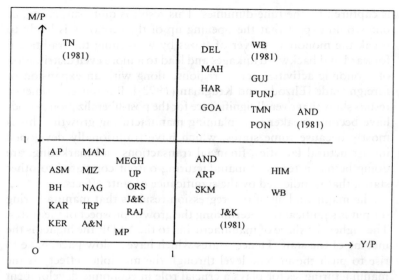

Chart 1: Income and Manufacturing Orientation for all the states of India for the period: 1980–1, 1990–1 and 1995–6

($y/p > 1$) in all three years. While Tamil Nadu has improved substantially in its income position in 1990, West Bengal has witnessed a sharp deterioration in manufacturing orientation in the 1990s.

(ii) The states which do not have a manufacturing orientation, have fluctuating positions in the interstate income distribution. Among these states, those which report good status in income distribution are the Andaman and Nicobar Islands, Arunachal Pradesh, West Bengal, Himachal Pradesh, Sikkim and J&K in 1980.

(iii) All other states including the entire NE region, with the only exception of Arunachal Pradesh and Sikkim, have never crossed the benchmark of $r/p = 1$ in any of the three years.

(iv) The gaps between top and bottom states in terms of their income status are quite substantially large in these three years. Punjab, the top most state, has 2 per cent to 2.5 per cent of the total population of 28 states and commands 4 per cent to 5 per cent of the aggregate of these states' NSDP, while Bihar, the bottom-most state, has 10 per cent of the population and commands only 6 per cent of the aggregate NSDP in 1980. Assam, the most important state of the north-eastern region, similarly has a share of population of 2.6 per cent, but it

TABLE 11.4: MANUFACTURING ORIENTATION AND RELATIVE INCOME POSITIONS FOR VARIOUS STATES AND UNION TERRITORIES OF INDIA

States/ UTs	Manufacturing Orientation (m/p)			Relative Income Position (y/p)		
	1981–1	1990–1	1995–6	1980–1	1990–1	1995–6
A&N	1.086744	0.572135	0.918211	1.672153	1.22368	1.340123
AP	0.611715	0.843458	0.849904	0.882982	0.977037	0.981599
ARP	0.404016	0.409854	0.495987	1.005118	1.284818	1.495515
ASSM	0.331175	0.25012	0.168773	0.821931	0.732159	0.653299
BIH	0.400064	0.47344	0.286835	0.586764	0.567638	0.401036
DEL	2.925355	2.981453	2.596719	2.578851	2.583243	2.703382
GOA	3.062976	3.835314	4.096394	2.012393	2.315437	2.488117
GUJ	1.585083	1.907148	2.444396	1.241249	1.252332	1.434153
HAR	1.323942	1.748565	1.525916	1.516629	1.663823	1.500345
HIM	0.293804	0.565911	0.609416	1.090109	1.06275	1.026924
J&K	0.32626	0.319401	0.302266	1.136187	0.846071	0.797399
KAR	0.840042	0.918537	0.910042	0.972881	0.966747	1.043322
KER	0.828235	0.689553	0.62565	0.964692	0.86089	0.897193
MAHR	2.634849	2.457529	2.754361	1.558317	1.651889	1.890235
MAN	0.258281	0.260796	0.1338	0.908305	0.824654	0.812958
MEGH	0.173315	0.180058	0.151233	0.87075	0.821867	0.737117
MIZ	0.128568	0.121305	0.156432	0.824643	0.765211	0.943848
MP	0.657584	0.676193	0.649055	0.8687	0.804258	0.756157
NAG	0.115238	0.396253	–	0.870956	0.93701	–
ORS	0.539905	0.387971	0.394608	0.840512	0.655981	0.666278
PON	1.783039	1.88805	1.885483	1.787679	1.509638	1.205891
PUNJ	1.162949	1.518975	1.673546	1.711191	1.768584	1.703052
RAJ	0.534751	0.545579	0.569424	0.781749	0.921071	0.80491
SKM	0.353557	0.386349	–	1.005207	1.597865	–
TN	1.622828	1.353103	1.316399	0.958598	1.060775	1.149877
TRP	0.236984	0.136098	0.145931	0.836035	0.778666	0.860727
UP	0.488444	0.617838	0.502674	0.817508	0.783399	0.67465
WB	1.472533	0.950109	0.883224	1.134787	1.01704	1.102575

Source: NSDP at constant and current prices for states and Union Territories provided by the CSO.

commands NSDP share of only 2.1 per cent. In 1995, Assam's NSDP share had declined to 1.8 per cent, Bihar's share had declined to 4.5 per cent, while Punjab's share had increased to 4.3 per cent. This relationship between manufacturing orientation and relative income positions seems to be generally consistent with Kaldor's hypothesis that there is a positive relationship between manufacturing orientation and growth rates (see, Kaldor, 1966). A number of studies based on cross-section data on countries confirm this hypothesis. Among the regions, which had inherited manufacturing orientation from the colonial period, Maharashtra and Gujarat have done relatively well even after Independence, whereas West Bengal has steadily declined. It may be interesting to investigate if there is any relationship between the rates of deceleration in manufacturing output with that of the rate of productivity growth. Mathur (1987) provides insights to this. Delhi, Goa, Haryana, Punjab, Karnataka and Pondicherry are the 'newly industrialized' regions in the Indian economy.

II B. STRUCTURAL CHANGE: A NORTH-EAST PERSPECTIVE

Table 11.3A (Appendix A) gives a snapshot situation of the shares of various components of NSDP for the beginning and the terminal years of our study. We observe that in 1980–1, agriculture was the major occupation of most of the states, followed by services. For the hilly states such as Mizoram, Nagaland and Meghalaya, services occupy a relatively more important position than agriculture for obvious reasons. In these regions, arable land may be relatively scarce. Similarly, mining and other primary resources are also relatively scarce in supply for all the states, as can be observed from the share of the primary sector in total NSDP. The most crucial factor of economic development is the manufacturing sector, that shows very low shares, less than 10 per cent, for all the states. The situation is not very different in 1999–2000. The share of agriculture shows some decline for all the states, while the share of manufactures virtually remained stagnant. Infrastructure and the services share show an increase for all the states, except for Mizoram in infrastructure and Nagaland in services. In Table 11.4A (see Appendix), we report our regression results for the changes in the shares overtime for the last two decades. The compound rate of change in the shares for the entire north-east, tells us the story about structural changes in the north-east.

Sector-Wise Growths

In Table 11.1, we clearly see that all the sectors of north-east are growing, although its growth performance has been poor, relative to the all-India level. However, the non-linear growth paths as reported in Table 11.5, reveal quite a different scenario. While most of the

TABLE 11.5: NON-LINEAR GROWTH RATES FOR DIFFERENT SECTORS IN THE NORTH-EAST STATES AT 1980–1 PRICE

Sector	Period	Intercept	T	T2	T3	R^2	D-W
Agriculture	1981–98	11.778* (559.03)	0.035* (6.994)	−0.0006* (−2.48)	−	0.96	2.35
Infrastructure	1981–98	10.107* (466.86)	0.0579* (28.958)		−	0.98	1.66
Manufacturing	1981–98	9.843* (267.27)	0.064* (7.208)	−0.002* (−4.733)	−	0.90	1.55
Primary	1981–98	9.659* (72.802)	0.232* (3.949)	−0.022* (−3.112)	0.0006* (2.7419)	0.80	1.75
Services	1981–98	11.687* (916.56)	0.052* (44.167)		−	0.99	1.43
Unregistered	1981–98	9.041* (279.47)	0.036* (12.223)		−	0.90	1.18
Registered	1981–98	9.2405* (182.33)	0.118* (5.286)	−0.008* (−2.934)	0.00018* (2.0036)	0.94	1.59
Population	1981–98	17.009* (1503.8)	0.009* (1.913)	0.0023* (3.883)	−0.0001* (−5.045)	0.99	2.31
SDP	1981–98	12.68* (981.62)	0.038* (32.495)			0.98	1.47

Note: * denotes significance less than 5 per cent, ** denotes significance between 5 per cent to 10 per cent, without * denotes insignificant.

sectors have a clear upward linear trend in their respective growth paths, the non-linear trends of agriculture, manufacturing and primary sector growths have shown a downturn in later periods (see the fitted growth paths in Figs. 11.1–11.3). The only saving grace is that the population growth in the region shows a clear decreasing trend after 1997 (Fig. 11.4).

Evaluation of The Shares

As expected, with economic growth, the shares of agriculture as well as the primary sectors in the NSDP have been decreasing at an average rate of 1.4 and 1.08 per cent respectively and the shares of services and infrastructures have been increasing by 1.3 and 1.9 per cent respectively. However, the most disturbing fact is that against the normal historical trend (Chenery and Syrquin, 1988), the shares of manufactures have been decreasing at an average rate of 1.55 per cent for the entire north-east. Our regression analyses reveal that non-linear estimates give the best fit for many cases as reported in Table 11.5.

As in the case of growth rates, we observe that most of the shares show non-linear trends, indicating non-constant growth in the shares as can be seen from Table 11.5A (Appendix A). While agriculture shows a linear trend rate of decline, the other sectors show non-linear relationships. It can be observed that the downturn in the shares of manufactures could be located sometime around 1985.

From the viewpoint of individual states (not reported in the table) we observe that the compound growth rates of the shares over the twenty years' period, show a decline in agricultural shares for Arunachal Pradesh, Assam, Manipur, Meghalaya, Nagaland and Tripura, but Mizoram shows a small, positive trend. But surprisingly, manufacturing shows decreasing trends for Assam, Manipur and Tripura, while all the other hill states show positive trends. Similar, conflicting trends could also be observed in cases of infrastructure and services.

III. ECONOMIC GROWTH AND INEQUALITY

An interesting issue relating to economic growth is whether economic growth causes inequality. In our regional framework, we may ask if the differential inter-regional growth processes results in increasing

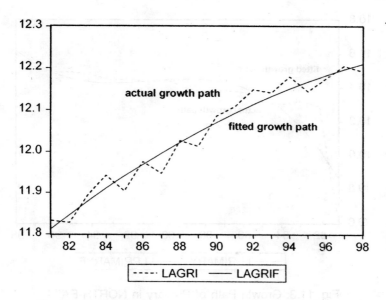

Fig. 11.1: Growth Path of Agriculture in NORTH-EAST

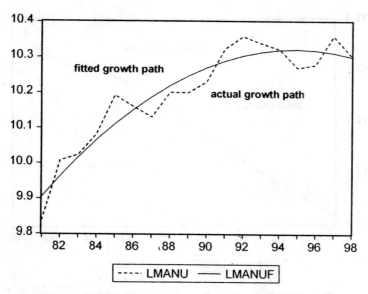

Fig. 11.2 Growth path of Manufacturing in NORTH-EAST

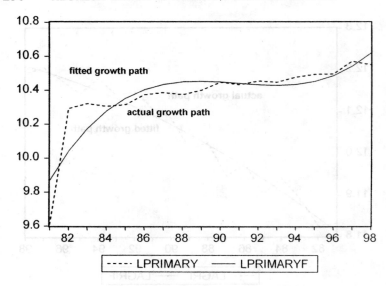

Fig. 11.3: Growth Path of Primary in NORTH-EAST

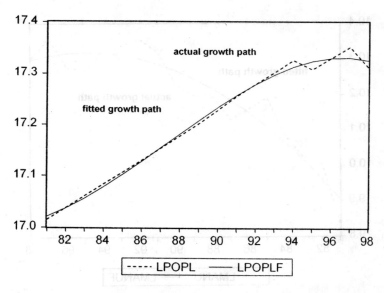

Fig. 11.4: Population Growth Path in NORTH-EAST

inter-regional inequality. It is obviously understandable why rising inter-regional inequality is not desirable in a federal economy.

THE THEIL INDEX OF INEQUALITY MEASURE

In a given situation, inequality can be measured in many ways. The measures, which are normally used in the context of inter-state disparity, are Coefficient of Variation, Gini Coefficient and Disparity Ratio. We have used a single measure, namely, the Entropy Measure, developed by Theil (1967, 1977). The advantage of an entropy measure of inequality over other measures was discussed in Das and Barua (1996). Inequality among states in any economic indicator, such as income, can be graphically represented by plotting the respective states' shares in that indicator [Net State Domestic Product (NSDP) for instance] against their shares in total population. The NSDP distribution among states is regarded as 'equal' if for any state, the NSDP share and the population share are identical. This 'equal' distribution corresponds to the diagonal of a Lorenz Curve diagram, where inequality is defined in terms of deviations from this diagonal. Being an information-theoretic measure, an entropy measure of inequality is based upon a logarithmic transformation of these state-wise shares.

We have computed entropy measures to capture interstate inequality in income, which is defined here as NSDP. We further divide the NSDP into 5 separate groups such as (i) agriculture (ii) manufacturing (iii) services (iv) primary and (v) infrastructure, and measure inequalities for each of the cases separately. These measures are defined as follows:

$$E_x = \Sigma\, x_i \log (x_i / p_i) \qquad (1)$$

Where $x = Y, A, M, P, I$ (indicators such as income, agriculture, etc.); $i = 1, 2, 7$ (states); $\Sigma x_i = \Sigma p_i = 1$; p_i is the state's share in the total population of 7 states and y, a, m, n, s and f are respectively the i state's share in the sum total of 7 states' gross domestic products, agriculture, manufacturing, services, primary and infrastructure. Thus, E_y and E_m measure inter-state inequality in income and manufacturing respectively. E_x takes non-negative values and is equal to zero where there is no inequality. An equal distribution is denoted by $E_x = 0$, which happens when every region's population share and its share in the economic indicator are equal.

Inequality at The All India Level

An excursion through the early Five Year Plan documents would reveal that the reduction of regional inequalities has been one of the major objectives of successive economic planning in India. However, India's planning process has not been able to tackle this issue in a satisfactory manner. The political economy of federalism should recognize that the resource allocation problem must consider the entire domain of the federal economy, so as to provide for an economic justification of a federal organization. Unfortunately, in our centralized parliamentary democracy, the big (in terms of population and the numbers of the Members of Parliament) and hence the powerful states tended to receive more attention in terms of economic resource allocation.

The basic economic principle of federalism is that it provides the externality of markets to all. The success of markets as a strong, integrating force requires that no state should be in a position to appropriate the advantages that the market provides. If the initial conditions are at variance across the regions, then the Centre has to play a role in providing similar level playing grounds for all. Such an accommodating behaviour leads to convergence in economic performances of the regions, while indifference or exclusionary policies lead to divergences or inequalities. The Nehruvian planners clearly saw the need for such a convergence as a cementing force for upholding the unity and integrity of the country.

Careful observation, however, reveals that the development planning models in India had not explicitly used any regional inequality constraint in the maximization of the growth function. All that the Mahalanobis Model did, was simply to maximize the rate of growth via maximization of the rate of savings. And it was indeed a legitimate exercise, as the early literature on economic development emphasized on increasing income inequalities for maximizing the rate of growth via the maximization of savings, where savings were viewed as the key constraint to growth a la Harrod.

The distribution issue was, therefore, left entirely for the Planning Commission and the Finance Commission to tackle outside the planning process. The Planning Commission and the Finance Commission used the instruments of grants and subsidies and of some revenue sharing mechanism between the states and the centre respectively, but never ever were such instruments used in order to minimize the variances of income inequalities. Thus, it is an entirely empirical question, whether the growth process had led to any adverse inter-regional income distribution in India.

A negative relationship between growth and inter-regional inequality is not desirable in a federal economy as mentioned above. The reasons are obvious. However, we wish to emphasize only on three points: First, while in a market economy, an individual being unable to influence the market outcome acts in a passive way, his counterpart in a federal economy – the region – can however act in the most decisive manner. Thus, in a federal economy, if a region is progressing at a relatively faster rate than another, the lagging region may demonstrate envy, which may cause conflicts and tensions within the federal system. Second, even if economic benefits in terms of higher growth could be achieved by creating regional inequality, the benefits so achieved, may not outweigh the cost of containing the dissenting voice of the people of the region lagging behind. And the third, particularly when an economy is in a phase of transition from a regimented towards a liberalized economy, political acceptability of policy changes on a much wider scale is desirable for making the transition successful. It will be difficult to politically sell the idea of liberalization, if it is believed that liberalization may cause growth, but only at the expense of rising inter-regional income inequalities.

Growth and Inequality in The North-East

In our effort to examine this relationship, we shall first consider the north-east in isolation and try to see the relative income positions of various north-east states in comparison to the average north-east income. Then, we shall look at the relative income positions of the north-east states in comparison to the Indian states. For the purpose, we calculate the Theil measure of inequality for NSDP and its various components for the north-east states and their compound growth rates (see Table 11.6A and 11.7A in the Appendix).

Table 11.7A shows that while the inequality indices, the entropies, show an increasing trend for all sectors of the north-east economy, the most pronounced growth in inequality could be observed in cases of services and infrastructure. The manufacturing shows the lowest rate of increase in inequality. Interestingly, inequality in NSDP has shown the highest rate of growth.

Like the growth rates and the shares, the inequality levels also show non-linear rising paths. Table 11.8A (in Appendix) gives the regression results for non-linear estimation of inequality growths. The only sector that shows a linear growth rate in inequality, is the infrastructure sector. The inequality graphs show decreasing tendencies for agriculture and primary sectors and rising tendencies for manufacturing, services and the NSDP.

THE ENTROPY MEASURE OF INEQUALITY AT THE ALL INDIA LEVEL

The entropy measures of inequality in income (E_y) and its various components for this period 1980–1 to 1996–7 are given in Table 11.6. Entropy Estimates at Constant Prices (28 states and UTs) 1980–1 = 100, given in Table 11.6 indicates that except for the primary products, regional disparities have increased during 1980–97 on almost all counts. These inequality trends are analyzed in Table 11.7. The annual average rate of growth of inequality has been the highest in

TABLE 11.6: ALL INDIA ENTROPY FOR DIFFERENT SECTORS

Year	Agriculture	Manu-facturing	Primary	Services	Infra-structure	NSDP
1980–1	3.931625	21.78497	18.25452	9.631526	10.43930	4.718401
1981–2	4.627755	19.01402	18.74329	9.481619	10.95758	4.696861
1982–3	5.306370	18.00740	18.13985	9.909728	11.75116	4.958717
1983–4	4.266501	18.16664	17.26742	9.559418	11.96291	4.601927
1984–5	4.019378	17.29663	18.24952	9.097317	12.17943	4.705339
1985–6	4.633679	19.33577	17.34749	10.12972	12.15075	5.238478
1986–7	4.679559	20.74582	16.52260	9.850759	11.57915	5.195191
1987–8	5.770094	17.45538	16.99838	9.498747	12.09190	5.524591
1988–9	5.300876	17.06378	15.56957	9.356859	11.74434	5.296166
1989–90	5.622022	17.68838	17.35239	9.712498	12.99181	6.278179
1990–1	5.433355	18.88574	15.94796	9.580413	12.73096	5.968650
1991–2	6.356461	18.56945	13.90024	11.35743	13.18419	6.564580
1992–3	6.611351	22.33897	15.98985	11.99382	14.25757	7.966499
1993–4	6.589916	23.69411	16.37862	13.29823	15.74734	8.498246
1994–5	6.439145	26.01787	17.00445	13.72944	15.30823	8.941305
1995–6	7.053061	26.78033	17.38306	14.70320	15.80496	9.727413
1996–7	7.859003	26.57705	17.51058	14.27685	16.18508	9.736183

REGIONAL AND NATIONAL PERSPECTIVES

TABLE 11.7: ALL INDIAN COMPOUND GROWTH OF ENTROPY

Sectors	Entropy Growth Rates	R^2
Agriculture	3.68* (8.59)	0.83
Manufacturing	2.02* (3.32)	0.42
Primary	−0.67 (−2.06)	0.22
Services	2.75* (5.88)	0.70
Infrastructure	2.5* (10.22)	0.87
NSDP	5.07* (11.31)	0.89

NSDP and all are highly significant. The increase of inequality in manufacturing has been found to be positive, and significant. However, a break up of the manufacturing sector into registered and unregistered indicates that the inequality in the unregistered sector has been increasing at a much higher rate.

The non-linear estimates of the inequality exercise are reported in Table 11.9A in Appendix A. The Figures 11.5–11.8 analyse the fitted

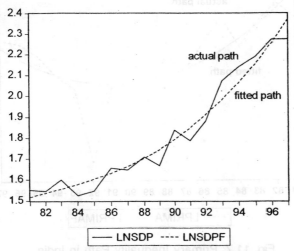

Fig. 11.5: Income Inequality Path in India

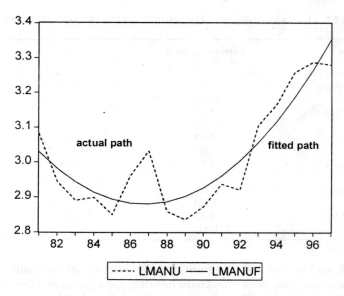

Fig.11.6: Manufacturing Inequality Path in India

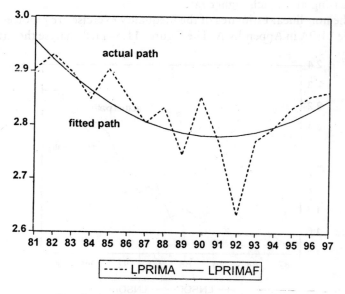

Fig. 11.7: Primary Inequality Path in India

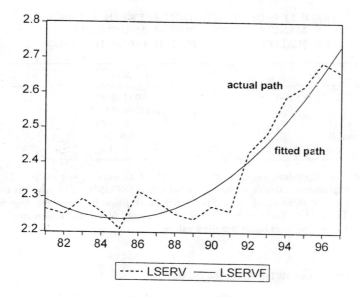

Fig. 11.8: Services Inequality Path in India

and actual all-India inequality growth path for income, manufacturing, primary and service sectors. The fitted path shows that the inequality is rising overtime for income, manufacturing and services. For primary, inequality was falling up to 1991 but after 1992, it is showing a rising trend.

INEQUALITY COMPARISON: ALL INDIA
AND THE NORTH-EAST

If we compare the north-east with other states of India in terms of inequality, we have to compare the entropy figures in the Tables 6A (in Appendix) and 11.6. We see that the crude entropy levels for agriculture, manufacturing, primary and services are higher at an all-India level, when compared to the north-east. The reason for high inequality across India than the north-eastern states is due to greater heterogeneity across states at all India level than within the north-east. However, for most of the sectors, the compound rate of entropy growth is higher in the north-east, when compared to the all-India level (Table 11.7A and Table 11.8).

TABLE 11.8: OLS ESTIMATION BETWEEN ALL INDIA MANUFACTURING OUTPUT AND INCOME INEQUALITY FOR THE PERIOD 1980–1 TO 1996–7.

	MO
INCOME IN EQ (E_y)	507258.9*
	(12.96083)
R^2	0.918
Adjusted R^2	0.9125
N	17

Note: The dependent variable in column (1) is manufacturing output. The explanatory variable in the right hand side is INCOMEINEQ, which is the entropy measure of inequality in income (E_y) that has been taken from Table 11.6. The numbers are the coefficients of the regression model. Figures inside brackets are the t-values.

ECONOMIC GROWTH AND INEQUALITY

It is interesting to empirically examine whether there is any conflict between income inequality (E_y) and manufacturing growth. Taking this into our hypothesis, we have run a regression in Table 11.8 on the level of manufacturing output by taking income inequality on the right hand side. The coefficient of INCOMEINEQ, the explanatory variable, is significantly positive (coefficient: 507258.9, t = 12.96 with $p > |t| = 0.000$). This shows that there is no conflict between inequality and manufacturing growth in India. We do not, however, wish to draw any strong conclusion from this as we believe that this issue requires much more detailed analysis. However, there must be adverse distributional implications for the concentration of manufacturing activities in a few big states, which suggest that the government should adopt adequate egalitarian income distribution policies.

IV. DEVELOPMENT STRATEGY: A NORTH-EAST PERSPECTIVE

Our findings above, have conclusively demonstrated that (i) the development strategy, if any, that has been followed for the north-east states, has not done any good for any of the state and (ii) it has led to increasing regional imbalances within the north-east. The most disturbing fact is, contrary to the usual belief, the decreasing role of the manufacturing sector in the process of development. If the objective of the Central Government is to increase employment potential in the region and to control insurgency movements, it has to reorient its development strategy for the north-east in such a way that it helps foster the growth of the manufacturing sector in the north-east. The fact that the manufacturing sector could not take-off despite the spectacular growth in the infrastructure and the service sectors, only remind us that certain biting constraints are coming in the way of the development of the manufacturing sector in the region. What one can *prima facie* think as a possible cause for this, is perhaps the constraint posed by the limited size of the domestic market. Obviously, the growth of infrastructure and the service sectors alone could not do much if these sectors were not supported by a strong and buoyant manufacturing sector. The major hurdle to investment and growth in the region is political uncertainty and chaos, and in that backdrop, the rising inter-regional inequality will increase rather than reduce such uncertainties. Policy makers have not paid enough attention to the impact of adverse movements in personal and regional income distributions and urban-rural disparities. Some adjustments, thus, have to be made in the strategy of development in order to achieve a more egalitarian distribution of income among regions and this should be from the north-east as well as from the Indian perspective. We have also demonstrated that interstate income distribution has moved adversely during the period of 1980–97 for the Indian economy as a whole, thereby confirming earlier findings by Das and Barua (1996). The gaps between the richest and poorest state is too large to be acceptable in any stable federal structure. For the sake of long-term unity and integrity of the country, these gaps must be reduced. This is possible only if meaningful development activities take place in the backward states. In the light of our empirical finding, we have certain suggestions to offer for increasing economic growth and reducing inter-state disparities.

1. Policies should be directed towards increasing the size of the north-east market, which could only be possible through increasing inter-regional and inter-national trade.
2. Central transfers to the states should have specific developmental objectives and adequate precautions should be taken such that these funds are not spent on direct consumption. As far as possible, the management of these funds should be entrusted with the village

Panchayats. Fund allocation should be village, rather than state-specific, so that misuse can be minimized.
3. Central investments in projects in a state should be consistent with their respective factor proportions. Heavy industries set up in relatively land-locked states like Nagaland and Meghalaya will not help industrializing the state. Moreover, such investments are not likely to reduce income disparities, both inter-state and intra-state. Investment patterns in states should be consistent with the local conditions. For instance, investments in labour-intensive industries like textiles, paper products, handicrafts, agricultural processing and food processing, software management and in vocational training facilities, specific skill formation, development of forest and water resources including fisheries, are consistent with the factor endowment of a state like Assam. Similarly, arable land-scare regions like Nagaland, Mizoram, Meghalaya, Manipur and Arunachal Pradesh must look for high value-added manufacturing such as toys and footwear, umbrellas, semi-conductor and software processing, garments and handicrafts, floriculture and fruit processing.
4. Large investment in a few sectors like oil, coal or petrochemicals is not likely to reduce income disparities. Such a policy, if undertaken, will retard the growth of the economy, make almost every state worse off and raise internal disparities. However, capital investment in infrastructure development in states will have an equalizing effect in the long run. In fact, the development of transport and communication facilities in the hill regions is badly needed.
5. Interstate disparities can be reduced, if the work force participation rate is improved in the backward states. In backward states, a large portion of the population is virtually excluded from the workforce due to lack of acquisition of skills. New industries, which can cater to modern tastes and designs, cannot be set up in backward regions not so much due to the scarcity of capital but mainly due to non-availability of local skills. In the final analysis, state-wise income inequality boils down to the unequal distribution of facilities for skill formation and training. It is often observed that the people from states like Assam, Manipur or Nagaland tend to migrate to relatively developed states in India to acquire skills and productive employment. The rapid decline in educational standards from primary upwards to the university levels, contri-

buted to a large-scale exodus of young students to the more advanced metropolitan centres for their education. These masses of students, after being educated outside their province, do not desire to go back to their respective province due to non-availability of job opportunities. As a result, the enlightened middle-class shrinks in size, which further poses a serious constraint to technological upgradation. An uneven distribution of educational facilities is responsible for this phenomenon. India is a country with tremendous diversity in culture, resource endowment and technology, which make inter-state disparity an acceptable fact of life. What this paper wants to highlight is the big gaps observed in our data between the top and the bottom states. In our view, such large differences in the levels of development and standards of living are likely to cause a lot of damage to our federal structure. More developmental grants should therefore be channeled to the relatively backward regions.

In this study, we have seen that certain states in India have been virtually left out of the mainstream of economic activities. The development of these states will not only improve the overall economic performance, but will also lead to a better income distribution, both personal and interstate. The primary step in this direction, as we have argued, involves the creation of infrastructure in the backward states and a dispersion of educational facilities. Otherwise, these islands of poverty and stagnation will stand out as big question marks in our federal experiment.

V. CONCLUSION

Taking 1980 to 1997 as the period of our study, we have looked at the economic growth performance and inequality among 28 Indian states and UTs in respect of income and its various components. Results show a steadily increasing trend in inequality among Indian states on all fronts during this period. Our main finding is that economic development in India has been rather unevenly spread among states. Gujarat, Maharashtra, Tamil Nadu and West Bengal were known for their manufacturing orientation even during the British rule. These states as well as Haryana, Karnataka and Punjab, which have acquired a manufacturing orientation in the post-Independence period are better placed than the rest in terms of development and standard of living. In order to address the conflict between growth and inequality, our study reveals that inequality in income is not necessarily bad for the growth of manufacturing. However, the Central Government should adopt adequate policies so that any conflict between growth and income distribution doesn't arise. Accordingly, states like Andhra Pradesh, Bihar and the north-east states such as Nagaland, Mizoram, Meghalaya, Arunachal Pradesh, Tripura, Manipur and Assam deserve serious attention.

The above analysis clearly shows that there have been growth and structural changes in the north-east economy, but the structural changes that one observes are not conducive for rapid economic development. Rapid economic development requires a continuous increase in the contribution of manufactures in the domestic product, which can ensure a progressive increase in income due to increasing returns to scale and specialization. The increase in infrastructure is a good indicator of development, but it cannot by itself contribute to growth. It often acts as a catalytic agent for development by facilitating the growth of manufactures. But the growth of manufactures requires a vast market, that unfortunately, is a limiting factor for the development for the north-east. Any scope for the expansion of markets will spurt off a manufacturing growth process since the infrastructure sector is becoming increasingly favourable for it.

NOTES

1. Y. Kube et al., 'Interdependence and Industrial Structure', *Industrialization and Growth: A Comparative Study*, a World Bank Publication, 1988.
2. This is however justified assumption as the share of trade in GDP has dramatically increased to above 30 per cent in recent years. But then it will be a difficult proposition to determine the share of each of the states in India's total trade.
3. Per capita NSDP and population and infrastructure.

REFERENCES

Ahluwalia, M.S., 'State Level Performance under Economic Reforms in India, in Anne Krueger (ed.)', *Economic Policy Reforms and the Indian Economy*, Chicago: University of Chicago Press, 2002.

Bajpai, N. and Jeffrey Sachs, 'Trends in Inter-State Inequalities of Income in India', Discussion Paper No. 528, Harvard Institute for International Development, Harvard University, 1996.
Bardhan, P.K. and T.N. Srinivasan, 'Income Distribution: Patterns, Trends and Policies', *Economic and Political Weekly*, 24 April 1971.
Barro, Robert and Sala-i-Martin, *Economic Growth*, New York: McGraw-Hill, 1995.
Bhatty, I.Z., 'Inequality and Poverty in Rural India' in P.K. Bardhan and T.N. Srinivasan, eds., *Poverty and Income Distribution in India*, Calcutta: Statistical Publishing Society, 1974.
Cashin, Paul and Ratna Sahay, 'Internal Migration, Centre-State Grants, and Economic Growth in the States of India', IMF Staff papers, vol. 43, no. 1, 1996, pp. 123–71.
Celasun, M., 'Sources of Industrial Growth and Structural Change: The Case of Turkey', World Bank Staff Working Paper 614, Washington, 1983.
Chatterjee, G.S. and N. Bhattacharya (1974), 'On Disparities in Per Capita Household Consumption in India', in T.N. Srinivasan and P.K. Bardhan (eds.), *Poverty and Income Distribution in India* Calcutta: Indian Statistial Institute, 1974 pp. 337–68.
Chenery, H.B., *Structural Change and Development Policy*, New York: Oxford University Press, 1979.
Chenery, H.B. and W.J. Raduchel, 'Substitution and Structural Change', in, *Structural change and Development Policy*, New York: Oxford, 1979, pp. 143–72.
Chenery, H.B. and S. Robinson and M. Syrquin, *Industrialization and Growth: A Comparative Study*, published for the World Bank, Oxford University Press, 1988.
Choudhury, Mahinder D. 'Behaviour of Spatial Income Inequality in a Developing Economy: India 1950–76', paper presented at the Ninth Conference of the Indian Asociation for Research in National Income and Wealth, 1974.
Choudhury, U.D.R., 'Inter-state and Intra-state Variations in Economic Development and Standard of Living' (monograph), New Delhi: National Institute of Public Finance and Policy, 1992.
Dandekar, V.M. and N. Rath, *Poverty in India*, Pune: Indian School of Political Economy, 1971.
Dasgupta, Dipankar, et al., 'Growth and Interstate Disparities in India', *EPW*, 1 July 2000, pp. 2413–17.
Das, S.K., A. Barua and M.N. Ghosh, 'Inter-state Economic Inequality in India: Some Implications for Development Strategy', Discussion Paper, New Delhi: International Trade and Development, Jawaharlal Nehru University, 1993.
Das, S.K. and A. Barua, 'Regional Inequalities, Economic Growth and

Liberalization: A Study of the Indian Economy', *Journal of Development Studies*, vol. 32, no. 3, 1996.

Dholakia, R., 'Spatial Dimensions of Acceleration of Economic Growth in India', *EPW*, vol. 29, no. 35, 21 August 1994, 2003–9.

Dholakia, R.H., *Regional Disparity in Economic Growth in India*, Delhi: Himalaya Publishing House, 1985.

George, K.K. *Centre-State Financial Flows and Inter-state Disparities*, Delhi: Criterion Books, 1988.

Govinda Rao, M., 'Proposals for State-Level Budgetary Reform', *EPW*, 1 February 1992.

Gupta, S., 'The Role of the Public Sector in Reducing Regional Income Disparity in India', *Journal of Development Studies*, vol. 9, no. 2, 1973, pp. 243–60.

Jain, L.R., K. Sundaram and S.D. Tendulkar, 'Dimensions of Rural Poverty: An Inter-regional Profile', *Economic and Political Weekly*, vol. 13, 1988.

Kaldor, N.,'Alternative Theories of Distribution', *Review of Economic Studies*, vol. 23, 1955–6, pp. 94–100.

——, *Causes of the Slow Rate of Economic Growth of the United Kingdom, An Inaugural Lecture*, Cambridge: Cambridge University Press, 1966.

Kubo, Y., 'Methodology for Measuring Sources of Industrial Growth and Structural Change', Washington, World Bank Development Economics Department, April 1980.

Kubo, Y. and S. Robinson, 'Sources of Industrial Growth and Structural Change: A Comparative Analysis of Eight Economies', in Proceedings of the Seventh International Conference on Input-Output Techniques, New York: United Nations (UNIDO), 1984.

Kuo, S.W., *Economic Growth and Structural Change in the Republic of China*, Washington: World Bank Development Research Department, 1979.

Kurian, N.J., 'Widening Regional Disparities in India – Some Indicators', *EPW*, vol. XXXV, no. 7, 12–18 February 2000.

Kuznets, S., 'Economic Growth and Income Inequality', *American Economic Review*, vol. XLV, 1955.

Majumdar, G. and J.L. Kapoor, 'Behaviour of Inter-State Income Inequalities in India', paper presented at the Twelfth Conference of the Indian Association for Research on National Income and Wealth, 1980.

Marjit, S. and S. Mitra, 'Convergence in Regional Growth Rates: Indian Research Agenda', *EPW*, vol. 31, no. 33, 17 August 1996, pp. 2239–42.

Mathur, A., 'Regional Development and Income Disparities in India: A Sectorial Analysis', *Economic Development and Cultural Change*, vol. 31, no. 3, 1983, pp. 475–505.

Mathur, A.K., 'Why Growth Rates Differ Within India: An Alternative Approach', *The Journal of Development Studies*, vol. 23, 1987.

Minhas, B.S., 'Rural Poverty, Land Redistribution and Development', *Indian Economic Review*, vol. 5, 1970.

Minhas, B.S. and L.R. Jani, 'Incidence of Rural Poverty in Different States and All India: 1970–1 to 1983', Technical Report No. 3915, New Delhi: Indian Statistical Institute, 1989.

Minhas, B.S. et al., 'Measurement of General Cost of Living for Urban India, All India and Different States', *Sarvekshana*, vol. XII, no. 1, 1988.

Mitra, Ashok, 'Will Growth and Centralized Fiscal Arrangements Do?', in I.S. Gulati, ed., *Centre-State Budgetary Transfers*, Delhi: Oxford University Press, 1987.

Mundle, Sudipto and M.G. Rao, 'The Volume and Composition of Government Subsidies in India: 1987–8', *Economic and Political Weekly*, 4 May 1991.

——, 'Issues in Fiscal Policy', in Bimal Jalan, ed., *The Indian Economy: Problems and Prospects*, New Delhi: Penguin, 1992.

Nagraj, R., A. Varoudakis and M.A. Veganzones, 'Long-run Growth Trends and Convergence across Indian States; mimeograph, Mumbai: GIDR, 1997.

Nair, K.R.G., 'A note on Inter-State Income Differentials in India 1950–1 to 1960–1', *Journal of Development Studies*, vol. 7, no. 1, 1971, pp. 441–7.

Oates, W.E., *Fiscal Federalism*, New York: Harcourt Brace and Jovanovich, 1972.

——, *Political Economy of Fiscal Federalism*, Lexington: Lexington Books, 1977.

Pasinetti, L., 'Rate of Profit and Income Distribution in relation to the Rate of Growth', *Review of Economic Studies*, vol. 29, 1961–2, pp. 267–79.

Persson, T. and G. Tabellini, 'Is Inequality Harmful for Growth?', *American Economic Review*, vol. 84, no. 3, 1994.

Planning Commission of India, 'Report of the Expert Group on Estimation of Proportion and Number of Poor', New Delhi: Perspective Planning Division, 1993.

Rao, M.F. Govind, R.T. Shand and K.P. Kaliranjan, 'Convergence of Income across Indian States: A Divergent View', *EPW*, vol. 34, no. 13, 27 March 1999, pp. 769–78.

Rao, M.G. and R.J. Chelliah, 'Survey of Research on Fiscal Federalism in India' (monograph), New Delhi: NIPFP, 1990.

Raman, J., 'Convergence or Uneven Development: A Note on Regional Development in India', Valparaison University, US, mimeograph, 1996.

Sachs, Jeffrey, Nirupam Bajpai and Ananthi Ramiah, 'Understanding Regional Economic Growth in India', paper presented for the Asian Economic Panel Meeting held in Seoul on 25–26 October 2001, pp. 1–49.

Sen, A.K., 'Poverty, Inequality and Unemployment: Some Conceptual Issues in Measurement', in P.K. Bardhan and T.N. Srinivasan, eds., *Poverty and Income Distribution in India*, Calcutta: Statistical Publishing Society, 1974.

Singh, Nirvikar and T.N. Srinivasan, 'India's Federalism, Economic Reform and Globalization', paper prepared for CREDPR project on Globalization and Comparative Federalism, 2002.

Srinivasan, T. N. and P.K. Bardhan, eds., *Poverty and Income Distribution in India*, Calcutta: Indian Statistical Institute.

Stambauch, R., 'Inequality and Social Status in Successive Generations', *European Economic Review*, vol. 10, 1977.

Theil, H., *Economics and Information Theory*, Amsterdam: North-Holland, 1967.

Vaidyanathan, A., 'Some Aspects of Inequalities in Living Standards in Rural India', in T.N. Srinivasan and P.K. Bardhan. eds., *Poverty and Income Distribution in India*', Calcutta: Indian Statistical Institute, 1974, pp. 215–41.

Williamson, J.G., 'Regional Inequality and the Process of National Development: A Description of the Patterns', *Economic Development and Cultural Change*, vol. 13, no. 4, 1965.

APPENDIX A

TABLE 11.1A: GROWTH RATES FOR DIFFERENT SECTORS IN NORTH-EAST STATES

Sector	Period	Intercept	T	T2	T3	R²	D-W
Agriculture	1981–98	11.778* (559.03)	0.035* (6.994)	−0.0006* (−2.48)	−	0.96	2.35
Infrastructure	1981–98	10.107* (466.86)	0.0579* (28.958)	−	−	0.98	1.66
Manufacturing	1981–98	9.843* (267.27)	0.064* (7.208)	−0.002* (−4.733)	−	0.90	1.55
Primary	1981–98	9.659* (72.802)	0.232* (3.949)	−0.022* (−3.112)	0.0006* (2.7419)	0.80	1.75
Services	1981–98	11.687* (916.56)	0.052* (44.167)	−	−	0.99	1.43
Population	1981–98	17.009* (1503.8)	0.009* (1.913)	0.0023* (3.883)	0.0001* (−5.045)	0.99	2.31
NSDP	1981–98	12.68* (981.62)	0.038* (32.495)	−	−	0.98	1.47

Note: * denotes significance less than 5 per cent; ** denotes significance between 5 per cent to 10 per cent, without * denotes insignificant.

TABLE 11.2A: SDP GROWTH RATE FOR DIFFERENT IN NORTH-EAST STATES (PER CAPITA)

States	Period	Intercept	T	T2	T3	R²	D-W
APR	1981–98	7.322* (362.84)	0.052* (27.905)	–	–	0.98	1.94
ASSM	1981–98	7.1611* (252.52)	0.037* (2.985)	–0.003** (–2.123)	0.0001** (2.084)	0.88	1.57
MAN	1981–98	7.243* (614.03)	0.0179** (6.292)	–0.0003** (2.109)	–	0.98	2.54
MEGH	1981–98	7.1489* (352.61)	0.0212* (11.314)	–	–	0.88	1.15
MEZ	1981–98	6.923* (63.70)	0.134* (2.792)	–0.011** (–1.979)	0.0004* (2.200)	0.93	1.32
NAG	1981–98	7.279* (274.13)	0.0304* (9.749)	–	–	0.88	1.45
TRP	1981–98	7.205* (160.83)	–0.039** (–1.972)	–0.006* (2.734)	0.0001** (–1.832)	0.97	1.24

Note: *denotes significance less than 5 per cent, ** denotes significance between 5 per cent to 10 per cent, without * denotes insignificant.

TABLE 11.3A: SHARES OF DIFFERENT SECTORS OF NSDP AT 1980-1 PRICE FOR THE NORTH-EAST STATE: 1980-1 AND 1999-2000

		AGRI	MNF	PRI	INFRA	SERV
APR	80-1	0.37	0.07	0.10	0.16	0.30
	99-00	0.24	0.07	0.10	0.26	0.30
ASM	80-1	0.44	0.07	0.04	0.08	0.38
	99-00	0.34	0.05	0.06	0.10	0.45
MAN	80-1	0.46	0.05	0.04	0.05	0.42
	99-00	0.28	0.04	0.08	0.12	0.49
MEGH	80-1	0.38	0.03	0.04	0.14	0.41
	99-00	0.23	0.04	0.06	0.18	0.33
MIZ	80-1	0.24	0.03	0.08	0.16	0.49
	99-00	0.20	0.02	0.02	0.08	0.68
NAG	80-1	0.29	0.02	0.04	0.14	0.52
	99-00	0.18	0.08	0.08	0.30	0.37
TRI	80-1	0.52	0.05	0.10	0.05	0.35
	99-00	0.26	0.04	0.04	0.07	0.58

TABLE 11.4A: GROWTH RATES OF SHARE OF DIFFERENT SECTORS OF NSDP FOR THE NORT-EAST AT 1980-1 PRICE

Sectors	Growth rate of Shares	$\bar{R}^2$
Agriculture	−1.54*	0.94
	(−17.05)	
Manufactures	−1.55*	0.71
	(−6.35)	
Infrastructures	1.91*	0.86
	(9.84)	
Primary	−1.08)*	0.16
	(−1.73)	
Services	1.32*	0.97
	(23.99)	

Note: The figures in Parentheses are the *t*-values.
 *denotes significance at use than 5 per cent level.

TABLE 11.5A: NON-LINEAR GROWTH SHARES OF DIFFERENT SECTORS OF NORTH-EAST

Sector	Period	Intercept	T	T2	T3	R^2	D-W
Agriculture	1981–98	−0.868* (−88.658)	−0.0154* (−17.048)	–	–	0.94	2.21
Infrastructure	1981–98	−2.462* (−64.216)	−0.030* (−1.7708)	0.0048* (2.366)	−0.0001** (−1.896)	0.92	2.13
Manufacturing	1981–98	−2.813* (−104.10)	0.0162* (2.475)	−0.0016* (−4.987)	–	0.89	1.86
Primary	1981–98	−3.011* (−25.6)	0.192* (3.685)	−0.022* (−3.594)	0.0007* (3.256)	0.61	1.84
Services	1981–98	−0.985* (−113.00)	0.008* (4.197)	0.0002** (2.118)	–	0.97	1.67
Unregistered	1981–98	−3.517 (−84.64)	−0.04 (−4.0618)	0.002* (3.94)	–	0.52	1.98
Registered	1981–98	−3.430* (−94.002)	0.078* (4.850)	−0.0084* (−4.335)	0.0002* (3.3001)	0.89	2.32

Note: *denotes significance less than 5 per cent, ** denotes significance between 5 per cent to 10 per cent, without * denotes insignificant.

TABLE 11.6A: ENTROPY OF NE STATES FOR DIFFERENT SECTORS

Year	Agriculture	Manu-facturing	Primary	Infra-structure	Services	SDP
1981	0.004991	0.025180	0.085026	0.058466	0.004993	0.000873
1982	0.005260	0.029253	0.031565	0.040386	0.006226	0.001786
1983	0.005934	0.026883	0.025693	0.063746	0.007979	0.001828
1984	0.007503	0.032607	0.036256	0.049290	0.006643	0.002543
1985	0.004837	0.040452	0.039243	0.061696	0.006612	0.002845
1986	0.004539	0.050583	0.044132	0.075026	0.005953	0.003719
1987	0.005399	0.035909	0.058175	0.103086	0.007274	0.004868
1988	0.007902	0.032997	0.034487	0.141278	0.009459	0.005658
1989	0.012623	0.037924	0.040601	0.167053	0.012436	0.006845
1990	0.008690	0.039441	0.024084	0.133022	0.010826	0.004738
1991	0.010349	0.027576	0.050600	0.122279	0.007866	0.007065
1992	0.013527	0.017606	0.055889	0.123607	0.008992	0.009822
1993	0.015327	0.025909	0.080647	0.181999	0.011090	0.011974
1994	0.018571	0.040955	0.063571	0.197165	0.014261	0.014509
1995	0.012212	0.036912	0.093016	0.142058	0.065276	0.013943
1996	0.010951	0.045692	0.080799	0.178481	0.070906	0.020137
1997	0.005280	0.043747	0.074819	0.175485	0.090552	0.021085
1998	0.008598	0.052761	0.076329	0.240743	0.098711	0.034112

TABLE 11.7A: GROWTH RATES OF ENTROPY THE NORTH-EAST ECONOMY

Sectors	Entropy Compound Growth Rates	R^2
Agriculture	4.98*	0.36
	(2.992)	
Manufacturing	1.88	0.13
	(1.5405)	
Primary	4.68*	0.34
	(2.885)	
Services	16.11*	0.72
	(6.435)	
Infrastructure	9.08*	0.82
	(8.654)	
NSDP	18.15*	0.96
	(21.307)	

TABLE 11.8A: GROWTH RATES OF ENTROPY TREND IN DIFFERENT SECTORS OF NORTH-EAST STATES

Sector	Period	Intercept	T	T2	T3	R^2	D-W
Agriculture	1981–98	-4.947*	-0.239	0.046*	-0.0018*	0.70	1.96
		(-15.868)	(-1.735)	(2.790)	(-3.223)		
Manufacturing	1981–98	-4.031*	0.3171*	-0.0406*	0.0014*	0.49	1.50
		(-15.694)	(2.783)	(-2.959)	(3.1214)		
Registered	1981–98	-2.047*	0.1008*	-0.012*	0.0004*	0.66	2.14
		(-25.359)	(2.814)	(-2.943)	(2.677)		
Unregistered	1981–98	-2.936*	0.119*	–	–	0.93	2.03
		(-33.64)	(14.791)				
Primary	1981–98	-2.550*	-0.339**	0.040**	-0.001**	0.56	1.73
		(-6.975)	(-2.094)	(2.084)	(-1.794)		
Infrastructure	1981–98	-3.062*	0.090*	–	–	0.82	1.28
		(-26.94)	(8.654)				
Service	1981–98	-4.786*	-0.149**	0.0163*	–	0.88	1.11
		(-16.163)	(-2.087)	(4.458)			
SDP	1981–98	-7.298*	0.425*	-0.028*	0.0009*	0.97	2.22
		(-39.558)	(5.204)	(-2.937)	(2.808)		

Note: *denotes significance less than 5 per cent, ** denotes significance between 5 per cent to 10 per cent, without * denotes insignificant.

TABLE 11.9A: NON-LINEAR ESTIMATES

Sector	Period	Intercept	T	T2	T3	R²	D-W
Manufacturing	1981–97	3.0855* (53.16)	−0.0675* (−4.092)	0.0044* (5.6127)	—	0.82	1.42
Primary	1981–97	2.9923* (67.467)	−0.0390* (−3.4439)	0.0018 (2.931)	—	0.52	1.92
Service	1981–97	2.3234* (51.722)	−0.0346* (−3.0159)	0.0034* (5.5708)	—	0.90	1.35
SDP	1981–98	−7.298* (−39.558)	0.425* (5.204)	−0.028* (−2.937)	0.0009* (2.808)	0.97	2.22

SECTION IV

RESOURCE ENDOWMENT AND DEVELOPMENT POLICY IN THE NORTH-EAST

PLANNING FOR GROWTH

Where does the north-east go from here? Before planning for growth for the region, stock must be taken of what resources the region possesses. It is only then, that a suitable action plan can be constructed to utilize these resources in the best possible manner and devise means to work around shortcomings.

In this vein, B.C. Barah and A.K. Neog point out a peculiar paradox that prevails in the north-east, the obvious lack of growth in the middle of plenty. They point out that the phenomenal biodiversity and the presence of numerous micro-environments have not been utilized in any manner. The resources that have been utilized efficiently, like petroleum and tea have not done the region much good *per se*, while the presence of fertile land and abundant water goes waste as the agricultural revolution has passed the region by. Equally damaging is the absence of effective participatory local self-government and lack of investment in Research and Development, both, according to the authors, indispensable in a globalizing the market economy.

Gulshan Sachdeva argues that the present policy approach to development based on the guidelines of the Planning Commission and the NEC are not appropriate for faster development of the region. He stresses upon a 'new policy approach' based on market signals in which private investment will play the key role. In order to encourage private investment, he argues, the state shared try to (i) improve insfrastructure of the economy, (ii) change land and labour policy and (iii) maintain law and order. In his alternative development framework, the agricultural sector will have to play the leading role in all round economic development of the region, particularly, Assam.

Sandwip Kumar Das and Monica Das have attempted to analyse the production and consumption pattern in the north-east states. They observed that most of the states in the region maintain their consumption standards by heavily depending on the rest of the country and through central transfers. Lack of income generation has led to falling consumption standard overtime. They argue that poverty and income inequality will, increase if the region fails to involve itself in value-adding production processes. They have focused on trade and industrialization through establishment of export procession zones as ways to increase value-addition by using locally abundant resources.

CHAPTER 12

An Analysis of Resource Endowment and Economic Management (A Study of North-Eastern India)

B.C. BARAH AND A.K. NEOG

INTRODUCTION

Economic Development of an area depends upon the quality and quantity of resources, level of technology adoption and the size of markets. In so far as resources can be exported or imported, abundance or lack of it need not be a cause for development or underdevelopment of an economy. Resources can broadly be classified into

1. Land, water and other natural resources including biotic as well as abiotic resources.
2. Human resources.
3. Financial resources.

Although the first category of resources is conventionally referred to as resource endowment of an economy, in the present context, all the above three categories are covered for the purpose of analysis in this paper. Natural resources are transacted and are transformed into output with the help of technology and management. Mismanagement of resources causes wastage and degradation, and deprives the users (people) of their current as well as future benefits. After all, economic growth is essentially a process of setting aside resources for the future from current consumption.

This paper addresses the following issues:

1. Role and significance of resource endowment to the economic development of the north-eastern region,

2. Status of resource availability and its utilization trends,
3. Importance of infrastructure for sustainable development of resources, and
4. Measures for optimal management of resources in order to ensure long-term economic and ecological security.

Development is measured in terms of its various indicators which are built up on the basis of data of desired quality and quantity. Accuracy of empirical measurement and precision of the estimated policy parameters depend on good and adequate data set. But, for reasons known to everyone, the paucity of relevant data pertaining to north-eastern India, limits the scope of analysis in the paper. Therefore, the analysis and policy inferences are restricted to the available data from various secondary sources.

BACKGROUND OF THE NORTH-EASTERN REGION (NER)

The NER occupies 2,55,083 sq. km. which is approximately 8 per cent of the land area of the country inhabited by 3.75 per cent of country's population. It is significant to note that the population of the region has tripled from 102.61 lakh in 1951 to 315.48 lakh in 1991, as compared to 2.34 times rise in population of the country as a whole. The population stand at 384.95 lakh in 2001. In 1950, the NER comprised of three political units, viz., Assam, Manipur and Tripura, and a centrally administered NEFA area. By 1972, the number of states in the region rose to 7, by the creation of 4 additional states of Nagaland, Meghalaya, Arunachal Pradesh and Mizoram. Unfortunately, even after 50 years of Independence, all the 7 states suffer from identical economic woes which concern many of us. Situated in a unique geographical setting, the region represents a peculiar diverse socio-economic, political and cultural mix. About 70 per cent area of the region is hilly and 86 per cent of the people live in rural areas. According to the National Commission on Agriculture (1976), the states of Arunachal Pradesh, Meghalaya, Mizoram, Nagaland and Tripura are identified as hill areas. The hill areas in Assam account for about 20 per cent of the land and in Manipur, for about 90 per cent of the land. These socio-economic, political and cultural diversities should form the basis of regional planning, which unfortunately in the past, did not find an appropriate place in the models of development planning. The next section gives a brief description of the present status of resources in the region.

RESOURCE ENDOWMENT

Perpetual Resources and Biotic resources: Besides fertile land and abundant water resources, the region is endowed with variety of natural resources awaiting its proper utilization. Noted Agricultural Scientist, Dr M.S. Swaminathan (1997) describes the region as a cultural and genetic paradise and a granary of mega biodiversrity in terms of flora and fauna as well as micro-flora and micro-fauna. Biological and physical natural resources perform numerous invisible and inevitable functions, which are necessary to sustain these very resources. As the government has made no concerted efforts to manage the resources for the benefit of mankind, contrary to conserving biodiversity, the stock of these biological resources are fast, depleting making social life devoid of harmony and lacking in coexistence.

The utilization pattern of the land resources shows that in 1985–7, about 65 per cent of the geographical area of the region is under forest, which, of course, is fast dwindling. Table 12.1 shows that the forest cover ranges from a minimum of 31 per cent in Assam to a maximum of 86 per cent in Nagaland. The availability of net sown area varies from 2.21 per cent of the geographical area in Arunachal Pradesh to 35 per cent in Assam. Such a low net sown area sets physical limit to crop production and is a problem for food security from own sources. Areas under food grain occupy 42 per cent of the available land area (ranging from 13 per cent in Arunachal Pradesh to 82 per cent in Nagaland). Among the crops, paddy occupies about 89 per cent of food grain area.

Although, agriculture is the backbone of the regional economy, owing to the lack of technical change, it contributes very little towards income generation. Agricultural backwardness, characterized by low level of productivity, burgeoning unemployment (registered unemployment in Assam was as high as 16.35 lakh as in 1999), absence of technical progress and over-dependence on the vagaries of an uncertain monsoon are the major obstacles to economic development in the region. The production of basic foodstuff has been lagging far behind population growth in recent years. This is an

TABLE 12.1: LAND AND HUMAN RESOURCES

Area in 000 ha in 1996-7

State	Land	Forest	Area not available for cultivation	Net Sown Area	Food grain Area	% of food grain to net sown area	Main Crop	Jhum Area sq. km. 1983	Population in Lakh 2001
Arunachal Pradesh	8,374.3	5,154	48	185	176.6	95.5	Rice	700	10.91
Assam	7,884.3	1,930	2,493	2,744	2,728.7	99.4	Rice	696	226.38
Manipur	2,232.7	602	1,445	140	172.5	123.2	Rice	900	23.89
Meghalaya	2,242.9	935	224	216	132.2	61.2	Rice	530	23.06
Mizoram	2,208.1	1,598	65	109	77.5	71.1	Rice	630	8.91
Nagaland	1,657.9	863	61	225	201.7	89.6	Rice	190	19.89
Tripura	1,048.6	606	133	277	272.7	98.4	Rice	223	31.91

Source: NEC, Basic Statistics of North-Eastern Region, GOI, Shillong, 2002.

important source of imbalance in food security. In order to correct the imbalances and further stimulate growth opportunities, the back-up infrastructural support to agricultural development is essential, but in reality it is almost negligible.

DEMAND AND SUPPLY OF FOOD

In 1991, the total population of the region was 315.48 lakh. The demand for food for population was estimated at 6.3096 million tons of food grain (approximately @ 1 ton food grain per family of a standard size of 5 members). As against this figure of demand, the total production of food grain from the 7 states was 4.8829 million tons in 1990–1 (Table 12.1). This imbalance in the food sector may remain unabated as the growth (compound) rate of food grain was hardly 1.02 per cent during 1980–1 and 1993–4. At the same time, the growth of the area under food grain production was also sluggish. Again, the technological breakthrough in agriculture had totally bypassed the region to make a mark in productivity improvement. Therefore, the region as a whole, was totally dependent on the outside economy in order to fulfil its food requirements. The commercialization of crops like tea and other allied enterprises have made very little dent on the regional economy.

Low infrastructure investment which has been steadily decreasing has reduced the performances of the agriculture sector to a very low level. Since infrastructure development has been neglected by successive regimes from the beginning of the planning era, the magnitude of the cumulative infrastructure investment requirement in the region at present is so enormous. The Ninth Five Year Plan document has specifically recognized that the benefits of economic development has not accrued to the NER in the same measure, as in the rest of the country, even though the region is endowed with abundant natural resources. It has also been realized that the socio-economic development of the region is crucial for the progress of the country. The Approach paper quotes, 'The Ninth Plan will focus attention on identifying the gaps in these regions in terms of power, communication, railways, roads, education, agriculture, etc., so that efforts could be made to bridge the gaps through supportive measures to enable the region to join the mainstream of economic development of the country'.

TABLE 12.2: TOTAL FOOD GRAIN PRODUCTION IN THE NER

	1980-1	1985-6	1990-1	1991-2	1992-3	1993-4	1994-5	1995-6	1996-7	1997-8	2000-1
Area ('000 ha)	3,427	3,689	3,713	3,757	3,722	3,747	3,677	3,713	3,762	3,756	3,893
Production ('000 ton)	3,826	4,309	4,882	4,884	4,852	5,068	5,085	5,086	5209	5259	5,875
Yield (kg/ha.)	1,116	1,168	1,315	1,300	1,304	1,353	1,383	1370	1385	1,400	1,509

Source: NEC, *Basic Statistics of NER*, 2004.

TEA ECONOMY

The unique requirement of the topographical setting of natural slopes for tea gardens, is highly congenial for the production of tea in parts of NER. That is why, over 56 per cent of tea gardens (2,37,593 ha. area out of 4,25,026 ha. at an all-India level) lies in the NER. In 2000, it produced about 4,58,978 thousand kg. of tea, Assam alone produced 98.10 per cent of regional total production. The growing domestic demand and ready world market, for Indian tea have attracted the attention of several industrial houses. A number of multinational and big Indian business houses own and manage the entire tea industry in the NER. It employs a large number of skilled, as well as unskilled labour. However, the multiplier effect and linkages of the tea economy to the regional economy has been negligible.

WATER RESOURCES

The sources of water in the region are abundant. A large perennial river system, high rainfall, a rich underground aquifer, tanks, ponds, beels, lakes and derelict water combine to contribute to the vastness of this resource. Extensive lush green forests also provide water through the interwoven water holding capacity of the land masses. The river Brahmaputra traverses a distance of 2,900 km. through Tibet, India, and Bangladesh, draining an area of about 5.80 lakh sq. km., out of which 70,634 sq. km. (i.e. 12.17 per cent of the total basin area) is in Assam. It has a length of 218 km. in Arunachal Pradesh and 725 km. in Assam. The hydroelectric power potential of the Brahmaputra is about 13,426 MW at 60 per cent load factor, which is not yet fully exploited. Originating in Manipur, the Barak river travels a distance of 403 km. up to Lakhipur in Assam. The total catchment area of the Barak river system is 25,900 sq. km. and the estimated annual run-off at Badarpur *ghat* is 41,188 mcum. The Barak system has a power potential of 2,442 MW. Unfortunately, even a fraction of the vast inland water resources has not been utilized so far, for the purposes of gainful economic activities. In addition, there is also enormous groundwater potential. The L.C. Jain Committee reported an estimated ground water potential upto 1990-1 at 1.775 lakh ha. The paradox is that, despite the abundant water resources, irrigation utilization in the rabi season in Assam is not more than a mere 6 per cent of the cropped area. On the other extreme, at the same time, devastation due to floods in the area are increasing every year by leaps and bound. Surplus water resources must be converted to growth opportunities, rather than to a source of destruction.

HUMAN RESOURCES

Human population has tremendous influence on the sustainability of an economy. Population pressure reduces the carrying capacity of natural resources, upon which the livelihood of people depends. The population in the NER was 102.6 lakh in 1951, that rose to 351.48 lakh in 1991. This exerts a continuous and increasing pressure on the resource base and the economy, bringing down the quality of life. Emphasizing the externality of global population growth, renowned development thinker Lester Brown quoted in his book *Full House* from a joint report (1992) by the US National Academy of Sciences and the Royal Society of London as, 'If current predictions of population growth prove accurate and the pattern of human activity on the planet remain unchanged, science and technology may not be able to prevent either irreversible degradation of the environment or continued poverty for much of the World.' For the NER, where technological innovations are almost negligible and the population is fast-growing, the above predicament may be more appropriate and relevant. The degradation of natural resources and high incidence of educated unemployment (see Table 12.3) are sources of continued poverty and depletion of income levels. The literacy rate of the region, though above that of the national level, has not contributed to the expansion of opportunities of employment.

ABIOTIC RESOURCES

The region has been surplus in gas and petroleum resources. As early as 1901, the Digboi oil refinery was set up, followed by the Guwahati refinery in 1962 and BPRL in 1979. The Numaligarh refinery in the joint sector is under implementation. Crude oil also occurs in Nagaland, Arunachal Pradesh and Tripura, natural gases are also available in these states. The production of these resources are given in Table 12.4. Most of the natural gas found, is wasted and some parts are partially utilized in some tea gardens, the Assam State Electricity

TABLE 12.3: HUMAN RESOURCE DEVELOPMENT,
DEGRADATION OF NATURAL RESOURCES
AND INCIDENCE OF POVERTY

States	Urban(%)	Literacy (%)	Registered Unemployment 1993 (in '000)	Poverty (%) R	Poverty (%) U	Soil Degradation (lakh ha)
Assam	11.10	52.89	13,770	27.7	28.3	22.17
Arunachal	12.80	41.59	77	–	33.4	24.44
Manipur	27.52	59.89	2,299	28.0	40.6	3.74
Meghalaya	18.60	49.10	279	23.5	5.5	8.37
Mizoram	46.10	82.27	399	5.2	3.5	4.21
Nagaland	17.21	61.67	207	–	23.5	4.05
Tripura	15.30	60.44	1,892	23.5	22.7	–
All India	26.13	52.21	3,62,755	18.1	16.2	1,234.47

Notes: R = Rural, U = Urban.
Sources: NEC, *Basic Statistics of North-Eastern Region*, Shillong, 1995,
GOI, *Economic Survey 1996–7*, GE&T, Ministry of Labour,
GOI, *Report of the Expert Group on Estimation of Proportion of and Number of Poor*; PPD, Planning Commission, July 1993, p. 59.

Board and a few other industrial undertakings (see Table 12.4). Other geological and mineral resources such as coal, limestone, chromite, sillimanite, uranium and the other valuable minerals are also not yet optimally utilized. A noticeable development is that these resources have a history of efficient utilization and have been contributing significantly to the national economy. However, for long time, the region has contended with a pittance.

FINANCIAL RESOURCES

Abundant water resource and other natural resources are the potential opportunities, but the perennial scarcity of financial resources has been a threat in several ways. If the resources are properly developed, these can be put to viable economic use more efficiently. The development process requires immense funds, which is of course, scarce. Therefore, to harness an abundant resource, one needs to harness scarce financial resources appropriately, in order to stream-

TABLE 12.4: PRODUCTION OF CRUDE OIL AND NATURAL GAS

State	1980–1	1990–1	1995–6	1999–0	% to all-India (1999–0)
1. CRUDE OIL PRODUCTION ('000 tons)					
Assam/Nagaland	1,760	5,076	5,044	5,028	17.94
Arunachal Pradesh	2	43	28	44	
All-India	10,507	33,031	35,145	28,028	100.00
2. GROSS PRODUCTION OF NATURAL GAS (million cubic metres)					
Assam/Nagaland	843	2.040	1,925	2,279	11.20
All-India	2,358	17,998	22,628	20,672	100.00

Source: GOI, *Basic Statistics of Indian Petroleum and Natural Gas*, Ministry of Petroleum and Natural Gas, New Delhi, Oct. 1996; NEC, *Basic Statistics of NER*, 2002.

line the economic management of the resources. Financial resources are necessary to propel the regional economy to greater heights.

Due to the lack of appropriate growth stimuli, even the dominant primary sector in the region has not been able to generate surplus resources to stimulate the process of accumulation in the secondary and tertiary sectors. In fact, the process of capital formation, not only in agriculture but also in other sectors of the economy, is yet to gather momentum. The inflow and outflow of financial resources is broadly reflected in the movement of credit (C) and deposits (D) in the banks and flow of funds from all-India financial institutions. As per the latest (June 1996) data available, the public sector banks mobilized deposits institutions. As per the latest (June 1996) available data, the public sector banks mobilized deposits amounting to Rs 6,284 crore (i.e. 1.76 per cent of the all-India level) in the NER against which the banks' credits offered, amounted to Rs 2,071 crore (i.e. 0.98 per cent of the all-India level). Thus, the C/D ratio for the region is 0.33, lying far below the national average of 0.59. The C/D ratio is a measure of capital formation and an instrument of capital creation. Statewise, the C/D ratios as given in Table 12.5, imply that more than two-thirds of the financial resource are draining out of the region regularly.

The Status of statewise C/D ratios for 1969 and 1996 are given in

TABLE 12.5: TRENDS OF BANK CREDIT-DEPOSIT RATIO OF
PUBLIC SECTOR BANKS AND DISBURSEMENT
BY THE ALL-INDIA FINANCIAL INSTITUTIONS

(Rs. crore)

States	Credit Deposit Ratio		Cumulative disbursement disbursement (till March 2003)
	June 1969	June 2003	
Assam	0.39	0.32	1984.9
Arunachal Pradesh	na	0.16	72.6
Manipur	0.14	0.31	133.9
Meghalaya	0.28	0.27	189.4
Mizoram	na	0.34	76.2
Nagaland	0.06	0.16	78.4
Tripura	0.04	0.24	311.0
All-India	0.78	0.54	5,70,254.3

Sources: 1. GOI; Economic Survey, 2003–4,
2. IDBI, Report on Development Banking in India 2002–3.

Table 12.5. Interestingly, rather than improving the fund utilization prospect, the C/D ratios of Assam and Meghalaya have deteriorated overtime. The comparable C/D ratios in the developed states are relatively higher and have a positive relationship with their per capita income. The NER is said to be over-dependent on Central resources, but the C/D ratios suggest that there is a net outflow of financial resources from the region. Keeping this in view, the banks should be asked to consider targetting a fixed proportion of their deposits (say two-thirds) for investment within the region.

Table 12.6 shows the inflow of Foreign Direct Investment (FDI) which is also meagre in the region, as compared to other regions of the country. As a result, the region has not been able to gain the benefits of technology transfer and skill development, consequent on liberalization of the national economy. Intensive lobbying at the political level is needed to influence the Foreign Investment Promotion Board under the Ministry of Industry at the Centre, motivate foreign investors to set up projects in the NER and provide incentives to attract the investors. When the Indian economy is globalizing as a whole, the economy of the NER cannot afford to remain isolated nor should it be subjected to isolation under the garb of mismanagement and scarcity of financial resources.

TABLE 12.6: STATEWISE FOREIGN INVESTMENT
(AUG. 1991 TO MARCH 2004)

States	No. of Approvals	Amount of FCI (Rs. million)
Assam	19	14.95
Arunachal Pradesh	2	110.60
Manipur	2	31.85
Meghalaya	5	529.60
Mizoram	1	15.22
Nagaland	2	36.80
Tripura	4	30.88
Total	35	769.90
All India	25,482	29,23,582.82

Source: SIA Newsletter, April 2004.

THE STATUS OF INFRASTRUCTURE DEVELOPMENT

The development of infrastructure is a *sine qua non* for overall development and economic growth. The lack of infrastructure is the Achilles' Heels that labels the NER's economy as a limping economy. The level of infrastructure is the ultimate measure of the performances of an economy and necessary instruments for sustaining growth and development. A simple linear, statistical relationship between the Infrastructure Development Index (IDI) and Per Capita Income (PCI) also re-affirms that infrastructure contributes positively and significantly towards improving the per capita income. The functional relationship as estimated, using state level data of 17 Indian states for 1993–4, is given below:

Functional Relationship: $PCI = \alpha (IDI)^\beta e^\varepsilon$
Estimated function: In PCI= 1.75+1.04 in IDI $R^2 = 0.53$
  (t value 4.13)   (N, df)=(17, 15)
(Source of Data: CMIE, State Profiles, March 1997)

Infrastructure development cannot be postponed, as it cannot be borrowed, hired or imported. It can precede, concur or succeed economic development. There exists, thus, an implicit simultaneity between economic development and efficient infrastructure such as roads, railways, ports, power, telecommunication, banks, information networks, irrigation, educational and health institutions. Development indicators show that the NER economy has attained the status of a non-performing economy, primarily due to infrastructure absenteeism. The status of the NER as an outlier in the economic sphere in India, must be tackled with unparalleled enthusiasm and incomparable investment for its development by the government (state as well as Centre), private investment and people's participation. Comparative performances of infrastructural development indicators, clearly support the backwardness thesis being discussed in the paper. Based on the findings of the Research by Prof. K.L. Krishna, the Tenth Finance Commission clearly gives a vivid comparative picture (Chart 2 of the Development Indicator). On a disaggregate analysis and a comparison with the all-India level, the average surface and unsurface roads per 100 sq. km. at the all-India level is 60.8 km. in March 1989, whereas the same is 50.5 km. in Arunachal Pradesh, 82.4 km. in Assam, 48.4 km. in Nagaland, 29.4 km. in Manipur, 27.8 km. in Meghalaya, 134.3 km. in Tripura and only 162 km. in Mizoram. Again, in the case of railways, four out of seven states, i.e. Manipur, Meghalaya, Mizoram and Arunachal Pradesh are yet to appear in the railways map of the country. By March 1992, the percentage of villages electrified in the respective states were Assam (98 per cent), Arunachal Pradesh (50 per cent), Manipur (80 per cent), Meghalaya (47 per cent), Mizoram (72 per cent), Nagaland (99 per cent) and Tripura (64 per cent) as against the all-India figure of 84 per cent. The availability of telecommunication facility, specifically in the rural areas, is far from satisfactory. The role of market infrastructure in the region is a tricky issue. Theoretically, the market is a place where transactions, both on the production and consumption sides take place simultaneously and the plough-back benefits of the market must reach the beneficiary. A peculiarity of the NER is that market transactions for several of its resources are continuously taking place and find not only the national market, but the world market as well. How many benefits from the market are retained in the region, is a moot question.

CONSTRAINTS ON ECONOMIC MANAGEMENT OF RESOURCE ENDOWMENT

Two types of constraints confront an economy, viz., supply side constraints and demand side constraints. Natural calamities like floods that disrupt economic activities, act as supply side constraints. Other constraints include security and insurgency, inadequate infrastructure facilities, lack of dynamic governance, high cost of production, inaccesabilities due to lack of communication and information, landlockness and other bottlenecks. On the other hand, the incidence of poverty, unemployment, high cost of living due to bottleneck inflation, population pressure, etc., operate as demand side constraints. A discussion on the agricultural sector would elaborate the nature of the constraints in the NER. A significant portion of the cropped area in Assam and other states are flood-prone. The agrarian structure of the region is marked by a large number of small and marginal farmers, operating uneconomic holdings under traditional technology. This has resulted in very low production. In the hilly areas, the land is owned by different tribal communities and farming is based on *jhuming*, i.e. shifting cultivation. Except for the plains of Assam, Manipur, and Tripura valley, a cadastral survey of the land has not yet been conducted. This perhaps, limits the flow of agricultural credit to *jhuming* cultivation. Industrial entrepreneurship is also almost negligible. Research and development in agriculture and other sectors of the economy is extremely poor, which results in below-average performance of the various sectors.

MEASURES OF ECONOMIC MANAGEMENT

(i) *Power of People – An Approach to Land Reform and Method of Output Sharing, Diversification as an Instrument of Sustainability, Market Reform*: The power of people in the economic management of resources is considered supreme, yet it has been ignored and reduced considerably by consecutive regimes in the north-eastern region. The 73rd and 74th constitutional amendments by the Central Government throw a ray of hope in this direction. In order to strengthen the entitlement power of people, measures to accelerate the process of development of the region is indispensable. The responsibilities of villages and urban development must be entrusted to and the organizational structure of the Panchayat Raj and Nagarpalika must be strengthened. The village and district council and village headman in the hilly areas are central to the transformation of the rural and urban economy. This is because, generation of surplus in the agricultural sector is a prerequisite for industrialization and over-all development of a region. Agricultural sector can generate surplus only when it is dynamic. Such dynamism requires sectoral transformation and reforms. The ultimate development will, therefore, hinge on the optimal management and utilization of resources by the these local bodies. A precondition for the purpose is the sensitization of the de-bureaucratization process.

(ii) *Investment on Research and Development and Infrastructure – An Approach to Land Reform and Method of Output Sharing, Diversification as an Instrument of Sustainaibility, Market Reform*: In the flood-prone areas, infrastructure for farm sector needs to be expanded and strengthened on a priority basis through public sector investment. This implies a speedy reordering of the priority in favour of agriculture as the dominant sector. At present, both the actual crop productivity as well as the productivity at the experimental field is lower than that of the national level. The experimental yield of various crops in the region is much below the actual realized yield of comparable crops in other developed regions like Punjab. This indicates that the effective investment on crop improvement programmes is not taking place up to the expected level. Productivity cannot be enhanced without backup R&D efforts. Upward revision of the crop productivity potential is an essential requirement for growth as well as sustainable development. The investment on human capitals is also required to improve the productivity of farm labourers by spreading farm skill, training and education. Crop strategy should be chalked out to minimize crop losses/damages during floods and to develop alternative flood escaping cropping strategy. All these strategies may be bundled in consortium mode of backup R&D in agriculture. The irrigation facilities must be enhanced adequately from the existing six per cent in the *Rabi* season. In order to create confidence among the flood panicky farmers, crop insurance coverage should be extended to compensate losses in terms of crops, assets as well as human lives and livestock.

(iii) *A new Approach to Land Reform and Method of Output Sharing:* In order to tackle the problems of unviable holdings due to fragmentation and law of inheritance, land reform measures should be introduced making provision for sharing the land ownership rather than owning the tiny land holdings. This means to devise a method of sharing the value of output from the commonly owned landholdings. Alternatively, where possible, the concept of co-operative farming should be introduced. In the hilly tribal areas, cadastral survey should be conducted and land reform measures should be initiated conferring permanent, heritable and transferable land rights. This would enable the farmers to access the bank credit facilities, government subsidies and other inputs.

(iv) *Crop Diversification as an Instrument of Sustainaibility:* Changes in the economically unviable agricultural activities must be promoted. For example, if a particular crop is unprofitable, then incentive should be created to shift to other crops with higher returns. The advantages of the market liberalization and globalization may be maximized only through identification and diversification and effective specialization in agriculture, whenever possible. Once such reforms come about, then the conventional constraints impending smooth flow of credit and other issues such as security/insurgency problems, infrastructural bottlenecks, lack of entrepreneurship, low recovery of advances, problems of manpower utilization, etc., will automatically disappear. The success of the reform policy would depend on an, efficient export policy specifically tailored for the region. The report of a special study on export potential in the NER by the Indian Institute of Foreign Trade emphasized the improvization of border trade in the region and promoting trade with the South-East Asia. The Marine Product Export Development Authority has identified over 125 varieties of fish from the lakes, rivers, streams and other riverine system in the NER. Our trade must take advantage of the bio-diversity, including several ornamental fish varieties, for the benefit of the people.

(v) *Market Reform*: The choice of markets is a mainstay of development. It is not true to say that the NER suffers due to lack of markets. Lucrative markets for the resources of the region existed even in historical times. But the benefits of market transactions have not been trickled down to the desired level. Therefore, a reorganization of the market structure would improve the economic condition of the region. Since the region shares several common economic woes, it may be possible to initiate a common market in the region for mutual benefit of the partners. Four components of the envisaged market must be recognized as formulated below:

A. To counter the market forces interacting against the development of the region, following alternatives may be adopted and appropriately institutionalized.

a. *Inside Resources-Outside Markets* (for several natural resources including citronella, crude oil, natural gas, silk, agro-products, minerals, etc.)
b. *Inside Resources-Inside Markets* (sustenance requirements, agricultural produce, forests, water, land, indigenous handicrafts, etc.)
c. *Outside Resources-Inside Markets* (technology, industrial and engineering products, textiles, vegetables, fish, eggs, wheat, rice, fruits, silk, skilled manpower, etc.)
d. *Outside Resources-Outside Markets* (several intermediary goods and industries, etc.)

B. The introduction of a *Common Market* for inter- and intra-regional transactions within the NER, in order to eliminate the marketing bottleneck.

(vi) *Credit Policy and Fiscal Discipline in the NER*: As illustrated above the region suffers from fiscal mismanagement rather than inadequacy of financial resources. The productive capitals are not been able to retain as depicted through the deteriorating CD ratios. Reversing the current rate of credit utilization to one-third to at least two-third (bank C/D ratios) would provide ample scope of capital formation in the region. The acute scarcity of investible funds can also eliminated in the process.

CONCLUSION

At the time when the national economy has been liberalized to a great extent and assimilated to the global scene, the north-eastern regional economy is still unable to keep its head out of worries of under-development. The economy of the NER must change and cannot remain insulated or should not be subjected to remain so for want of financial resources. The notion that inflow of Central resources to the region and its utilization has not been sufficient to stimulate adequately the internal process of surplus generation, should continue to haunt. Since the induced investment is lacking, in order to stimulate the economy autonomous investment from the public/central sector should come forth to break through the vicious circle of underdevelopment and regional imbalance and foster a cycle of vibrant growth and balanced development. Development presupposes a congenial socio-political milieu free from threats and insurgency cobwebs, and an investor-friendly atmosphere. Creation of such an environ is the duty of not only of the government but also of the north-eastern society. The government and society have to be not only proactive but also overactive (in the matter of economic development) to usher in a new millennium. The known competitive strength, must be utilized and various growth-enhancing measures must convert the strength to growth and investment opportunities. We have illustrated the results of SWOT analysis and represented our view points to the Expert Committee on the Eco-regional Technology Mission for the north-eastern India (Govt. of India) under the chairmanship of Dr M.S. Swaminathan, Shillong. The results, which are appended (Appendix I), are relevant in the context of this paper.

REFERENCES

Barah, B.C. and A.K. Neog, 'Prospects of Agricultural Development in Floodprone Eco-system', *Agricultural Economics Research Review*, vol. 10, Jan.–June 1997, pp. 65–78.

Barah, B.C., 'Constraints to Agricultural Development in Assam', *Journal of NEICSSR*, 1993.

———, *Traditional Water Harvesting Systems in India*, New Delhi: New Age Publishers, 1996.

———, *Irrigation Development and Econological Implications*, Hyderabad: Delta Publishers, 1996.

——— and A.K. Neog, 'Role of Water Resources and Regional Perspectives of Food Security: an Analysis of Backward Agriculture in Water Surplus North-Eastern India', in *Prof. P.C. Goswami Memorial Volume of Economic Development of Assam*, forthcoming.

Bardoli, G. and A.K. Neog, *Economy of North Eastern India*, Guwahati: LBS Publications, 1986.

Brown, Lester, *Full House*, New York: W.W. Norton, 1996.

Behera, M.C. and N.C. Roy, eds., *Trends in Agrarian Structure in the Hills of North-Eastern India*, New Delhi: Commonwealth Publishers, 1997.

Goswami, Atul, 'A Debate on North Eastern Economy', *Economic Times*, 9 May 1997.

Goswami, P.C., *Agriculture in Assam*, Guwahati: Assam Institute of Development Studies, 1989.

India, Govt. of, *Report of the Tenth Finance Commission*, New Delhi: Ministry of Finance, 26 November 1994.

Neog, A.K., 'Population Dynamics of the north-eastern Region', *Journal of Commerce*, Guwahati University, 1995, pp. 18–31.
——, 'Resource Mobilization in Underdeveloped Areas', *Journal of North-Eastern India*, Council of Social Sciences Research, Shillong, vol. 15, April 1991.
India, Govt. of, *Report of Dr. M.S. Swaminathan Committee on Remedying Agricultural Progress in the Backward Areas: Eco-Regional Technical Mission in the North-East India,* New Delhi: Ministry of Agriculture, 1997.
Thakur, P., ed., *Profile of a Development Strategy for India's North-East,* Guwahati: Span Publications Ltd., 1988.

APPENDIX I

Eco-regional Technology Mission for the North-Eastern India
SWOT analysis
Constraints:

Socio-cultural: Population, tribal, non-tribal, technical manpower, women agricultural workforce.

Physical: Land-locked, agro-eco system, rainfall, flood, ecology, cropping pattern shifting cultivation *vs.* settled agriculture, size of holding, soil, fishery, livestock, forest.

Technological: Irrigation, HYV, fertilizers, agro-processing industries, disaster warning system (flood), technical laboratory for testing, grading, soil testing, etc., fishery, livestock improvement, risk and uncertainty in *Kharif* season.

Infrastructure: Road and communication, transport (rail, road, air and water), banking and other financial institutions, health, education, rural electrification.

Strength: Water
     Tea
     Oil and petroleum products
     Gas
     Forest resource
     Potential international markets for Xs and Ms.
Weaknesses: Isolation
     Socio-cultural closeness (particularly of the tribals)
     Shifting cultivation
     Complete lack of database
     Lack of capital formation
Threats: Ecological/flood, earthquake
     Insurgency
     International border
     Invisible poverty
     Corruption
     Inner line permit restriction

Strategy:

A. Markets:
1. Inside resources outside markets (citronella, oil, gas, timber, tea, silk products, agro-processing products, etc.)
2. Inside resources inside markets (agricultural products, forests, water, land, etc.)
3. Outside resources inside markets (technology, industrial and engineering goods, textile, other consumer goods, wheat, rice, fruits and vegetable, fish eggs, silk products)
4. Outside resources outside markets (intermediary products)

RESOURCE ENDOWMENT & ECONOMIC MANAGEMENT

B. Common markets in the north-eastern region.
C. Flood Prone Area Development programme.
D. Research and Development on locational specific appropriate technology.

Reference Literature and Committee Reports

Reports:

1. L.C. Jain Committee on Clause Seven of Assam Accord; Economic Development of Assam, Planning Commission, New Delhi (refer as Commission)
2. Raja Chellaiah Committee on Resource Mobilisation in the NE India; Commission
3. North-Eastern Council reports, Shillong.
4. Rajadhayaksha Committee on Backward Areas, Planning Commission.
5. P.D. Saikia Committee on Agriculture in Assam, Govt. of Assam.
6. Agricultural Altas of Assam, Assam Agricultural University, Jorhat.
7. Chakraborty Committee Report on Backward Areas, Commission.
8. Report of the National Commission on Agriculture, Ministry of Agriculture, New Delhi.
9. ICAR North-Eastern Complex Report.
10. Annual Report of NEIBM.
11. Annual Report of the Indian Institute of Entrepreneurship, Guwahati.
12. Various publications of the Agro-economic Research Centre, Jorhat.
13. Annual Report of the North-Eastern Institute of Science & Technology, Itanagar, Arunachal Pradesh.
14. Research Report of the Institute of Cultural and Development Studies (ICSSR), Guwahati.
15. Research Report of the North-Eastern Indian Council of Social Science Research, Shillong.
16. S.P. Shukla Report on Development of the North-Eastern India, Govt. of India.

CHAPTER 13

North-Eastern Economy: New Policy Options

GULSHAN SACHDEVA

INTRODUCTION

The north-eastern region of India presents an appropriate case study to assess the main reasons for the failure of the present policy framework concerning the upliftment of economically backward and isolated regions. The failure of the economic policy framework has also been frequently cited as one of the main reasons for the emergence of insurgency and its continuation in the region. However, this failure is generally discussed in the context of 'economic neglect' of the region. It is further argued that to end this neglect, a massive developmental assistance from the government is required, which in due process would also end discontent, insurgency and terrorism in the region. This paper has argued that the failure is not because of any so-called 'economic neglect', but because of wrong economic policy framework which has created an unbalanced and unsustainable economy and destroyed the basic institutions of a modern market economy in the region.

THE REGION

The north-eastern region, also known as the land of seven sisters, comprises the states of Arunachal Pradesh, Assam, Manipur, Meghalaya, Mizoram, Nagaland and Tripura, with about 8 per cent of the country's geographical area and about 4 per cent of its population. The region is known for its ethnic, linguistic, cultural, religious and physiographical diversity.[1]

Historically, successive legal and administrative decisions taken between 1874 and 1935 gave the areas of the north-east a distinct identity. The British administration initially treated the hill areas as a 'Non-Regulated Areas', then declared them as 'Backward Tract' and, lastly, 'Excluded Areas' and 'Partially Excluded Areas'.

Statistics are available in plenty about the number of races, tribes and their subgroups, ethnic groups, cultures, religions, languages and dialects spoken in this region. But broadly speaking there are three distinct groups of people – the hill tribes, the plains tribes and the non-tribal population of the plains. The majority of those living in the plains are Hindus and Muslims while a substantial proportion of hill tribes in Meghalaya, Mizoram and Nagaland are Christians. Geographically, apart from Brahmaputra, Barak (Assam) and Imphal (Manipur) valleys and some flat lands in between the hills of Meghalaya and Tripura, about two-thirds area of the region consists of hilly terrain. Most of this hilly portion is either owned, or controlled or managed, by tribes, clans or village communities. The most populous part is the Brahmaputra valley which constitutes about 22 per cent of the region.

The pace of development in the hill areas and plains differs considerably. The valleys are economically active areas, the Brahmaputra valley being the most active. Tribal populations constitute only about one-fourth of the population of the north-east, even though in four states – Mizoram, Meghalaya, Nagaland and Arunachal Pradesh – tribals are in majority. In Mizoram, which has one of the highest literacy levels (82 per cent) in the country, second only to Kerala (90 per cent), they constitute as high as 95 per cent of the population.

On the one hand, the region is diverse and heterogeneous. On the other hand, it is quite homogeneous; the social stratification found in other parts of the country is not present in the north-east. The tribal societies in the hill areas are egalitarian. As a result, the type of poverty found in many other parts of India does not exist in most of the hilly states of the region.

PRESENT ECONOMIC POLICY FRAMEWORK

Due to special constitutional arrangements, historical background as well as geographical location,[2] the Central Government has been trying to integrate the north-east region with the national economy through certain policy frameworks. It has accepted the right of tribals to retain their way of life and identity and has sought to integrate them through democratic means into the federal frame of the Constitution of India. The policy framework for the region so far is guided by a combination of political economy and culture. The focus of the *political economy approach* is on the relations between the state and the economy. Therefore, in this approach, the role of the bureaucratic state arrangements is strongly emphasized. The *cultural approach*, however, focuses on the socially constructed character of economic organization where the economic system is a product of the social order.

As a result of this *combined approach*, the importance of the bureaucratic arrangements in the process of economic development has been unduly exaggerated. Besides, wherever possible, an attempt has been made by policy makers to work through the unique social and cultural institutions existing in the region instead of imposing new institutions.[3] This special approach has been adjusted with the Central Government's policies of a regional planning development model. The major assumption of regional planning is that it would permit the transfer of surplus generated in one region to another. This mechanism was expected to increase aggregate national efficiency through optimum resource allocation.

Under the influence of this policy, various schemes for the development of infrastructure and economy of the north-east region have been formulated. The schemes include the formation of the North-Eastern Council, Hill Area Development Project and Sub-Plans, Tribal Area Sub-Plan, and Tribal Development Agency Projects to name only a few. In addition, these seven states have been declared as Special Category States; they get Central assistance on the basis of 90 per cent grant and 10 per cent loan. Some public sector units have also been set up in the region. The policies of industrial licencing, concessional finance and investment subsidy, growth centres, as well as freight equalization of some major industrial inputs have also been used towards economic development. Under the announcement made by the then Indian Prime Minister Deve Gowda in October 1996, all developmental ministries and departments of the Central Government have been directed to earmark at least 10 per cent of their annual budget for the programmes in the north-east. In case any Central Government Ministry is failed to achieve this target, the unutilized 10 per cent portion is pooled in the non-lapsable central pool of resources which will be reutilized to finance developmental projets in the north-east. Creation of a separate Department of

Development of North-Eastern Region (DONER) is another new initiative by the government.

Further, to protect tribal interests, policies of less interference with the cultural traditions and customs of the local people are being followed, and additional political and administrative framework has been provided for the region. Under the Sixth Schedule of the Constitution, the concept of Autonomous District Councils has been applied.[4] The councils are responsible for looking after the social, economic and minor criminal and civil matters of the tribal people. More specifically these councils are empowered to make laws with respect to: (a) land; (b) forest; (c) water course; (d) shifting cultivation; (e) establishment of village and town and its administration; (f) appointment of, or succession to chiefs or headmen; (g) inheritance of property; (h) marriage and divorce and matters relating to any other social customs.

Restrictions have been imposed on the rights of Indian nationals to acquire landed property in these areas. The regulation of Inner Line Permit prohibits entry of outsiders into Arunachal Pradesh, Mizoram and Nagaland without a permit, and debars a non-native to acquire any interest in land or the produce of land. Tribal belts and blocks have been constituted in the plains to prevent land alienation from tribals there.

It has to be acknowledged, however, that the development strategy implemented so far, mainly through the Planning Commission and North Eastern Council, has failed to produce the desired results. The state and sectoral plans of the Planning Commission have not been able to provide enough impetus for local development, which would have led to self-sustained growth. Instead of creating an efficiency-oriented economic process, this policy framework has resulted in the creation of a politically led distribution-oriented process. The result is that natural resources, profits, savings and the like are, in fact, moving away from the region to high productivity regions. Besides, the almost total dependence on Central funds and planned direction has promoted a trait of passiveness towards development and encouraged patronage and corruption. It has also created a government monopoly in employment, which has destroyed the work ethic necessary to build a modern economy. Expectations were raised and they could not be fulfilled with centrally sponsored schemes.

Moreover, contrary to popular perception, the lack of development in the past was not because of shortage of funds. In fact, sufficient resources were always provided to the region, but a substantial portion of the funds earmarked for various schemes has not really gone into those schemes. Some scholars have pointed out that the regime of corruption in India, even under normal circumstances, severely limits the actual impact of development expenditure on target groups. In situations of widespread breakdown of law and order, as in the case of many parts of the north-east, the impact of government-sponsored development projects is very little.[5]

Therefore, it can be argued that although some developmental changes have taken place in the region,[6] yet the present policy framework has not been able to provide good transport and other infrastructural facilities. The region remains isolated from the rest of the country; it has not been able to encourage investors; it has not produced skilled labour, there is little entrepreneurial development; and the primitive agricultural practices of the region have not been transformed into modern commercial agriculture. More importantly, this policy framework has also become one of the important factors that have contributed to the emergence of insurgency as well as its continuance in the region. In a nutshell, this policy framework has outlived its utility. The political economy approach has inordinately relied on the capacity of the Central Government and its bureaucratic arrangements for economic development.

On the cultural side too, changes have taken place overtime. In today's north-east, tribals are not 'head hunters'; on the contrary, a large number of them are highly educated and have adopted Western dress and modes of living. Therefore, in the new economic environment, to depend once again on the very same institutional mechanisms like the Planning Commission (whose own future is not certain) may not be the right approach.

In a liberalized economy, any new policy has to be based on some kind of a *market-oriented approach*. The new policy framework should concentrate more on economic factors and less on political and cultural factors (although they cannot be ignored altogether). The economic factors include labour cost, comparative advantages, technology, efficiency and returns on investment. Inefficient economic processes and barriers to market entry clearly make an economic difference. The market approach generally assumes economic rationality, and the atomised individual, whether firm or individual, as the crucial economic actor. In this approach, the economic system is an aggregated outcome of the production, exchange, and consumption of goods and services. Through the self-interested rational actions of individuals social order emerges.

In the area of regional economic development, the neo-classical theory asserts that regional disparities would be reduced on the basis of factor movements across regions. Assuming that all regions possess similar technology and similar preferences, and there are no institutional barriers to the flow of capital and labour across state borders, the Solow-Swan neo-classical growth model would predict that states would have similar levels of per capita incomes in the long run. This model also predicts that poor regions will grow faster than rich ones; in other words, regions with lower starting values of capital-labour ratio will have higher per capita income growth rates.[7] Therefore, instead of regional planning, this approach suggests greater concentration on free flow of goods and productive factors among regions. Ideally a uniform legal and governmental framework would be important for the free movement of factors of production. Perhaps this would be sufficient to ensure static efficiency. The equalization of returns to factors is believed to be accomplished through trade and mobility of factors other than natural resources. These trade and factor movements between regions are expected to achieve self-adjusted equalization of their income and employment levels. However, regions differ in their ability to respond to external stimuli, due partly to differences in elasticities of supply.

In the north-east region even the stimulus to expansion at the national level is likely to run up against supply bottlenecks due to insufficient infrastructure, entrepreneurship, business supporting institutions as well as the insurgency which prevails in many parts of the region. This is where the state would have to play a role, and more importantly the state governments. In a liberalized economy, development will not be a boon from the Centre. On the contrary, development of a particular state will depend on the actions of the government of that state. Later in the article, some areas have been identified where policy action needs to be initiated by state governments. The Central Government can also help the north-east but it must be clearly understood that in a market-oriented economy the vast powers of the Centre, acquired under the auspices of the Planning Commission and huge public sector will be curtailed.[8] Therefore, there is an urgent need to reappraise the role of the

Central Government in developing the region with the right degree and intensity in the context of a decentralized liberal economy. The Central Government will play the role of a facilitator rather than a promoter of development.[9]

UNBALANCED ECONOMY

The development strategy followed by the Centre and state governments has created an unbalanced economy in the north-east. There are differences among the seven states of the region with respect to their resource endowments, levels of industrialization as well as infrastructural facilities. On the whole, all these economies are underdeveloped agrarian societies with very weak industrial sectors and inflated service sectors. The industrial sector has mainly developed around tea, oil, timber (TOT) in Assam and mining, saw mills and plywood factories in other parts of the region. The tea plantation industry employs a large labour force; in Assam alone it employs more than 5,00,000 workers.[10] State-sponsored industrialization — whether sugar mills, jute mills, paper mills or food processing – has not been successful. Small-scale industries have also not been viable and there is large scale industrial sickness in this sector. The economy of the region remains primarily agricultural. The full potential of this sector has not been exploited. Primitive farm practices of slash-and-burn (*jhum*) shifting cultivation in many of the hills and mainly single-crop traditional farming in the plains continue. As a result, the region is not even able to produce adequate food grain to feed its population. The states of the region import food items worth about Rs 2,000 to 2,500 crore annually from other parts of the country.[11] Since neither agriculture nor industry has taken off, the pressure for employment is on the service sector. As a result, this sector has expanded disproportionately. Because of low economic activity, the states of the region have resource deficit. Of these limited resources a large portion is spent mainly to maintain the service sector. While the national economy is growing fast after initial contraction, the economies of the region are slowing down. Assam, the largest economy of the region is in a very critical state, both in agriculture and industry. However, improved agricultural production and productivity in some pockets of the north-east indicate that there is large untapped potential in agriculture.

HARD AND SOFT INFRASTRUCTURE

Almost all the writings concerning the north-east have mentioned infrastructural problems faced by the region. A close look at the infrastructural situation reveals that the region has a mixed level of infrastructure. Assam, the biggest economy of the region, is not far behind the national average. The region has about 6 per cent of the national roads and about 13 per cent of the National Highway. Because of lack of proper maintenance, however, the quality of these roads may not be very good. Barring Assam, railway is almost nonexistent in other parts of the region. The position of persons per bed in hospitals is better in the region except for Assam and Tripura. Although the number of banks have increased, the credit-deposit ratio is low, particularly in the urban areas. In telecommunications, some states have made good progress. For example, Mizoram has more telephone connections per lakh population than the national average. Arunachal is also not very far behind. Tripura and Assam have more schools per 100 sq. km. than the national average. Meghalaya is very near to the national average but the remaining states are far behind. As for the number of teachers per 100 students, all the states are much ahead of the national average. Nagaland and Manipur have three times more teachers per 100 students than the national average.

Therefore, despite severe infrastructural backlog, the region has relatively reasonable infrastructure in certain pockets. The Brahmaputra valley qualifies as an area with moderate infrastructure. For industrial development to be more effective, it would be useful if efforts were concentrated in this area, rather than to thinly spread the limited resources in all the seven states.

In the area of human resources, the region scores over most other states of India in literacy rate. Except Arunachal and Meghalaya, all other states of the region have literacy rates above the average national literacy rate, Mizoram being next only to Kerala. Only Arunachal Pradesh is below the national level for female literacy.

The region has done well in education because of many sociohistorical factors, but the *importance of the literacy factor should not be overemphasized*. Although Mizoram, Nagaland and Manipur have higher literacy rates, the largest state – Assam – is only at the average national level. The combined literacy rate of the region is 64.8 per cent, which is below the all-India figure of 65.4 per cent.

This level is also below its neighbour, West Bengal, which has 69.2 per cent literacy (2001 census). However, female literacy of the region is significantly higher than the national average. In addition, compared to the general population, the scheduled castes are better educated in Arunachal Pradesh and Assam and scheduled tribes in Mizoram. Literacy rates among scheduled tribes is also significantly high in all the north-eastern states.

It should be noted that despite having a large education infrastructure and better literacy rates in some of the states, the *education levels may not be very high*. There are enough teachers in the north-east, but many of them are not trained. According to the *Sixth Educational Survey* of the NCERT, of the total 2,66,057 school teachers at all stages in the region, only 45 per cent were trained teachers. The corresponding figure for the national level is about 87 per cent. The situation was particularly bad in Assam and Nagaland where only about 30 per cent teachers at the higher secondary levels are trained.[12] The large educational infrastructure, both for lower as well as for higher education, is a strength which should be maximized by improving its quality. In-service training of teachers should be a priority area.

STATE GOVERNMENT FINANCES

While discussing finances of the north-east states, it has to be kept in mind that many of these states were created mainly to fulfil the ethnic, political and cultural aspirations of the people. During the reorganization of the states in the north-east, a pertinent criterion – that the territory in question must have revenue resources to meet its administrative and other non-developmental expenditure was ignored. It was perhaps thought that with their potential, particularly in the areas of agriculture, hydroelectric power and handicrafts, these states would be able to achieve financial viability after help and protection in the initial years. But any form of protection or subsidy has the tendency to be perceived by economic agents as a permanent feature of the system. In due course of time, it creates its own network of beneficiaries and any change in the existing set of rules evokes strong resistance.

Creation of smaller states in the region might have been a sensible policy from a larger national perspective. But how and when these states would become financially viable was clear neither to the

Central planners nor to the state governments. Decades have passed and the economies of the region continue to suffer. It seems that both the Centre as well as the state governments of the region have accepted the status quo. The Planning Commission holds routine discussions with these states year after year. Because Central assistance has been assured they have not made much effort to develop their internal financial resources.[13] Since the states do not have to raise internal resources to meet their non-developmental expenditure, there has been a tendency to multiply administrative units and employees beyond reasonable requirements. Their main task seems to be simply to find ways to utilize Central funds in a routine manner. This sort of financial situation is neither desirable nor sustainable.

Three major points about the government finances in the region are worth noting. First, an overwhelming portion of the overall receipts comes from the Centre. Second, the states' own tax revenues are very low, even negligible in some states. Third, non-Plan revenue expenditure is high in most of the states.

The share of gross transfers from the Centre to aggregate disbursements has been the highest in Mizoram where the average for the years between 1985–6 and 1990–1 was about 95 per cent. During the same period the average for Arunachal was about 80 per cent. For Assam the average contribution to the budget was about 73 per cent. In the other States of the region, share of gross transfers was more than 80 per cent of total disbursements. The all-India average during this period was around 45 per cent. In the initial years of the 1990s, these ratios declined in all the states except Arunachal Pradesh. In the last few years roughly half of the disbursements in Assam comes from the Centre. In Arunachal, Manipur, Mizoram and Nagaland, they are still nearing 80 per cent. In Meghalaya and Tripura, the ratios are somewhat lower.[14]

DEVOLUTION AND TRANSFER OF RESOURCES

The transfer and devolution of resources from the Centre to states are essentially via three channels. First, are the statutory transfers (comprising tax sharing and grants-in-aid) through the Finance Commission recommendations. Second, are Plan grants through the Planning Commission guidelines. The Planning Commission fixes the assistance to the states to carry out their plans while the Finance

Commission determines the assistance required for current account budgetary support. There are also 'discretionary' grants through Central ministries, primarily for Centrally-sponsored schemes. There are also some indirect channels, such as loans from the Central Government and allocation of credit by financial institutions controlled by the Central Government.

Between 1990–1 to 2002–3, Assam received about Rs 43,000 crore from the Centre. Arunachal and Manipur received about Rs 9,900 crore and Rs 11,500 crore respectively. Meghalaya received about Rs 9,000 crore and Tripura's share was more than Rs 14,000 crore. Similarly, figures for the same period for Nagaland and Mizoram are about Rs 12,000 crore and 9,000 crore, respectively. The total figure for the region for these thirteen years is about Rs 1,08,504 crore.

These are gross figures. A portion of that money is also given back to the Central Government as repayment of loans and interest payments. Thus, the cumulative net devolution from the Centre to the north-east for the period between 1990–1 and 2002–3 is about Rs 92,000 crore.[15]

Similarly, while looking at the per capita Central assistance during the Eighth Plan, Arunachal tops the list. Against the national average of Rs 1,080, the total per capita assistance to the state was more than Rs 36,000 while Mizoram and Nagaland received Rs 32,567 and 23,177, respectively. This was much more even compared to other special category states like Himachal Pradesh, Jammu & Kashmir and Assam which received Rs 5,921, 9,754 and Rs 3,161, respectively. Per capita assistance to the economically poorest state of India, Bihar, was only Rs 876.[16]

Another area where Central assistance could be seen is in the public sector activities. The gross block of Central Public Sector Enterprises (CPSE) worth Rs 13,318 crore is in the region, mostly in Assam. This is about 5 per cent of its total assets as well as more than 5 per cent of its employment in India.[17]

The state governments have failed to develop their own financial resources. The potential areas to broaden the tax base are sales tax, revenues from irrigation and better realization of taxes from power and transport. The growth of non-Plan revenue expenditure has been high in the region but recently there has been an effort by some of the states to keep it under control. It seems that the present financial situation of many north-east states is not sustainable even in the medium run. So either Central funding have to be increased, which in present circumstances neither looks possible nor desirable. The only way out could be cutting expenditure and raising internal resources. This needs prudent financial management by states of the region. Further, the time has perhaps come when income tax for the tribals in the region could be introduced.

NEW CHALLENGES

The need for a balanced multilevel planning system has always been felt in planned regional development. The decentralization of power and funds to states and then to local bodies was on the agenda. Central and state governments relied on the rhetoric of decentralization but in reality resisted it and undermined any real decentralization.

In the prevailing climate, however, the logical conclusion of economic liberalization is decentralization at the political level and greater autonomy to investors. Under new economic policy regime, the states of the north-east will be in a better position to manage their own affairs. They will also have the flexibility to attract investment and improve their supply responses. However, the north-east states will have to compete with relatively advanced states also undergoing the same process. The region will have to do a lot of homework and show more openness, transparency and also accelerate efforts to attract private investment. Many new opportunities are opening up. The crucial question is whether the north-east region will be able to take advantage of these opportunities. As discussed earlier, the present policy framework has not led to desired results. Moreover, with the changing economic scenario the option of continuing the with same set of policies will not hold. Is the north-eastern region preparing itself for the new challenges?

There are some positive attitudinal changes both at the Centre as well as in the states. But a great deal needs to be done. It is evident that with the present infrastructure, the region will not be able to support any major economic activity. To attract international financing for major infrastructural projects, a different approach is required. Proposals for such projects need to be different compared to the proposals submitted so far to the Planning Commission; they need to specify the end user, maintenance costs as well as user charges. But implementation of projects based on market principles is not an easy task. This is evident from the example of Assam where farmers are showing reluctance to accept a World Bank funded irrigation rehabilitation project, which requires a part of the cost to be borne by them.[18]

ROLE OF PRIVATE INVESTMENT

It must be understood that private capital is a critical component for progress in the region.[19] Although private capital is no panacea, it is a critical component of economic progress. Higher levels of private investment are essential to generate productive employment, raise productivity and improve technology and work culture.

Despite announcements and the appointments of many commissions, the Centre is less likely (or less able) to increase public expenditure to remove even infrastructural bottlenecks. The bulk of capital that will be required to improve supply responses in the region will ultimately have to come from private rather than government sources. Therefore, attracting private capital should be given the highest priority. Compared to what has been done so far, at least as much effort should be devoted to this task as is devoted to securing aid from the Centre.

Fortunately, the general perception that the industry is not keen to invest in the region is gradually changing. Recent initiatives taken by the Confederation of Indian Industry (CII), Bengal Chamber of Commerce and Industry (BCCI) and Federation of Indian Chambers of Commerce and Industry (FICCI) show that the private sector is interested in the region. BCCI has set up a new Guwahati chapter.[20] In 1997, it organized EXPO-Northeast. FICCI had organized a round table on economic development of the north-east. CII earlier suggested a new initiative called SUNRISE (Summit of NE States for Regional Initiative and Shared Enterprise) to address challenges of development in the region.[21] It recommended a three-dimensional initiative for overall development of the region. Cultural integration (SUN safaris, SUN academy, SUN sport), geographical integration (SUN port, SUN route, SUN river, SUN air); and industrial integration (SUN farms, SUN crafts, and SUN ventures). Some major industrial houses, such as the Reliance Industries have committed major projects, in the region. Since then CII, FICCI and FINER (Federation for the Industries of the North-East Region) have taken many initiatives in the north-east. These developments indicate that the Indian industry is willing to move into the north-east provided attitudes towards business (read outsiders) change.

To attract private investment and capital to the region, some fundamental changes are necessary. They are mainly in the areas of land policy, labour laws, and infrastructure, both hard and soft, besides the general law and order situation in the states.

Land Policy

Apart from some industries in Assam, the region is primarily agricultural. So the initial economic activity has to start from agriculture. The present agricultural techniques are very destructive and relatively unproductive. For a start the agriculture of the region must be commercialized. There is tremendous scope for tea plantations, horticulture, rubber plantations, floriculture, sericulture, etc. As it is the share of cash crops in the total agriculture production in the region is quite substantial.

With the exception of the Rubber Board, the government departments which promote such activities have more or less failed in all the states. These are all highly capital intensive and technical activities; there is no choice but to invite private capital into these areas. However, the present land tenure system in the region is very complex.[22] Apart from Assam, it is difficult to get land in other north-east states either on ownership or on lease. In order to attract private capital, there is an urgent need to look into land policies.

Any market-based economy cannot grow in a place where there is no genuine market for the basic factor of production—land. There is a realization now in the region that the land tenure system among the tribals is responsible for the slow growth in agriculture. It was also observed that in Manipur private lands are more developed compared to community lands; even hill lands under private ownership or management are prosperous.[23] Therefore, major policy actions in the area of land policy have to be taken by almost all the states. In any new system, land should be made available to investors for industrial or agricultural purposes in a transparent manner, either on lease or on ownership. This would be an important step in removing a major hurdle in the way of economic development of the region. Even in the case of Assam, the issue of non-availability of suitable land (in terms of size and location) for setting up industries has been pointed out repeatedly by the Dinesh Goswami Report (1988), L.C. Jain Report (1990) and Cooper and Lybrand Report (1995).[24]

Labour Policy

Another important issue related to economic development in the region is labour. It has to be understood that the north-eastern region is a labour scarce economy rather than a labour surplus economy. This is perhaps one of the main reasons for the failure of the various labour-intensive government schemes in the areas of animal husbandry, fishery and under the Jawahar Rozgar Yojana. Despite all the talk of outsider invasion, labour (both skilled and unskilled) is a big problem in the region with the possible exception of the Brahmaputra valley and Tripura. Already, outside labour (mainly from Bangladesh, Myanmar and other parts of India) is a crucial factor in both agricultural as well as non-agricultural activities of the region.

Discussions with local entrepreneurs revealed that with increase in economic activities, the problem of labour shortage is expected to be aggravated. Unless the region is opened up for outside labour, economic development is going to suffer. Labour, however, is a highly sensitive issue; the states are afraid of a repeat of what happened in Tripura where tribals have become a minority. For the economic development of the region, it is imperative to evolve a tolerant labour policy. Policy makers of the region are aware of the problem but do not accept it officially for obvious reasons. Unofficially, however, some states have already started some exercise to deal with the problem. They are considering a control mechanism to allay tribal apprehensions of influx of outsiders.[25] The labour policy has to become more open if the north-east region really wants to take advantage of new opportunities.

Infrastructural Improvement, Mainly Power

Another major problem in the region is infrastructure, particularly power. Every study on the north-east has highlighted the problem of infrastructure in the region. The S.P. Shukla Commission, which was set up mainly to look into infrastructural gaps in the region has reported that infrastructural requirements for the region are in the tune of Rs 93,619 crore. The Commission estimated the requirements for the Ninth Plan period at about Rs 18,000 crore.[26] However, of the total estimates, more than Rs 60,000 crore are for the power sector alone. This is the crucial area. All the states in the region except Meghalaya face a shortage of power. Yet the north-east region has a huge reserve of hydroelectric potential – between 30,000 to 40,000 MW. Arunachal Pradesh claims that it alone has the potential of about 30,000 MW, of which only 25 MW has been harnessed so far. If only a portion of the hydroelectric potential is realized, the region can become attractive to investors. Obviously, this is one area where foreign investment can be readily attracted. Today more than 15 new power projects, including the private sector projects, are at different stages of implementation. Project reports of Lower Kopili and Tipaimukh projects are also ready. Twenty-seven other projects are under investigation. All these projects would require about Rs 40,000 crore worth of investment. The Ogden Energy of US has signed a letter of understanding with the Assam government for exploring various possibilities of setting up power projects in the state. The company has also shown interest in taking the Bongaigaon thermal power station on lease for renovation and upgradation.[27]

If things go as planned, the power situation is likely to be eased. But for the next five to ten years, power will remain a major problem in the region which no investor can ignore. Radical changes in the thinking of different Central ministries as well as local politicians are required to remedy this situation. Otherwise the region will have to import power from Bangladesh or elsewhere even to meet domestic consumption.[28]

LAW AND ORDER

The north-east region is the land of the oldest insurgency in Independent India. The last few decades have seen the emergence of a number of insurgent groups. Many of these have faded out but some are still active and continue to spill blood.[29] Frequent bandhs and economic blockades by various groups are another annoying factor. A project report on bandhs in Assam reveals that 73 bandhs were called by different organizations between June 1997 and May 1998.[30] Bandhs are called not only by insurgent organizations, but also by political parties, including the AGP, BJP and the Congress. A bandh call for 12 hours was the most common, called 36 times during the period June 1997 to May 1998. However, longer duration bandhs – 36 or 48 hours – were also not very uncommon. According to this report, per day loss in state domestic product due to bandhs is Rs 4,479 lakh. The total loss due to bandhs between June 1997 and May 1998 was Rs 1,255 crore.[31] A related aspect is the fear of extortion, kidnapping and killing of businessmen in the region. To survive, almost every industry or business, big or small, in most parts of the north-east, makes regular contributions to different underground groups – call it extortion, ransom or protection money. There are reports that even public sector units and government employees in many of the states also pay. The allegations of the tea industry funding militants[32] deter possible investors for two reasons. First, it has made the fact widely known to potential investors that payment to militants is the rule in the region. If big respected companies like the Tatas could not operate without paying some kind of protection money, no other company is likely to have any faith in the government's announcements that they would provide a safe and secure environment to investors. Second, it has made the task much more difficult for the those companies already operating in the region. Multinational companies who were planning to enter the region, particularly in the power sector and oil exploration may now think twice. They find it much more difficult to 'buy peace' with militants.

The Central Government and state governments in the region have announced many tax incentives. However, the 'insurgency tax' is one of the biggest disincentive to investment in the region. Therefore, serious efforts to end insurgency would be much more meaningful than the announcements of numerous schemes for economic development.

GEOGRAPHICAL ADVANTAGE

Another area where radical policy action is needed is the external sector. For long, it has been argued that the disadvantageous geographical situation of the north-east region is one of the main stumbling blocks in its economic development. This isolated, landlocked region shares less than 2 per cent of its borders with India, and the rest with Bhutan, Bangladesh, Myanmar and the Tibetan region of China. For the most part this international border has been artificially created. The result has been the elimination of the region's trade, commerce and other linkages which existed in the pre-Partition days.[33]

Using the region's 2 per cent perimeter as a major linkage point with the rest of India and at the same time checking the inflow of goods and people from across the remaining rest of 98 per cent has been a gigantic task.

Lately, there has been talk of converting this locational disadvantage into a boon because of an increasingly integrated world economy. This is particularly so when all the seven states of the region are on international borders. In addition, these states are very close to the dynamic South-East and East Asian economies. Most policy makers in the region are excited and optimistic about the idea of linking their economies with dynamic Asia. There are even suggestions that if for security reasons the Government of India is reluctant to open up the natural trade routes, the north-east states should ask the Central Government to compensate them for the loss of trade.[34]

It is imperative to develop a coherent policy thinking in this area. The reason being that there is not only a failure of the economic policy framework in the region but also a weakness of country's foreign policy which has ignored South-East Asia for a long time. As a result, the north-east region was not only cut-off from its natural economic partners but also encircled by unfriendly countries.

So far the major border trade activity of the region with Bangladesh and Myanmar is 'unauthorized trade'. The state authorities are fully aware of these activities which function smoothly through unofficial channels. China is an important player in the border trade even though its trading activities are mainly through Myanmar.

The major policy issue, therefore, would be to synchronize these realities into Indian trade policies. In fact, to transform this low economic activity area into a dynamic region in the next ten to fifteen years, a coordinated effort by different Central ministries and departments – mainly External Affairs, Home, Commerce and DONER – as well as a strong commitments from each of the north-east states is needed. With a well thought-out long term policy, this region has the potential to emerge as a strategic base for domestic and foreign investors to tap the potential of contiguous markets of China, Myanmar, Bangladesh, Laos, Thailand, Vietnam, Cambodia as well as Malaysia, Indonesia and beyond.

To begin with, the emphasis should be on creating conditions, both at the policy level and at the ground level, on converting the unauthorized trade into authorized trade. This is not a simple task. The genuine trader will have many practical problems. The unauthorized trade works on the basis of a strong network which involves traders, police and forest departments and, of course, many underground groups, and each has its own share in the pie. Apart from infrastructural problems at Moreh, the large number of checkposts on National Highways 39 and 53 would create problem in switching over from illegal to legal trade. Traders claim that the expenditure on transportation from Moreh to Dimapur is about Rs 50,000 per truck, which includes hire charges, payments to various underground groups, and money paid at almost every police and forest checkpost.[35] Similarly, transport expenditure from Imphal to Guwahati is more than Rs 35,000 per truck. The main reason is that the commodities which are coming from the border are not legal. The list of items agreed on by the governments of India and Myanmar is not of much use to traders. However, even if the products were legal, the usual 'tax' would still need to be paid at every checkpoint.

In most cases, the state governments turn a blind eye to the border trade in illegal items because it creates a lot of economic activity in the region. But since these commodities are not declared legal officially, there is corruption at every turn. It would a good idea to declare certain areas in the region as free trade areas since for all practical purposes they are free trade areas anyway. After declaring so and creating a minimum infrastructure, the second major step would be to devise an aggressive strategy to form a growth triangle or quadrangle involving neighbouring regions. Earlier some scholars emphasized the idea of the 'Bay of Bengal Growth Triangle'.[36] It was proposed to have joint studies and coordinated investment plans to tap the natural resources of the region, that is the eastern and north-eastern states of India, Bangladesh, Nepal, Bhutan and possibly Myanmar. But, with the signing of the Bangladesh-India-Myanmar-Sri Lanka-Thailand Economic Cooperation (BIMST-EC) agreement, the focus has shifted to this forum.

While keeping the interests of north-east in mind, some interrelated steps could be taken to create a growth quadrangle involving north-eastern India, northern Myanmar, south-west China,[37] northern Thailand and Bangladesh.[38] In August 1999, the 'Kunming Initiative' to promote a growth quadrangle between India, China, Myanmar and Bangladesh was launched at an international conference in Kunming, the capital of Yunnan province of China. The conference resolved to establish a Forum for Regional Cooperation between China, India, Myanmar and Bangladesh through interaction among academics, governments and leaders of business and industry. The basic objective of the conference was to strengthen regional economic cooperation among contiguous regions of eastern/north-eastern India, Bangladesh, China and Myanmar.[39] It was agreed that regional cooperation 'should be guided by the Five Principles of Peaceful Coexistence, emphasizing equality and mutual benefit, sustainable development, comparative advantages, adoption of international standards, and infrastructure development in order to enhance connectivity and facilitate the widest possible economic cooperation'.[40] In this way, in the long run, the vision of making the north-east region a partner in a wider-cross-border Brahmaputra, Yangtze, Mekong quadrant can be realized.[41]

CONCLUSIONS

The present economic policy framework for the north-east region is based on its political economy and a cultural approach, adjusted with regional planning models. It is implemented mainly through the Planning Commission and the North-Eastern Council. Despite huge financial investments this has failed to produce the desired results. Further, this is inappropriate to face the challenges presented by the process of liberalization/globalization of the economy. A new policy framework for the north-east will have to be based on the market approach (although certain political and cultural factors cannot be ignored altogether). If the correct policies are pursued, the region will be able to improve its economy. Under the new economic strategy, private investment should be viewed as the critical component. But first of all the region has to become investor friendly. To encourage private investment, policy makers have to focus on infrastructure (both hard and soft), land and labour policies and improve the law and order situation. Secondly, the geographical proximity of the region to the dynamic South-East Asian economies can be utilized if bold policies are initiated both by the Centre as well as by the state governments. These policies include converting unauthorized trade activities into authorized trade, both at the policy level and at the ground level; declaring certain areas of the north-east region as free trade areas; and an aggressive strategy for creating a growth quadrangle involving the north-east, Myanmar, south-west China, northern Thailand and Bangladesh. Removal of Restricted Area Permit and Inner Line Regulations would also help integrate the north-east with Indian and global economies. With Myanmar becoming a member of ASEAN, a common market of 500 million consumers is at the doorstep of the north-east. Thirdly, Assam is the key to the development of the north-east; within Assam priority should be given to modernize its agriculture. Given the rich natural resource base there is considerable scope for increasing agricultural growth. This could be done by improving the cropping intensity, extending dry season farming through irrigation, and diversifying into other areas like horticulture, fisheries, and dairy production.

NOTES

1. For detailed description of the region's ethnic, cultural and religious diversity, see R. Gopalakrishnan, *The North-East India: Land, Economy and People*, New Delhi: Vikas, 1991; and B.G. Verghese, *India's North-East Resurgent: Ethnicity, Insurgency, Governance a Development*, New Delhi: Konark, 1996.
2. These special historical and geographical aspects of the region as well as background of special constitutional arrangements are summarized by L.P. Singh, 'Problem (The North-East: A Symposium on the Problem of Neglected People and Region)', *Seminar*, no. 366, February 1990, pp. 12–18.
3. While writing the foreword to the 2nd edn. of Verrier Elwin's *A Philosophy for Nefa*, Shillong: North-Eastern Frontier Agency, 1959, Pt. Jawaharlal Nehru wrote that 'avenues of development (for tribal areas) should be pursued within the broad framework of the following five fundamental principles:

    (a) People should develop along the lines of their own genius and we should avoid imposing anything on them. We should try to encourage in every way their own traditional art and culture.
    (b) Tribal rights in land and forests should be respected.
    (c) We should try to train and build up a team of their own people to do the work of administration and development. Some technical personnel from outside will, no doubt, be needed, especially in the beginning. But we should avoid introducing too many outsiders into tribal territory.
    (d) We should not over-administer these areas or overwhelm them with a multiplicity of schemes. We should rather work through, and not in rivalry to, their own social and cultural institutions.
    (e) We should judge results, not by statistics or the amount of money spent, but the quality of human character that is evolved.

4. See Arvind K. Sharma, 'District Councils in the North-East', in *Fifty Years of Indian Administration: Retrospect and Prospect*, ed. T.N. Chaturvedi, New Delhi: Indian Institute of Public Administration, 1998.
5. See, Ajai Sahni, *The Terrorist Economy in India's Northeast: Preliminary Explorations*, paper presented at the ICSSR Seminar at New Delhi on 2–3 March 2000.
6. For major changes which have taken place in the region see, B.P. Singh, *The Problem of Change: A Study of North-East India*, New Delhi: Oxford, 1987.
7. See Paul Cashin and Ratna Sahay, 'Regional Economic Growth and Convergence in India', *Finance and Development*, March 1996.
8. 'Liberalization and the Changing Roles of Centre and the States', in J. Raja Chelliah, *Towards Sustainable Growth: Essays in Fiscal and Financial Sector Reforms in India*, New Delhi: Oxford, 1996, pp. 19–45.
9. The recommendations of the Conference of the Ministers of Industries of the North-Eastern States held at Guwahati on 30 November 1996, however, looks the problem in a different way. They mainly argued for a 'promotional approach, with substantial grants from the Central Government'.
10. *Statistical Hand Book of Assam*, Guwahati: Directorate of Economics and Statistics, Government of Assam, 1994, p. 120.
11. This is according to the report of the *Committee for Educated Unemployed in the North-Eastern Region* (1997), p. 11.
12. *Sixth All India Educational Survey*, vol. VII, NCERT, 1998.
13. These points are also raised by L.P. Singh, 'National Policy for the North-East', in Upinder Baxi, Alice Jacob and Tarlok Singh, eds., *Reconstructing the Republic*, New Delhi: Har-Anand, 1999.
14. Author's calculations based on various Reserve Bank of India publications.
15. For details see Gulshan Sachdeva, *Economy of the North-East: Policy, Present Conditions and Future Possibilities*, New Delhi: Konark, 2000.
16. *Parliament Questions*, 21 February 1997.
17. *Public Enterprise Survey, 1995–96*.
18. *The Assam Tribune*, 6 June 1997.
19. While inaugurating a round table on economic development of north-eastern states, the then Finance Minister Manmohan Singh also stressed the need to involve the private sector in the process of development of this region. See Press Release by FICCI, 4 July 1995. Atul Sarma, however, is sceptical about the role private sector can play in the region. See, Atul Sarma, *Development Strategy in the North-East in the Context of Globalization* (mimeo). He argues that 'having lagged behind in terms of the level and quality of administrative, social and economic infrastructure, these states are not likely to benefit immediately from

private investment flows in the new regime. Being placed as they are, the role of the public sector in these economies has to be much greater' (p. 15).
20. *Bengal Chamber of Commerce and Industry Newsletter*, 13 January 1997.
21. Confederation of Indian Industries, *Sunrise: Heralding a New Dawn, a Presentation to North-Eastern States,* Guwahati: CII, August 1995.
22. For details see Table 7.2, Gulshan Sachdeva, op. cit., pp. 213–14.
23. See Foundation for Environment and Economic Services (FEEDS) and Institute of People's Action (IPA), *Shifting Cultivation: Tea Cultivation as an Alternative: A Report,* Imphal: FEEDS and IPA, 1997.
24. Cf. *Report of (Jayanta Madhab) Advisory Committee on Industry*, vol. 1, Dispur: Government of Assam, p. 9.
25. See Meghalaya Economic Development Council, *Outline Proposal for the Meghalaya Economic Policy,* Shillong: EDC Group, 1995, Appendix 1.
26. *Transforming the North-East: Tackling Backlogs in Basic Minimum Services and Infrastructural Needs: High Level (S.P. Shukla) Commission Report to the Prime Minister,* New Delhi: Planning Commission, 1997, pp. 8–9, 27. *The Assam Tribune,* 4 June 1997.
28. Asian Development Bank is already looking at the possibility of importing power to Tripura and Mizoram from Bangladesh. See *Times of India,* 12 June 1997.
29. For details about different insurgent groups active in the region as well as all aspects of north-eastern insurgency see mainly Sanjoy Hazarika, *Strangers of the Mist: Tales of War and Peace From India's Northeast,* New Delhi: Viking, 1994; and Ved Marwah, *Uncivil Wars, Pathology of Terrorism in India,* Delhi: Harper-Collins, 1995, pp. 224–316.
30. North-Eastern Development Finance Corporation (1999), *Project Report on Bandhs in Assam,* Guwahati: NEDFC.
31. Ibid.
32. For details about allegations of Tata Tea funding ULFA militants, see cover stories of *India Today,* 20 October 1997; and *Business India,* 20 October 1997.
33. To understand how Partition of the country has affected negatively the traditional trade and economic links of the north-east see, Sanjoy Hazarika, op. cit., pp. 257–60.
34. *Report of (Jayanta Madhab) Committee on Industry,* op. cit., p. 6.
35. For details see, Table 5.3, Gulshan Sachdeva, op. cit., pp. 155–7.
36. Centre for Policy Research, *Indo-Bangladesh Dialogue: Economic and Trade Cooperation,* New Delhi: CPR, 1995.
37. South-west China includes Yunnan province, Sichuan province, Chongqing municipality and Guizhou province.
38. For details see, Gulshan Sachdeva, 'India-China Economic Coopera-

tion in a Growth Quadrangle', in *The Peacock and the Dragon: India-China Relations in the 21st Century*, eds. Kanti Bajpai and Amitabh Matto, New Delhi: Har-Anand, 2000.
39. Also see Che Zhimin, *Proposition on Formation of Sub-Regional Zone of China, India, Myanmar and Bangladesh* (mimeo), 1988.
40. *The Kunming Initiative*, 17 August 1999. (This declaration is the outcome of an international conference to promote growth quadrangle between India, China, Myanmar and Bangladesh held in Kunming, Yunnan, from 14 to 17 August 1999. Apart from scholars from all four countries, China and Myanmar were officially represented in the conference.)
41. For details of this argument see B.G. Verghese, op. cit., especially Chapter 17 of the book.

CHAPTER 14

Convergence in the Consumption Behaviour: A North-East Perspective

SANDWIP KUMAR DAS AND MONICA DAS

ISOLATION OF THE NORTH-EAST

In more than one way the north-eastern region presents an enigma that has baffled those who have studied the federal economy of India. There is now a consensus that the process of economic reform started in the early 1990s has been successful in raising the rate of economic progress in the country. The result of economic reform has been so encouraging that we are now heading towards a set of second-generation reforms, particularly in the financial sector. Initially there was an apprehension that the reforms might raise growth rates of national income but poverty and inequality might also increase. In fact, many political observers feel that the Narasimha Rao government that ushered in economic liberalization for the first time lost the elections due to increased poverty caused by the new economic policies. However, recent evidence shows that poverty has not increased. The National Sample Survey estimates of poverty shows a 10 per cent drop in the percentage of population below the poverty line between 1992–3 and 1999–2000. Since the economy has performed fairly well in this period, as indicated by the macro-economic indicators, the fall in poverty estimates lends support to the view that there need not arise a conflict between growth and poverty alleviation in the Indian economy.

Given this scenario, all eyes will now be turned towards the north-eastern states because here the economic indicators tell a different story. Evidence shows that the reforms have hardly touched the region and as a result regional inequality in our federal economy has presumably increased, even though there has been rapid growth and poverty reduction on an average during the last decade. This is a phenomenon that should worry the federal policy makers a great deal. The demographic profile of the north-eastern states presented in Table 14.1 clearly shows that these states are falling behind the rest of the country and this is a problem that needs to be addressed very seriously.

Though all-India poverty measure has fallen from 36 to 26 during 1992–2000, all north-eastern states with the exception of Mizoram have poverty levels much above the Indian average; Assam, the biggest among the north-eastern states, exhibits the highest poverty. Some of the puzzling facts that emerge from the table are: (i) Assam has the lowest population growth rate in the region, though the figures are from the last census. (ii) All other states in the region have population growth rates higher than the Indian average. (iii) Most states in the region have high literacy rates and excluding Arunachal Pradesh female literacy rate is higher than the national average. All these indicates very clearly that the development process in the region has not been able to involve the local people effectively. In fact, the work participation rates measured by total workers as a percentage of total population are fairly high in the region in both male and female categories.[1] This again points to the hypothesis that no proper utili-

TABLE 14.1: DEMOGRAPHIC PROFILE OF NORTH-EASTERN REGION

	Percentage of Population Below Poverty Line (Estimates for 1999–2000)	Annual Exponential Growth Rate of Population (%) 1981–91	Literacy Rate		
			Male	Female	Total
Assam	36.09	2.17	61.87	43.03	52.89
Manipur	28.54	2.57	71.63	47.60	59.89
Meghalaya	33.87	2.84	53.12	44.85	49.10
Mizoram	19.47	3.34	85.61	78.60	82.27
Nagaland	32.67	4.45	67.62	54.75	61.65
Sikkim	–	2.51	65.74	46.69	56.94
Tripura	34.44	2.95	70.58	49.65	60.44
Arunachal	33.47	3.14	51.45	29.69	41.59
All India	26.10	2.14	64.13	39.29	52.21

Source: National Sample Survey for Poverty Estimates and Economic Survey, 1999–2000.

zation of manpower is taking place. There can be several reasons for this. First, the region may be using obsolete technology, giving rise to low labour productivity. Second, being sparsely populated, the region may be suffering from transport bottlenecks standing in the way of development of a marketing network that can generate incomes for the local population. Both these factors are expected to cause isolation of the north-east from the markets of the rest of the country. Goods will be produced and consumed in the region itself with no real possibility of trade with the rest of India. The purpose of this paper is to show that this is what is basically happening. Unless steps are taken on a priority basis to improve transport and marketing network, the isolation of the north-east will perpetuate. Geographical and economic integration of the region with the rest of the country will bring new technology into the region and raise the standard of living. In what follows we look at the consumption and production patterns of the states to show that the region's share in India's consumption expenditures is higher than its share in production of a large number of products.

PATTERNS OF PRODUCTION AND CONSUMPTION IN THE NORTH-EAST

The north-eastern states are Assam, Manipur, Meghalaya, Mizoram, Nagaland, Sikkim, Tripura and Arunachal Pradesh. The region is hilly with a fragile land mass, making communication difficult and expensive. For many parts of north-east, air transport is the only practical means of transportation. The region is sparsely populated. The density of population is the highest in Assam (286 person per sq. km.) which also has the highest population in the region. The next is Tripura with a density of 263. The population density in the rest of the states varies between 10 in Arunachal Pradesh and 82 in Manipur.[2] Agriculture and the service sector are the two major components of the gross domestic product in the region. The industrial sector is dominated by tea and timber in Assam, while mining, sawmills and plywood factories represent most of the manufacturing in the other states. Lack of employment opportunities in agriculture and manufacturing puts pressure on the service sector, particularly the government services.

The product range of the north-eastern states is extremely narrow. Plantation crops constitute a major part of the region's agriculture.

Assam's major crops are tea, coffee, rice, jute, cotton and oilseeds. Rice is grown in all the states in the region. Sugar cane, rubber, millet, wheat and forest products are some of the other items produced in the region. There is a tendency towards self-sufficiency in the production of food grains in all the states, though it is unlikely that the states have comparative advantage in the production of all crops. The Revealed Comparative Advantage (RCA) measures for mainly agricultural products are reported in Table 14.2. RCA is a static con-cept and is defined as a ratio between the product's share in the total output of the region and the region's share in national output of the product. For instance, in Assam the share of cereals in the total production of cereals in the north-eastern region is 17.33 times the share of the north-eastern region in the national production of cereals. Such a large number indicates that Assam has comparative advantage in cereals among the states in the north-east region. In fact, the table shows that Assam has RCA in all the products produced in the region. However, it must be stated that RCA is a static measure and it is not very reliable.[3] Theoretically, an RCA measure greater than unity is supposed to indicate comparative advantage. Assam exhibits RCA in all the products. Other states have RCA in selected products. Table 14.3 shows that there is scope for specialization in the production of food items in most of the states in the region and the tendency towards self-sufficiency prevents such specialization from taking place.

Next we look at the pattern of consumption expenditure in the north-eastern states. National Sample Survey has data on state-wise per capita consumption expenditure on major items for both rural and urban sectors. From this one can estimate the total consumption expenditure by multiplying per capita expenditure with the state population. We are particularly interested in inter-state disparities in consumption expenditure. First we compute a measure of disparity for fifteen major states of India and then compare that with a measure of disparity for eight north-eastern states. The measure of disparity used in this study is known as the entropy, which is defined as follows:

$$(100 / \log N) \, \Sigma \, X_i \log (1/X_i)$$

where X_i is the i-th state's consumption share in the product under consideration, so that $\Sigma \, X_i = 1$ and N is the number of states in the sample. If all states have an equal share, the entropy measure will be equal to 100, showing absolute equality in the distribution of

TABLE 14.2: REVEALED COMPARATIVE ADVANTAGE, 1993–4

Items	Assam	Manipur	Meghalaya	Mizoram	Nagaland	Sikkim	Tripura	Arunachal Pradesh
Cereals	17.33	1.75	0.54	0.42	0.82	0.00	2.19	0.65
Rice	11.26	1.17	0.35	0.28	0.54	0.00	1.44	0.42
Wheat	349.66	0.00	15.75	0.00	2.27	0.00	25.65	19.85
Gram	501.48	0.00	107.46	0.00	573.12	0.00	143.28	0.00
Cereal Substitute	5.90	2.86	8.25	5.21	13.94	0.00	0.62	25.01
Pulses and Products	88.03	0.00	3.86	16.68	15.44	0.00	10.04	8.18
Edible Oil	20.98	0.24	0.61	0.20	1.02	0.00	1.13	3.04
Pan, Tobacco & Intoxicants	26.57	0.00	11.07	19.93	0.00	0.00	2.21	0.00
Clothing (cotton)	84.01	10.50	567.05	220.52	10.50	0.00	168.01	0.00
Milk	48.42	4.22	3.65	0.61	2.79	2.22	2.58	1.36

Source: Central Statistical Organization.

TABLE 14.3: INTER-STATE DISPARITY IN URBAN
CONSUMPTION EXPENDITURE 1993–4

	15 State Entropy	8 State Entropy for north-east
Cereals	93.2	69.9
Gram	91.0	34.8
Cereal Substitute	44.5	70.6
Pulses & Products	90.4	67.6
Milk & Products	92.0	66.7
Edible Oil	91.2	68.6
Meat, Egg, Fish	88.0	75.0
Vegetables	92.6	73.5
Fruits	90.2	58.7
Sugar	90.7	68.0
Salt	93.2	74.3
Spices	92.2	73.6
Beverages, etc.	92.4	60.1
Pan, Tobacco & Intoxicants	93.6	74.9
Fuel & Light	92.8	76.4
Clothing	92.8	66.8
Footwear	93.7	78.5
Misc. Goods & Services	92.3	70.3
Durable Goods	89.4	53.2

Source: Estimated from data provided by National Sample Survey.

consumption spending across states. The other extreme is absolute inequality in which one state in the sample gets all and the others get nothing, in which case the entropy measure will be equal to zero.

Table 14.3 shows inter-state inequality measure in respect of urban consumption expenditure for the year 1993–4 for fifteen major states (including Assam) and eight north-eastern states. Since the value of the entropy is fairly high in both cases and in respect of most products, there is no evidence of any significant inter-state disparity in consumption expenditure. It is, however, generally true that consumption disparity is higher in the north-east region than in the fifteen major states. With the exception of gram and cereal substitute, the pattern of disparity is the same[4] in the two samples, which indicates the fact that the consumption habit of the region is converging towards the Indian standard. We shall present more evidence of this convergence of consumption habits when we discuss the profiles of north-eastern states. From the data presented so far the facts that emerge are that the consumption basket in the north-eastern states is fairly diversified though greater diversification has taken place in the fifteen major states. However, the production pattern in the north-east is not based on specialization but on a notion of self-sufficiency. This finding is consistent with the hypothesis stated in the previous section that labour productivity in the region is low and technology is backward.

STATE PROFILES

North-east of India is not homogeneous. Many states such as Arunachal Pradesh and Sikkim are new and their development experience in the Indian union is short. Mizoram, Nagaland, Meghalaya and Arunachal Pradesh are dominated by tribal population. The states in the region also differ in terms of growth of per capita income; some states like Nagaland, Manipur and Tripura have not shown any growth during the decade of the 1990s. Assam is the oldest state in the region and it has also shown signs of stagnation. The federal government has not yet developed an economic policy for the north-east. One also observes a lack of coordination between the national government and the state governments. A few studies have been done to look at the problems and prospects of the states in the region. For instance, Wadia[5] has studied the forest resources in the region. A study by the Tata Consultancy Service[6] makes the point that most exports from the region to the rest of the country are low value-added primary goods and this leads to drainage of resources from the region through resources-intensive exports. A Planning Commission study shows the weakness of the banking system in the region resulting in low credit deposit ratio. There is some evidence in support of the suspicion that bank deposits of the region are being deployed elsewhere.[7] Finally, a specific study on Nagaland has suggested a development strategy for the state.[8]

In the rest of the paper we want to look at the profile of each state separately. We shall focus on the state's share in national consumption expenditure on selected products and compare that with its share in national production. In addition to this we shall also compare the state's per capita consumption with the national average. Our main hypothesis is that the region is backward in production but not so backward in consumption, resulting in dependence of these states on the rest of the country. Obviously, such dependence cannot continue for ever. Unless the production structure of the north-eastern states is improved, they will soon face a severe economic crisis.

Assam

Located in the Brahmaputra valley, Assam is surrounded by Bhutan and Arunachal Pradesh in the north, Nagaland and Manipur in the east, Mizoram and Tripura in the south, and Meghalaya, Bangladesh and West Bengal in the west. It is the oldest and by far the most important state in the north-east of India. It is rich in natural resources like natural oil, natural gas, coal, rubber and minerals like granite, limestone and kaolin. It is also rich in forest resources. Assam is regarded as the gateway to the north-east as it has the best infrastructure in the region. Though industrially most developed in the region, Assam is primarily agricultural with 74 per cent of the people engaged in agricultural and allied activities. The main cash crops are jute, tea, cotton, oilseeds, sugar cane, fruits and potatoes. Textile, cement and oil refining are the main industries. Table 14.4 provides an analysis of the production and consumption of main products in Assam in 1988–9 and 1993–4. The first two columns in the table give the state's share in national consumption expenditure. It appears that Assam has maintained its relative position in national absorption of goods, particularly in food products with a few exceptions such as milk, in which its consumption share has declined. The third column shows the ratio between Assam's per capita expenditure and the national average per capita expenditure (the ratio has been multiplied by 100). In 7 out of 19 products reported in the table, Assam's per capita consumption expenditure is higher than the national average. The fourth column gives Assam's share in the national production of selected items. It should be mentioned that consumption shares are computed from value figures. In other words, consumption shares are shares in total consumption expenditure at the national level for the relevant product. On the other hand, production is measured in metric tons and production shares are, therefore, computed from physical production of the relevant product in the state and its corresponding national total. Since shares are independent of the unit of measurement, we can compare the consumption and production shares for each product. Production data are not available for all items in the table. This means that either the data are not reported or the state does not produce the product which is showing a blank in the fourth column. Assam's consumption share is higher than the corresponding production share for all products

TABLE 14.4: ASSAM

Items	1993–4 Consumption Shares (%)	1988–9 Consumption Shares (%)	1988–9 Per Capita Consumption Relative to Indian Average	1993–4 Production Shares (%)	1993–4 Dependency Index
Cereals	3.8	3.7	143.60	2.51	151.60
Gram	2.5	1.9	92.90	0.03	8,756.79
Cereal Substitute	0.2	0.2	6.70	0.15	129.35
Pulses and Products	2.0	2.2	76.50	0.44	459.64
Milk & Products	1.5	2.0	57.70		
Edible Oil	2.3	2.0	85.10	2.83	81.19
Meat, Egg, Fish	6.5	5.3	243.60		
Vegetables	3.1	3.2	117.80		
Fruits	2.2	1.8	83.20	2.56	86.02
Sugar	2.0	2.1	75.80	0.73	274.17
Salt	3.6	3.6	134.90		
Spices	1.6	1.7	62.20	0.56	288.15
Beverages, etc.	2.8	2.6	105.90		
Pan, Tobacco and Intoxicants	4.6	3.8	175.20	0.74	618.70
Fuel & Light	2.4	2.7	88.80		
Clothing	2.6	2.3	97.80	0.01	34,814.00
Footwear	2.9	1.9	108.80		
Misc. Goods and Services	2.2	2.1	82.00		
Durable Goods	1.8	0.9	69.20		
Higher than Indian Average (no.)			7.00		

Source: National Sample Survey and Central Statistical Organization.

except edible oil and fruits. The last column shows the dependency index, which is simply the ratio between consumption share and production share multiplied by 100. Thus, any item reporting a dependency index that is greater than 100 would indicate dependence of the state for that item. The table shows Assam's dependence for most of the products, which is rather surprising in view of the fact that the state has revealed comparative advantage for all these products.

Manipur

Bounded by Nagaland in the north, Mizoram in the south, Upper Myanmar in the east and Cacher district of Assam in the west, Manipur is known for its natural beauty and splendour. The state is essentially agricultural. The main industries are pharmaceuticals, steel re-rolling, plywood, bamboo chipping, cement, *vanaspati* and electronics. Manipur is well connected by air and road transport but deficient in railway facility. The traditional occupation of the people is related to logging, cash crops, handloom, handicraft, weaving and pisciculture. The state suffers from poor infrastructure and its per

TABLE 14.5: MANIPUR

Items	1993–4 Consumption Shares (%)	1988–9 Consumption Shares (%)	1988–9 Per Capita Consumption Relative to Indian Average	1993–4 Production Shares (%)	1993–4 Dependency Index
Cereals	0.39	0.42	195.27	0.2500	153.45
Gram	0.01	0.14	63.46		
Cereal Substitute	0.01	0.03	12.50	0.0749	9.66
Pulses and Products	0.11	0.21	98.18		
Milk and Products	0.03	0.04	16.55		
Edible Oil	0.11	0.10	47.03	0.0328	326.03
Meat, Egg, Fish	0.34	0.36	163.57		
Vegetables	0.15	0.17	76.85		
Fruits and Nuts	0.05	0.05	23.81	0.1453	33.52
Sugar	0.09	0.09	41.30		
Salt	0.28	0.42	192.86		
Spices	0.15	0.14	65.49	0.0565	273.21
Beverages, etc.	0.07	0.05	23.42		
Pan, Tobacco and Intoxicants	0.25	0.28	128.41		
Fuel and Light	0.19	0.20	90.17		
Clothing	0.06	0.12	55.53	0.0009	5946.31
Footwear	0.28	0.58	269.29		
Misc. Goods and Services	0.11	0.07	32.79		
Durable Goods	0.03	0.03	14.87		
Higher than Indian Average (no.)		5.00			

Source: Same as Table 14.4.

CONVERGENCE IN THE CONSUMPTION BEHAVIOUR 341

capita income growth has been much lower than the national per capita income growth rate in recent years. Table 14.5 illustrates the problem of slow growth. The first two columns giving Manipur's consumption shares in two years show a decline during the period for most items of consumption. Per capita consumption in Manipur is higher than the national average only in respect of 5 out of 19 items. Due to the non-availability of comparable production data, production shares are computed for only a few items. Except in the cases of cereal substitute and fruits Manipur shows dependence. Lack of industrialization is the main cause of slow income growth. The state needs infrastructure development before any viable process of industrialization can begin.

Meghalaya

Meghalaya is known as a fruit growing state and the major fruit crops are orange, pineapple, banana, jackfruit, plum, pear and peach. Rice and maize are the major food crops. Shillong, the capital of the state, is a tourist spot. There are some small and medium scale industries apart from tourism. But transport isolation is a bottleneck because there is no railway linkage and road and air transport are not very well developed. The state is endowed with important minerals like coal, limestone and granite, but these are extracted and mostly sold outside the state, leaving the state with low value addition. Meghalaya seems to have potential for agro-based and horticultural industries, but in the absence of transport and marketing infrastructure, the future does not look very bright. All this is reflected in the low per capita income of the state and its economic backwardness relative to the rest of the country. Table 14.6 shows that Meghalaya's record in maintaining consumption standard is slightly better than what we have seen in the case of Manipur. The state's consumption share between 1988–94 increased moderately in the case of some items and it exhibits per capita consumption expenditure higher than the national average in seven items. The production shares are also on the high side compared to Manipur and as a result the dependency index is not very high. The position of the state in respect of fruit and spices is quite comfortable. Literacy rate in Meghalaya is 49 per cent and the urbanization rate is the second highest in the region. With English as the administrative language the state has tremendous potential in tourism, services and various agro-based

TABLE 14.6: MEGHALAYA

Items	1993–4 Consumption Shares (%)	1988–9 Consumption Shares (%)	1988–9 Per Capita Consumption Relative to Indian Average	1993–4 Production Shares (%)	1993–4 Dependency Index
Cereals	0.271	0.28	131.39	0.09	310.52
Gram	0.015	0.05	25.00	0.01	
Cereal Substitute	0.084	0.00	0.00	0.22	38.82
Pulses and Products	0.122	0.14	67.88	0.02	
Milk & Products	0.133	0.18	84.48		
Edible Oil	0.207	0.17	78.83	0.08	252.35
Meat, Egg, Fish	0.749	0.72	343.14		
Vegetables	0.300	0.27	128.57		
Fruits and Nuts	0.111	0.12	59.52	0.66	16.95
Sugar	0.171	0.19	91.30		
Salt	0.243	0.32	153.57		
Spices	0.156	0.11	52.60	0.78	19.90
Beverages, etc.	0.291	0.18	84.59		
Pan, Tobacco and Intoxicants	0.806	0.52	246.27	0.31	260.12
Fuel and Light	0.212	0.23	111.66		
Clothing	0.242	0.20	93.82	0.05	479.48
Footwear	0.193	0.49	235.83		
Misc. Goods and Services	0.212	0.21	99.68		
Durable Goods	0.049	0.08	36.89		
Higher than Indian Average (no.)			7.00		

Source: Same as Table 14.4.

industries. But in order that these industries become cost-effective, road transport needs improvement. An extension of the railway lines would also be very useful.

MIZORAM

The hill state of Mizoram was created in 1987 and is one of the youngest states in the Indian Union. The terrain is not very suitable for a viable transport network as the area is covered by steep hill ranges separated from one another by narrow valleys, Agriculture is the main occupation of 70 per cent of the people. Other occupations

TABLE 14.7: MIZORAM

Items	1993–4 Consumption Shares (%)	1988–9 Consumption Shares (%)	1988–9 Per Capita Consumption Relative to Indian Average	1993–4 Production Shares (%)	1993–4 Dependency Index
Cereals	0.10	0.08	97.41	0.07	419.30
Gram	0.03	0.03	38.46		
Cereal Substitute	0.03	0.02	18.75	0.14	21.91
Pulses and Products	0.07	0.10	126.93	0.08	
Milk & Products	0.05	0.05	65.95		
Edible Oil	0.07	0.07	81.34	0.03	255.25
Meat, Egg, Fish	0.33	0.27	330.59		
Vegetables	0.17	0.19	233.73		
Fruits and Nuts	0.05	0.05	63.55	0.15	30.99
Sugar	0.09	0.10	126.11		
Salt	0.23	0.27	328.57		
Spices	0.05	0.05	60.08	0.22	20.50
Beverages, etc.	0.05	0.04	54.10		
Pan, Tobacco and Intoxicants	0.21	0.22	275.65	0.56	37.71
Fuel and Light	0.15	0.17	205.83		
Clothing	0.12	0.05	62.25	0.02	627.00
Footwear	0.33	0.43	525.98		
Misc. Goods and Services	0.07	0.04	55.16		
Durable Goods	0.04	0.02	27.01		
Higher than Indian Average (no.)			8.00		

Source: Same as Table 14.4.

are related to handloom and handicrafts. The state's per capita income is higher than the national average primarily due to Central Government assistance which, as it appears from Table 14.7, is used to maintain the consumption standards. A comparison of the first two columns of the table shows that the state is by and large maintaining its consumption shares. In 8 out of 19 products its per capita consumption expenditure is higher than the per capita consumption expenditure of the country. The level of dependence is not very high in minor products but the state shows dependence in major products such as cereals, edible oil and clothing. Mizoram does not exhibit revealed comparative advantage significantly in any product except clothing. Because of the difficulty in transportation of goods from Mizoram to other parts of the country, the future of Mizoram lies in trade with the neighbouring countries, particularly Bangladesh and Myanmar with whom the state shares its border. Mizoram has the highest literacy rate in the region, which is perhaps the biggest asset the state has in its possession.

NAGALAND

A few recent studies on Nagaland's economy are available.[9] Nearly all of Nagaland is mountainous and one-sixth of land is under forest cover. Despite abundant rainfall and fertile soil, cultivation is diffi-

TABLE 14.8: NAGALAND

Items	1993–4 Consumption Shares (%)	1988–9 Consumption Shares (%)	1988–9 Per Capita Consumption Relative to Indian Average	1993–4 Production Shares (%)	1993–4 Dependency Index
Cereals	0.24	0.22	153.89	0.13	182.87
Gram	0.03	0.03	21.15	0.03	93.86
Cereal Substitute	0.00	0.00	0.00	0.36	0.00
Pulses & Products	0.10	0.13	89.34	0.08	133.15
Milk and Products	0.07	0.10	72.81		
Edible Oil	0.09	0.14	97.49	0.14	69.05
Meat, Egg, Fish	0.53	0.68	473.84		
Vegetables	0.22	0.24	168.76		
Fruits and Nuts	0.09	0.15	101.47	0.02	379.96
Sugar	0.11	0.13	89.42		
Salt	0.29	0.35	242.86		
Spices	0.10	0.15	102.49	0.07	131.99
Beverages, etc.	0.12	0.21	145.30		
Pan, Tobacco and Intoxicants	0.36	0.61	423.86		
Fuel and Light	0.17	0.19	130.47		
Clothing	0.08	0.36	248.61	0.00	8,158.52
Footwear	0.26	0.41	283.46		
Misc. Goods and Services	0.14	0.24	170.00		
Durable Goods	0.05	0.12	84.34		
Higher than Indian Average (no.)			12.00		

Source: Same as Table 14.4.

cult. *Jhum* cultivation and terraced wet rice cultivation are widely practiced in the state and about 73 per cent of the population is engaged in agriculture. Literacy rate, particularly female literacy rate in Nagaland is very high. But hardly any industrial activities are conducted in the state. The growth rate of state domestic product is much below the average Indian growth rate and the per capita income is much below the national level. Agriculture, forestry, fishing and logging constitute almost the entire economy. Rice and maize are the major crops. Nagaland is characterized by absence of markets and wholesale dealers. All industrial units are concentrated around Kohima and Dimapur. The main exports transacted at Dimapur are cotton, jute, timber, forest produce, chillies and mustard seeds. Financial services in the state are grossly inadequate. In the sample, Nagaland shows an alarming picture so far as the consumption of food products is concerned. Its consumption shares have dropped in all products except cereals between 1988–94. But since the state's consumption shares were initially high, in 12 out of 19 products Nagaland's per capita consumption are found to be above the national average. With low production shares the state shows high level of dependence (Table 14.8).

Sikkim

Sikkim, is bounded on the north and north-east by Tibet, on the south-east by Bhutan, on the south by West Bengal and on the west by Nepal. It is perhaps the most mountainous state with one-third of land covered by dense and inaccessible forest. Population of Sikkim is mostly rural with Gangtok as its largest town. Sikkim is a multi-ethnic state with 70 per cent of its population being of Nepalese origin; there are also many tribal groups such as Lepchas and Bhutias. The density of population is very low and the literacy rate is above the Indian average. Only about 11 per cent of the state's area is under cultivation. Agriculture is the occupation of 58 per cent of the people. The principal crops are maize, rice, wheat, potato, large cardamom, ginger and orange. The state's industrial activities are concentrated in the areas of fruit jams and juices, bakery products, beer, plastic goods, wrist watches and leather goods. Traditional handicrafts and tourism are also important. Various development programmes started in the state during the last decade have raised wage employment opportunity. This is perhaps the reason why the state

TABLE 14.9: SIKKIM

Items	1993–4 Consumption Shares (%)	1988–9 Consumption Shares (%)	1988–9 Per Capita Consumption Relative to Indian Average
Cereals	0.054	0.04	87.93
Gram	0.045	0.03	59.62
Cereal Substitute	0.000	0.00	0.00
Pulses and Products	0.036	0.04	78.12
Milk and Products	0.048	0.05	96.78
Edible Oil	0.048	0.05	97.41
Meat, Egg, Fish	0.085	0.09	185.08
Vegetables	0.062	0.07	143.03
Fruits and Nuts	0.033	0.02	38.28
Sugar	0.035	0.03	66.21
Salt	0.043	0.05	103.57
Spices	0.038	0.03	55.51
Beverages, etc.	0.079	0.03	56.90
Pan, Tobacco and Intoxicants	0.078	0.05	105.03
Fuel and Light	0.047	0.06	119.59
Clothing	0.033	0.02	38.63
Footwear	0.051	0.10	213.78
Misc. Goods and Services	0.062	0.06	115.61
Durable Goods	0.010	0.01	10.56
Higher than Indian Average (no.)			7.00

Source: Same as Table 14.4.

has by and large maintained its consumption shares between 1988–94. But its consumption shares are low, resulting in only 7 out of 19 products in which Sikkim's per capita consumption is above the national level. Non-availability of production data is the reason why we could not compute the dependency index. Table 14.9 presents whatever could be obtained from the data.

TRIPURA

Bangladesh surrounds Tripura on all sides, while it has borders with Assam and Mizoram in the east. Originally a Princely State and later a Union Territory, Tripura achieved statehood in 1972. Its population is partly tribal but predominantly Bengali. The economy of the state

CONVERGENCE IN THE CONSUMPTION BEHAVIOUR

TABLE 14.10: TRIPURA

Items	1993–4 Consumption Shares (%)	1988–9 Consumption Shares (%)	1988–9 Per Capita Consumption Relative to Indian Average	1993–4 Production Shares (%)	1993–4 Dependency Index
Cereals	0.474	0.56	172.50	0.32	146.49
Gram	0.000	0.11	34.62	0.01	0.00
Cereal Substitute	0.119	0.29	87.50	0.02	731.70
Pulses & Products	0.220	0.27	83.03	0.05	442.44
Milk & Products	0.202	0.36	111.41		
Edible Oil	0.300	0.35	108.45	0.15	197.18
Meat, Egg, Fish	1.087	1.55	474.59		
Vegetables	0.439	0.50	153.70		
Fruits and Nuts	0.246	0.35	107.51	1.05	23.30
Sugar	0.210	0.28	86.86		
Salt	0.553	0.54	164.29		
Spices	0.262	0.31	93.76	0.11	234.34
Beverages, etc.	0.196	0.26	79.32		
Pan, Tobacco and Intoxicants	0.604	0.72	222.40	0.06	974.80
Fuel and Light	0.357	0.43	131.19		
Clothing	0.372	0.20	59.88	0.01	2,489.59
Footwear	0.475	0.33	100.00		
Misc. Goods and Services	0.304	0.31	94.41		
Durable Goods	0.212	0.12	36.66		
Higher than Indian Average (no.)			10.00		

Source: Same as Table 14.4.

is dominated by agriculture, which absorbs 64 per cent of workers and accounts for 48 per cent of state gross domestic product. The main crops are paddy, wheat, jute, potato, sugar cane and oilseeds. Tourism is growing as an industry and handicraft has good potential. But the state's geographical isolation has hindered its industrialization. Its per capita income is stagnant and below the national level. As can be seen in Table 14.10, Tripura shows a very high level of dependence and falling consumption shares. Since the shares in consumption are initially on the high side, Tripura's per capita consumption is higher than the national average in 10 out of 19 products reported in the table.

Arunachal Pradesh

Located farthest in the north-eastern part of India, Arunachal Pradesh is perhaps the most backward of the states in the region in terms of infrastructure, with the lowest density of population and also the lowest literacy rate. The state shares its border with Bhutan in the west, China in the north and north-east, Myanmar in the east and south-east and Assam in the south. Though the biggest in terms of land area Arunachal has no railway linkage and is accessible only through air and road transport. Known for its forest resources, Arunachal has the highest per capita income in the region and it is also above the national average per capita income. The occupation

TABLE 14.11: ARUNACHAL PRADESH

Items	1993–4 Consumption Shares (%)	1993–4 Per Capita Consumption Relative to Indian Average	1993–4 Production Shares (%)	1993–4 Dependency Index
Cereals	0.13	128.78	0.11	119.15
Gram	0.22	210.71		
Cereal Substitute	0.00	0.00	0.65	0.00
Pulses and Products	0.11	107.04	0.04	270.27
Milk and Products	0.08	82.35		
Edible Oil	0.11	108.01	0.41	26.88
Meat, Egg, Fish	0.35	346.01		
Vegetables	0.17	165.96		
Fruits and Nuts	0.08	75.27	0.16	47.94
Sugar	0.07	64.07		
Salt	0.17	165.08		
Spices	0.09	92.26		
Beverages, etc.	0.07	66.46		
Pan, Tobacco and Intoxicants	0.23	220.67		
Fuel and Light	0.14	137.18		
Clothing	0.15	146.15		
Footwear	0.23	228.16		
Misc. Goods and Services	0.06	61.99		
Durable Goods	0.06	62.76		
Higher than Indian Average (no.)		11.00		

Source: Same as Table 14.4.

of a large section of its population is linked to forestry and 75 per cent of the workforce is engaged in shifting cultivation. The main crops are rice, maize, millet, wheat and mustard. A growing tertiary sector and some forest-based industries absorb the rest of the workforce. The state has considerable tourist potential, which can be exploited only if a transport network is established. The data for 1988–9 are not available. Table 14.11 provides consumption and production shares for 1993–4. The state's consumption shares are on the high side and as a result its per capita consumption is higher than the national level in 11 out of 19 products. Dependency is not very high.

CONCLUSIONS

An attempt has been made in this paper to analyse the production and consumption patterns of eight states in the north-eastern region of India. The recent trend towards globalization of the Indian economy has not touched this region because the markets are either non-existent or weak. The result is economic isolation, largely due to the absence of transport and marketing network. The entire region is agricultural and there are some important mineral resources, forestry and forest-related products are extremely important in all the states. In most of these states the economic potential lies in agro-based industries. Tourism is the other area where the states can exploit their natural wealth. There is an urgent need to establish an elaborate network of rail and road transport. This would require substantial amount of public investment. But before that happens the states may look for opportunities for greater amount of trade within the region and with the neighbouring countries such as Bangladesh, Myanmar and Bhutan. The initiative must come from the Central Government in the form of establishment of export processing zones in the region and provision of other export facilities. So far as the present status is concerned, all the states in the north-east are heavily dependent on the rest of the country. In many states consumption standards are being maintained through central transfers, which will not be viable in the long run. In general, the lack of income generation has resulted in falling consumption shares in most states. It is very likely that poverty and inequality have increased and this trend will continue unless the people are involved in value-adding production processes converting the resources of the region into final goods that are sold in the rest of India or exported to countries having common borders with the states. High rates of literacy in the region, particularly female literacy, are being wasted now. The study shows that there is a great of commonality in the problems faced by all the states, which calls for an integrated scheme of development of the north-eastern region. Such a scheme will explore the areas of comparative advantage in the states and plan for the establishment of an elaborate system of transport and marketing network.

Economic development in the north-eastern region has to be considered in the light of the concept of sustainable development. Industrialization of a very large part of India has resulted in considerable damage to the environment. All the major cities of India are reporting large-scale air and water pollution. Even the ground water has developed toxicity as a result of the dumping of untreated chemicals. Indian agriculture poses a similar problem. Population pressure has resulted in intensive cultivation in most part of the country and multiple cropping has become the new mode of cultivation, particularly in Punjab and parts of Uttar Pradesh. The effect of Green Revolution on the soil quality has been disastrous. Large-scale use of chemical fertilizers has not only reduced the reproductive power of the soil but the use of deep tube wells has depleted the underground water causing salinity and other problems. There is no doubt that land productivity has been declining in the recent years.[10] The effect of this on the per capita net availability of food grains is being assessed now. According to one estimate[11] the growth rate of per capita net availability of food grains (grams per day) during 1991–9 has been negative for all food grains: –0.75 for rice, –0.0068 for wheat, –1.24 for other cereals, –0.89 for cereals, –0.58 for gram, –0.75 for pulses and –0.88 for food grains as a whole. The north-eastern region has a specific advantage over the rest of India in having an unpolluted environment. What is required is the globalization of the region so that it can find avenues for exploiting its potential without worrying about the damage that globalization is likely to cause to its environment at this stage. The time has come for us to think about relocation of industrial and agricultural activities in order to protect the environment. An economic policy for the north-east has to take this environmental consideration into account as a part of the overall policy of sustainable development.

NOTES

1. See *Economic Survery, 1990–2000*, p. S-115.
2. The figures quoted are from the Directorate of Economics and Statistics, Government of India (NIC).
3. See Bela Balassa, *The Theory of Economic Integration*. Homewood, Illinois: Richard D. Irwin., Inc., 1961.
4. The entropy measure is 20–30 points lower in the sample of eight states in respect of all items except the two items mentioned in the text. This probably indicates that there is greater incidence of poverty in the northeast region than in fifteen major states.
5. S.K. Wadi, 'Prospects of Forest Development in N.E. India', in *N.E. Hill Region of India: Problems and Prospects of Development*, ed. T. Mathew, New Delhi: Agricole Publishing Academy, 1981.
6. See *A Perspective Plan for North-Eastern region, Phase I*, TCS Report, Shillong.
7. See *Transforming the North-East,* High Level Commission Report to the Prime Minister, Government of India, 7 March 1997.
8. 'Nagaland: A Trade Model of Growth', Association for Environment and Development Research, New Delhi, May 1999.
9. Ibid.
10. See Majid Hussain, 'Socio-Economic Implications of Agricultural Development in India', paper presented at the national seminar on Implications of Globalization on the Indian Economy, Department of Economics, Jamia Millia Islamia, New Delhi, 1–2 March 2001.
11. See Table 14.3 of Shahid Ahmed, 'Emerging Economic Scenario and Food Security in India', paper presented the seminar Implications of Globalization on the Indian Economy, Depatment of Economics, Jamia Millia Islamia, New Delhi, 1–2 March 2001.

SECTION V

POPULATION AND MIGRATION

IN A STATE OF PERMANENT FLUX: POPULATION AND MIGRATION IN THE NORTH-EAST

That the north-east has been a kaleidoscope of myriad races is not only true today but is also borne out by mythological sources as is hinted by H.P. Ray in the first section of the book. It indicates that the north-east thus has never been a stranger to migration.

J. Gogoi too delves into mythology when relating the legend of King Kirat bringing in Aryans to his kingdom to develop the Aryan culture in ancient Kamrup. However, the most significant migration took place in 1228 with the coming of a group of Mongoloid people originally from the upper Irrawady valley who quickly took control of the valley and ruled for six centuries. Gogoi points out to other migrants, the tea garden workers, the Bengali Hindu migrants who came in with the British and later after Partition, the Nepalis brought in by the British and most importantly and controversially the Bengali Muslims. Gogoi points out that in the initial stages, the influx of the Bengali Muslim peasants into Assam was beneficial as the migrants brought in new agricultural skills and land hitherto fallow was brought under cultivation. However, as the land–man ratio grew adverse with rising population, so did the benefits from this influx, and soon the original inhabitants started to feel the squeeze. Gogoi points out that it is not difference in per capita income but land–man ratio as well as distance that explains migration.

Santanu Roy lays down the theoretical foundations of migration. He points out to the comprehensive and dynamic nature of the decision to migrate given the fact that such decisions are taken by the family keeping in mind the future consequences of such decisions. Additionally, factors like risk, information about existing networks of the community (to which the illegal migrant belongs) in the host economy and relative destitution affect migration. On the other hand, trade, acting as a proxy for transfer of labour may reduce migration. Accordingly, Roy develops a comprehensive plan to temper the flow of immigrants.

Jaishree Konwarh looks at the tribal population of Assam, commenting that the recent upsurge in their numbers is not due to better social welfare but due to initial gross under-numeration. The tribals who were forcibly assimilated into the mainstream and dispossessed of their land had hoped for the better following Independence. But this was not to be. This disillusionment has seen the tribals rejecting their Assamese identity in favour of their original identity.

Thus, the melting pot reverses itself into a more colourful kaleidoscope.

CHAPTER 15

The Migration Problem in Assam: An Analysis

JAYANTA KUMAR GOGOI

INTRODUCTION

The population problem has become one of the most fundamental of all human problems. Therefore, studies on population have assumed great importance in recent times. The impact of population growth on economic development and social change in overpopulated developing countries needs a thorough study for effective policy measures. Population studies in India have so far been mainly conducted at the national level which tend to conceal the distinctive social, economic and environmental patterns at the state or regional level. Such macro-level studies tend to overlook the regional peculiarities in the behaviour of demographic variables. A study of the causal factors explaining such regional variation would, therefore, be rewarding. This is particularly true of Assam, whose demographic experience is unique in many respects, including the migration problem. The present study is an attempt in this direction.

MIGRATION INTO ASSAM:
A HISTORICAL BACKGROUND

The process of migration into Assam dates back to the days of early Aryan settlement in India when the streams of Aryan people came to this part after crossing the north Bengal plain. It is said that Narakasura, the earliest mythological Kirat king of Kamrup—a kingdom which included many parts of present north Bengal and Bangladesh – brought a large number of Aryans from northern India for the promotion of Aryan culture in this region (Das, 1980,

p. 2). However, the most notable stream of migration took place in AD 1228 when a group of Mongoloid people entered Assam through the north-eastern gateway. They came from the ancient kingdom of Muangman or Pong, which was situated in the upper portion of the Irrawady valley. They not only defeated the local tribes but ruled over the Brahmaputra valley region for 600 years till the region was taken over by the East India Company in AD 1826 by the Treaty of Yandaboo. The descendants of these migrants, who are known as Ahom, now constitute on of the major population groups of the Brahmaputra valley in Assam. Even during the Ahom rule, migration to the region took place from both the west and east borders. The Ahom kingdom was invaded several times by the Mughal emperors of Delhi and the rulers of Bengal. Many of them stayed back as prisoners or captives and later became an integral part of the state's indigenous population. On the other hand, the Buddhist people from Upper Burma belonging to the present Khamti, Phakial and other communities came down to Upper Assam and settled there.

However, the number of these migrants was comparatively small and a new phase of migration started with the annexation of Assam by the British. Therefore, an attempt has been made here to study the different streams of migrants in Assam since the arrival of the British in AD 1826. Altogether there were five large-scale streams of migrants, namely,

(a) Tea garden labourers,
(b) Muslim peasant migrants from then East Bengal,
(c) Bengali Hindus,
(d) Nepalese migrants, and
(e) Migrants from different parts of India.

The out-migration or emigration from Assam is very insignificant, the total number being as small as 45,986 in 1951 against 73,223 in 1931 (*Census of India*, 1951, p. 80). There has been no change in the volume and direction of out-migration or emigration since 1921. About 72 per cent of them are found in the adjacent states of Manipur, Tripura and West Bengal (*Census of India*, 1951). West Bengal is actually responsible for the largest number of out-migrants from Assam, numbering 18,570. A few hundred of Assam-born people were found in Bihar, Orissa, Uttar Pradesh, Madhya Pradesh and Tamil Nadu in the 1951 census report. Probably most of them were the children of repatriated tea garden labourers and a few of the educated classes and traders. Unfortunately, the number of emigrants outside India is not available but it is sure to be insignificant. According to the 1971 census report, only 54,014 Assamese speakers lived outside Assam, which accounted for a bare 0.6 per cent of the total Assamese speakers. This figure increased marginally in the 1991 census but this increase attributed was mainly to the increasing number of Assamese students in different parts of the country. Therefore, we can now turn our attention to the five major streams of migrants into Assam already outlined above.

TEA GARDEN MIGRANTS

The tea garden labourers were brought by the British capitalists mainly from Bihar, Chhotanagpur, Central Province (presently Madhya Pradesh) and Orissa consequent upon the development of the plantation industry in the state of Assam. Although started as early as in the 1830s, large-scale migration of tea garden labourers took place from the 1870s. It continued till 1937, the number falling low after 1931 by which time tea garden labourers numbered just under 10 lakh in Assam (*Census of India*, 1961, p. 134). The importation of people to work in the tea gardens from densely populated low-wage areas became necessary not because of general indolence of the indigenous people, as is alleged by some writers, including the Census Superintendents, but because of a number of factors such as de-population of Assam caused by the civil wars and the Burmese insurrections during the latter part of the eighteenth and the early part of the nineteenth centuries, the non-existence of a class of landless peasants, self-sufficiency, lack of demand for cash and the inhuman treatment meted out to the garden labourers by the planters (Goswami, 1975, pp. 44–5). It is to be noted that the total number of tea garden labourers, consisting wholly of migrants were 67,500; 2,43,400; 4,61,800 and 7,47,200 in 1876, 1891, 1911 and 1931, respectively. This is excluding those migrants who after the expiry of the contract took up independent agriculture outside the tea gardens (*Annual Reports on Immigration in Assam,* 1876, 1891, 1911 and 1931). Imported tea garden labourers, whose number along with their descendants is about 50 lakh at present, have completely identified themselves with the indigenous population of the state and constitute an inseperable part of the composite Assamese society and culture.

MUSLIM PEASANT MIGRANTS

The second stream of migration was Muslim peasants from the then East Bengal districts of Mymensingh, Pabna, Borga and Rangpur. Driven apparently by the pressure on the soil at home, and lured by cheap and plentiful supply of both virgin and exceptionally fertile lands in Assam with the freedom of settlement of ryotwari system, land-hungry peasants from East Bengal began to pour into the state from the beginning of the twentieth century. They first entered through the districts of Goalpara. The population of the district increased by 1.4 and 2.0 per cent between 1881–91 and 1891–1901 respectively, but, suddenly shot up by 30 per cent in 1911 (*Census of India*, 1961, pp. 67, 249). The number of migrants in Goalpara district rose from 49.1 thousand in 1901 to 118.2 thousand in 1911, an increase of 240 per cent, forming 19.7 per cent of the actual population of the district. In the decade 1901–11, however, few peasants went beyond Goalpara district, those censused in other districts of the state being mostly clerks, traders and professional men, numbering only a few thousands (*Census of India*, 1961, p. 249).

Though there was long-standing congestion of population, scarcity of land, famines and pestilence in east Bengal, people never migrated from there in large numbers prior to the twentieth century (Davis, 1968, p. 118). It is on record that the zamindars of the Goalpara district failed to induce ryots of the overcrowded districts of East Bengal to settle in the wasteland of the district during the middle of the nineteenth century (Mills, 1854, Appendix D, p. 17). The Census Commissioners of 1891 and 1901 categorically stated that the people from overcrowded East Bengal districts could not come to occupy wastelands in Assam as there was no inducement and recruitment avenues like those existing for the tea gardens (*Census of India*, 1921, pp. 39–40, 68).

In fact, though the small farmers and landless labourers of Bengal were facing economic hardships from the beginning of the establishment of Permanent Settlement (1793), the situation was perhaps tolerable till the last part of the nineteenth century. But the economic and agrarian conditions of East Bengal districts gradually became unbearable for the depressed and landless labouring classes from the beginning of the twentieth century. There was extraordinary rise in the prices of food grains, and the indebtedness of the people of Mymensing district had become a subject of inquiry by the government in 1906 (*Report on the Land Revenue Administration* . . . , 1907, pp. 1–2). However, the rapid growth of population and the increasing pressure on land as well as the oppression of the zamindars led to the movement of peasants towards Assam.

Another factor which attracted the East Bengal peasants to settle in Assam was associated with the political development in India during the 1920s. The Congress leaders of Assam withdrew their support to the Britishers in forming a government under the Government of India Act, 1919, due to the call of Non-Cooperation movement by Mahatma Gandhi. A new government, was however, being formed in 1921 with the support of leaders of other parties like the then Assam Mohammedan Association and Tea Planters of Assam who were mostly Britishers. Therefore, the then Assam government, particularly between 1921–38 gave implicit support to this incoming migration in the name of 'grow more food' campaign, which tilted the religio-ethnic composition of the valley's population. Even special officers were appointed to look after the welfare of these migrants and it is on record that a greater portion of the sum realized as premia from the allottees of wastelands was spent in the area for the benefit of these migrants (*Report of the Line System Committee*, Shillong, 1938, p. 8).

Thus, the inflow of these migrants from East Bengal was so severe and so vigorous was the way they seized vacant areas of the valley that they altered permanently the future of the valley's socio-economic structure.

BENGALI HINDU MIGRANTS

The third stream of migrants were the Bengali Hindus, who were brought by the Britishers for their office and other professional works. It happened because of the Bengali Hindu's early initiation in English education and the British-India administrative system. The movement of this stream was intensified along with the opening of new railway lines, post and telegraph offices, and development of tea and petroleum industries in particular. The Bengali clerks, doctors and lawyers monopolized the British government jobs and professions. However, the most conspicuous mass migration of this stream took place at the time of Partition and immediately thereafter. The feeling of insecurity of life and property of the Hindus in then East Pakistan led the movement of this section of population to

India, and Assam being the adjacent state received a larger number of displaced Hindus. The 1951 census report gives the total number of refugees in Assam, including present Meghalaya as 2,74,455 of which 2,72,075 came from then East Pakistan. Cachar being the nearest district received the highest number (93,177) followed by Goalpara (44,967) and Kamrup (42,871). Sibsagar district received the lowest number (7,514) while Darrang and Lakhimpur received 18,833 and 13,965 persons, respectively. The process was further intensified when the refugee rehabilitation schemes were implemented by the state and when they were given physical and social shelter by their relatives and acquaintences. In 1958, their number was estimated at 4.87 lakh and it rose to 6.28 lakh in 1961. This further increased to 2.33 million in 1971, constituting 19.71 per cent of Assam's population. As per the 1991 census report the number of Bengali-speaking population stood at 4.35 million constituting 21.67 per cent of the total population of Assam. The migrants belonging to this category are mostly engaged in service and commercial activities and they are concentrated in urban areas, especially in the Brahmaputra valley towns. For example, according to the 1961 census report, out of 9.13 lakh urban population in Assam, 3.5 lakh were Bengali as against 3.04 lakh Assamese-speaking population. Thus, Assamese speakers constitute 33 per cent of the urban population as against 38 per cent Bengali and 13 per cent Hindi speakers, as per the 1971 census report. With the emergence of Bangladesh, a fresh stream of Bengali Hindu migrants entered Assam and their exact number is not known as the 1981 Census did not take place in Assam and the details of the 1991 census report on migration is not readily available so far.

NEPALESE MIGRANTS

The fourth stream of migrants into Assam consistsed of Nepalese immigrants. This started with the British occupation of Assam. The recruitment of Nepalese into British army dates back to 1815, when the latter defeated Kazi Amar Singh Thapa and according to the fifth provision of the agreement, the British secured the right to recruit Nepalese into British army (Kanskar, 1982, p. 77). However, the Government of Nepal was unwilling to allow its men to serve the British army and, therefore, Gorkhas of the Indian army on leave in Nepal were encouraged to smuggle out recruits from Nepal and were rewarded by the British. The Nepalese Government disliked the clandestine operation and took strong measures to discourage it. Some Gorkhas serving in the Indian army on leave in Nepal were even put to death and property of some others confiscated (Mojumdar, 1973, pp. 42–3). As a result the British Government encouraged migration of Gorkha families from Nepal and established Gorkha settlements in certain parts of India including Assam. The British administration first brought the Gorkhas as soldiers and then subsequently as watchmen, peons, etc., for their personal service. Many of them stayed behind after retirement and settled permanently in Assam. However, later on, fresh Nepalese migrants began to come of their own accord and started settling in different parts of Assam as graziers. They came in large number during the last few decades of twentieth century to take up cultivation and livestock in the uncultivated and unowned hill slopes. They went more or less unnoticed because they preferred to settle in the forest areas near the foothills along the northern border of Assam and occupied large areas of the forest land. Many of them live in the outskirts of urban areas supplying milk and fuel to the urban dwellers. At present a major part of the business of milk and milk products is in the hands of Nepalese migrants. Besides, a large number of Nepalese are employed as porters, chowkidars and office peons throughout the state following the tradition initiated by the British administration.

The period 1911–31 was the most important for Nepalese migrants and their number was estimated at 83,306 in the 1931 census report. The number further increased to 1,01 lakh in 1951, 3.49 lakh in 1971 and 4.32 lakh in 1991. Thus, according to the 1991 census report, Nepalese-speaking population constitute 1.9 per cent of Assam's total population. Forty per cent of these Nepalese migrants were found in Darrang and Sonitpur districts followed by 24 per cent in Lakhimpur district. In other districts it varied from 1 to 8 per cent. The immigration of Nepalese migrants still continues as the citizens of Nepal do not require any passport to enter India, under the terms of the Indo-Nepal Friendship Treaty of 1950, the Tripartite Delhi Agreement of 1951 and the 1956 Revised Indo-Nepal Agreement. Thus, free interchange and flow of both country's nationals as well as their right to own property in either country is allowed, unhindered and without restrictions. These agreements only made official a situation which had existed *de facto* from the British period. The reciprocity which the agreements formulated indeed continues today, with 3.24 lakh Indian-born population in Nepal and 5.25 lakh Nepal-born population in India, according to the Census Report of 1971 of both the countries. Bihar alone accounted for 23.27 per cent of the Nepal-born population in India in 1971, the highest among all states. Assam stood next to Bihar by absorbing 17.41 per cent of the Nepal-born population.

MIGRANTS FROM DIFFERENT PARTS OF INDIA

The fifth stream of migrants into Assam were from other parts of India seeking economic opportunities in trading, construction works and white-collar jobs, particularly from Orissa, Andhra Pradesh, Madhya Pradesh, Rajasthan, Bihar, Punjab, Uttar Pradesh, Tamil Nadu, Kerala and West Bengal. It is to be noted that the migrants from Rajasthan need a separate historical analysis because of their significant role in the economy of Assam since the British period. The majority of the migrants from Rajasthan are from Marwar and they are popularly known as Marwaris. Marwari migrants came to Assam in a small number in the pre-British period, but their movement became significant with the establishment of British rule and the subsequent development of tea industry and other commercial and industrial establishments. They acted as money changers, bankers and general agents to the managers of tea gardens, especially in old Sibsagar and Lakhimpur districts. They operated the mustard trade in Kamrup and Goalpara districts, sold hardware and other articles imported from other parts of India and became dealers in rice and grains throughout the state. Thus, they were successful in monopolizing practically the entire trade and commerce in Assam by the turn of the nineteenth century (Allen, 1906, p. 75). The 1891 census reported only 4,877 migrants from Rajputana; their number increased to 22,000 in 1961 and further to 70,000 in 1971. They are mostly concentrated in the urban and industrial centres and virtually the entire business and commercial transactions of the state at present can be said to be in their control.

The migration from the states of Bihar and Uttar Pradesh also started with the beginning of British rule in Assam. The migrants were absorbed as washermen, barbers, sweepers, cobblers, load carriers, wage labourers in construction sites. Their inflow increased with the extension of railway lines and steamer service which opened new avenues of employment in Assam. Their inflow was further intensified after Independence when their services were in great demand as a result of industrialization and urbanization in the region. Thus, their concentration is found in the urban and industrial areas of the state.

The in-migration of people from other states of India is mostly a post-Independence phenomenon. Of these, the Punjabi migrants are economically more significant as they are mostly engaged in commercial and industrial establishments of their own, while most of the other migrants are either salary holders in companies or public sector undertakings as contractors or wage labourer in construction activities. Most of the migrants from other states of India are found in the urban areas of Assam.

To sum up, most of the above migration streams into the state took place with the annexation of Assam by the British administration from the early part of the nineteenth century. The inflow of such migrants increased considerably by the turn of the twentieth century.

The Role of Per Capita Income, Land–Man Ratio and Distance in Migration Analysis in Assam

We have already explained the various socio-economic causes responsible for different streams of migration into Assam. Now, we can combine all the streams of migrants together and relate them with the important common push factors which might have influenced their movement into Assam. Lower per capita income and land-man ratio at the place of origin, and the distance between the place of origin and place of destination may be considered as three important push factors in this regard. To relate these push factors with the volume of migration into Assam, we have standardized the latter by taking the proportion of out-migrants/emigrants to total population of the place of origin, as the size of population at the place of origin is also a determining factor in the process of migration. The regression model thus attempt to explain. The proportion of out-migrants/emigrants to Assam to total population of the state/country of origin in terms of per capita income (with due adjustment for Bangladesh and Nepal currency), land–man ratio and the mean geographical distance between the place of origin and place of destination (Assam).

The basic purpose at the first stage is to find out the correlation between in-migration/immigration into Assam from different states/countries and (a) the per capita income at the place of origin, (b) land–man ratio at the place of origin, and (c) mean geographical distance between the place of origin and the place of destination. This will enable us to know whether there exists any relationship between the variables that we have chosen.

It is interesting to observe that the coefficient of correlation between the proportion of out-migrants/emigrants and per capita income, found to be −0.42, is significant at 90 per cent level. Thus, lower the per capita income of the place of origin, higher the proportion of out-migrants/emigrants from the place of origin which corroborates our hypothesis mentioned above.

The coefficient of correlation between proportion of out-migrants/emigrants and land–man ratio was found to be −0.47, which is significant at 95 per cent level. This also indicates that lower the land–man ratio at the place of origin, higher are the out-migrants/emigrants and, therefore, corroborates our hypothesis.

Finally, the coefficient of correlation between proportion of out-migrants/emigrants and mean geographical distance between the place of origin and place of destination (Assam) was found to be −0.63 and is statistically significant at 99 per cent level. Thus, distance also played an important role in the process of migration into Assam. To sum up, it can be said that per capita income and land-man ratio at the place of origin and the mean geographical distance between the place of origin and the place of destination (Assam) are three important push factors which have direct bearing on the streams of migration into Assam.

To assess the variation explained by these three variables taken together, a regression analysis by taking the proportion of out-migrants/emigrants as the dependent variable and per capita income, land-man ratio and mean geographical distance as independent variables, was carried out and the following regression equation was obtained

$$Y = 1.8 - 0.2X_1 - 0.9X_2 - 0.7X_3$$

where,

Y = Proportion of out-migrants/emigrants to total population of the state/country of origin

X_1 = Per capita income at the state/country of origin

X_2 = Land–man ratio (per capita cultivable land) at the state/ country of origin

X_3 = Mean geographical distance between the place of origin and the place of destination (Assam)

The coefficient of multiple correlation (R) works out to be 0.75, which is significant at 99 per cent level. Employing the test of significance for coefficients of X_1, X_2 and X_3, it was found that except the coefficients of per capita income (X_1), the other two coefficients of land-man ratio (X_2) and mean geographical distance (X_3) were found to be significant at 95 per cent level. This indicates that these are two significant factors in explaining the variation of the dependent variable Y. The value of the coefficient of multiple determination (R^2) is 0.5625 indicating that these three independent variables together explain 56.25 per cent of the variation in the dependent variable (Y) in our analysis. The remaining 43.75 per cent of unexplained variation may be attributed to non-quantifiable variables like exploitation by landlords, failure of land reform measures and other push factors at the place of origin that has already been explained.

REFERENCES

Das, H.P., 'The Problem of Immigration in Assam: A Geographical Review and Interpretation', Presidential Address to the National Association of Geographers, India, Chandigarh, January 1980, p. 2.

Census of India, vol. III, Assam, Part I, Report, 1921, pp. 39–40.

——, vol. XII, Assam, Manipur and Tripura, Part I-A, Report, 1951, p. 80.

——, Assam, General Report, 1961.

Goswami, H., 'Population Growth in the Brahmaputra Valley, 1881–1931', *Assam Economic Journal*, vol. 1, March 1975, pp. 44–5.

Government of Assam, *Annual Reports an Immigration in Assam*, 1876, 1891, 1991 and 1931.

Davis, K., *The Population of India and Pakistan*, New York: Russell and Russell, 1968, p. 118.

Lt. Col. Matthie, 'Memorandum to A.J.M. Mills', in A.J. Mills, *Report of the Province of Assam*, Calcutta: Government of Bengal, 1854, Appendix D, p. xvii.

Report on the Land Revenue Administration of the Provinces of Estern Bengal and Assam for the Revenue year 1906–7, Dacca, 1907, pp. 1–2.

Report of the Fine System Committee, Shillong, Government of Assam, 1938, p. 8.

Kanskar, Vidya Bir Singh, 'Emigration, Remittances and Rural Development', Centre for Economic Development and Administration, Tribhuvan University, Kathmandu, 1982 (mimeo.), p. 77.

Allen, B.C., *Assam District Gazetters*, vol. VII, 1906, p. 75.

Mojumdar Kanchanmoy, *Political Relations between India and Nepal, 1827–1923*, Delhi: Munshiram Manoharlal, 1973.

CHAPTER 16

'Why Do They Come?' Economic Incentives for Immigration to Assam

SANTANU ROY

I. INTRODUCTION

The demographic growth in Assam over the course of the twentieth century is the highest recorded by any region in the Indian subcontinent. Between 1901 and 1991, the population of India grew by 354 per cent. In contrast, the population of Assam expanded by 676 per cent – from 3.3 million to 22.3 million. Most of the difference between the rate of population growth in Assam and that of India as a whole can be attributed to the unprecedented migration of population from other regions to Assam – particularly from the densely populated neighbouring plains of East Bengal (later East Pakistan and currently the sovereign nation of Bangladesh). It is estimated that only about half the population of Assam in 1971 were descendants of the residents of the current territory of Assam in 1901.[1]

This demographic influx has had adverse effects on the delicate ethnic balance within the population. It has, overtime, created a deep sense of social and cultural insecurity among the indigenous people and has threatened their political leverage.[2] In a state characterized by increasing unemployment and underemployment, immigration is seen as directly reducing the labour market earning opportunities for indigenous people. Migration of poverty stricken marginal economic agents is also responsible, to a significant extent, for the pattern of ruthless (often, irreversible) ecological destruction – deforestation and myopic overexploitation of open-access biological resources – that the state has experienced in course of the century. One specific aspect of this process is the loss of land and forest facilities traditionally used by the tribal population of the state who did not practice settled agriculture in private landholdings. This has resulted in sharp deterioration in their economic welfare. As the availability of surplus wastelands have disappeared and even the *chars* (riverine wastelands) are overpopulated, migrants have increasingly encroached illegally upon public lands. Partly in reaction to these developments, the last four decades of the twentieth century have seen increasing social discontent, ethnic tensions and political movements against immigrants. The student-led mass movement against illegal immigration during 1979–84 (the 'Assam movement') created a major social and political upheaval and brought the problem into sharp focus.

Migration has played an extremely important role in the process of economic growth in Assam. The growth of the tea industry in the nineteenth-century Assam was critically dependent on migrant indentured labourers from Bihar and Orissa as the Assamese, with bountiful land endowments, were not willing to work as wage labourers in the plantations. The migration of Western-educated Bengali Hindus in the nineteenth century as government employees and professionals not only served in the growth of the colonial economy but also helped to accelerate the expansion of modern education and creation of modern economic infrastructure. In the twentieth century, migration of peasants from land scarce East Bengal with advanced knowledge and experience of intensive cultivation had a major impact on agricultural output, techniques as well as new crop diversity.[3] In the latter half of the twentieth century, migrant labourers bid down wages, particularly for semi-skilled jobs – and to that extent reduced the costs of production – not only for agriculture in the peak season but also in construction and other urban activities.

If there is a widespread adverse reaction to immigration today, it is because of the scale at which migration has occurred. If the scale of migration had been smaller, the flow calmer then the process would have been much more socially assimilative and the threats to the indigenous population at any point of time would have been much lower. The high spate of immigration after Independence occurred even while land and other resources as well as the limited socio-economic infrastructure were under increasing demographic pressure and in a state where the process of economic development was slow, often stagnant. Therefore, the economic costs of immigration on society have gradually outstripped the benefits.

Much of the existing discussion on the demographic influx in Assam is centred around estimation of the magnitude of migration – particularly, illegal immigration in the post-Independence period – the legal, political and humanitarian issues related to the definition of illegal immigrants and the feasibility of their detection and deportation within an appropriate legal framework. The debates represent sharply differing opinions, partly because of the setting of ethnic conflict in which they are carried out and partly because there is virtually no reliable data on immigrants; the evidence is mostly indirect.

In the post-Independence period, most immigrants have operated outside the formal or legal immigration process, taking advantage of an extremely porous border. Even refugees from East Pakistan who were entitled to Indian citizenship have mostly not followed up their entry by formal registration (mostly destitute and illiterate, they were often unaware of any such requirement). The accord signed between the Government and leaders of the Assam movement in 1985 effectively legitimized all immigrants entering Assam before 24 December 1971. Only those entering illegally after that date, were liable for deportation. However, subsequent political dynamics, partly motivated by the fear of harassment by minorities, and the nature of the legal framework adopted for detection of such illegal migrants have effectively ruled out any progress on this front beyond the trivial.

In this article, we are not particularly concerned about the exact magnitude of immigration or the political and legal problems associated with 'illegal' immigration. Indeed, so far as economic incentives are considered, it hardly matters whether migration takes place across political boundaries or within a nation. Further, given the nature of border controls between India and Bangladesh and the low probability of detection or deportation, illegal immigrants do not face significantly different costs and benefits compared to internal migrants coming to Assam from other regions of India.

A significant portion of the demographic influx experienced by Assam has occurred due to economic factors. In fact, almost all migration prior to Independence and bulk of the migration from Bangladesh in recent decades can be attributed to the quest by marginal economic agents for better income opportunities. Even in the case of refugees fleeing political and religious persecution in East Pakistan, economic factors have played a role in motivating them to settle down in Assam. The development of an effective policy framework for prevention of migration and, more generally, of any kind of long-term perspective on the demographic scenario requires us to understand these economic factors.

The economics of migration is a fairly well developed field of study. However, much of this literature has studied issues concerned with internal migration within developed countries and immigration to developed countries.[4] The literature on internal migration in developing countries has mostly confined attention to rural-urban labour migration – the process by which hordes of underemployed workers from the agricultural sector join the ranks of the informal sector in urban and semi-urban areas. In contrast, the migrants moving from Bangladesh to Assam mostly move from rural to rural areas and further, a significant part of the incentives for migration to Assam comes from elements outside the labour market such as purchase of land, encroachment of public land and forests, exploitation of common property resources, public goods and infrastructure, etc.

In the received paradigm of rural-urban labour migration, the movement from rural sector to the urban informal sector is perceived as an investment in search for high wage jobs in the formal sector.[5] More recently, this literature has been significantly augmented by the 'new economics of migration' which has emphasized the role of factors such as family-based decision-making, risk diversification, attitude towards risk, incomplete information and relative destitution in explaining certain features of rural-urban migration.[6] The literature on international migration has also emphasized the role of networks of past migrants and the social infrastructure in host economies in explaining migration flows.[7]

This article is a selective adaptation of the economic factors emphasized in the existing literature which are relevant to our specific context. The aim is to develop a better perspective on the nature of microeconomic incentives for migration from Bangladesh to Assam and the complexity of issues involved. Those who deny the fact that any significant illegal immigration has occurred in Assam in recent years often argue that there is no significant difference between average rural wages or per capita agricultural income between Bangladesh and Assam. This paper will point out the important arguments why the incentive to migrate may be high *even if actual or average real wages are lower in Assam*. In fact, the old fashioned hypothesis that migration can be explained mainly by wage differences has been systematically rejected in a wide class of studies.[8] We will outline economic forces that cannot only initiate migration between economies that are similar on the average, but can make it self perpetuating. We will, however, be unable to shed any light on the relative empirical strengths of individual economic factors in the context of migration from Bangladesh. This is an important topic that requires thorough empirical investigation in the future.

Section II provides a brief outline of the history of immigration to Assam through the twentieth century. The reader who is familiar with this story may directly move to Section III where we begin our analysis of economic incentives for migrants.

II. OUTLINE OF HISTORY

In the nineteenth century, migrants entering Assam were primarily indentured labourers recruited from among the tribals of Bihar and Orissa for the tea plantations, as well as Bengali Hindus who served in the colonial government machinery and in other professions in urban areas.[9] At the end of the nineteenth century, Assam was viewed as a land-abundant province by the colonial government—it had the fourth lowest population density among provinces in British India and stood in sharp contrast to neighbouring East Bengal where population pressure on land was beginning to be felt.

The census reports of 1891 and 1901 regretted the fact that there was not sufficient economic incentive to attract farmers from East Bengal to come to Assam and cultivate the huge tracts of uncultivated land. The Census Superintendent of Assam in 1901 observed that 'there is room in the Brahmaputra Valley for another four million persons' and that 'after making allowances for hills, rivers and swamps, there are five million acres of cultivable land available . . .'.[10]

A small stream of peasants had, however, started moving from land-scarce Bengal to the western district of Goalpara even as early as the end of the nineteenth century. By the census of 1911, the migration of peasants from Mymensingh, Pabna, Bogra and Rangpur had become quite noticeable, particularly to *char* lands in Goalpara. The process accelerated dramatically in the following decade and the movement had extended to Kamrup and Nowgong. The 1921 census estimated that about 55 per cent of population growth in the Brahmaputra valley in the preceding decade was due to migration. By the 1931 census, the immigration rate had been so dramatic that the Census Superintendent C.S. Mullan was alarmed. He wrote:

Probably the most important event in the province during the last 25 years
– an event, moreover, which seems likely to alter permanently the whole
future of Assam and to destroy more surely than did the Burmese invasion
of 1829, the whole structure of Assamese culture and civilization – has been
the invasion of a vast horde of land-hungry Bengali immigrants, mostly
Muslims from the districts of Eastern Bengal. . . . Where there is waste land
thither flock the Mymensinghias. . . . Without fuss, without tumult, without undue trouble to the district revenue staffs, a population which amounts
to over half a million has transplanted itself from Bengal into the Assam
Valley during the last twenty-five years . . . it is sad but by no means improbable that in another thirty years Sibsagar district will be the only part of
Assam in which an Assamese will find himself at home.[11]

The trend continued in the subsequent years. The Muslim League ministry in colonial Assam led by Sir Mohammed Sadulla actively encouraged migration of Muslim peasants from Bengal under the 'Grow More Food' campaign.

After Independence and the Partition of India in 1947, East Bengal and the Sylhet district of Assam became a part of Pakistan, a nation designed as a homeland for Muslims. Huge streams of Bengali Hindu refugees entered Assam (as well as Tripura and West Bengal). Although it was expected that the transfer of population would be over in a few years time, the flow continued for decades. During periods of war between India and Pakistan as well as times of religious riots in East Pakistan, the flow exhibited significant increases. The 1971 Indo-Pak war, which created the nation of Bangladesh was also accompanied by a large influx of refugees.

One way to get some idea of the scale of migration of refugees is to observe that in 1947, 27 per cent of the population in East Pakistan were Hindus. This proportion declined to 14 per cent in 1971 and 10 per cent in 1991. Most of this difference is due to migration. Refugees coming from areas with geographical contiguity to Assam and which had been the source for past migration to Assam found it easier to move to Assam. Although the Indian constitution made special provisions for granting of citizenship to refugees from Pakistan, this was only for a limited time period and refugees entering later were legally required to go through a process of naturalization. Very few of them actually did so.

Successive legal amendments (such as that following the accord signed between the Central Government and leaders of the Assam movement in 1985) have legalized all migrants entering before a certain date (24 March 1971). It is worth emphasizing here that although the migration of Hindu Bengalis to Assam is mainly attributed to 'persecution by the majority in East Pakistan', the fact that these refugees chose to settle in Assam and did not move to any other part of India – particularly after they had been here for sometime – is certainly based on economic considerations such as the economic incentives provided by an existing network of past migrants.

The flow of migrants in the second half of the twentieth century consisted not only of genuine refugees but also of poverty stricken people in search of economic opportunity. The most dramatic influx of 'refugees' from East Pakistan is likely to have taken place in the immediate years after 1947. Immigration in the later years is likely to have been increasingly motivated by economic considerations. During the period 1951–71, the population of Assam grew by about 35 per cent every ten years as compared to the all-India rate of 21.5 per cent in the period 1951–61 and 24.8 per cent in 1961–71. This difference in population growth is largely attributed to immigration.[12]

During the period 1971–91 (no population census was held in Assam in 1981), the population of Assam grew at a rate of 52.44 per cent compared to an all-India growth rate 48.24 per cent. This narrowing of the gap between demographic growth in Assam as compared to the country as a whole has led to speculation that the flow of immigration from Bangladesh has declined to a negligible level. However, there are other facts which indicate that the narrowing of the difference in overall growth was more likely a consequence of the rapid decline in the flow of Hindu refugees to Assam and that significant illegal immigration motivated by economic reasons did continue.

First, when one looks at the district-level figures, one observes that the population grew at a very high rate in several districts. These districts also recorded extraordinarily high rates of growth in the previous decades which indicates of high immigration into some focal areas.[13] Second, the Muslim population in Assam recorded an unprecedented growth of 77.4 per cent in this period (1971–91) – higher than its recorded growth in the period 1951–71 and significantly higher than the growth rate of 55 per cent recorded by Muslims in India as a whole. Third, the enumeration of electors' lists by the Election Commission showed unprecedented increases. For example, between two revisions of 1994 and 1997, a three year gap, there was more than 30 per cent increase in 17 Assembly constituencies and more than 20 per cent increase in 40 Assembly constituencies (roughly a third of all constituencies in Assam). The all-India average growth of electoral rolls over this three-year period was 7 per cent, while for Assam it was as high as 16.4 per cent. Fourth, the Government of India figures indicate that between 1972 and 1993, of the people who entered India from Bangladesh *legally*, 8.36 lakh people stayed back illegally.[14]

The growth of the overall Hindu population in Assam between 1971 and 1991 is not only sharply lower than that recorded in the period 1951–71 but it is also lower than the all-India growth rate of Hindu population by about six percentage points. Thus, the migration of Hindus from Bangladesh to Assam is likely to have declined significantly over this period – partly in response to the social turmoil and economic stagnation in Assam in the recent decades and partly because the base Hindu population in Bangladesh had dwindled to just about 10 per cent of the country's population making them a much less 'visible' minority there and hence, less likely to be the target of active group persecution.

While none of these and other facts provide direct evidence of overall immigration, taken together they do indicate that immigration is highly likely to have been significant in the period 1971–91, even though the scale of immigration may have been smaller than in the previous decades, and that immigration was increasingly generating population movements into tribal areas – both in the hills as well as the plains – which, in part, provided the background for violent ethnic conflicts in these areas in recent years. Further, immigrants from Bangladesh to Assam in the final decades of the twentieth century, like those in the first half of this century, were much more likely to be destitute, marginal and landless peasants, mostly Muslims, attracted by their perception of better long-run economic opportunities in India.

III. THE DYNAMIC ASPECT

The basic economic approach to migration is to view it as an investment which allows economic agents to gain access to earning and consumption opportunities that are specific to the geographical location to which they migrate. For an economic unit, the opportunity cost of migrating to a particular location or region is the (next best) welfare that the unit would have attained if it had instead migrated to an alternative location or not migrated at all. The latter includes the costs of moving that could be avoided had the unit not migrated to this particular location. The return to such investment is the welfare that the migrating unit attains after moving to the new location and being able to access the new economic opportunities overtime. For ease of exposition, the rest of our analysis will be carried out on the assumption that the migrant's second best option is to stay back at its source village.

Migration is the consequence of decisions taken by socio-economic units motivated by their self-interest. The unit making such a decision is more likely to be the family rather than the individual, even though the entire family may not actually migrate. The welfare that an individual migrant or a family of migrants gives up or attains in course of migration is not a static notion, it encompasses current as well as future welfare. More formally, as in any investment decision, the net return from migration is the gain in terms of present value of the stream of welfare overtime which the migrant unit attains by moving from the source to the destination.

The dynamic nature of the returns implies that comparison of *current* earning opportunities between the source and destination points do not adequately capture the economic incentives for current migration. Extensive empirical evidence shows that international migrants are often worse off in the initial years after migration relative to their material well-being prior to migration.[15] However, unless a migrant is perfectly myopic, he will take into account the future as well as current earnings. Even if economic opportunities at the source and destination points are identical, after incurring the physical costs of relocation (particularly when it is illegal immigration) migrants are likely to be poorer after migration. Further, in the initial years, the migrant will spend a lot of time and resources on labour market search, information acquisition, and gaining access to common property and public resources. As in any investment decision, the migrant will expect to recover this through future earnings. Similarly, the welfare sacrificed by the migrant includes her perceived future earnings and entitlements at her original location. Thus, economic incentives for migration may be high even if the current earning opportunity for the migrant – say, in terms of current rural wages in a bordering district of Assam – is actually lower than that in Bangladesh. What matters more is the comparison and perception of future earnings.

The future, however, is uncertain and unknown. The perception of future welfare that a potential migrant has depends on her subjective assessment of the way the world works, the information she manages to gather directly or through observation of the fortunes of past migrants from her observable neighbourhood, her attitude towards risk as well as the extent to which she cares about the future (the rate of impatience). Without going into details, it is reasonable to assume that these subjective factors and information sets are likely to vary widely across the population of the source country. Other things being equal, the people who choose to migrate are likely to be the ones who are more patient, i.e. care more about long-run welfare of themselves and their children (greater intergenerational altruism), are less risk-averse and likely to have gathered relatively favourable information about the destination. Indeed, the average immigrant might have a rosier evaluation of her future welfare in Assam than even the average indigenous person facing similar economic opportunity overtime – the self-selection process ensures that migrants are likely to be less myopic, less risk-averse and have more favourable priors on future economic changes.

An effective policy framework for reducing the incentive to immigrate needs to be based on an understanding of the dynamic nature of the returns to migration. In particular, measures which limit the future or long-run economic prospects of illegal migrants and their offsprings can reduce the flow of migration even if the State is unable to directly prevent their entry or their access to current earning opportunities in the informal sector. Restrictions which raise the cost of future access to formal sector jobs, access to public subsidies and institutions and ownership of immovable assets can be more effective than what is generally presumed.

IV. THE LABOUR MARKET ASPECT

Historically, the most important incentive for immigration has been the return to human capital, arising from physical access to the labour market in the host economy. Potential immigrants from Bangladesh, particularly those infiltrating the border illegally, are unlikely to hold significant amount of assets in the source country. While a significant proportion of immigrants have eventually acquired *de facto* control over land and other productive resources, the primary source of income for most of them, particularly the new migrants, has been the informal labour market in rural as well as urban areas.

This might lead some analysts to conclude that the wages in the informal sector (such as agricultural wages, or average wage for unskilled labour in the urban informal sector) ought to be taken as the index of income opportunity for immigrants.

There are two problems with this. First, as emphasized in the previous section, for most immigrants, entry and participation in the informal labour market is not an end in itself, but rather a first step, an investment, which allows them to access better earning opportunities. Thus, unskilled workers may acquire skills through low-wage apprenticeship in skilled jobs (construction, carpentry, etc.) which allow them to eventually enter the higher paid skilled labour market. Workers who work in the urban informal sector may someday hope to acquire a higher paid job in the formal urban sector. Second, there is increasing unemployment and underemployment characterizing the labour market. This means that the probability of a migrant finding full-time employment at the prevailing wage is less than one. Further, the higher paid labour markets – the formal urban sector as well as the market for rural skilled labour which are more likely to be capacity-based – are also likely to exhibit greater distortions due to institutional and other sources of rigidities.[16] These distortions also create unemployment and necessitate job search.

The upshot of this is that one must look at the labour market opportunity for a migrant as a multistep lottery. The migrant is likely to enter at the lowest rung of casual worker with very low wages and relatively higher probability of finding employment but in the future, she will hope to search and change her observable attributes (including legitimate documents) and skills so as to move into higher wage jobs, though the probability of being able to find such a job – determined partially by the rate of unemployment in that category – is likely to be much smaller. How does a migrant evaluate such a lottery? If the agent is risk-neutral, then one may suppose that she simply looks at the net present value of expected earnings generated by this lottery (now and in the future). If is she is risk-averse, then she is likely to be concerned about the extent of uncertainty (the spread of the distribution). We return to this issue in Section VI.

The size and geographical concentration of the existing immigrant base in the state has played a crucial role in reducing the initial cost of job search in the casual rural labour market as well as in the informal sector in urban and semi-urban areas. The network not only increases the probability of finding an initial job but also aids future job search through provision of information as well as guarantees which allow employers to be reasonably certain about the trustworthiness of the new migrant and her abilities. As the individual migrant is rather dependent on the network base in the initial years, she can be effectively punished for any deviation through social enforcement by the network. This allows the system to be incentive compatible. The existing base of migrants can act as intermediaries and reduce the moral hazard and adverse selection problems in the interaction between potential employers and new migrants. We return to this network aspect in Section VIII.

There are some direct policy implications of the above discussion. First, rigidities in the formal sector labour market which sustain higher than market clearing wage can create incentives for immigration and even though immigrants do not directly enter the formal sector, the lure of formal sector earnings is a part of the dynamic lottery which impels them to migrate. To the extent that the formal sector rigidities are a result of government actions (for example, the unwieldily growth of an overstaffed unproductive public sector and interventions by the government to maintain higher wages for existing employees at the cost of greater unemployment), removal of imperfections in the labour market created by state intervention can exert an indirect beneficial effect on immigration. Second, if the state can screen the employment process in the formal sector so as to make it more costly for recent illegal immigrants and their offsprings to seek employment in this sector, it can have a non-trivial effect on the long run incentive to immigrate even though only a small proportion of such immigrants actually find employment in the formal sector.

V. THE ASSET ACQUISITION ASPECT

Immigrants gain access to earning opportunities not only through the labour market but also through acquisition of return-yielding productive assets (which would have been impossible without physical migration). These assets include land, water resources (rivers, lakes and their biological components) and forests. When the assets have well-defined private property rights (as in the case of privately owned farmland), immigrants acquire these assets through voluntary trading. On the other hand, when private property rights are not well defined as in the case of common property resources or publicly owned resources (such as forests or *khas* land), acquisition takes the form of physical occupation or encroachment of the land or forests or of the access to natural resources.

Demographic pressure on land in Bangladesh has been systematically and significantly higher than in north-eastern India.[17] Even nearly after a century of high population growth, population density in Bangladesh was thrice that of Assam in 1991. The extent of land erosion, deforestation, silting of river beds and overexploitation of fisheries has also been at a much higher level. In general, the natural resource base has been seriously depleted and to the extent that the use of such resources were available as common property or open access public property, the asset base of the poor rural population has been extensively damaged. Demographic growth has reduced the average product which has increased the incentive for individual household members to acquire land and set up new farms where their marginal productivity is much higher.

VOLUNTARY TRANSFER OF PRIVATE PROPERTY

The possibility of purchase of land by a migrant depends on the price of land. The market for agricultural land is, however, afflicted by major imperfections and informational incompleteness. For one thing, the valuation of agricultural land – by the potential seller as well as a prospective buyer – depends on its earning potential as well as its resale value. The earning capacity from a plot of land depends, in part, on the ability of the farmer to gain access to informal credit, social insurance against risk, common property resources, implicit tied labour contracts and, in particular, on the extent of cooperation among local farmers in the use of resources (including plough instruments) as well as provision of security against theft. All these factors depend on the kind of people who own land in the neighbouring areas and the extent of cooperative behaviour enforced as social norms through repeated interaction. This externality in the payoff from landholding implies that an existing farmer will have a lower valuation for his land and will be eager to sell it at a low price once he realizes that most of the neighbourhood is being sold to immigrant farmers. This is because he does not expect the complementary institutions, inputs and cooperative arrangements which served him in the traditional village community to continue in the future. On the other hand, the immigrant buyers will have a higher valuation for the same land (compared to the seller just described) as they expect many others of their community to be able to buy and to move to new institutions and cooperative arrangements sustained as part of social norms within the immigrant community, often transplanted from the common source for such migrants. This underlies the rapid transfer of entire villages and blocks from indigenous people to new immigrants and a pattern of land acquisition that is like wholesale invasion. It is important to recognize the role of self-fulfilling expectations about actions of other agents in leading to such outcomes. In fact, it is entirely possible that in some other village, the expectations are that no village landholder is going to sell at a low price and in that case, none of them will actually sell (that is, at the price the immigrants are willing to offer).

The State can play an important role in preventing coordination of expectations towards the wrong equilibrium – in halting the cascade – and thereby reducing the expected earning from land acquisition by potential immigrants. Direct controls by way of legislation on the quantity of land transfer, enumeration of farmers and landless labourers within each district and restrictions on acquisition of land by people from outside the district, high taxes on transfer of agricultural land and involvement of the village panchayat in the process of taking permission for sale of land can go a long way in ensuring that people can coordinate their expectations and that there is no sequential frenzy of selling. The government might also impose a quota on the total amount of land that can be sold within each panchayat area in a certain number of years. Of course, these measures are costly – they will reduce the liquidity of the land market and prevent transfer of land to the most efficient farmer. However, this is a social cost worth bearing until the demographic influx stabilizes and the state acquires greater potency in protecting its borders and its assets.

Acquisition of Public Assets

As discussed in Section II, the overwhelming motivation for immigration of peasants from East Bengal in the first half of twentieth century was provided by the availability of vast tracts of wasteland owned by the State and the its policy of encouraging settlement and cultivation of such land.

As mentioned in Section II, the Census Superintendent of 1911 had estimated that about 5 million acres of surplus uncultivated land was available for cultivation. As the flow of immigrants expanded overtime, most of this land was settled. In 1947, in his letter to the prime minister of independent India, the then chief minister of Assam Gopinath Bordoloi estimated that there were only about 200,000 acres of wasteland available, of which no more than 25,000 acres were fit for reclamation.[18] Even the *char* areas were saturated. In the second half of the twentieth century, immigrants were no longer looking forward to acquiring virgin public land available for cultivation but increasingly moving towards illegal encroachment of reserved public forest land, public land set aside for grazing and for construction, and even public land along roads and railway tracks.[19]

Immigrants, unlike the indigenous tribes, were not used to living off the ecology of forest resources in a sustainable fashion. The result is deforestation. The weak government machinery was unable to conserve the property rights of the State, and partly bowing to political pressure, virtually surrendered to this invasion. Deforestation has become particularly noticeable since the 1980s. In 1980, it was estimated that about 33 per cent of the geographical area of Assam was covered by forests. In 1990 a survey done by the Assam Remote Sensing Application Centre revealed that the percentage of area under forest cover had fallen to about 21 per cent. Dense forest canopy could be found only in some isolated forest areas. Encroachments and illegal felling of trees have been widely detected. The government figures on protected and reserved forest areas often disguise the fact that a part of this area is encroached upon, cleared and sometimes under cultivation for decades. Recently, in seeking a World Bank loan, even the state government agreed that it had lost over 2,230 sq. km. of forest area since 1989.[20] Encroachment by illegal migrants not only puts pressure on forest resources and land, but also divides the local population along ethnic lines preventing any form of collective action which could have conserved the resources (the effect being more severe in forests governed by Area District Councils). Encroachment of forests by immigrants from Bangladesh is responsible for the increasingly violent conflicts in the tribal areas of the state.

The asset acquisition incentive for migration has also taken into account the open access water resources – the rivers and lakes of the state. The rivers of the state, particularly in Brahmaputra valley, are much less intensively fished than in Bangladesh and this provides a major earning and subsistence opportunity for immigrants. The increase in over-fishing and the gradual threat of extinction of some of the traditional varieties of fish is largely attributed to the increasing demand for fish by immigrants (partly, subsistence consumption) as well as the increased fishing activity by immigrants.

Finally, it is not just natural resources that provide scope for asset acquisition for migrants. Immigrants – even when they are illegal – are able to gain complete access to the public socio-economic infrastructure – schools, medical facilities and other public goods as well as the public distribution system with subsidized food and necessities. These public goods and welfare measures on the whole provide a superior package than that available in rural Bangladesh and form an important element of the incentive to migrate.

Thus, the failure of the state to protect its property rights over land and public resources and its inability to prevent overexploitation of renewable resources has been one of the major sources of incentive for migration. If the state moves against illegal encroachers of public property with a firm resolve and also administers effective restrictions on fishing and other forms of resource extraction, it will significantly reduce the incentives for immigration while also securing economic and ecological dividends. Increasing the cost of access to health, education and public distribution system for illegal migrants by instituting background checks, thorough monitoring, state-issued identity card requirements, etc., would also have a similar effect.

VI. THE RISK ASPECT

Migration is an investment in a risky project – the returns are subject to a high degree of uncertainty. For an illegal migrant, there is the primary risk of being detected and eventually deported though evidently that risk is not bad given the overwhelming scale of illegal immigration that appears to have taken place. Probably more important is the income risk faced in the labour market characterized by unemployment and underemployment as well as uncertainty about actual acquisition of productive assets – particularly those in the public domain – and the possibility of holding on to such assets in the future. Even if there is no uncertainty in the actual market, uncertainty emerges because of lack of information about the destination.

There are three economic insights that are worth pointing out. First, the potential migrants ought to face much lower income risk at their source location compared to their destination because at the source, they have access to traditional social capital and social insurance – a complex network of income smoothing arrangements – enforced through social punishment in a repeated dynamic setting. These forms of social capital are a crucial element of how they have traditionally survived despite the merciless vagaries of nature, crop price fluctuations (with no futures markets), incomplete credit markets and macroeconomic instabilities. Migration implies giving up these forms of social insurance and exposing oneself to primary income uncertainties. Other things being equal, this should act as a major disincentive for migration. However, if there are well-established social and economic networks formed by earlier migrants at the destination, then these networks can partially provide for social capital and informal insurance and thus enable migrants to face the risks in their new location.

Second, one of the important factors highlighted by the new economics of migration is the role of migration as a means of risk diversification within a large family. Sending out part of a family abroad is equivalent to investing in an asset whose return is relatively uncorrelated with local income risk and thereby holding a diversified asset portfolio which reduces aggregate risk for the larger family. In large family farms with growing pressure on land and low marginal product of family labour, the output forsaken by sending out a part of the family is low, i.e. the cost of making this investment is low. Extensive empirical evidence points out that this risk diversification argument leads to migration in developing societies even when the expected income of the migrant at the destination point is no different from that at the origin.[21] The probability and ease of repatriation of income to source families influence the desirability of risk diversification through out-migration.

Third, it has been shown that economic agents who are facing threats of survival, i.e. in danger of not being able to meet a basic threshold level of subsistence consumption are likely to exhibit risk-loving behaviour in order to maximize their chances of survival. Consider an agent who needs at least Rs 250 to physically survive and faces the choice between a prospect which yields Rs 200 for certain and another risky prospect which can yield either Rs 100 or Rs 300 with equal chance. Though the two prospects yield the same average, the second one is riskier (higher spread) and normally a risk-averse agent would choose the former. However, the survival constraint implies that the agent will definitely perish if she chooses the first prospect while the risky prospect gives her at least half a chance of surviving. Therefore, she is likely to choose the risky prospect. Given the greater riskiness of post-migration income prospects, this offers another explanation why migration can be attractive even when the expected incomes are identical at the source and destination points.

VII. THE INFORMATIONAL ASPECT

Trans-border migration, particularly when it is undertaken outside the legal immigration process, takes place under a veil of ignorance. Potential migrants have limited information about the future income prospects and their objective probability distribution as well as the relationship between their own personal attributes and the income prospect. Their perception is based on mass media, popular myths and their own observation of the fortunes of past migrants in their geographical or social neighbourhood. In this section, we shall talk about two interesting aspects of the process of information acquisition.

First, there is always a selection bias in the observation of the fortunes of past migrants. In the population of past migrants from one's observable neighbourhood, a person is more likely to hear about or observe the fortunes of those who migrated and were relatively more successful in the destination economy. The large numbers who live in squalor and deprivation after migration are not likely to be observed by people in their source village. So, the statistical inference process is comparable to a survey with a large class of non-respondents who are self-selected with a bias. Thus, if one uses only the observed sample, then one is likely to form a more favourable perception of the earning opportunity through migration compared to the reality. This creates an incentive for migration which would not have existed under full information.

Second, migration from any area is a sequential process. One way to think about it is that people receive informative signals about the opportunities across the border, observe the actions of those who migrate and decide whether or not to migrate. This creates a ideal opportunity for the phenomenon of 'informational herding' where perfectly rational agents ignore their own signals and follow others. To illustrate this, think about a village where succeeding 'generations' receive signals about the earning prospect across the border which says either 'good' or 'bad'. Further, suppose that the actual earning prospect across the border is unknown to villagers though it is known to remain unchanged overtime. The signal is imperfect – receiving a 'good' signal simply means that the actual earning opportunity is more likely to be good than to be bad. Each generation observes the actions of previous generations but not their signals. Suppose the first three generations would not have migrated if they had got 'bad' signals. However, they do receive good signals purely by chance and decide to migrate. The fourth generation has four observations – the signals of the three previous generations revealed by their actions and its own signal. So even if its own signal is bad, it is likely to place a high probability on the even that the earning opportunity is actually good and decide to migrate. In other words, its own action will be independent of its own signal. The fifth generation, knowing this, will base its own inference on only the first three generations' signals (as the fourth generations' action is independent of its signal) and arrive at exactly the same conclusion as the fourth generation. In fact, all subsequent generations will ignore their own private signals and migrate, even if the reality and all the signals, apart from the first few, were bad. This is an example of herding as an incentive for migration under incomplete information even when the migrant is worse off after migration.

One of the implications of the above analysis is that there is a major role for dissemination of correct information in reducing the incentive to migrate. Herding is notoriously sensitive to exogenous information perturbation and small changes in the information set can break the entire chain. Dissemination of information can also correct the selection bias in learning. Instruments of mass media such as radio and television can carry the message far and wide across the border. One is not talking about propaganda here but rather documentaries and dramatized features on actual socio-economic problems in Assam, the ecological disasters, the economic conditions of the mass of immigrants living on the margins of survival, and having them broadcast or telecast in Bengali to viewers in Bangladesh. However, information sent out by government agencies in Assam might be suspected of being biased and manipulative in the interest of curtailing migration. One way to avoid that would be to involve neutral agencies, even foreign producers and to use multinational satellite television channels for telecast.

VIII. THE NETWORK ASPECT

Our discussions in the previous sections have highlighted the crucial role that networks of past immigrants play in determining the incentive to migrate for new immigrants. A number of existing studies have found that the network of past migrants – their size, composition and economic characteristics – performs much better in explaining the rate and destination of migration compared to say, wage differentials. The effect is much more pronounced for illegal immigration because the network of past migrants is an important protection against detection and deportation. The larger the size of the immigrant community in the bordering districts, the easier it is for them to merge undetected in the local population and gather the credentials necessary to engage in economic activities.

The networks of past migrants perform many roles. First, they provide insurance against starvation and lack of shelter in the initial phase after migration. Second, they provide information and access to the informal labour market – sometimes past migrants act as employers of new migrants – and also on-the-job training in simple skills. Note that there is nothing altruistic about this behaviour. The past immigrants who provide information, shelter, access to employment or direct employment profit from this arrangement. For example, an employer of a new immigrant may be able to pay him lower than market wage as the latter has no other option and also has a bargaining disadvantage in view of his illegal status. Similarly, intermediaries who supply new immigrants to other employers and vouch for their quality (guarantee that they will not shirk or indulge in crime) earn a decent price for this. Their reputation is sustained as new illegal immigrants have very little by way of alternative income that they can fall back upon if they cheat on the local network.

Third, new immigrants share social characteristics and norms with past migrants from their source area and are easily absorbed into the cooperative arrangements or institutions for collective action in immigrant villages – which works to the mutual benefit of both old and new migrants. As a by-product, the access to social insurance, labour tying and informal credit arrangements within this community helps overcome income risks. Fourth, the networks of past migrants establish reputations of high quality output or skills in certain areas which is a bonanza for new migrants. Fifth, the installed base of past migrants provides a network of informal arrangements through which earnings can be repatriated to the larger family in the home country and also some form of social monitoring. This provides motivation for large families to send part of their family abroad for risk-diversification and income repatriation. Sixth, past migrants occupying public lands, forests and other resources through illegal encroachment enable new migrants to have easier access to these resources, though they may have to pay a positive access price. Further, the network backs up new encroachments. Finally, a large base of past migrants implies that political representatives can be influenced to creating public goods for immigrant areas as well as preventing any hard measures against illegal migrants.

As immigration occurs overtime, the installed base of past migrants expands and also acquires greater prosperity, assets and reputation and this tends to sustain positive incentive to migrate for new migrants through the network effect. This occurs despite the fact that as population grows in Assam – naturally or due to migration – the marginal return to migrant labour tends to get depressed particularly in a sterile technological and capital investment climate. Larger the network, stronger the effect. Thus, immigration may become self-sustaining.

One important feature of the network effect is that its strength depends on geographical concentration. Concentration of past migrants and their economic activities in border areas is enormously more helpful for new illegal immigrants than if they are scattered throughout the state. Similarly, their political leverage is higher if they are not scattered uniformly across constituencies. The incentive to migrate through the network effect can be significantly reduced by policies that induce economic mobility of immigrants throughout the region through other economic incentives. Redesigning the borders of electoral constituencies can reduce the political impact of immigrant networks, though it will incite allegations of persecution of minorities.

IX. RELATIVE DESTITUTION

The new economics of migration has emphasized the role of relative destitution in the internal migration processes of developing nations. The basic idea is that agents care about their relative wealth or income within their community – their status in the context of the local distribution. They have an incentive to migrate to a different community where they would be 'relatively better off' even if the absolute income at the destination is not higher than that at their current location. Thus, the poorest in a village with high inequality would like to move to a community where the distribution is more equal, even if everybody in the other community is just as poor. Destitute new migrants entering Assam often enter communities of recent immigrants where most people have similar economic characteristics and often difference in wealth due to asset holding are not very large. The marginal migrant is able to reduce his relative destitution by immigrating. The process has a self-perpetuating nature to it. The poorest in a village migrate and the people in the next income rung now find themselves at the bottom, their relative destitution worsens, creating new incentives for migration.

X. INTERNATIONAL TRADE

It has been frequently argued that free international trade between Assam and Bangladesh is one of the measures that will help contain migration.[22] One of the predictions of the textbook theory of international trade is that free trade in goods will lead to equalization of input prices across nations-including wages, even though labour and other resources which enter as inputs, are not explicitly traded. This factor price equalization theorem holds only under certain conditions. In particular, in a two-country setting, wages are likely to be equalized under free trade if, among other things, both countries have access to the same production technology but differ only in their relative endowments of the various factors of production such as labour and capital. However, if there are differences in production technology across countries, then wage differences may well persist or even expand – wage and productivity of labour will be relatively higher in the country which is technologically superior in the production of the labour intensive goods. A similar effect comes about when one country has a superior infrastructure (roads, telecommunications etc.).[23]

The geographical proximity between Assam and Bangladesh implies that the cost of movement of goods between the two economies is low. The most serious bottleneck facing Assam's economy is that of transport access to rest of India and rest of the world. This is an area where Bangladesh, by natural geography, has a great comparative advantage over India. Thus, if Bangladesh 'exported' the use of its road and rail transport and port services to Assam, it would be of enormous economic value to the latter. Of course, there is a wide array of other goods that Assam and Bangladesh could export and import from each other. The question is whether free trade between Bangladesh and India is likely to reduce differences in wages between Bangladesh and Assam and thus the overall incentive for migration.

One way to address this problem is to understand that if free trade reduces the incentive to migrate than it must raise wages in Bangladesh and/or reduce wages in Assam. Relative to India, Bangladesh is more labour abundant in the sense that it has a higher ratio of labour to other factors such as capital, land or natural resources. Trade with India will expand labour-intensive productive activities in Bangladesh and thereby raise the wages (or reduce unemployment in a labour market characterized by structural rigidities), which should reduce the incentive to migrate. On the other hand, competition from goods produced in Bangladesh would actually reduce production of some labour-intensive goods in Assam, particularly, in the agricultural sector. In the short run, earning opportunities for labour will probably decline in Assam. Thus, the short-run effect of free trade will be a reduction in the incentive to immigrate.

In the long-run, manufacturing and tertiary activities are likely to expand in a big way once the transport bottleneck is removed. While these activities are not labour intensive, they will eventually drive up wages and the probability of employment in the formal sector as well as the urban informal sector. This will not only increase the incentive for rural-urban migration but, as we have argued earlier, increase the incentive for trans-boundary migration from Bangladesh. More generally, given the technological and infra-structural differences between India and Bangladesh – once Assam's economy is better integrated into the national economy of India – it is unlikely that the long-run labour market earning opportunities in Assam will be significantly worse than in Bangladesh. *Ceteris paribus*, free trade might actually increase immigration in the long-run.

XI. PROSPECTS AND POLICY

Given the scale of immigration that has occurred in Assam through the twentieth century, one might expect that the economic incentives for migration may have declined and that in the long run, the flow of migration might be reduced to a negligible level. Assam has experienced a rapid increase in density of population, domestic unemployment and underemployment, economic stagnation, ethnic violence affecting immigrants in various areas and the intensity of harvesting of natural resources as well as a sharp decline in the availability of land and forests available for encroachment. These factors should decrease the incentive to migrate. Other factors that have similar effect are construction of fences and increase in patrolling along the Indo-Bangladesh border,[24] the establishment of a legal framework (however ineffective) to detect illegal migrants, the political movement towards granting some form of permanent resident status to indigenous people, the introduction of identity cards and the current national political dynamics which appear to be biased against religious minorities in India.

Unfortunately, the incentive to migrate depends not only on the prospects for a migrant in the host economy but also in the source economy. So, the question that we have to ask is how are the relative earning opportunities between Assam and Bangladesh likely to change in the future? In this context, observe that even if the incentive to migrate for an individual migrant remains constant and the distribution of income and other characteristics in Bangladesh remain unchanged overtime, the number of immigrants entering every year is likely to increase simply because of increase in the overall population of Bangladesh. To add to this, there are important factors which may tend to increase the incentive to migrate for an individual migrant.

At the beginning of the 1990s, Bangladesh had a population density of over 900 people per sq. km., about three times the density of population of Assam. Crop-land, at about 0.08 ha. per capita, was already desperately scarce. The United Nations predicts that Bangladesh's current population will nearly double, to 235 million by 2025.[25] As the scope for extensive cultivation has been more than exhausted, population growth will cut by half the amount of crop land available per capita by the year 2025 and sharply increase fragmentation of holdings. The problem of flooding appears to be increasing overtime, particularly aggravated by deforestation in the Himalayan watersheds of the region's major rivers and increasing deposits on river beds. The forests and biological resources of Bangladesh are under serious threats of extinction. Despite overexploitation of resources, Assam will continue to look like a greener pasture for decades to come.

Increasing economic uncertainty and pressure on land is likely to increase the incentive for large rural families in Bangladesh to ask individual members to immigrate in order to diversify overall income risk. The increase in destitution and threats to basic survival in Bangladesh will mean an increase in the number of people willing to take big risks. The network of immigrants in Assam – who are now close to, if not the majority of population in several districts and virtually occupy the entire border area – implies that the network benefits to current immigrants is actually much higher than immigrants who came in the past. This trend will continue. The network will continue to render measures for detection of illegal immigrants largely ineffective.

Finally, when peace returns to the land and economic growth picks up in Assam, wages and employment opportunities will expand and there will be even greater incentives for migration. In fact, the more widespread the growth process, the more it 'trickles down', the more it brings income and opportunities to the rural areas and the poorest, the more of an incentive it will provide to the marginal migrant.

Assam stand at the crossroads. Our analysis indicates that if decisive steps are not taken to curb the incentives for further migration, a significant flow of illegal immigration is likely continue in the future. In course of our discussion of economic factors behind migration, we suggested some measures that might reduce incentives for immigration. For ease of reference, we list some of the key suggestions below:

(i) The use of mass media-based information dissemination in Bangladesh through credible channels to inform ignorant migrants about the actual economic conditions of recent immigrants to Assam, their poverty and the new measures on the border. This will prevent migration due to incomplete information and wrong learning.

(ii) Urgent steps for conservation of natural resources, particularly forests, rivers and lakes, and drastic steps to prevent deforestation, over-fishing and other ecological damage. This will yield a double dividend in terms of ecological conservation as well as reduction of the scope for asset acquisition by migration.

(iii) Restrictions on transfer of land, particularly, agricultural land, to people who cannot establish residence for a certain period in a certain demarcated zone and, in addition, a ceiling on the total amount of land that can be transferred in a village area within a certain time frame.

(iv) Greater decentralization of power to local communities so that they have greater control over local resources including forests and access to water resources; this will also ensure greater coordination against mass sale of land because of self-fulfilling expectations.

(v) Eviction of all illegal encroachment of public land and forests, and licencing their management to private agents if the state finds itself unable to protect its property rights.

(vi) Removal of wage rigidities in the formal sector as a part of the liberalization process in the economy so as to reduce the incentive for migration as a 'search' process.

(vii) Changing boundaries of electoral constituencies and influencing location of new economic activities so as to disperse the existing networks of immigrants in high concentration areas and border districts.

These measures are no substitute for rigorous border patrolling, increasing the intensity of observation towers on the border and development of a legal system which can identify and deport illegal immigrants. It is, however, unclear whether the state will be able to deport any of the existing illegal immigrants. If we understand that deportation will be impossible, then it is much better to grant general amnesty, legalize all immigrants and ask them to register. They can be granted limited rights till they go through a delayed naturalization process. A comprehensive computerized database of all legal residents of the state can then be prepared and identity cards issued. Anyone who does not register by a certain date, may be presumed to be a foreigner unless otherwise proved. This scheme will also create a cleavage between the self-interests of existing migrants and that of future migrants. A rigorous system of compulsory registration of all births and deaths must be simultaneously introduced.

An interesting suggestion made recently is the introduction of temporary visa for workers from Bangladesh who want to work in Assam during the peak agricultural season or some major construction activity, and who are sponsored by a bona fide employer. This would significantly reduce the incentive for immigration by workers in Bangladesh who currently immigrate in order to access temporary opportunities or peak season demand for agricultural labour.[26]

In the life of every society, there are times of prolonged decay and conflict when the only way out is to transcend the burdens of the past, move beyond history and memory, and face the future armed with only awareness of the brutal reality and the power of reason. This is the way Assam must approach its immigration problem.

NOTES

1. See, Weiner (1978) and the discussion in Sanjib Baruah, *India Against Itself: Assam and the Politics of Nationality*, Philadelphia: University of Phildelphia Press, 1999.
2. In the neighbouring state of Tripura, the indigenous tribals constituted 70 per cent of the population in 1901. Immigration reduced that proportion to a bare 30 per cent in 1991.
3. For example, jute became an important cash crop in the course of the century entirely due to innovative farmers from Mymensingh.
4. One exception to this is the migration process in Sub-Saharan Africa which has come under fairly close scrutiny. A useful set of survey articles is contained in Rosenzweig and Stark (1997).
5. The classic paper is Harris and Todaro (1970). However, the first formal treatment of migration as a consequence of differences in returns to human capital is found in Sjaastad (1962). See also, Stark (1991) for a thorough contemporary treatment of labour market issues in migration.
6. See, Stark and Bloom (1985); and Stark (1991).
7. See, Massey et al. (1993).
8. See, for example, Ghatak, Levine and Price (1996).
9. Of course, not all Bengali Hindus in Assam were really migrants as some of them came from Sylhet which was a part of the province prior to 1947.
10. See, Baruah (1999).
11. C.S. Mullan quoted in the 'Report on Illegal Migration into Assam' submitted to the President of India by the Governor of Assam, November 1998.
12. Although some have argued that a part of it is also due to the higher growth rate among Muslims and tribals. See, for example, Das (1989).
13. The annual growth rate of population in Assam between 1971 and 1991 is 2.66 per cent. In contrast, the hill districts of N.C. Hills and Karbi-Anglong experienced annual growth rates of 4.9 per cent and 3.7 per cent respectively. Among the plains districts, Dhemaji recorded a growth rate of 5.37 per cent, while Kokrajhar, Bongaigaon and Kamrup recorded high annual growth rates of 3.8 per cent, 3.2 per cent and 3.3 per cent.
14. See, the 'Report on Illegal Migration into Assam' submitted to the President of India by the Governor of Assam, November 1998.
15. See, Massey et al. (1993).
16. See, Ray (1998).
17 See, Homer-Dixon (1994).
18 See, Baruah (1999).

19. *The Assam Tribune* reported on 28 March 2000 that out of a total area of 2,800 sq. km. in the Upper Assam forest circle, about 1,500 sq. km. are under encroachment (mostly along the Assam-Nagaland border). Most of these encroachers are from Nagaland, having little to do with immigrants from Bangladesh. But it serves as a good indicator of the inability of the state government machinery to prevent occupation of public assets by private encroachers.
20. *The North-East Daily*, Sunday, 5 December 1999.
21. See, for example, Ghatak, Levine and Price (1996).
22. See, for example Banerjee et al. (1999).
23. See, Razin and Sadka (1997). Empirical evidence has generally falsified the factor price equalization theorem and even the weaker hypothesis that trade reduces gap between wages. This is generally attributed to persistent and self-perpetuating differences in technology, knowledge and economic infrastructure as well as other non-convexities such as increasing returns.
24. The decision to fence the border was taken in 1985 under the accord signed by the Central Government and the leaders of the Assam agitation, but has not yet been completed.
25. See, Homer-Dixon (1994).
26. See, Banerjee et al. (1999).

REFERENCES

Banerjee, Paula, et al., 'Indo-Bangladesh Cross-Border Migration and Trade', *Economic and Political Weekly*, 4 September 1999.

Baruah, Sanjib, *India Against Itself: Assam and the Politics of Nationality*, Philadelphia: University of Philadelphia Press, 1999.

Das, Susanta K., *Spotlight on Assam*, Maharashtra: Premier Book Service, 1989.

Djajic, Slobodan, 'Illegal Immigration and Resource Allocation', *International Economic Review*, vol. 38, 1997, pp. 97–117.

Ethier, Wilfred, 'Illegal Immigration: The Host Country Problem', *American Economic Review*, vol. 76, 1986, pp. 56–71.

Fernandes, Walter, 'Conflict in North East: A Historical Perspective', *Economic and Political Weekly*, 18 December 1999.

Ghatak, Subrata Levine, Paul and Stephen W. Price, 'Migration Theories and Evidence: An Assessment', *Journal of Economic Surveys*, vol. 10, 1996, pp. 159–98.

Harris J.R., and P. Michael Todaro, 'Migration, Unemployment and Development: A Two-sector Analysis', *American Economic Review*, col. 60, 1970, pp. 126–42.

Thomas, F. Homer-Dixon, 'Environmental Scarcities and Violent Conflict: Evidence from Cases', *International Security*, vol. 19, no. 1, 1994, pp. 5–40.

Massey, Douglas S. et al., 'Theories of International Migration: A Review and Appraisal', *Population and Development Review*, vol. 19, no. 3, 1993, pp. 431–66.

Razin, Assaf and Efraim Sadka, 'International Migration and International Trade', in *Handbook of Population and Family Economics*, vol. 1B, ed. M.R. Rosenzweig and O. Stark, Amsterdam: Elsevier Science B.V., 1997, pp. 851–88.

Ray, Debraj, *Development Economics*, Princeton: Princeton University Press, 1998.

Report on Illegal Migration to Assam Submitted to the President of India by the Governor of Assam, 8 November 1998.

Rozensweig, Mark R. and Oded Stark, eds., *Handbook of Population and Family Economics*, vol. 1B, Amsterdam: Elsevier Science B.V., 1997.

Sjaastad, Larry A., 'The Costs and Returns of Human Migration', *Journal of Political Economy*, vol. 70, Supplement, 1962, pp. 80–9.

Stark, Oded, *The Migration of Labour*, Cambridge: Basil Blackwell, 1991.

Stark, Oded and David Bloom, 'The New Economics of Labour Migration', *American Economic Review*, vol. 75, 1985, pp. 173–8.

Weiner, Myron, *Sons of the Soil: Migration and Ethnic Conflict in India*, Princeton: Princeton University Press, 1978.

CHAPTER 17

Growth of Tribal Population in Assam

JAISHREE KONWARH

In recent times, population study is assuming great importance due to the increasing impact of population growth on the socio-economic development, particularly in the over-populated under developed countries. Population studies in India have so far been mainly conducted at the national level. But such macro-level studies tend to overlook the regional peculiarities in the behaviour of demographic variables. This is particularly true of Assam, whose demographic experience is unique in many respects. The population of Assam had increased from 32.9 lakh in 1901 to 224.14 lakh in 1991,[1] representing a fantastic growth of 581.25 per cent over 90 years as against an increase of 258.18 per cent for India as a whole during the same period. But the picture of Assam's population will not be complete without analysing the tribal population pattern, which also shows some interesting trends. The tribals of Assam,[2] who are the earliest inhabitants of the state and have a distinct ethnological identity, constitute 12.82 per cent of the total population, according to the 1991 census. This paper is an attempt to highlight the behaviour of tribal population growth of Assam.

The Scheduled Tribe population of Assam (as per the Scheduled Tribe Lists Modification Order, 1956), though indigenous and the earliest settlers of this region, did not get much prominence before the attainment of Independence. It is only after Independence that the government, in trying to improve the economic condition of the country paid any attention to these backward sections of society. The census authority started collecting detailed information regarding tribal population to help the government formulate proper policy measures to bring these backward groups of people to the national mainstream.

This paper will concentrate on the growth pattern of the tribals of Assam only after the attainment of Independence. But to study the present trend, we must have some idea of the past pattern of growth of the tribals of Assam, however, erroneous that information might be. Moreover, the list of Scheduled Tribes announced by the Government in 1956 embraces some tribes not included earlier. So whether pre- and post-Independence trends they can be compared is yet another questionable matter. Table 17.1 presents the growth pattern of the tribal population of Assam compared to the general (tribal and non-tribal) population, along with percentage variations from the turn of the nineteenth century. The characteristics of tribal population growth that can be inferred from the table are: (a) like the general population trend, the growth rate of the tribal population was always positive, even in 1921 (the year of great divide); (b) though positive the percentage variation for the tribals was much lower than for the general population in the pre-Independence period; (c) in the post-Independence period the growth rate of the tribal population was much faster than the general population.

TABLE 17.1: TRIBAL AND GENERAL POPULATION GROWTH IN ASSAM, 1901–91

Year	Tribal Population		General Population	
	Persons	Decadal Variation	Persons	Decadal Variation
1	2	3	4	5
1901	5,50,000	–	32,90,180	–
1911	6,00,000	+ 9.09	38,48,617	+ 16.99
1921	6,17,135	+ 2.85	46,36,980	+ 20.48
1931	7,04,977	+ 14.28	55,60,371	+ 19.91
1941	7,50,000	+ 6.38	66,91,790	+ 20.40
1951	8,05,657	+ 7.42	80,28,856	+ 19.93
1961	11,64,641	+ 44.55	1,08,37,326	+ 34.98
1971	16,06,648	+ 37.95	1,46,25,152	+ 35.95
1981	21,09,000	+ 31.27	1,80,41,000	+ 23.36
1991	28,74,441	+ 36.29	2,24,14,322	+ 24.24

Source: Various census reports.
Notes: (a) Cols. 2 and 4: figures are adjusted from census reports for the present political jurisdiction of Assam.
(b) Cols. 3 and 5: figures are computed.
(c) The population figures for 1981 have been worked out by interpolation.

As revealed in the table, the percentage variation of the tribal population in the post-Independence decades (1951–61, 1961–71, 1971–81 and 1981–91) were 44.55 per cent, 37.95 per cent, 31.27 per cent and 36.29 per cent, whereas in the case of the general population, the percentage were 34.98, 34.95, 23.36 and 24.24 per cent respectively. Before 1951 the tribal population grew at a much slower pace, the percentage variation being 6.38 per cent and 7.42 per cent, respectively in the two decades prior to Independence (1931–41 and 1941–51), while the variation for the general population were 20.40 per cent and 19.93 per cent for the same period. This abnormal and sudden increase in the numbers of tribal population has shaken up the authorities and many demographic thinkers. They have been compelled to examine the causes influencing this sudden spurt.

The picture of the growth of tribal population will not be complete if we do not show how much of the total population of Assam is being constituted by the tribal population. In other words, to what extent are the number of tribal people growing in relation to the general population in Assam. Table 17.2 presents the proportion of tribal population to general population in Assam between 1901–91.

Table 17.2 reveals that though a consistent proportion of the total population of Assam is being constituted by the tribals, their proportion to the general population declined in early twentieth century; it fell from 16.72 per cent in 1901 to 10.04 per cent in 1951. It is only after the attainment of Independence that the proportion of tribal population showed a favourable tendency. It increased from 10.75 per cent in 1961 to 10.99 per cent in 1971, then to 11.69 per cent in 1981 and again to 12.82 per cent in 1991.

In the case of the general population of Assam, migration along with natural growth caused the population to grow at a tremendous pace. But migration could not have had any effect on the sudden increase in the tribal population of Assam because these groups of people are not found in any other parts of India, except in some pockets of the north-east. Nor could natural growth alone have brought about such a sudden increase to their growth rates, though we have to admit that the policy measures adopted by the government to imporve the economic conditions of the people did exert certain positive effect on the natural growth rate. The principal policy measures responsible for this were the introduction of new medicines, improved healthcare facilities, sanitation, education, transport and communication facilities, and decline in infant and maternal mortality rates.

TABLE 17.2: PROPORTION OF TRIBAL POPULATION TO
GENERAL POPULATION OF ASSAM, 1901–91

Year	Tribal Population	General Population	Percentage of Tribal Population to g.p.
1	2	3	4
1901	5,50,000	32,90,180	16.72
1911	6,00,000	38,48,617	15.59
1921	6,17,135	46,36,980	13.31
1931	7,04,977	55,60,371	12.68
1941	7,50,000	66,94,790	11.20
1951	8,05,657	80,28,856	10.04
1961	11,64,641	1,08,37,326	10.75
1971	16,06,648	1,46,25,152	10.99
1981*	21,09,000	1,80,41,000	11.69
1991	28,74,441	2,24,14,322	12.82

Note: *Estimated.
Source: Census of India; reports on Assam for relevant years.

Another factor indirectly responsible for increasing their number is the longevity of the life of the tribal people, due to the betterment of socio-economic condition as a result of development activities on the part of the government as well as the local authorities.[3] But this could not be the sole factor, causing the growth rate of the tribal population to increase at such a pace.

The most important factor which influenced the growth of tribal population in Assam was the gross under-enumeration about their number in the censuses prior to Independence. During the colonial era, the inflow of tea plantation and agricultural peasants from outside the region and their subsequent settlements in the midst of tribal villages alienated the poor and oppressed tribals because the nontribal peasants could afford to pay the exorbitant land prices to the tribals to own the land. Thus pressurized, the inherently shy tribals were pushed into the inaccessible pockets, devoid of proper transport and communication facilities. Such deprivation of land and resources threatened the very survival of the poor and oppressed tribals. When this process of de-peasantization and pauperization was accentuated, the tribals grew suspicious about the intentions of the colonial rulers. They also understood that unless they participated in the freedom movement along with their counterparts in other regions of the country, they could not free themselves from the shackles of colonial oppression and injustice. Thus, gradually they got themselves assimilated and merged into the greater entity, the 'Assamese'. Also, most of the tribals after converting to the Hindu religion into dropped their clan names and the enumerators mistakenly included them into other major population groups. For example, most of the Rabha people after adopting the Hindu religion using stopped the name 'Rabha'.[4] In the districts of Darrang and Kamrup, a great majority of tribes have been subjected to conversion or a gradual process of assimilation so much so that there is hardly any difference between the Assamese Other Backward Class Hindus and the Rabhas.[5] This reflected as the slow growth of the tribal population and their gradual decline in proportion to the general population from 1901 onwards.

The Independence of India hopes gave rise to hopes of social justice and equality among the tribals. The Constitution of India incorporated several provisions towards these ends. It also provided many safeguards and protections to the tribals. All in all, the post-Independence period has been one of acceleration in the pace of social change and modernization of various tribal groups in the north-east and their effective induction within the framework of the nation-state.

But unfortunately their hopes and aspirations have been progressively belied. The gap between policy pronouncements of subsequent governments and the implementation of the same has become wider. In fact, in contemporary India there have been constant attacks on and threats to the tribals in one form or the other by various socio-economic forces. As retaliation to such threats, most of the tribal communities in Assam today are involved in ethnic movements of varying complexions and intensities. In recent decades, many of these tribal groups have swung back from the 'Assamese Hindu' identity to their original tribal identity. In 1961, many of the indigenous tribal people like the Bodos, Garos and Rabhas who accepted Assamese as mother tongue in 1941 and 1951 census, identified themselves now with their original mother tongue.[6] There are active movements to de-Sanskritize the lifestyle and revive tribal customs and modes of worship.

Such revival and retribalization by rejecting the 'Assamese' identity have led the tribals to identify themselves as 'tribals' in the last three censuses. As argued by Goswami and Gogoi, 'it is reflective of greater consciousness of the tribal population about their ethnic identity leading to more accurate reporting of their numbers in the last two censuses'.[7]

Moreover, with the spread of education, better transport and communication facilities, the language barriers – each tribal group has its own dialect – and inaccessibility of tribal habitat, which had prevented the enumerators from directly contacting the respondent and collecting the accurate information have been removed to a greater extent, even though in some remote places this situation still prevails. This has also helped the tribals in coming into contact with the outside world and losing their inhibition, especially the womenfolk. All these have made the tribals aware of their ethnic identity and recording themselves correctly in the post-Independence censuses. The gross under-enumeration which had occurred prior to Independence got nullified in the last three censuses.

The district-wise distribution of the tribal population of Assam (Appendix 17.I) shows that Cachar district had experienced the most extreme fluctuation, with the record increase of 110.09 per cent during the 1951–61 decade as against by only 8.58 per cent and 22.41 per cent in the two successive decades. The other districts showing the same kind of erratic behaviour are the United Mikir and North Cachar Hills, Goalpara, Darrang and Lakhimpur. These are districts with higher proportion of tribal population to general population (Appendix 17.II). In United Mikir and North Cachar Hills, while the proportion of tribal population declined from 1961 onwards, for the districts of Goalpara, Kamrup and Darrang the proportion of tribal population to general population decreased until the 1971 census. But in the census of 1991 it had grown. In the case of Lakhimpur district, the other district with higher proportion of tribal population, it had moved up. The concentration of tribal population in different districts measured with the help of location quotient also substantiates the same trend (Appendix 17.III). At one end Cachar shows the lowest concentration, while at the other end United Mikir and North Cachar Hills show the highest concentration, which presents a declining trend from 1961 onwards. On the other hand, Goalpara, Darrang and Lakhimpur are the three other districts which have higher concentration of tribal population than the other plains districts.

It is worth mentioning here that district-wise, the largest concentration of the East Bengal immigrants is in Goalpara, Nowgong, Kamrup and Darrang. The immigrants from Nepal are mainly concentrated in the two districts of Lakhimpur and Darrang. The indigenous people of Assam find themselves on the verge of losing their ethno-cultural identity in their own homeland. This threat has made them aware of their own identity and to fight in order to preserve it. The Boro-Kacharis, a major tribal group of Assam along with some other tribal groups, who live mostly in the districts of Goalpara (gateway of Assam), Kamrup and Darrang, face constant threat from immigrants, especially the Muslim immigrants from Bangladesh. This has created a very fragile situation in the state. Tensions and conflicts runs rife between these people and the indigenous people of Assam, especially the tribals. Their fears have manifested in the form of violence and demand for autonomy and a separate state.

Difference in fertility rates in the two populations arise not so much from biological differences as from social and economic differences.[8] In other words, two populations with similar social and economic backgrounds must have similar fertility rates and must increase at the the same rate. So when we compare the natural growth of the tribal population of Assam with the tribal population of its neighbouring (NER) regions on the one hand and the general population in the plains of Assam on the other, we find that the natural increase of the tribals of the north-east region is very low.[9] The annual natural growth rates estimated from birth and death rates for the villages of the region were 1.66 in Kanther Terang (Karbi village), 1.40 in Benshidua (Garo village), 0.58 in Hmmpui (Mizo village) 0.62 in Khonsa (Noke village) and 3.44 in Mawtnum (Khasi village).[10]

On the other hand, there is no evidence to show that the natural rate of increase of the indigenous population of Assam is higher than the national average. In a study 'Fertility Patterns of the Brahmaputra Valley: 1881–1931', H. Goswami has convincingly shown that the fertility rate of the population of Brahmaputra valley had closely approximated the national average till the end of the third decade of the twentieth century. There is no reason for this trend to have reversed in the near past. The percentage of unmarried among both males and females aged 15 and above, which has an important bearing on fertility rate, increased in Assam from 26.52 in 1951 to 30.58 in 1961 in case of males. In the case of females, the increase was from 9.45 to 12.53.[11] The proportion of single persons in all age groups has also been higher in Assam than that for India as a whole.[12] All these justify a lower fertility rate for Assam.

Similarly, the literacy rate for Assam, among both males and females, is higher than many other states. So there should be no reason for the state to have higher fertility rate than the national average.

Moreover, as Guha has commented, conditions of life are not very much different for tribals and non-tribals, particularly in the plains of Assam. The natural growth rate for Assam's population as a whole must be closer to the tribals than to the national average.[13] In other words, the natural rate of growth among the tribals must be closer to the general population of Assam. Thus, it will not be incorrect to assume the recorded natural rate of growth for the general population to represent the tribal population of the state.

Table 17.3 presents the recorded and estimated tribal population of Assam, estimation made at each decade's natural rate of increase among the general population of the state between 1901–91. The tribal population would have grown as shown in the column 3 (estimated tribal population), had the rate of natural increase for the general population prevailed for the tribals also.

The size of estimated tribal population, with marginal exception, remained higher than the size of recorded population prior to Independence. This strengthens the argument of gross under-enumeration which had occurred during that period because of the gradual assimilation and deliberate identification of the tribals as part of the greater 'Assamese Hindu' entity, to fight the common enemy 'the Britishers'. But after the attainment of Independence, with the loss of that common cause and unfulfilment of their expectations and hopes, the tribals have reverted to their original identity and recorded themselves as

TABLE 17.3: DECADE-WISE GROWTH OF TRIBAL POPULATION BASED ON THE RATE OF NATURAL INCREASE AMONG THE GENERAL POPULATION OF ASSAM, 1901–91

Period	Recorded Tribal Population	Estimated Tribal Population	Difference Col. 2–Col. 3
1	2	3	4
1901	5,50,000	–	–
1911	6,00,000	6,24,800	– 24,800
1921	6,17,135	6,13,200	+ 3925
1931	7,04,977	7,02,300	+ 2677
1941	7,50,000	8,36,808	– 86,808
1951	8,05,657	8,61,750	– 56,093
1961	11,64,641	9,86,124	+ 1,78,517
1971	16,06,468	15,07,046	+ 99,422
1981	21,09,000	19,50,252	+ 1,58,748
1991	28,74,441	24,94,947	+ 3,79,494

Source: Col. 2: Various census reports; Cols. 3 and 4: Estimated.

tribals in the subsequent censuses. Thus, after Independence, particularly after 1961, the recorded number of tribal population has outpaced the estimated one.

NOTES

1. *Census of India, 1901 and 1991*, General Population Tables.
2. The tribes of Assam are divided into two groups, viz., the hill-tribes consisting of the Karbis and the Dimasas, and the plain tribes also divided into two groups, viz., the Poro group and the Mishing or Miri group. The Boro group consists of Kacharis, Sonowals, Lalung, Mech, Rabha, Burman and Deoris.
3. B.N. Bordoloi, *District Handbook, United Mikir & Mikir Hills*, Shillong: Tribal Research Institute, 1972, p. 8.
4. B.M. Das, *Rabha: Amar Jana Jati*, ed. P.C. Bhattacharya, Jorhat: Ahom Sahitya Sabha, 1962, p. 165.
5. S. Choudhury, *Tribes of Assam Plains*, Guwahati: Directorate of Welfare of Plain Tribes and Backward Classes, Govt. of Assam, 1980, p. 65.
6. *Goalpara District Gazettes*, 1979, p. 92.
7. A Goswami and J.K. Gogoi, 'Migration & Demographic Transformation of Assam 1901–71', in *North-East Regions, Problems and Prospects of Development*, ed., R.L. Abbi, Chandigarh: Centre for Research in Rural and Industrial Development, 1984.
8. W.S. Thompson and D.T. Lewis, *Population Problems*, New York: Miami University, 1965, p. 273.
9. P.D. Saikia, *Immigration into Tribal Areas of North-East*, mimeo, Jorhat: Agro-Economic Research Centre for the North-East.
10. Ibid.
11. *Census of India, 1961*, Assam, General Report, p. 164.
12. S.N. Agarwala, *India's Population Problem*, Bombay: Tata McGraw Hill, 1995, p. 74.
13. Amalendu Guha, 'Little Nationalism Turned Chauvinist: Assam's Anti-foreigner Upsurge, 1979–80', *Economic and Political Weekly*, special number, 1980.

APPENDIX 17.I: DISTRICT-WISE PERCENTAGE OF DECADEL VARIATION AMONG THE TRIBALS AND GENERAL POPULATION OF ASSAM DURING 1951–61, 1961–71 AND 1971–91

District	1951–61 Tribal Popn.	1951–61 General Popn.	1961–71 Tribal Popn.	1961–71 General Popn.	1971–91 Tribal Popn.	1971–91 General Popn.
Goalpara	33.20	39.32	36.12	44.12	100.58	62.19
Kamrup	29.36	38.39	34.04	38.38	69.22	54.23
Darrang	56.08	39.51	32.32	34.62	103.33	56.85
Nowgong	27.34	36.51	42.93	38.83	34.54	50.69
Sibsagar	39.82	24.43	30.53	21.81	79.33	41.90
Lakhimpur	37.95	38.85	71.93	35.74	82.29	52.40
United Mikir & N.C. Hills	93.65	69.08	24.27	62.79	67.75	78.66
Cachar	110.09	23.53	8.58	24.29	22.41	45.42
Assam	44.56	34.98	37.95	34.95	78.91	53.26

Source: Computed from relevant census reports.

APPENDIX 17.II: DISISTRICT-WISE PROPORTION OF TRIBAL POPULATION TO GENERAL POPULATION OF ASSAM DURING 1951–91

District	1951	1961	1971	1991
Goalpara	15.3	14.7	13.9	17.14
Kamrup	11.5	10.8	10.4	11.46
Darrang	9.7	10.9	10.7	13.86
Nowgong	7.6	7.2	7.4	6.65
Sibsagar	5.7	6.4	6.8	8.62
Lakhimpur	10.7	10.7	13.4	16.13
United Mikir & N.C. Hills	66.0	75.6	57.7	54.15
Cachar	0.6	1.0	0.9	0.75
Assam	10.0	10.8	11.0	12.82

Source: Computed from relevant census reports.

APPENDIX 17.III: CONCENTRATION OF TRIBAL POPULATION IN DIFFERENT DISTRICTS OF ASSAM IN 1951 TO 1991

District	Location		Quotient	
	1951	1961	1971	1991
Goalpara	1.53	1.37	1.26	1.34
Kamrup	1.15	1.00	0.95	0.89
Darrang	0.97	1.01	0.97	1.08
Nowgong	0.77	0.67	0.68	0.52
Sibsagar	0.56	0.59	0.62	0.67
Lakhimpur	1.07	0.99	1.23	1.26
United Mikir & N.C. Hills	6.57	7.03	5.25	4.22
Cachar	0.06	0.01	0.08	0.06

Source: Computed from relevant census reports.

SECTION VI

TRADE AND INDUSTRIALIZATION IN THE NORTH-EAST

THE WAY AHEAD

What then is the way ahead? Depressingly, there is no obvious or easy way ahead. While many have advocated trade as a means of industrial growth based on the results of trade-based growth models, such solutions leave many questions unanswered.

Looking at India's overall trade and macro-economic policy and its regional implications M. Agarwal and L. Berlage argue that if liberalization is to reduce regional inequalities then the public sector has to undertake a major role in upgrading physical, infrastructure and human capital. They opine that as of now most states have not realized the potential unlocked by liberalization and indeed a laissez-faire policy may even see resources flowing out of poor states to the rich.

As Alokesh Barua points out, one of the prerequisites of such models is political stability—a factor conspicuous by its absence in the northeast. Secondly, he points out to the infrastructural requirements such strategies assume, namely transport, power and an efficient financial sector. More importantly, he points out that trade is not new to the north-east; indeed much of India's trade at one time came from this region with little or no benefit accruing to the region due to the enclave nature of this trade. Thus, it is not enough to call for trade; there are certain parameters to be satisfied. This trade to be of benefit to the region, must have linkages with the rest of the economy and must absorb local labour. Barua advocates pushing furniture manufacture, food processing and livestock rearing (as there are supply side advantages in these areas) and advocates opening trade with Bangladesh, Burma, South-East Asia and south-west China as a means to ensure a market for such goods.

H. Goswami and J.K. Gogoi are less than optimistic about the impact of opening of markets in neighbouring countries by the formation of SAFTA or through bilateral measures, as in the case of Myanmar. They claim that the existing trade with Bangladesh, which is substantially contraband and consists of items smuggled through Assam will now be imported directly through West Bengal as concealment will be unnecessary. Where trade with Myanmar is concerned, it is Manipur that will benefit.

It is then clear that simple fables simply told are not likely to yield appropriate policies for the development for the north-east and may even lead to its further impoverishment.

CHAPTER 18

Trade Policy in India, Growth and Regional Development

MANMOHAN AGARWAL AND
LODEWIJK BERLAGE

I. INTRODUCTION

Trade Policy has always been considered an important component of a country's development strategy. During the past half a century however, there has been a sea change in mainstream thinking on trade policies. Fifty years ago there was consensus among economists and policy makers that an appropriate trade policy for industrializing countries was one which protected infant industries. Today the consensus is in favour of an export-oriented trade policy. This paper discusses why a protectionist trade policy, often called the policy of Import Substituting Industrialization (ISI) was adopted and how it fell out of favour. We also elaborate on the current views of what is an appropriate trade policy. We then discuss changes in trade policies in East Asia and in India in the light of changing views on what should be an appropriate trade policy. In addition, we analyse the effect of liberalization on regional development.

II. CHOICE OF AN APPROPRIATE TRADE POLICY

Why Industrialization

Economists trying to devise a strategy for development at the end of the Second World War had to take into account the dependence of almost all developing countries on exports of primary products. Prebisch, among others, argued that expansion of primary production and exports would not lead to development.[1] Expansion of export volumes would lead to a decline in the terms of trade. As a result export earnings would increase rather slowly and even fall as price elasticities of demand for primary commodities were supposed to be low. At the same time imports of capital goods would have to increase rapidly to raise the growth of GDP per capital. Indeed, it was generally accepted that developing countries did not have the capacity to produce many capital goods. Rapid growth in imports while exports stagnated would result in balance of payment (BOP) deficits that would force a cutback in investment plans and slow down growth. Since development could not be based on growth of primary production and exports, development required a policy of industrialization.

Why Import Substituting Industrialization

Industrialization based on the production of import substitutes for domestic markets rather than producing for exports was recommended. Such ISI would tackle many of the constraints to faster growth. Nurkse had argued that one of the factors limiting investment in developing countries was lack of demand.[2] But if the supply on domestic markets was reserved for domestic producers by keeping out imports, entrepreneurs would be sure that demand existed and so could be depended upon to invest in import substituting industries. Also, economists were in general pessimistic about the prospects for the world economy. Extrapolating from the experience of the pre-Second World War years, they expected the world economy to grow very slowly, with a bias towards stagnation.[3] Economists also expected the pre-Second World War pattern of trade policy, namely countries adopting extensive restrictions on trade, to continue. More specifically, they expected that exports of labour-intensive goods from developing countries would face significant barriers in industrialized countries which they would not be able to overcome. Furthermore, it was believed that in order to set up new industries developing countries would need to adopt protectionist policies. Only in this way would such sectors be able to develop a skilled and productive labour force that would enable them to become competitive in the world market. All these reasons led many economists to recommend the adoption of an ISI strategy for development.

Appropriate Tools for Implementing
an ISI Strategy

The main issue in the choice of appropriate tools for implementing an ISI strategy was how far to depend on price signals, i.e. whether to use import duties or to use import duties. Countries tended to adopt quantitative restrictions (QR) to curtail imports. This was because QRs were believed to provide more certain signals to prospective investors in the protected industries than tariffs. The impact of tariff protection was uncertain as foreign exporters might retaliate by lowering their prices. The choice between price signals and QRs depended in part on the relative importance of the private and public sectors.

Most countries started ISI policies by adopting an import substitution strategy in consumer goods industries. Here it was believed that restricting of imports would lead the transnational corporations (TNC) who were supplying the imported goods to undertake the production of similar goods in the developing country itself. Such investment by the TNC would also contribute to solve the problems of lack of investment funds and of the acquisition of new technologies.

ISI policies were often strengthened by negative shocks in world markets, e.g. a sudden fall in the price of important export goods. Countries experiencing such shocks would often be reluctant to devalue. They would instead react to the excess demand for foreign exchange by adopting a regime of more or less generalized import licences. Such licences became an additional instrument to keep out imports and supported ISI policies.

III. INDIAN TRADE POLICY IN THE FIRST THREE PLANS

At the time of Independence Indian exports were heavily concentrated both in terms of commodities and geographically. Three primary goods, cotton, jute and tea, accounted for almost 70 per cent of India's exports and in all of these goods India was a significant exporter so that further increase in its share of world exports would be difficult. Almost 60 per cent of the exports went to the UK. Furthermore, there was very limited development of manufactures in the country. In these circumstances it was believed that it would be difficult to increase exports, both of primary and manufactured goods. It was believed that planning could lay the basis for the growth of new manufacturing industries producing for the domestic market. In the longer run, these new industries could start exporting.

In contrast to most other countries, India started its import substitution in capital goods industries. This was because its growth strategy was based on the Mahalanobis growth Model, which showed that investment in the basic goods-industries would lead to a higher rate of growth.[4] This industrialization was implemented under the aegis of the state. Such state-sponsored industrialization raised issues of generating sufficient investment funds as well as acquiring the technology necessary for establishing new plants producing capital goods.

In the First Plan and the initial years of the Second Plan the Government depended on its accumulated foreign exchange reserves, the Sterling Balances, to pay for the higher imports of capital goods and also to finance the increased public investment. But the foreign exchange reserves were depleted by the middle of the Second Plan, precipitating a BOP crisis. From this period till the end of the Third Plan the Government depended on foreign aid, mainly from the US and the World Bank to finance its investment and the resulting BOP deficit. Foreign aid during the Second and Third Plans was about 3 per cent of the GDP and financed about 25 per cent of India's investment and a third of public investment. The Government also put into place a stringent QR regime in order to match imports with the available amount of foreign exchange. Imports of only those goods that were considered essential and were not produced at home were allowed.[5]

The large BOP deficits were not sustainable and in the Third Plan the Government made policy changes to increase exports and reduce the BOP deficit. The main instrument to promote exports were export subsidies. There were many different rates of subsidies. Also the number of rates for levying import duties were increased. The QR regime was very complex. All these measures resulted in a non-transparent system of incentives. It was not clear to potential investors in which sectors to invest. Furthermore, in the final years of the Third Plan as drought resulted in a large increase in food imports and a decline in agriculture-based exports BOP situation worsened Pressure from the US and the World Bank forced the Government to devalue the rupee, and to consolidate and simplify the trade regime in order to improve its administration and to provide clearer signals to investors.

Reforms in the Indian trade regime were part of a broader move towards restructuring trade policies which was observed in many developing countries as most of them faced BOP difficulties. In the next section we discuss this move in East Asia.

TRADE POLICY IN EAST ASIA

In the 1950s and 1960s, most developing countries adopted ISI policies. But after a few years' experience, countries started adapting their policies to better meet the specific problems their economies were facing. The first countries to move away from pure ISI policies were the East Asian economies. Some of them such as Taiwan and Malaysia used their comparative advantage in agricultural products to increase export earnings. These countries were able to do this partly because other countries sought to diversify away from primary exports and neglected such exports. The higher export earnings of Taiwan and Malaysia were partly at the expense of other primary exporting countries, mainly from Africa. Such export earnings provided the resources for investment in industries. Of course, Malaysia followed the route to industrial investment somewhat later than Taiwan.[6] Korea, on the other hand from the beginning of the 1960s when it started changing its trade policy focused on industries that would produce for export markets in the short run. It provided protection for new industries by restricting imports and channeling cheap credit, but on condition that these industries would sell a growing share of their output on world markets.[7] So by the mid-1960s some East Asian economies had started to move away from pure ISI policies to a more balanced policy posture providing protection for new industries but at the same time encouraging or forcing them to export.

There was also a move among some Latin American countries to place greater emphasis on export performance. Brazil and Colombia adopted a variable exchange rate system under which the exchange rate was adjusted frequently in order to maintain the competitiveness of exports. With the adoption of such an exchange rate policy, exports from these countries grew more rapidly than they probably would have done otherwise.

During the 1960s and the 1970s of the past century, the world economy was growing very rapidly and countries that adjusted their trade regime to place greater emphasis on exports were able to successfully increase their exports and raise their growth rate.

V. INDIAN TRADE POLICY: MID-1960s AND THE EARLY-1970s

Due to the drought, Indian policy makers realized that a change in agricultural policy was needed. The changes ushered in the Green Revolution. While there was some pressure from the US and the World Bank to change agricultural policies there was also a recognition in India that changes in agricultural policies were needed.

As noted in Section III there was pressure from the US and the World Bank on India to change trade polices and to allow the exchange rate to play a more prominent role. Under pressure the Indian Government in 1966 did simplify and consolidate many of the subsidies and tariffs applied to trade and substantially devalued the rupee. The entire devaluation episode is shrouded in mystery.[8] Analysis of the comments of various actors in the drama suggests that the devaluation and the clean up of controls and other trade measures was undertaken in the expectation that greater aid would be forthcoming to meet the expected deficit after trade liberalization. When the increased aid did not materialize the Government was forced to again tighten import controls. This resulted in a withdrawal of aid by the US and the World Bank, precipitating a BOP crisis in 1966 and the need for the Government to adopt what would later be called structural adjustment measures. The drought restricted agricultural supplies and so prevented a large export response as the major export industries depended on the agricultural sector for inputs. This, together with the adjustment measures initiated by the Government, which resulted in a recession, meant that trade reforms were stillborn and did not lead to the kind of reorientation that occurred in some East Asian and Latin American countries.

So in a way, the aborted reform resulted in an intensification of the import substitution policy. The severe foreign exchange shortage resulted in an intensification of the restrictive import regime. At the same time to mop up the profits that importers could make in an era of shortages of imported goods, import duties were raised to transfer these excess profits from the private to the public sector.

The Government also undertook a number of steps to raise both private and public savings and to get greater control over the allocation of savings. Bank nationalization should be viewed in this light. The rapid expansion of the branch network seems to have raised the savings rate and a larger share of savings started flowing through the banking system. The Government also tried to use the banking system to control the allocation of credit to meet its economic and social goals as had been done in most of the East Asian economies.

But as a result of the steep increase in the price of oil in 1973–4 the Indian economy was hit by another BOP crisis. Again the Indian Government adopted a policy mix of foreign financing of the excess demand for foreign exchange and of macroeconomic adjustment. India borrowed from the various facilities set up at the IMF to finance the larger deficit resulting from the oil price increase. It also adopted very contractionary fiscal and monetary policies to curtail demand and in this way to reduce imports and manage the BOP. But this was only the short run side of the policies. For the longer run it did not change its ISI policy, but rather extended it to the oil sector. It raised its investment into oil exploration and oil refining to reduce its dependence on imported oil. It also nationalized the foreign oil companies in order to ensure that decisions and actions in this crucial sector accorded with national priorities.

VI. DEVELOPMENTS IN TRADE POLICY

From the mid-1960s onward, there was extensive research from the mid-1960s on the impact of trade policy on economic performance. This research consisted both of cross-country regressions on large samples of countries to test for a relationship between export performance and growth as well as in-depth country studies.

The main conclusions of this research were that ISI policies resulted in substantial inefficiencies that had a detrimental effect on economic performance. The regression analysis showed that export performance was positively related to growth. Export performance was measured either by the growth in exports, or share of exports in GDP, or change in share of exports in GDP.[9] Though a number of shortcomings of these studies were pointed out the overall impression that resulted was that restrictive trade polices had a deleterious effect on growth.[10] The main shortcoming of the cross country analysis was that whereas its purpose was to establish the effect of trade policy on growth, export performance rather than a trade policy indicator was used as the explanatory variable in the empirical studies. But exports could be the result of other factors apart from trade policy. Also exports could be the result as well as the cause of economic growth. In later work various indicators of trade policy were used in order to study the effect of trade policy on growth. The results depended on choice of indicators, time periods, and estimation methods, and so could not establish a persuasive link.

The detailed country studies also showed that countries which followed an export-oriented trade policy performed better than countries which followed ISI policies. Also, countries did better in periods when they adopted more liberal policies than when they adopted more restrictive policies.[11] This research together with the severe debt crisis in many developing countries in the 1980s, and the world-wide move towards market-oriented policies starting in the late-1970s in the developed countries resulted in a growing number of developing countries adopting export-oriented policies. Currently, hardly any developing country has recourse to extensive QRs, either because of BOP problems or to speed development. There has also been a very substantial reduction in tariff rates in developing countries. Currently, many Latin American and transition economies of Europe have average tariff rates of about 10 per cent. Rates in East and especially South Asia are higher.

Trade policy in India did not take the same path as in East Asia and Latin America. India maintained its import substitution policy. However, there were two significant changes in the Indian policy framework in the late 1970s and 1980s. Firstly, there was some liberalization of imports. Secondly, Government investment was shifted towards the agricultural and oil sectors leading to the neglect of many infrastructure investments and an increasing dependence on the private sector for investment in manufacturing. Indian policy makers pegged the exchange rate of the rupee to a basket of currencies. The net effect of this was a real devaluation of the rupee. For the first time since Independence India's share in the imports of most regions increased. Coupled with higher remittances as Indian labour went to work in the Middle Eastern countries, which wee experiencing an oil revenue financed boom, India ran a BOP surplus for a few years in the middle of the 1970s and accumulated a substantial foreign exchange reserve. It did not reduce the overall protectiveness of its trade regime, but introduced change in a more piecemeal fashion.

Capacity utilization was very low. This was believed to be one of the consequences of the stringent exchange control regime put in place after the cut back in aid, which had resulted in a tremendous shortage of intermediate goods and components. To raise capacity utilization, the government liberalized the import of intermediate goods and of components. However, there was no overall liberalization. Tariff rates were periodically raised to mop up the excess profits earned because of the stringent import control regime.

Even though there was no overall trade liberalization, there was a growing realization that import control were counter-productive in the long run. Consequently, when the country faced a BOP crisis in the early 1980s because of higher oil prices there was no attempt to further increase the restrictiveness of the import control regime. This was a change from the reaction in previous BOP crises.

Another change in policy making was the management of the exchange rate. In the mid-1970s the exchange rate had been allowed to depreciate and this seemed to have had a favourable effect on export performance. After the BOP crisis of the early 1980s, the real exchange rate was kept constant through periodic adjustments. However, the BOP situation did not improve in the first half of the 1980s as exports remained relatively stagnant. During the second half of the 1980s Indian policy makers followed a more aggressive exchange rate policy and the real exchange rate was allowed to depreciate. This resulted in a better export performance, though not dramatically so.

Starting in the early 1980s, a number of adjustments in the trade regime, and more importantly in the internal regime for capacity expansion were undertaken. Consequently, even though export performance did not improve dramatically, there was an acceleration in the rate of growth of the economy. Whereas GDP had grown at under 2 per cent a year between 1966 and 1973, so that per capita income had declined, in the rest of the 1970s the growth of GDP had been about 4.5 per cent, in the first half of the 1980s over 5 per cent, and in the latter half of the 1980s nearly 6 per cent.

The 1990s have seen a fundamental change in India's trade policies. This change has been precipitated by a number of factors. Despite rapid growth the economy remained fragile and vulnerable. The Middle East crisis of 1990–1 coupled with domestic political instability shook the confidence of foreign lenders, and India faced a very severe BOP crisis. The response to this crisis was very different from that to previous crises. Whereas previous crises had resulted in some changes, the basic policy framework of ISI behind very protective walls had been maintained.

The 1991 crisis, combined with an increasing belief that the former protectionist policies were not appropriate and were responsible for India's relatively poor performance compared to the East and South-East Asian economies, and even more compared to China's economy, resulted in a fundamental shift in trade policies. The Chinese example was very pertinent. In the past when faced with the experience of the East Asian countries many Indian policy makers and analysts had argued that these were small countries and India could not follow a similar policy. The Chinese example revealed the weakness of the argument. Also, rapid growth in China put pressure on Indian policy makers to achieve a higher growth rate for strategic reasons and to maintain Indian influence in the world. It is ironic that a need to accelerate growth was felt when the economy was actually performing well. The crisis provided an opportunity to reform the trade regime.

There was also international pressure in the 1990s. The Indian trade regime was one of the most protectionist, much more so than that of other developing countries. There was, therefore, pressure during the multilateral trade negotiations, known as the Uruguay Round, for India to reduce its tariffs. The international pressure can be seen most clearly in the case of the elimination of QRs. Even after the start of the liberalization process and some pruning, India had, at the end of the 1990s, QRs on some 3,000 tariff lines for manufactures. There was a demand for the elimination of these QRs. The Indian Government argued for being allowed to eliminate them over a period of seven years.

The EU, after negotiations, agreed for a six-year period for the elimination of the QRs. But the US did not agree and took the matter to the WTO Dispute Settlement Board which asked India to get rid of them in less than two years. India lost the appeal and so had to get rid of them much earlier than it had wanted to. While the other developing countries did not figure overtly in the dispute, most of them had already got rid of their QRs either as part of the agreement that allowed them to become members of the GATT/WTO or as part of Bank-Fund structural adjustment programmes. They saw no reason why India should be allowed to maintain QRs. An interesting aspect of the elimination of the QRs has been that the widespread fear that this would lead to considerable industrial distress has not occurred. One can draw the conclusion that Indian industry did not need this protection, and that at best it allowed Indian companies to earn super normal profits.

While the Indian Government eliminated QRs on manufactures only as a result of defeat at the Dispute Settlement Board of the WTO, it started on its own the process of reducing tariffs. Tariffs before 1991 reached a maximum of almost 400 per cent and the average was about 100 per cent. This was in comparison to average tariffs of about 6 per cent in the developed countries and of about 10–15 per cent in most developing and transition countries. In 1992 India sharply reduced its tariffs and then later, as part of its offer in the Uruguay Round (UR) agreement signed at Marrakesh, it reduced the maximum of most tariffs to about 35 per cent. Today the average tariff is about 20 per cent.

QRs on agriculture had been eliminated much earlier as part of the UR agreement which required the elimination of all QRs and their replacement by equivalent tariffs. The agreement then called for a 24 per cent reduction in tariffs by developing countries. There will be further cuts in tariffs as part of the new round of multilateral talks, the Doha Round. Also, Yashwant Sinha the former finance minister declared that Indian tariff levels should be reduced to the levels in ASEAN countries in a few years. So we can expect further reductions in tariffs.

As tariffs and QRs are now no longer being used to manage the BOP, the Government is depending on the exchange rate for this purpose. There was a sharp depreciation of the rupee in 1991 itself. Later there has been steady devaluation of the rupee over the year – it is only in 2004 that there has been some revaluation of the rupee t *vis-à-vis* the dollar. But this reflects more the weakness of the dollar than the strength of the rupee. The policy shift seems to have been very successful. During almost the entire period since Independence, India had run a deficit. Indian export performance had also been very poor. India's share in world exports, which had been about 2 per cent at the time of Independence, had declined to 0.4 per cent by the end of the 1970s. It had then stabilized in the 1980s at this low level. After the change in policies it has increased somewhat and is now 0.6–0.7 per cent. Furthermore, India has been running a BOP surplus and has been accumulating foreign exchange reserves which by the middle of 2003 were about $80 billion, an unprecedented level of reserves.

So Indian trade policy today is much more in consonance with that adopted by most other countries – a low level of tariff and a limited number of tariff bands; elimination of QRs.

VII. LIBERALIZATION AND REGIONAL DEVELOPMENT

Considerable fears have been expressed that liberalization would widen regional disparities. It is argued that under planning the Central Government could allocate its investments in favour of the less developed states and regions. But under a free market regime the poorer states would not be able to attract private capital, particularly private foreign capital with its technological advantages, because of their poor infrastructure, and so regional disparities would increase.

Analysis later in the book shows that if we rank the states by per capita income, there is no significant change during the era of planning – the richest states remained the richest and the poorest states remained the poorest (Agarwal and Basu).

Will liberalization increase regional disparities? It may be true that private investment will be attracted to states with good infrastructure. But there is no reason why liberalization should inhibit the upgrading of infrastructure in the poor states. After all, liberalization does not mean the total withdrawal of the public sector from all economic activity, but a specialization between the private and public sector with the public sector undertaking those tasks that the private sector either cannot or will not undertake. In fact, liberalization requires the public sector to play a strong role in creating an investment-friendly environment. Public investment could occur against the logic of profitability and so often results in loss making investments, whose ultimate contribution to the state's economy and even to the welfare of the poor was doubtful. Such investments cannot be afforded under a market-oriented regime, particularly one with severe fiscal constraints. The fiscal and market constraints on governments following inappropriate policies are welcomed by some analysts and feared by others. A liberal trading regime would bring more forcefully to the fore the question of governance. Poorly governed states would not be able to attract investments.

It is imperative, therefore, that if a state desires to grow faster and if interstate disparities are to be reduced, greater investment need to be made in a state's infrastructure, both human and physical. Furthermore, the state now has the option to attract private investments into these areas. Of course, governments must ensure that these services are not priced so expensively that the poor are frozen out of using these services. But ensuring investments in infrastructure is the minimum that a state should do; it can undertake additional actions to accelerate growth in an era of liberalization. This would mean structuring its investments in order to derive maximum benefits from the more liberal environment. For instance, it is very clear by now that there is great scope for providing business outsourcing services. States with a strong network of institutions training accountants could provide accounting services; others could provide billing and invoicing services. States with a large English-speaking population could provide services through call centres, or even set up centres to provide such speaking expertise.

Governments also have to plan for moving up the value-addition chain. Many of these services may only be viable as long as wages are low, and as soon as some development takes place raising wages, the state could lose its comparative advantage. So the government has to use the initial fillip provided by the supply of simple and cheap services to plan for a sustained growth pattern.

There is no evidence as yet that state government have realized this potential for growth unlocked by liberalization.

Suppose that government intervention is minimal, i.e. that it follows a laissez-faire policy. The consequences would depend on factor mobility. Neo-classical theory usually assumes that backward states would have a lower capital-labour ratio so that the return to capital would be higher in the poorer states and the return to labour lower in the poorer state. Therefore, investment would move from the richer to the poorer state and labour from the poorer to the richer state. In the long run this process would equalize factor returns. But there is another view that stresses agglomeration and cumulative growth processes. Existing growth poles may offer economies of scale. Provision of infrastructure is characterized by decreasing unit costs. Then capital does not move, or many even move to the growth poles. It is labour that mainly moves from the poorer state to the richer state. This process is usually very slow so that adjustment takes long. Furthermore, mobility may be limited in India because of differences in culture and in language between the states. So, in India factor movements, particularly labour movements would not act to reduce regional inequalities.

The above-mentioned analysis points to the need for active state involvement if inter regional inequalities are to be reduced. The market acting on its own will not help in reducing such inequalities. Government will have to act to improve the infrastructure, provide services of public utilities and public goods such as education. But in addition governments must channel investments into areas where they can take advantage of the opportunities opened by liberalization. Export markets should be explicitly factored into the state's decisions and policies.

NOTES

1. See Prebisch (1950, 1951, 1959). Also see Spraos (1980, 1983) for a thorough discussion of the issue of the terms of trade.
2. See Nurkse (1953) for a discussion of the implications of lack of demand for a development strategy.
3. See Nurkse (1959).
4. See Bhagwati and Chakravarty (1969) for a discussion of the strategy underlying the Second and Third Plans.
5. See Bhagwati and Desai (1970), and Bhagwati and Srinivasan (1975) for a discussion of India's trade policies.
6. See Wade (1990) for a discussion of Taiwan's development strategy.
7. See Amsden (1996).
8. See Lele and Agarwal (1991) for a discussion of the circumstances surrounding these policy changes and their effects.
9. For a review of these studies see Rodrik (1995).
10. For a discussion of these shortcomings, see Rodrik (2001), Agarwal and Berlage (2003).
11. See Bhagwati (1978).

REFERENCES

Agarwal, Manmohan, 'Trade and Development: A Review of the Issue', in Dipak Banerji, ed., *Essays in Economic Analysis and Policy*, Delhi: Oxford University Press, 1991.

Agarwal, Manmohan and Lodewijk Berlage, 'Trade and Development: Changing Paradigms' (mimeo), 2003.

Amsden, A.H., 'Asia's Next Giant: South Korea and Late Industrialization', Washington: Economic Policy Institute, 1996.

Bhagwati, J.N., *Anatomy and Consequences of Exchange Control Regimes*, Cambridge: Ballinger Publishing Company, 1978.

Bhagwati, J.N. and S. Chakravarty, 'Contributions to Indian Economic Analysis', *American Economic Review*, 59, Supplement V, 1969.

Bhagwati, J.N. and P. Desai, *India: Planning for Industrialization and Trade Policies Since 1951*, New York: Oxford University Press, 1970.

Bhagwati, J.N. and T.N. Srinivasan, *India: Anatomy and Consequences of Exchange Control Regimes* (for NBER), New York: Columbia University Press, 1975.

Lele, U. and Manmohan Agarwal, 'Four Decades of Economic Development in India and the Role of External Assistance', in U. Lele and I. Nabi, eds., *Transitions in Development: The Role of Aid and Commercial Flows*, San Francisco: International Centre for Economic Growth, 1991.

Nurkse, R., *Problems of Capital Formation in Less Developed Countires*, Oxford: Blackwell, 1953.

——, 'Patterns of Trade and Development', *Wicksell Lectures*, Stockholm: Almqvist and Wiksell, 1959.

Prebisch, R., 'The Economic Development of Latin American and Its Principal Problems', Santiago: Economic Commission for Latin America, United Nations, 1950.

——, 'The Spread of Technical Progress and the Terms of Trade', *UN Economic Survey of Latin America 1949*, New York: United Nations, 1951.

Rodrik, D., 'Trade and Industrial Policy Reform', in *Handbook of Development Economics*, vol. 3B, pp. 2925–82.

Rodrik, D. and F. Rodriguez, 'Trade Policy and Economic Growth: A Skeptic's Guide to the Cross-National Evidence', in B. Bernanke and K.S. Rogoff, eds., *NBER Macro-economics Annual 2000*, 2001.

Spraos, J., 'The Statistical Debate on the Net Barter Terms of Trade Between Primary Products and Manufactures', *Economic Journal*, vol. 90, 1980.

Wade, R.C., 'The Role of Government in East Asian Industrialization, Princeton: Princeton University Press, 1990.

CHAPTER 19

History, Trade and Development: An Exploration of the North-East Economy

ALOKESH BARUA

INTRODUCTION

The north-east region has remained industrially and economically backward for decades despite its rich and abundant natural resource endowment. This is, however, not something unique about the north-east. There are many examples in history characterizing similar situation. As Arthur Lewis (1978) put it, the Industrial Revolution in Britain provided an opportunity for growth to all countries at the end of the eighteenth century; but only a few countries succeeded while many others failed to respond to such opportunities.[1] Lewis had given some interesting explanations for this. This paper seeks to examine why Assam (north-east was yet to born then!) failed to respond positively to the opportunities for growth unfolded by the forces of colonialism since the mid-nineteenth century. The region has been exposed to a massive scale of investment in plantation and infrastructure amounting to nearly 20 per cent of the national income of the region.[2] India's exports in tea were experiencing a spectacular 10 per cent cumulative annual rate of growth over the period 1901 to 1958. Assam's contribution to India's exports of tea was nearly 90 per cent.[3] Why then such a massive scale of investment and trade could not play the role of an engine of growth for the region? An answer to this question will help us clarify several misgivings or misperceptions about the view popularized by various Central Government agencies that trade is the ultimate path of salvation for the north-east.[4] The pertinent issue is how to actualize the potentialities for trade in order to generate a process of industrialization in the region, which in turn could provide the region a possible way out of the present mess in the economy.

THE NORTH-EAST ECONOMY AT A GLANCE

In a recent study Barua and Bandopadhyay[5] observed that during the last two decades the north-east region has been growing but at a very slow pace.[6] The most disturbing factor, however, is not the slow growth as much as the declining share of the manufacturing sector in GDP overtime.[7] Given that the share of the manufacturing as such very low – for some states like Mizoram it is as low as 2 per cent – the falling share is worrisome for many reasons. First of all, it is against the historical pattern of development that the manufacturing sector plays a vital role in economic development (Chenery, et al., 1988[8]). The study by Barua and Bandopadhyay also conclusively demonstrates by estimating the pooled cross-section and time series data across Indian states that the growth in income is positively and highly significantly related to the levels of manufacturing output. So, we may say that the slow pace of growth in income in the north-east is partly due to the sluggish growth of the manufacturing sector.[9] Secondly, as the land–man ratio is not favourable to many of the north-east states for agricultural development, these states should look upon the manufacturing sector for providing employment. Given the fact that the region experiences the highest rate of population growth in India,[10] maximization of employment should be the most important issue concerning the policy makers. Low growth in output has resulted in a very high proportion of unemployment in the region.[11] A very high rate of unemployment would obviously cause discontentment in any society against the prevailing form of social order. And once the intensity of such discontentment reaches the critical limit of tolerance, mass unrests and chaos are bound to follow. This is precisely what has happened in the north-east. The long and continuing political unrest and insurgencies in various north-east states have concerned policy makers that the root cause of the malice is the slow pace of economic development. The solution to the problem thus is perceived in terms of rapid industrialization of the region. And it is against this background that the idea of trade-oriented strategy of development has been conceived of. The high-level commission report[12] recommends establishing special economic zones with all necessary infrastructures at suitable locations in the north-east to attract export industries.[13]

WHY TRADE?

D.H. Robertson epitomized the role of trade in development by his famous statement that 'trade is an engine of growth'. The importance of trade can be explained in terms of the standard (i) vent for surplus and (ii) the market size models. The vent for surplus model stresses the fact that the region failed to maximize the rents it could have earned from the use of its natural resources due to lack of demand within the economy. As a consequence, the region, rather than being on the production possibility schedule is trapped inside. Export opportunities in such a situation enable the region to move towards the production frontier and thereby lead to increase in income and savings. This increase in income in turn is expected to generate a growth process. Caves gives many examples of economic growth from the export of surpluses.

The second model is derived from the well-known Smithian dictum that the division of labour is limited by the size of the market. A large market would allow firms to produce in a large quantity, which would then enable them to reduce the average cost of production. Trade with the outside world is thus expected to provide an opportunity to (i) reap scale economies in production, (ii) generate externalities that would provide scope for the growth of ancillary manufacturing activities and (iii) adopt new and advanced technology. The rapid growth in industrialization will increase productivity via realization of dynamic economies of scale. Dynamic economies refer to increasing returns brought about by 'induced' technical progress, learning by doing, external economies in production and so on. Manufacturing seems to be the sector where major cost-saving technical advances take place. Scope for industrialization can be enhanced if the region can overcome the limitations of the domestic market and one possible way to do this is trade. This is the reason why policy-oriented economists often suggest for trade-based industrialization.

MARKET SIZE AND GROWTH: EMPIRICAL EVIDENCE

There are many country and cross-country studies supporting the role of the market size on the growth of manufacturing. The study by Barna and Bandopadhyay mentioned above has also observed from pooled time series and cross-state data from the Indian economy that the size of the market positively and significantly determines the levels of manufacturing output. A large manufacturing sector provides the scope for realizing various external and internal economies through forward and backward linkages. Such economies in turn determine the competitiveness of the region for exporting and export opportunities provide the necessary impetus and the momentum for growth. Most of the states in the north-east suffer from a serious constraint of market size for many products. Even the region as a whole does not provide sufficient scale to profitably set up many industries. Exporting is a possible way to overcome the limitation of domestic market size but poor infrastructure and communication operate as stumbling blocks for any consideration to set up industry in the region. Besides, there is dearth of local risk-bearing capital and an entrepreneurial class. Capital from outside shy away due to lack of sufficient inducement to invest in the region. While poor communication and infrastructure reduces the inducement to invest, lack of good governance, work ethics and growing insurgencies of various forms have negative impact on such inducement. As a result, the region is caught in the vicious circle of poverty – poor because of low investment and low investment because of all the factors mentioned above.

THE MISSING LINKS

The theoretical arguments put forward for trade as a strategy of industrialization is absolutely valid. But there are a number of missing links. Are the local entrepreneurs, if any, not able to perceive this possibility? Why is profit-seeking private capital from other regions not flowing into the north-east to exploit this advantage? Was it that the region was never exposed to trading opportunities in the past? If yes, then why has the region failed to respond to such opportunities? Does the strategy imply not a single but a series of strategies such that it would require a sequencing of the implementation of the strategies? Who and how would then one decide the products in which export opportunities are viable? Should we depend on markets to give the signals or if markets do not exist then who should create such markets? These questions should be answered before one can legitimately suggest that a trade-oriented strategy will work for industrializing the region.

Possibly, the efficacy of the policy will depend on sequencing of the strategies into a number of stages or phases and all such stages may or may not be simultaneously implemented. They may have to follow certain logical order. The most crucial factor on which the success of the strategy would depend is political stability in the region as a whole. Political stability, however, cannot be attained by using police or military force but by involving the vast majority of people to see the rationale in the strategy and to politically support for the implementation of such a strategy. The enlightened middle class may have to play a crucial role in educating the people about the question of growth and development. How to achieve this end is beyond the scope of this paper but it should be remembered that political stability is the *sine qua non* to a successful trade-oriented strategy of industrialization.

But political stability alone is not enough without good governance and presence of dynamic and visionary political leadership. A dynamic leader will not only be in a position to create awareness and enthusiasm among the people for participating in the development process but may also attract foreign (meaning outside the region, not necessarily outside the country) capital to the region by ensuring adequate safety and security to life and property of the foreign investors. Since such a dynamic leadership cannot be created overnight, the Central Government has to play an important role through the national planning process. It can help inducing foreign private capital investment in the region. These inducements should not be merely in the form of giving tax holidays or other concessions to the investors. Such polices are bound to be counterproductive if the profitability within the region is very low because of other factors such as insurgency, power crisis, transport bottlenecks and inadequate supply of critical inputs. It was observed how such ad hoc policies have increased corruption rather than increasing industrial output in the region.

As argued elsewhere, most of the states in the region would not be in a position to initiate an industrialization process individually because each state has to depend on others in many important ways.

For example, except for Assam no other state has independent transport networking with the rest of India. So transport network must be improved among these states in its many dimensions. Massive expansion both in vertical and horizontal directions of roads and railways should be made available to all the states in the region. Fast moving multi-line highway tracks should be introduced among the major metropolis of various states. A place such as Guwahati should be a nodal point providing transport connections in air, railway and highways to all the states. And fast moving trains between the major metropolis of the country to the regional nodal point should be made available, which would require not only investment in upgrading railway tracks but also a little less Central hegemony in deciding about train routes. There is no reason why the Delhi-Guwahati Rajdhani Express should have a longer route to please some constituency in Bihar or UP! The traffic and passengers from the north-east should receive some preferential treatment as regards space reservation in trains. Perhaps all the small states in the north-east should collectively fight for such a cause through parliamentary democracy. The political parties should leave aside their ideological differences to raise a common voice for the developmental issues of the region.

Apart from transport and communication, there should be elastic supply of power without which no development process cannot be sustained for long. There has been remarkable development in the region in terms of connecting even remote villages through power and telecommunication networks of the country. But the region suffers from serious supply constraint as regards the power input, while it has enormous scope for hydroelectric power generation. The region has no irrigation project worth mentioning but it suffers heavily from floods, which disrupt all economic activities during the rainy season. A major power-cum-irrigation project can solve this problem, which of course will require huge investment. The Central Government must invest in such activities. Thus, public investment in infrastructure and communication development and in power generating projects should sequentially come earlier than any tall talk on trade-oriented development strategy.

Finally, another important issue that has not been touched upon so far is the creation of financial institutions that can provide necessary capital to entrepreneurs for business. The region suffers from an adequate credit supply facility for business and industrial development. The industrial loan given by the state under various schemes eventually ended up in consumption loans and such loans were also not easily recoverable. Uncertainty about recovery and any returns from such loans act as a major disincentive for the banks to initiate any credit facility to help an entrepreneur without proper collaterals. This is a difficult problem to tackle but it is also true that without efficient financial markets for credits no industrial development could be possible. There cannot be a readymade solution to the problems described above. The thrust of this paper, however, is that before talking about a trade-oriented strategy of industrialization for the north-east region all the issues mentioned above should be adequately addressed. Otherwise, the strategy will be a futile exercise.

LESSONS FROM HISTORY

Historically, Assam has always been highly exposed to international trade. There is now enough evidence to the fact that Assam had intensive trading relationships with China and the far eastern countries. The so-called silk route bears with that fact. As H.P. Ray (in this volume) argues that by the seventh century Assam's silk industry had reached the pinnacle of perfection. Mughals' repeated attempts to conquer this region was guided by the sole interest to look eastward for growth in trade and the expansion of the empire. The entry of the British in the early nineteenth century and the discovery of tea changed the course of history. The British looked westward rather than eastward because booming market for tea was in the west where it had to compete with the Chinese tea. Trade thus is not a new idea for the region. The policy-oriented economists who favoured a trade-oriented strategy of industrialization for the north-east have unfortunately little, if at all any, knowledge about the historical role that international trade has played in this region. However, the change in the attitudinal approach from westward to eastward for trade expansion and development needs to be recognized. Once again, we are trying to re-discover the lost silk route to China through the north-east for growth and development of the Indian economy.

Forces of free trade determined significantly the destiny of the economy of Assam during the middle of the nineteenth century. A sizeable share of India's exports[14] had been coming from the exports of tea in which Assam had been enjoying a monopoly position in India. The investments associated with tea and the ancillary industries such as coal, petroleum and saw mills and also infrastructure activities such as railways, roads, telecommunications and steamer services were quite substantial as it were valued at approximately 20 per cent of the prevailing national income (Guha, 1968). The total investment in the organized sector of the economy of Assam, according to Guha (1968) was approximately Rs 200 million during the period of 1881–1901. This was indeed a substantial amount of investment as the population increased from 1.8 million in 1881 to only 2.2 million in 1901. Why then did such large investments and trade so favourable to growth not help the region take-off on a sustained growth path? One must answer this question before venturing into giving any prescription that trade is essential for industrialization of the region.

The sole interest of the East India Company[15] to annex the region in 1826[16] was to exploit the rich natural resources of the region. Whatever little development it had contributed to in terms of improving the infrastructure facilities was the unintended fall back upon the region in the process of maximization of British interest. The major inducement to invest in Assam came from the highly profitable trade in tea in the world market. The booming opportunities of tea exports had given rise to the development of various ancillary industries. The construction of railway was initiated primarily to link the remote tea gardens to the transit points to the steamer services and thus the railway lines passed through deep and thick jungles rather than places of human habitation. Coal mining was carried out in response to the steady demand for coal from steamers and tea factories. Similarly, British investment in roads and telecommunication were also to serve administrative and mercantile interests. The installation of saw-mills was to facilitate the production of tea chests. Thus, the export of tea was the centripetal force to attract huge investment in those ancillary industries.

THE CAUSES OF ASSAMESE FAILURE

The Assamese economy failed to respond to the opportunities for development unfolded by the forces of trade due to several reasons. For a better understanding of the reasons for the failure, some preliminary knowledge of the pattern of resource allocation in Assam prior to the advent of the British may be relevant. For nearly six centuries the Ahom dynasty ruled in Assam uninterruptedly.[17] The Ahom king, by virtue of being the ruler, was the sole owner of all land[18] and the distribution of land among the people was based on trading in services in kind. To be precise, the entire male population was divided into *khels*, or guilds according to their respective occupation and each *khel* was divided into units (*gots*) consisting of four persons, each called a *pike*. Every *pike* was bound to serve the state either as a private or public servant for one-third of the year or to supply a certain quantity of his produce in lieu of the service. He was entitled in return to have 2 *puras* (1 *pura* is equivalent to a little over an acre) of *rupit* (arable) land apart from land for his house and garden. The *Borahs*, *Saikias* and *Hazarikas* supervised the *pikes* under the command of higher officials, civil and military, like the *Baruas*, *Rajkhowas* and *Phukans*. These officials were remunerated with *pikes* apart from rent-free grants. They could also occupy free of rent *khats* or wastelands where they employed their attendants and slaves. Large amount of arable land were also assigned rent-free or *lakhiraj* for the maintenance of temples and priests and the *satras*, the Vaishnava monasteries. Thus, revenue of the state was realized in personal service and produce. This highly inefficient system of resource management was one of the major reasons for the eventual decline of the Ahom empire.[19] The inefficient Ahom administration and the economic system that they installed in Assam which was essentially barter system acted against the rise of market economy. The existence of a market system is an essential pre-requisite to reap the advantages of trade and exchange.

The entry of the East India Company in the political scene of Assam resulted in a simple transfer of the rights of ownership of land and other resources from the Ahoms to the British Crown. The devastating rate of depopulation caused by successive civil wars and the Burmese attack left behind for the British a vast amount of arable and wasteland. The British, however, did not disturb the *khel* system in upper Assam but later imposed a poll tax of Rs 3 per *pike* instead of services or produce. In lower Assam, the poll tax was Rs 2 per *pike* and against 3 *puras* of land.[20] This system of land management and realization of revenues continued till 1870 when a radically different system of land management was introduced under the Act of Assam Settlement Rules.[21] Although the settled cultivation and the structure of village formation during the Ahom rule remained intact, vast tract of wasteland as well as cultivable land were available unclaimed due to massive depopulation caused by long civil wars and the Burmese invasions.[22] According to the estimate of Gunabhiram Barua, the total population was reduced to nearly half.[23] Such a devastating rate of depopulation in an otherwise sparsely populated region resulted in a large quantity of unclaimed arable land uninhabited by people, apart from the availability of vast tract of wasteland. This abundance of resources shaped the subsequent British policies of land settlement and of encouraging labour immigration from outside the region, which in turn determined the future course of Assam's economy.

A major discontinuity in the development path resulted from the discovery of tea in Assam and the consequential growth in trade in tea and other resources. The Assamese could not exploit this opportunity of development because of a number of reasons. The plantation revolution was not accompanied by any agricultural revolution within Assam to raise the agricultural productivity and marketable surplus. There was no scarcity of land but the impact of demonstration effect on the populace was almost negligible. The reason for the lack or absence of demonstration effect was the insulation of the region from any outside influence by the long isolationist political and economic strategy adopted by the Ahoms. This strategy was also singularly responsible for the lack of development of markets and exchange economy within Assam. Towards the latter stage of the plantation revolution, agricultural growth was also hampered by non-availability of land for agricultural expansion as a result of the occupation of the vast track of wasteland by the tea planters.

The rise of Assamese entrepreneurship in plantation was prevented by the non-existence of an Assamese capitalist class due to the fact that the Ahom economy was essentially a feudal self-subsistence economy. But more importantly, the British discouraged the rise of Assamese planters.[24] There were several hundred planters of which only a handful of small owners were of local origin. The British policy was not to allow the rise of Assamese entrepreneurship at all. Maniram Dewan, the first Indian tea planter, was hanged for alleged conspiracy during the 1857 revolt and his two tea gardens were confiscated (Guha, 1968). Since the entire capital was drawn in England, the profits that accrued to the plantation sector were, therefore, either reinvested for the expansion of the sector or paid to the shareholders in England. Since the cost of acquisition of land was zero and the planters paid barely the subsistence wage to the tea garden labourers (Guha, 1968; Barpujari, 1993), they earned as a consequence enormous profits from selling tea in the booming world market where the demand was highly elastic. At the dawn of India's independence,

India's share in world trade and production of tea were 50 and 40 per cent, respectively. Over the years the share of tea in India's exports has declined as India's exports have become more diversified. The share has slid down from 8 per cent in 1901 to 3.2 per cent in 1947 but it was still quite high. The huge profits so earned were either repatriated or used for investment in tea plantation. It was observed that barring the initial investment of Rs 2 million up to 1854, there was no fresh sterling investment and thus all subsequent investment for the expansion of acreage came obviously from the retained profits (Guha, 1968). There was in fact outflow of capital as investment opportunities were limited in Assam.

Secondly, the East India Company leased out the wasteland to planters, who were mainly European, for a fairly long period at a very nominal fee (Barpujari, 1993; Guha, 1968). The planters did not pay any compensation to the Government of Assam for all the wasteland they had acquired. The local Assamese people were denied the rents of these resources, which should have accrued to them. Since there was virtually no cost of acquisition of land, the planters tended to occupy more land than they needed for plantation. The total area of wasteland settled with planters rose from 3 lakh acres in 1971 to 6.4 lakh acres in 1901 (Guha, 1968). This resulted in gross inefficiency in the use of resources as vast tracts of land under the occupation of the planters was neither used for tea plantation nor for any other agricultural crop. Thus the acreage under tea rose from only 0.9 lakh acres in 1881 to 2 lakh acres in 1901, leaving nearly 60 per cent of the occupied land unused (Guha, 1968). In fact, as we shall see later the tea planters had to import rice in large quantities from Bengal due to the inelastic supply of rice locally even when rice prices were rising. The British also followed a discriminating policy as regards land revenue collection. For instance, the planters did not have to pay any tax or revenue to the government whereas the ordinary local farmers had to pay land revenue.

Thirdly, the plantation sector was developed as an enclave and it had no interaction with the local village economy. Most labourers for the tea plantation were imported from other states[25] and were subject to easy exploitation by the planters.[26] To describe the most vulnerable condition of the tea-garden labourers, we may quote a well-known economic historian who writes:

Ignorant men and women, once induced to sign a contract are forced to work in the gardens of Assam during the term indicated in the contract.

They are arrested, punished and restored to their masters if they attempt to run away; and they are tied to their work under penal laws such govern no other labour in India.[27]

There did not exist any competitive market for labour and the planters in their attempt to maximize profits used cheap labour from outside paying them just the minimum wage for survival. The Assam Emigration Act was passed in 1882[28] on the plea of that *local labour was scarce* and therefore import of cheap labour was essential for the growth of tea plantation. Many historians including Guha and Borpujari have accepted the labour scarcity assumption without questioning it. However, the fact is that there were *dual markets* – the plantation economy and the agricultural sector. While the planters arbitrarily determined the wage rate at a minimum subsistence level, the wage rate in the agricultural sector was determined by the marginal productivity of labour, which was almost twice that of the plantation wage rate. Naturally, with such wage differentials, it was not possible to induce local labour to move to the gardens in search of jobs. The tea planters could not have possibly forced the local labour to accept as low a wage as offered to the immigrants because the local labour could easily get themselves unionized.[29] Thus, labour scarcity was artificially created by government patronage. In fact, such scarcity served two objectives of the British government. First, to maximize profit from plantation by paying only subsistence wage to the immigrant labourers and secondly, squeeze out profits from the local agriculture by imposing land revenue burden on agricultural labourers. This exploitative policy of the British had led to the coexistence of two sectors with differential wage rates where labour for all practical purposes was fixed in each sector. Movement of foreign capital to the plantation sector did not increase the real wage but the profits of the planters. On the other hand, there was no movement of capital to the agricultural sector. The local village economy had to bear the burden of population expansion as the increase of agricultural output was limited by technology, since technological improvement was not feasible due to lack of local capital. Further, the scope for expansion of arable land was also limited since the tea planters occupied most of the wastelands. These along with the rise in land revenue squeezed out whatever little scope for primitive capital accumulation was present in the economy in the face of rising exposures to the world forces. There was thus a continuous fall in marketable surplus leading to rise in prices of the only staple good – rice. The rise in the price of rice was further accentuated by continuous immigration of outside labourers for the tea gardens. These factor specificity conditions largely determined the low-level equilibrium trap of the economy.

In the same way, the consumption demand for the plantation sector from foodstuffs to various manufacturing items were met by imports from abroad. As a result the linkage effect was almost absent. As the price of rice was rising due to population growth towards the late nineteenth century, the local supply of rice was not responding to the rising prices. Rice had to be imported in large quantities. There could be four reasons for this. First, the farmers were not interested in maximizing their income and so did not respond to the rising prices of rice. Two, the supply inelasticity could be due to low technology in agriculture and disguised unemployment in the village economy. Lack of technological innovation in agriculture was mainly due to the fact that the British policy was not to develop this sector and therefore capital was not flowing into this sector. Mobility of labour to tea plantation would have raised rice productivity but the tea planters found imported labour at a lower price than the local labour and hence the latter was not hired for the plantation economy. Thirdly, as the planters occupied a huge quantity of land for plantation of which only 40 per cent or so were actually used for tea plantation, it was not possible for the local labour to move outward for the expansion of agricultural activity.

Fourthly, the installation of railway and road networks was mainly to serve the tea industry and, therefore, the rail linkages left the local villages virtually untouched. So the communication and transport network did not help in developing markets for manufacturing. In fact, there was decline in the village handicraft industry with the importation of cheap products like textiles.

So the large investment and trade during the nineteenth century did not help the region progress on a sustained development path. The situation, however, is no more different today. For example, there has been large investment in oil and petrochemical industry without having any impact on the local development of industry. Many traditional industries such as textiles have, in fact, declined due to competition from other states. The local producers suffer from smallness of markets and scarcity of capital, because of which they are unable to improve the technology of production. However, the region produces a variety of handicraft products for which there are markets elsewhere in the country. The whole Indian market, even the markets abroad are available to them. The real issue is to integrate the small producers to these markets. Market forces will not do this due to a number of market imperfections. Thus, market intervention of some kind may be necessary for this purpose. The government has to play an important role as a mediator between the small producers and the markets and also as the financier of the productive enterprises of the small producers. These are issues, which require serious thinking.

TRADING IN WHAT?

Land locked countries tend to engage in border trade with the neighbouring countries. The border trade should play particularly an important role for the north-east region since 98 per cent of its border (thus only 2 per cent with the Indian mainland) is connected with international border shared with Myanmar, Bangladesh, China and Bhutan. In particular, Assam, Tripura and Meghalaya share a common border with Bangladesh while Mizoram, Manipur and Nagaland share border with Myanmar. Tibetan region of China and the Himalayan range of mountains border Arunachal Pradesh. In addition, Assam has border with Bhutan also. Obviously, there is a lot of scope for border trade but unfortunately the extent of such trade is not available.

There had been a lot of illegal border trade with Myanmar before the legalization of border trade by agreements between the two countries. There is no reliable estimate of the extent of illegal trade but information based on the confiscated items by the Customs shows that this trade mainly consists of goods like precious metals (silver and gold), wood, spices, vehicle, consumer goods such as electronics and fabrics and narcotic drugs. However, we get some interesting way of estimating the extent of illegal border trade from a study by FINER.[30]

India had entered into a Border Trade Agreement with Myanmar on 21 January 1994. The agreement came into effect on 12 April 1995 when Indo-Myanmar border trade was officially declared open for trade at Moreh in Manipur. India has no formal Border Trade Agreement with Bangladesh. Let us have a look at Indo-Burma trade during 1991–2.

The FINER study as mentioned above looked at the commodity

composition of trade between India and Burma and we reproduce here a Table 19.1 prepared by them on the commodity structure of trade between India and Burma during 1991–2. It is clear from the Table that the imports from Burma are largely consisting of agricultural items and exports to Burma are mainly manufacturing products. Similarly, the commodity structure for 1996–7 examined by them shows that the structure had remained the same except for inclusion of some new products. Thus, in 1996–7 – wheat and steel – were found in the export basket of India. Undoubtedly, the region at present does not have comparative advantage in such products like steel, treated steel, bars and rods, electronic goods, etc., exported by India to Myanmar.

In the same way it can be seen that India's major items of exports to Bangladesh include textiles, machinery and instruments, transport equipment, rubber products, chemicals and pharmaceuticals and mineral ores and the major imports from the Bangladesh consist of fertilizers, raw jute and organic chemicals.

Looking at India's trade with the south-east Asian countries like Thailand, Malaysia and Indonesia, we observe that the commodities exported by India to these countries consist mainly of shrimp, meal of Soya bean, granite, and cotton and aluminum ingots. These products are certainly not produced in the north-east region.

Thus, if trade has to facilitate industrialization and growth then the goods being exported from the north-east must have its production origin in the north-east itself. If goods produced elsewhere are being

TABLE 19.1: INDO-BURMA TRADE 1991–2

(Rupees millions)

Item	Exports	Items	Imports
Malted Milk	2.39	Peas	3.00
Barytes Powder	13.09	Peas, dried	34.25
Medicine	0.82	Beans	13.80
Cosmetics	1.74	Kidney Beans	37.06
Wood (Teak)	23.61	Guar Seeds	4.38
Bed Sheet	1.11	Others	410.07
Jute Bags	7.08	Moong	33.98
Bars and Rods	31.03	Tur	102.42
Electrical Goods	1.81	Urad	6.39
Insulators of other Materials	1.81	Wood	74.30
TOTAL	84.49		719.65

exported from the region then the north-east will merely serve the role of a transit location for exports and therefore its impact on industrialization may be only marginal. However, the north-east has potentialities for exporting goods based on its own resource endowment. For example, it has abundance of bamboo and cane and local artisans produce a variety of cane and bamboo products, which have high export potentials' not only outside India but also within India. But exports of these products suffer from (i) high cost of transporting as value addition increases the bulkiness of the product and (ii) the finished goods suffer from design limitations. Proper marketing can increase the demand for bamboo-based products since bamboo is a very good substitute, for wood and steel in the furniture and construction industries. Moreover, it is a replenishable resource and the optimum replenishable time for bamboo is much shorter than for cane and wood while steel is an exhaustible resource. Herein lies the importance of technological development to develop new bamboo-based substitutes for wood and the steel. Similarly, new technology also needed for reducing the bulk in transporting these products to distant places. In order to facilitate trade what is further needed is to develop networking with the artisans for marketing their products. But such technical changes do not normally take place in a market economy and therefore state intervention is required for technological developments.

The north-eastern region has been identified as an area having very good scope for the development of food processing industries. The agro-climatic condition is congenial for the production of agro-horticultural crops. Besides food crops, there are fruit crops, and vegetable and tuber crops. Among fruit crops, pineapples, oranges, bananas, guavas, jackfruits and many local varieties of fruits are grown in the region. They go waste during the production season due to lack of storage and processing facilities and due to inadequate transport facilities. Promotion of food processing industries in the small scale sector will not only check the wastage of these valuable resources and add value to them, but will also encourage the growers to grow more fruits and export them to the international markets. There are also vegetables and other crops, the production of which has gradually been rising in recent years. Among the vegetable crops, cabbage, tomato and cauliflower are grown and among the tuber crops, potato, sweet potato, and tapioca are grown. Tapioca grows wild in the border areas of Meghalaya. Based on these resources, industries can come up. Annually more than two lakh tonnes of spices are produced in the region. Principals among the spices are ginger, turmeric and black pepper. The region has good prospects for the development of industries based on plantation crops such as rubber, coffee, tea and so on. Rubber-based units have good prospects particularly in Tripura. More than half of the tea produced in the country is from the north-east region, particularly from Assam. Tea cultivation and processing have occupied an important place in the economy of the north-east. Tea industry offers scope for the development of ancillary and auxiliary industries in the region. A few industrial units have been set up such as caffeine making unit, tea machinery and equipment manufacturing unit. Based on the requirement of the tea industry, cane and bamboo basket-making unit, polythene bag-making unit, umbrella-making unit, etc., can be considered. Livestock is another important resource of the region. The entire region is rich in fodder and could support and sustain a large population of livestock. Rearing of livestock will provide scope for development of livestock-based industries.

THE CHANGE IN GEOGRAPHICAL DIRECTION OF TRADE

The interesting recent development in India's trade is that some of the South-East Asian and East Asian countries are emerging as India's major trading partners. For example, Hong Kong and China are in the 7th and the 9th positions respectively in terms of the share of total trade while Singapore and Malaysia are in the 10th and 11th positions respectively. In fact, the ASEAN and China, Japan and Korea have emerged as India's dominant trading partners, accounting for 19.7 per cent of India's total merchandise trade, compared to trade share of 19 per cent for EU and 12.8 per cent for North America. The signing of India-ASEAN Framework Agreement of Comprehensive Economic Cooperation is likely to further facilitate growth in trade with this region.

The developments in the geographical patterns of trade as described above seem to be consistent with the country's 'Look East Policy'. It is therefore important to recognize the fact the north-east region because of its strategic geographical position with respect to these countries can play a significant role in enhancing India's trade further with this block. For this the north-east must realize that to be able to play a role of the kind and derive benefits from trade, the region must exploit its transport advantage towards production advantage. Otherwise it can merely play the role of a transit rout for products produced elsewhere and destined for the ASEAN and other neighbouring markets.

Although the existing patterns of India's trade with the ASEAN and China, Japan and Korea do not indicate any specific advantage for the north-east in particular, it can however be argued that the north-east has potential advantage in many resources which are yet to be taped properly. For example, the region is rich in forest resources and can supply processed wood products and increase value addition by exporting furniture. Like the South-East Asian countries, Malaysia, and Indonesia, the north-east states can apply 'screwdriver technology' to reduce their transportation cost for exporting. Similarly, large-scale marketing is very crucial to pool the region's vast resources to the exporting nodes.

CONCLUSION

Increased regional and international trade can shape the future destiny of the north-east region by providing the scope for industrialization and growth. But mere facilitation of trade through the region with he neighbouring countries will have only marginal impact on the economy of the region unless the region can be converted into a production hub. For this the Central Government and the various State Governments of the region must adopt proactive role. Instead of providing tax holidays for investment in the region, the Governments should provide infrastructures, political stability and good governance. They should adopt more outward rather than inward looking policies for development. The economic integration of the states of the region is necessary to maximize the benefits from investment in various economic activities. The political parties, NGOs and Civil Societies also have to play important role in educating the people about the need for development. Special export processing zones should be created in the region such that investors find sufficient inducement to invest in locating production plans in the region. In order to achieve greater participation of the local people in production and distribution activities, the education sector should be given the prime importance. However, the vast rural masses have to be brought into the process of industrialization for political viability of the trade as a strategy of industrializing the region. For this the utmost importance should be given to raise the agricultural productivity in the region with proper flood control measures and other steps. As it had happened in the past, without a parallel agricultural revolution in the region, trade alone will not be sufficient to transform the region into a sustained development path. The growth in trading activities will only benefit those, possibly from outside the region, who are economically more powerful to exploit the resources of the region. The common people particularly the agricultural class being overshadowed by the powerful lobbies from outside will silently (or violently!) witness their inevitable decay and degradation.

NOTES

1. See W. Arthur Lewis, *The Evolution of the International Economic Order*, New Delhi: Kalyani Publishers, 1978.
2. See Amalendu Guha, 'A Big Push without a Take-off' in this volume.
3. See, Romesh Dutt, *The Economic History of India*, vol. 2, New Delhi: Low Price Publication, 1990, p. 391.
4. To quote a Central Government report: 'The north-eastern region shares only 2 per cent of the border with the mainland of the country and the balance of 98 per cent is shared with an international border, i.e. Bangladesh, Myanmar, China and Bhutan. It is considered natural and necessary for the region to look at the neighbouring countries for markets. Promotion of border trade is likely to create opportunities for the people to earn their livelihood, simultaneously providing greater avenues for private investments in infrastructure.' See, *Industrial Development and Export Potential of the north-eastern Region*, vol. 1, report prepared by IIFT for the Ministry of Commerce, Government of India.
5. Alokesh Barua and Arindam Bandyopadhyay, 'Structural Change, Economic Growth and Regional Disparity in the North-East: Regional and National Perspectives' in this volume.
6. The north-east has experienced 3.88 per cent annual growth rate in Net State Domestic Product against the national average of 5.1 per cent over the period 1980–1 to 1997–8. See Alokesh Barua and Arindam Bandyopadhyay.
7. The share of manufacturing has been declining significantly at the rate of –1.55 per annum during the period 1980–1 to 1997–8. See Barua and Bandyopadhyay.

8. H.B. Chenery, S. Robison and M. Syrgnin, *Industrialization and Growth: A Comparative Study*, published for the World Bank, London: Oxford University Press, 1988.
9. The manufacturing sector in the north-east grew at an annual rate of 2.33 per cent against the all-India average of 6.4 per cent. See Barua and Bandyopadhyay.
10. The population growth rate of north-east as a whole was 2.4 per cent against the national average of 1.8 per cent for the period of 1980–1 to 1997–8. Nagaland experienced the highest rate of population growth of 4.2 per cent for the same period. See Barua and Bandyopadhyay.
11. The rural unemployment rate in Assam is 6.2 per cent and 14.3 per cent for males and females respectively against the national average of 2 per cent and 1.4 per cent respectively. Similarly, the urban unemployment rates are 6.2 and 28.9 per cent for males and females respectively against the national average of 4.5 and 8.2 per cent respectively. See, 1993–4, 50th round, Report no. 409, *Employment and Unemployment in India*, National Sample Survey Organization.
12. *Transforming the North-East: High Level Commission Report to the Prime Minister*, 7 March 1997.
13. The committee also finds the opportunities to exploit the export market through floating joint ventures with the neighbouring countries. Among the key drivers of this process is the need for the region and enterprises to find new markets for their exports. The region can interact with the rest of the country and global market through trade in products, which can be produced by using local natural resources and skilled labour. While labour intensive exports can and should provide the initial platform, the region must evolve a framework for diversification and quality improvement of her export basket. Export opportunities are expected to create a competitive environment, which are supposed to raise the level of productivity and efficiency of north-east region's industry.
14. The share of tea in India's exports in 1859 was only 0.2 per cent. But it rose to around 5 per cent by 1985 and by the turn of the century the share of tea went up to 8 per cent. These figures are calculated from the figures of India's total exports and exports of tea in Romesh Dutt, *The Economic History of India*, vols. I and II, see vol. II, pp. 256, 259, 397, 400.
15. The Govt. of India Act of 1858 declared, 'India shall be governed by the Queen' and vested the Crown all the territories and powers of the East India Company.
16. See Barua, Introduction in this volume.
17. Ibid.
18. Regarding land ownership rights, Gait writes: 'In matters of land, the

Ahom kings following the general northern Indian tradition claimed that all land belonged to the Crown. Not only did the king exercise this right over lands, cultivated or waste, but he extended his prerogative of ownership over all woods, forests, ferries, mines, etc. . . . Nevertheless, the king could alienate only those lands for legal tenure of which the occupier had no documentary evidence. However, the king had at his disposal all uncultivated lands', p. 270.

19. See Barua, 'Rise and Decline of the Ahom Dynastic Rule: A Suggestive Interpretation' in this volume.
20. H.K. Barpujari, ed., *The Comprehensive History of Assam*, vol. V *Modern Period: Yandabo to Diarchy* AD *1826–1919*, Guwahati: Publication Board, Assam, 1993, p. 7.
21. Ibid., p. 21.
22. Ibid., p. 37.
23. S.K. Bhuyan, *Anglo Assamese Relations*, Guwahati, 1974, p.1.
24. Amalendu Guha, *A Big Push without a Take-off*, The Indian Economic and Political History Revised, vol. V, Sept. 1968.
25. By the turn of the century in 1901 the local labour in tea plantation was only 20,000 against the total recruitment of 307,000 workers in plantation, which was less than 1 per cent. See Guha, 1968. The details of the states from which labour was drawn are available in Barpujari, 1993.
26. The contract labourers under the Emigration Act were receiving half the wage rate of free agricultural labourer. See Guha, 1968.
27. See Romesh Dutt, p. 263.
28. See Barpujari, p. 241.
29. In fact, there were mass uprising of peasants against the decision of the government to increase the land revenue by 100 per cent in 1892. *The Amrit Bazar Patrika* observed that while in places such as Deccan Bengal and Pabna the rebellions of the ryots were directed against moneylenders, indigo-planters and zamindars respectively, in Assam it was open rebellion against the government. See Barpujari, p. 34.
30. FINER, 'Building External Market Linkages for Entrepreneurs in the North-Eastern Region', presented at International Conference on Business Opportunities in north-east India – Guwahati Initiative, 22–23 February 2001.

CHAPTER 20

Trading Across China, Myanmar, Bangladesh and India: Impact on North-East India

HOMESWAR GOSWAMI AND
JAYANTA KUMAR GOGOI

INTRODUCTION

China, India, Bangladesh and Myanmar can be called a sub-regional zone with a varied topography and an inconvenient transport and communication system. But the entire zone possesses abundant natural resources. The zone has abundant sunshine and rainfall, is rich in bio-diversity and has fertile soil for growing various crops. Apart from being full of mineral resources, the region is rich in tourism resources due to combination of factors such as human, natural, cultural and ethnic beauty, heritage sites, beaches and deep forests. The region also has huge potential for hydro-energy because of the presence of the Brahmaputra, Ganga, Irrawati, Jinsha, Mekong and Nujiang rivers. In spite of all these, the entire zone is regarded as underdeveloped. This is indicated by the levels of following three major indicators of development.

The per capita incomes of the constituents of the zone, in comparison to the per capita income of the USA and the European countries, are extremely low. These are $911 for China, $462 for India, $350 for Bangladesh in 2001 and $260 for Myanmar in 1997. China's export share as a proportion of the total world exports was 1.42 per cent in 1985 which increased only to 3.02 per cent in 1995 and 4.72 per cent in 2001. The increase in share of China's exports in world trade may be attributed to the reform measures undertaken by the country since 1978. Similarly, India's share in the world exports has increased from 0.45 per cent in 1985 to 0.62 per cent in 1995 and

0.70 per cent in 2001. Myanmar's export share in the world exports is highly insignificant. In terms of Human Development Index (HDI) prepared by the UNDP in 2003, China with 0.721 HDI ranks 104th out of the total 175 countries, India with 0.590 HDI ranks 127th, Bangladesh with 0.502 ranks 139th and Myanmar with 0.549 HDI ranks 131st in 2001.

All the three factors show that these four countries are economically underdeveloped though they are very rich in natural and human resources.

One of the ways of teckling the existing poor level of development in these four countries is through regional co-operation and increasing of bilateral trade amongst themselves. In spite of being geographical closeness, trading among the four countries take place mainly through sea routes (except Bangladesh), which are several hundred times longer in terms of distance, and is also costlier and time-consuming. Therefore, the volume of existing trade between India and China/Myanmar is abysmally lower in comparison to their trade relations with the European and American countries which are geographically far away from the region.

TRADE WITH CHINA

China is bordered by the Indian states of Arunachal Pradesh, Uttar Pradesh, Himachal Pradesh and Jammu & Kashmir. Trade between China and India at present takes place mainly through sea-routes. Table 20.1 presents the composition, value and percentage share of the value of each product of India's export to China in 1996–7 and in 2002–3. It must be noted that despite the low volume of trade, China has emerged as the fastest growing market for India's export in recent years. It is evident from the fact that the exports of India to China has increased from $615.32 million in 1996–7 to $1966.20 million in 2002–3 indicating a growth rate of nearly 220 per cent against India's overall export growth of 59.32 per cent during the seven years. The percentage growth of India's exports to other major exporting countries were USA (65.88), UAE (124.89), UK (21.02), Hongkong (31.46) and Germany (9.05) during the same period.

From Table 20.1 it appears that the primary and semi-finished iron and steel (24.78 per cent) and iron ore (20.41 per cent) contribute nearly 45 per cent of the total export earnings of India and China. Plastic and linoleum products have appeared as major item

TABLE 20.1: COMPOSITION, VALUE AND PERCENTAGE OF INDIA'S EXPOTS TO CHINA 1996–7 AND 2002–3

(in million US $)

Items of Exports to China	1996–7	2002–3
1. Primary, Semi-finished Iron & Steel	39.92 (6.49)	487.30 (24.78)
2. Iron Ore	65.59 (10.66)	401.25 (20.41)
3. Plastic & Linoleum Products	2.58 (0.42)	165.68 (8.44)
4. Other Ores & Minerals	71.23 (11.57)	124.09 (6.31)
5. Marine Products	74.07 (12.04)	105.26 (5.35)
6. Agro-chemicals (Inorganic & Organic)	13.38 (2.17)	87.55 (4.46)
7. Drugs, Pharmaceuticals & Fine Chemicals	26.03 (4.23)	82.35 (4.19)
8. Processed Minerals	15.93 (2.59)	82.01 (4.17)
9. Cotton Yarn and Fabric, etc.	45.41 (7.38)	62.99 (3.20)
10. Manufactures of Metals	1.00 (0.16)	30.97 (1.58)
11. Machinery and Instruments	4.36 (0.71)	29.54 (1.50)
12. Non-ferrous Metals	Nil	20.92 (1.06)
13. Electronic Goods	1.64 (0.27)	20.89 (1.05)
14. Residual Chemical & Allied Products	5.29 (0.86)	20.59 (1.04)
15. Dyes, Intermediates, etc.	2.22 (0.36)	19.47 (1.00)
16. Finished Leather	3.76 (0.61)	14.74 (0.75)
17. Spices	0.40 (0.07)	5.29 (0.27)
18. Others	242.51 (39.41)	205.31 (10.44)
All commodities	615.32 (100)	1966.20 (100)

Note: Figures in the bracket show the percentage share of each item in the total exports from India to China.
Source: CMIE, Foreign Trade and Balance of Payments, September 2003.

of exports to China during this period. China has replaced USA as a major importer of these products in recent years. China is also the major destination of India's exports of 'other ores and minerals' and 'marine products'. Table 20.2 shows the composition, value and percentage share of India's imports from China in 1996–7 and 2002–3.

China has also emerged as the fastest growing source of imports during this seven-year period. Imports from China grew from $757.55 in 1996–7 to $2789.72 million in 2002–3 registering a growth rate of more than 268 per cent against India's total increase of imports by 56.89 per cent during the same period of time. The growth of imports from China (268 per cent) is found to be much higher than the growth of imports from a few other major sources of India's imports such as USA (20.06), Belgium (65.12), UK (30.38), Germany (18.85) and

TABLE 20.2: COMPOSITION, AND PERCENTAGE SHARE OF
INDIA'S IMPORTS FROM CHINA IN 1996–7 AND 2002–3

(in million US $)

Items of Exports from China	1996–7	2002–3
1. Electrical Goods	52.08 (6.87)	776.12 (27.82)
2. Organic Chemicals	135.28 (17.86)	305.41 (10.95)
3. Coal, Cock and Briquettes	94.31 (12.45)	168.31 (6.03)
4. Medicinal and Pharmaceticals	58.68 (7.75)	144.64 (5.18)
5. Silver	Nil	121.21 (4.34)
6. Raw Silk	43.20 (5.70)	104.34 (3.74)
7. Non-electrical Machinary	32.19 (4.256)	101.80 (93.650)
8. Others	341.81 (45.12)	1067.89 (38.29)
All commodities	757.55 (100)	2789.72 (100)

Note: Figures in the bracket show the percentage share of each item in the total imports of India to China.
Source: CMIE, Foreign Trade and Balance of Payments, September 2003.

Switzerland (107) during this period. China as a source of India's imports occupied 20th position in terms of value in 1996–7 but it has been promoted to 3rd position; USA and Belgium occupying the 1st and 2nd position respectively in 2002–3.

From Table 20.2 it is clear that the basket of imports from China is far more diversified than the export basket to China since there is higher concentration of export value in a few items like primary and semi-finished iron and steel (24.78 per cent) and iron ore (20.48 per cent) in 2002–3. Table 20.2 further shows that while organic chemicals occupied the first position as an item of import in 1996–7, electronic goods have replaced it in 2002–3, contributing about 28 per cent share in the total imports from China.

In recent years, i.e. since 1999–2000, silver has become an important item of import from China. China is now the largest source of silver imports into India, the UK being the second. India's import of silver from China and the UK is $121.21 million and $108.44 million in 2002–3 which were $20.16 million and $115.17 million in 1999–2000 respectively.

With this rapid growth in trade, China has become India's fastest growing trade partner in recent years. And there still exists immense potentialities to further increase the volume of trade between the two countries in the near future.

TRADE WITH MYANMAR

Myanmar's main trading partners are Japan, Singapore, China, Thailand, India and Hongkong, in that order of importance. Table 20.3 shows the composition, value and percentage share of each item of India's imports from Myanmar in 1996-7 and 2002-3.

It is seen from Table 20.3 that at present (2002-3), the value of formal imports from Myanmar to India is $336.88 million which is 0.55 per cent of India's total imports in 2002-3. However, the total value of India's import which was $177.34 million in 1996-7 has increased to $336-.88 million in 2002-3, registering a growth rate of nearly 90 per cent during this seven-year period. The major items of imports from Myanmar are mainly two—pulses and wood and wood products which are 60 and 27 per cent respectively of the total imports from Myanmar in 2002-3.

But the CMIE is silent about the value of India's exports to Myanmar possibly because the volume of formal exports to Myanmar is very insignificant. However, a survey conducted by Indian Institute of Foreign Trade (IIFT) on behalf of the Ministry of Commerce, Government of India, in 1995, has estimated that the volume and value of India's informal trade with Myanmar are much higher than those of the formal one. The survey estimated the value of informal trade with Myanmar at Rs 2,000 crore via Moreh in Manipur, Rs 500 crore through Champhai in Mizoram and Rs 100 crore via Lungwa in Nagaland.

TABLE 20.3: COMPOSITION, VALUE AND PERCENTAGE SHARE OF INDIA'S IMPORTS FROM MYANMAR IN 1996-7 AND 2002-3

(in million US $)

Items of Imports	1996-7	2002-3
1. Pulses	119.01 (67.11)	201.92 (59.95)
2. Wood and Wood Products	43.40 (24.47)	92.28 (27.39)
3. Vegetable Oils (edible)	1.00 (0.56)	2.22 (0.66)
4. Fruits and Nuts	2.90 (1.64)	2.13 (0.63)
5. Others	11.03 (6.22)	38.33 (11.38)
All commodities	177.34 (100)	336.88 (100)

Note: Figures in the bracket show the percentage share of each item in the total imports of India from Myanmar.
Source: CMIE, Foreign Trade and Balance of Payments, September 2003.

A wide range of goods is being informally exported to Myanmar through Moreh including bicycles and bicycle parts, motor vehicle accessories, tyres, drugs and pharmaceuticals, cotton yarn and textiles, branded foods, edible oils, petroleum products, cement and other construction materials, paints, CI sheets, sewing machines, alcoholic beverages, cosmetics, etc. The items coming into India from Myanmar through informal channels are electronic goods, consumer durable, telephone instruments, blankets and other high quality textile products, tobacco products, toiletries which are not the local products of Myanmar but smuggled in or imported at a lower tariff to Myanmar from Japan, Korea, Singapore, etc. Myanmar also exports or smuggled out via north-eastern points certain local products such as betel-nuts, pulses, teak, groundnuts and a few other products of unknown origin such as gold, silver, narcotics, etc.

TRADE WITH BANGLADESH

The Indo-Bangla border is about 4,100 km. long and Bangladesh is bordered by three Indian states West Bengal is on Bangladesh borders in the west and north-west, and on the north-eastern states of Assam, Meghalaya, Tripura and Mizoram are on its eastern border. Since the Independence of Bangladesh, India has been exporting through its border points several items to Bangladesh. The border trade agreement between India and Bangladesh was signed in 1972 to meet the day-to-day requirements of the border people. Trade between India and Bangladesh takes place through the north-eastern border trading points like Dawki and Bholaganj (in Meghalaya), Karimganj, Steamerghat and Suterkandi (in Assam), Agartala, Kailash Sahar, Bilonia and Sonamua (in Tripura). It is estimated that Bangladesh exports items worth Rs 17 crore and imports items worth Rs 1 crore per year through Tripura border alone. The major share of Indo-Bangla trade takes place through the trade routes of West Bengal border points and sea-routes from various ports of India.

Both primary and manufacturing goods are traded between India and Bangladesh. While most of the exports and imports of primary goods through sea Ports are formal and legal, a part of the exports and imports of manufacturing articles through land-routes are informal and illegal. It is because several tariff and quantitative restrictions have been appended to the South Asian Preferential Trade Agreement (SAPTA), 1993, on exports and imports of manufacturing goods to protect local units of India and Bangladesh. Though the exact volume and value of articles informally and illegally traded annually across the land routes cannot be ascertained, it has been estimated that the share of informal and illegal segments of trade between India and Bangladesh would not be less than 70 to 80 per cent of the total volume and value of articles traded. Table 20.4 shows the composition, value and percentage share of India's exports to Bangladesh in 1996–7 and 2002–3.

No item is dominant in the list of India's export to Bangladesh. However, cotton yarn (13.65 per cent), non-basmati rice (9.85 per cent) and wheat (8.79 per cent) have importance in the export list. Table 20.4 further shows that the increase in formal exports to Bangladesh during 1996–7 and 2002–3 only about 26 per cent. In 2002–3, exports to Bangladesh constitute only 2.06 per cent of the India's total export in that year.

In addition to these formal exports several other items of goods are smuggled out to Bangladesh through north-eastern border points, such as orange, pineapple, jackfruits, potatoes, ginger, spices, rice, betel, petroleum products, fish, bicycles, tyres, papers, audio-video cas-

TABLE 20.4: COMPOSITION, VALUE AND PERCENTAGE SHARE OF INDIA'S EXPORTS TO BANGLADESH IN 1996–7 AND 2002–3

(in million US $)

Items of Exports from China	1996–7	2002–3
1. Cotton Yarn and Fabric	337.19 (38.77)	149.83 (13.65)
2. Non-basmati Rice	40.96 (4.71)	108.10 (9.85)
3. Wheat	9.67 (1.11)	96.44 (8.79)
4. Sugar	4.69 (0.54)	63.96 (5.83)
5. Primary, Semi-finished Iron & Steel	139.08 (4.49)	61.73 (5.63)
6. Transport Equipments	66.68 (7.67)	55.27 (5.04)
7. Coal	14.88 (1.71)	43.93 (4.00)
8. Oil Meals	0.28 (0.03)	37.96 (3.16)
9. Machinery and Instruments	55.89 (6.43)	37.19 (3.39)
10. Drugs, Pharmaceutical and Fine Chemicals	16.15 (1.86)	30.95 (2.82)
18. Others	284.22 (32.68)	412.03 (37.55)
All commodities	869.69 (100)	1097.41 (100)

Note: Figures in the bracket show the percentage share of each item in the total imports of India to Myanmar.
Source: CMIE, Foreign Trade and Balance of Payments, September 2003.

settes, cosmetics, milk powder, utensils, cattle, pulses, tea, salt, tobacco, aluminium goods, wood, electrical fittings, leather, etc.

The formal imports from Bangladesh is too small to be reported by the CMIE which results into a huge trade deficit of Bangladesh to the tune of $1 billion dollar with India against its total trade deficit of $5.24 billion in 2001. The reason for such trade deficit of Bangladesh with India is that Bangladesh's exports to Indian main markets like Mumbai, Delhi, Chennai, etc., are not cost-effective because of distance. However, it can establish a profitable trade relationship with the north-eastern states of India which have long borders with Bangladesh. The informal segment of imports, on the other hand, is quite significant. Through the border points articles like electronic goods, coconut oil, goat, jute, poultry products, synthetic fabrics, several consumer goods, high quality cloths, etc., are smuggled into India, many of which are third country products.

A COMPARATIVE TRADE SCENARIO

Tables 20.5 and 20.6 show the trends in India's imports from and exports to China, Myanmar and Bangladesh during the period 1996–7 to 2002–3 respectively. Table 20.5 shows that the proportion of import from China to the total imports of India has been rising over the years, but it is constant in case of Myanmar while this is falling rapidly in case of Bangladesh, although in absolute terms the import values have been increasing for all the three countries. The growth rate of import from China between 1996–7 and 2002–3 has been 269 per cent giving an annual average growth rate of 38.32 per cent as against an annual average growth of 12.85 per cent for Myanmar, (–) 1.80 per cent for Bangladesh and 8.33 per cent for the rest of the world.

Table 20.6 shows that the proportion of India's export to China has been increasing at a rapid rate, but it is remaining constant in case of Myanmar and falling in case of Bangladesh in terms of volume and value though India's exports in absolute terms to these countries are increasing over the years. The growth rate of export to China during this seven-year period has been growing at the rate of 219.54 per cent giving an annual average of export of 31.36 per cent as against an annual average growth rate of 9.46 per cent for Myanmar, 3.74 per cent for Bangladesh and 8.47 per cent for the rest of the world.

TABLE 20.5: IMPORTS OF INDIA FROM CHINA, MYANMAR AND BANGLADESH AND REST OF THE WORLD 1996-7-2002-3

(in million US $)

Year	India's Exports to			
	China	Myanmar	Bangladesh	Rest of the World
1996-7	757.55 (1.93)	177.34 (0.45)	62.28 (0.16)	39165.46 (100)
1997-8	1120.70 (2.70)	224.28 (0.54)	50.87 (0.12)	41534.56 (100)
1998-9	1096.47 (2.59)	173.72 (0.41)	62.39 (0.15)	42379.20 (100)
1999-2000	1288.27 (2.59)	171.80 (0.34)	98.25 (0.16)	49798.64 (100)
2000-1	1494.92 (2.99)	181.41 (0.36)	73.99 (0.15)	50056.27 (100)
2001-2	2043.33 (3.96)	375.70 (0.73)	59.32 (0.11)	51588.41 (100)
2002-3	2789.72 (4.54)	336.88 (0.55)	54.44 (0.09)	61445.40 (100)

Note: Figures in the bracket show the percentage share of imports from each country.
Source: CMIE, Foreign Trade and Balance of Payments, September 2003.

TABLE 20.6: EXPORTS FROM INDIA TO CHINA, MYANMAR, BANGLADESH AND REST OF THE WORLD 1996-7-2002-3

(in million US $)

Year	India's Exports to			
	China	Myanmar	Bangladesh	Rest of the World
1996-7	615.32 (1.84)	45.24 (0.14)	869.69 (2.60)	33497.97 (100)
1997-8	718.94 (2.05)	49.37 (0.14)	789.41 (2.25)	35048.67 (100)
1998-9	427.06 (1.29)	30.07 (0.09)	995.37 (3.00)	33210.97 (100)
1999-2000	539.41 (1.47)	34.14 (0.09)	636.92 (1.73)	36459.52 (100)
2000-1	839.03 (1.88)	50.70 (0.11)	874.41 (1.98)	44147.44 (100)
2001-2	955.19 (2.17)	61.10 (0.14)	1005.59 (2.29)	43976.01 (100)
2002-3	1966.20 (3.75)	75.21 (0.14)	1097.41 (2.10)	53370.00 (100)

Note: Figures in the bracket show the percentage share of exports to each country.
Source: CMIE, Foreign Trade and Balance of Payments, September 2003.

REGIONAL CO-OPERATION

Considering the geographical proximity and huge potentialities, the existing value and volume of bilateral trade, shown in the tables, between these three neighbouring countries (China, Myanmar and Bangladesh) on the one hand, and India on the other, appear to be too small. It is because trading between these countries has been quite difficult due to transport bottlenecks and the protectionist policy followed in the pre-globalization period. Lack of wider markets has impeded the economic development and the process of exploitation of potentialities of all these countries. However, in recent years all the Governments have begin showning keep interest in removing these bottlenecks by establishing regional co-operation. This has raised the hopes of China, Myanmar and Bangladesh becoming the major trading partners of India in the near future.

The rapid economic growth of China in recent years has opened the possibilities of expanding the trade relationship with India. China's huge population and growing per capita income and rapid infrastructural development have created opportunities for exporting several new products from India. India with its current economic reforms and growing GDP can emerge as a good market for Chinese goods. The recent bilateral trade agreements between India and China can act as a catalyst in this emerging scenario of trade potentialities between the two countries. To evolve the *modus operandi* of this trade and to identify the items to be traded, interactions between the academics and diplomats and professionals of both the countries are highly desirable. It is heartening to note that India and China have already launched a determined bid in 2003 to chart out a roadmap to forge an enduring and strong partnership based on the principles of Panchsheel and mutual sensitivity to each other's concerns and equality. The roadmap in the form of a joint declaration, the first-ever between India and China, was signed during the then Prime Minister Atal Behari Vajpayee's historic visit to Beijing in June 2003, leading to a flurry of high-level exchanges, including the launch of a new political initiative for the early resolution of boundary issue that bedeviled bilateral relations.

As a first step, India and China signed a memorandum on expanding border trade through Nathula Pass on the Indo-China boundary. This was followed by a move by the Chinese Foreign Ministry which stopped showing Sikkim as an independent country in Asia on its official website. In turn India also recognized Tibet as part of the territory of the People's Republic of China. Another area where India and China have made solid progress in 2003 is in the defence sector, where mutual suspicion had prevented the two largest armed forces in Asia from engaging and interacting with each other. The two sides also decided to step up bilateral military exchanges at different levels to boost mutual trust and understanding. For example, on ovember 2003, the Indian and Chinese Naval ships successfully ucted a search and rescue exercise off the coast of Shanghai in ast China sea.

The year 2003 also saw the continued expansion and intensification of India-China economic co-operation. During Vajpayee's visit, it was decided with his Chinese counterpart Wen Jiabao to form a joint study group to examine the potential complementarities and also draw up a programme for development of India-China Trade and Economic Co-operation for the next five years. This economic co-operation between India and China, the two giant nations with nearly 38 per cent of world population, in collaboration with the ASEAN, can transform the entire Asian continent into the biggest trading zone in the world. The existing intervening obstacles, both natural and political, between these countries will disappear when strong economic forces through active and vibrant trading activities are generated in the region.

Myanmar's entry into ASEAN block, its signing of an MoU with India in 1994 recognizing certain border trading points between Myanmar and India, the opening of the 160 km. Tamu-Kalewakalemy Road in February 2001, the opening of the Myanmar-India Friendship Centre at Yangoon and the signing of a bilateral trade agreement between India and Myanmar in October 2003, the bilateral trade agreements between India and China and ASEAN block in October 2003 are likely to play a major role in improving the regional economic co-operation between the three countries.

Bangladesh has a long border with the north-eastern region of India. The establishment of good economic co-operation, therefore, benefits both Bangladesh and the north-east because of their proximity. But no lasting foundation of co-operation has yet been laid between Dhaka and New Delhi for a beneficial trade relation. Several thorny socio-political and border issues, some real and some imaginary, have stood in the way of regional economic co-operation between these two countries. The Indo-Bangla Joint Economic Commission (JEC) has so far failed to settle any of the above issues, delaying economic co-operation between the two countries. The proposed Indo-Bangla Free Trade Agreement (FTA) can go a long way in establishing regional co-operation between these two countries. Nurul Islam and Rehman Sobhan, who were with the Bangladesh Planning Commission, have suggested joint venture manufacturing units like cement, fertilizer and sponge-iron to accelerate further trade between the two next-door neighbours. Nurul Islam fu[rther suggested] that the administrative and professional skills supporte[d by sepa]rate study on formal and informal trade between Ban[gladesh and] India are essential before establishing a free trade area be[tween the] two countries. The implementation of the proposed FTA b[et]ween Bangladesh and India is possible only when Bangladesh gets itself rid of the suspicion against the big neighbour, India.

As regards the development of land routes for promoting regional co-operation between these countries, the reopening of the famous Stilwell Roads is of utmost importance. This is the land route connecting India with Myanmar and China which was constructed between 1942–5. It runs from Ledo in India and passes through Lekhapani-Pangshu Pass in India, Myitkyina and Lashio in Myanmar in Kunming in Unnan province of China. Since Kunming is already connected with Hongkong by an express highway, the north-east India, for that matter India as a whole, could establish direct road link with Hongkong if the Stilwell Road is well-developed. Only a short stretch of the Stilwell Road (about 160–232 km.) from Ledo in India to Myitkyina in Myanmar needs rebuilding because beyond Myitkyina up to Kunming the road is already well-developed. From Myitkyina the road takes a southern turn towards Kunming. Since Lashio is well-connected by rail and road with provinces of south and central Myanmar, bordering Laos, Thailand, Malaysia and Singapore, the Stilwell Road can connect north-east India with the entire South-East Asian countries. Thus, if the Stilwell Road is reconstructed as a Trans-Asian Expressway and along with it a Trans-Asian Railway line, then in the near future the north-east India, for that matter the entire nation, could have direct access by both road and railway not only to Myanmar and South Chinese trading centres, but also to the entire South-East Asian region.

From the border point of Arunachal Pradesh in the east, the exports of India could reach by the Stilwell Road in Kunming in South China, nearly 1,600 km. within two days, Tangoon in Myanmar within two and a half days, Bangkok in four days and Singapore in five to six days. This land route of trade would be shorter and cheaper in comparison to the existing sea routes. India's trade may take a diametrically opposite direction from the West to the East and that too with much more gains, since the buyers and sellers of these markets of the East are culturally and racially more akin to the buyers and sellers of India.

Another land route opened in 2001 is the 160 km. Tamu-Kalewa-kalemy. If this road is extended by another 250–300 km. across Myanmar, it can meet the Stilwell Road at Bhamo from where Kunming is already well-connected. The Governments of India and Bangladesh have recently proposed to extend this road across Manipur and southern Assam to Bangladesh border, a distance of about 300 km., so that it can be the shortest land route between Bangladesh and Myanmar through north-east India. In that case the distance to Chittagong sea ports from Agartala, Imphal, Shillong, Guwahati, etc., will be shorter than that to Kolkata. The leaders of the South Asian Association for Regional Cooperation (SAARC) countries in January 2004, finalized the formation of South Asian Free Trade Area (SAFTA) from January 2006 which would accelerate trade among the SAARC countries.

With these developments, the north-east India with its geo-strategic locational advantage could emerge as a business transit centre for both the SAARC and ASEAN groups of nations. In that case, in certain strategic places of the north-east, large warehouses with business offices of exporters and importers from both sides would be built-up. Such places would emerge as the commercial hub of the region bustled by business executives, hotels, clubs, departmental stores, etc.

But it must be noted that unless exportable surpluses are produced within it, the north-eastern region could not be able to derive the full benefits of all these developments simply by acting as a corridor of exports of other countries. The north-east has to identify a few well-defined thrust areas and concentrate on specializing in those areas of production so that it can produce in excess of local demand.

EXPORT POSSIBILITIES FROM THE NORTH-EAST INDIA

On the basis of specialization based on the thrust areas, the north-east can emerge as an exporter to the East on the following items:

1. The north-east is famous for its exotic flora and fauna. Out of the 925 varieties of orchids available in India, over 600 can be grown in the region due to favourable climactic conditions. In fact, approximately 200 varieties are unique to this region and 60 per cent of these are ornamental in nature with high demand at the international markets. It is also ideally suited to produce spices,

fruits and vegetables, flowers and herbs. Therefore, the north-east of India can emerge as an exporter of orchids, flowers, apple, orange, pineapples, spices, herbs, etc. Moreover, the forests of the north-east offer a vast array of aromatic plants which can be used in the aromatic industry for the manufacture of perfumes, incenses, etc. In fact, there is an increasing shift in focus from chemcial perfumes and room freshness and the international trend is towards natural one's. With proper planning there exists a scope for establishing the aromatic industy on the region.
2. The north-east of India is well-known for its bio-diversities and heritage sites.
Tawang in Arunachal Pradesh, Majuli, Kaziranga, Manas, Pabitara, etc., in Assam can be developed further as tourist spots for people from Europe and America. If modern transport and communication system between the ASEAN countries and India along with the requisite infrastructure facilities are developed, then tourists visiting the ASEAN countries are likely to extend their tour programmes to the north-eastern part of India, a few hundred km. away. In 1996, an internationally reputed consultancy firm, Coopers and Lybrand submitted a report to the Government of Assam, which states that if the vast tourism potentials of north-east India are fully tapped and developed, within 20 years the region will receive more tourists than Singapore or Bangkok. Because almost all the Western and Japanese tourists visiting South-East Asian region would fly or drive a few hundred km. more to enjoy the scenic and cultural beauties of the north-eastern region. This alone can boost the economy of the entire north-east. But for this, road and airways between the south-east region and India have to be developed.
3. Assam alone produces about 50 per cent of the country's tea and the tea industry in India needs new international markets. Thus the tea industry of Assam can find new outlets for exporting its products to the South-East Asian countries, if such regional economic co-operation is built up.

CONCLUSION

Since the acceptance of globalization by Indian and South-East Asian countries in the 1980s, India's trade has been taking a diametrically opposite direction from West to East. India's trade relations with

China and ASEAN countries have been growing at a rapid rate. The potentialities of further growth in India's trade with these countries are also immense. But the absence of a strong regional economic co-operation greatly impeded the tempo of this growth. It is true that along with the globalization of vices as well. These are the costs of development, one has to bear with grace. What is necessary is find out a trade-off. The economic benefits of the regional economic co-operation through trade would definitely outweigh the costs in the form of importation of vices, imaginary or real. To achieve such regional economic co-operation through trade, the physical linkages among the trading partners in the form of Trans-National Roadways, Railways, Waterways and Airways (wherever possible) are essential. A huge amount of capital expenditure could be necessary to build such infrastructural facilities. It is possible only through financial co-operation among all the trading partners and the international financial institutions.

REFERENCES

Baruah, Srinath, 'Trade Liberalisation, Trans-border Informal Trade and Economic Prospects of North-Eastern Region', paper presented at the seminar on 'Trans-border Trade in north-east Indians', organized by Society for Conflict Analysis and Resolution, New Delhi, and OKD Institute of Social/Change and Development, held at Guwahati, 28 July 1999.

——, 'Certain Observations on Informal Border Trade with Neighbouring Countries and Economic Prospects of North-Eastern Region with Special Reference to Assam', paper presented at the seminar on 'Assam Beyond 2000 – Economic Issues', held at Guwahati, 21–22 November 1998.

Centre for Monitoring Indian Economy (CMIE) Pvt. Ltd., *Foreign Trade and Balance of Payments*, Mumbai, October 2002.

Chongli, Wang, 'Developing and Promoting the Trade Relationship Between China and India', paper presented at the International Seminar on 'Regional Development in India and China', New Delhi, 19–20 November 1998.

'Coopers and Lybrand, Assam – A Guide for Investors', report submitted to the Government of Assam, 1996.

Ganguly, J.B., 'Traditional Patterns of Assam's Trans-Himalayan Border Trade', paper presented at the seminar on 'Trans-border Trade in North-East India', organized by Society for Conflict Analysis and Resolution,

New Delhi, and OKD Institute of Social Change and Development, held at Guwahati, 28 July 1999.

Ghanashyam, A.R., 'Cross Country Trade: Arunachal Pradesh – Retrospect and Prospect', paper presented at the national seminar on 'Cross Border Trade of Arunachal Pradesh: Retrospect and Prospect', Department of History, Arunachal Pradesh, Doimukh, 28–29 September 2001.

Goswami, H., 'Trans-border Trade of Arunachal Pradesh: Retrospect and Prospect', Department of History, Arunachal University, Doimukh, 28–29 September 2001.

Goswami, H. and Jayanta Kumar Gogoi, 'Formation of South Asian Free Trade Area (SAFTA) and its Impact on the Economy of the North-East India', paper presented at the seminar on 'Border Trade in North-East India: Perspectives, Issues and Problems', North-East India Council for Social Science Research, Shillong, 14–15 December 1998.

——, 'Economic Prospects of the Stilwell Road: An Analysis', *Assam Economic Journal*, vol. XV, 2002.

Govemement of India, 'Transforming the North-East, 'High Level Commission: Report to the Prime Minister of India', Planning Commission, New Delhi, March 1997.

Government of India and the Government of Myanmar, *Agreement Between the Government of the Republic of India and the Government of the Union of Myanmar on Border Trade*, signed in New Delhi on 21 Junuary 1995.

Misra, Udayan and Jayanta Kumar Gogoi, 'India's North-East: Exploring New Possibilities in Trade and Communication with Special Reference to China', paper presented at the International Seminar on 'Regional Development in India and China', New Delhi, 19–20 November 1998.

Research and Information System, 'India's Border Trade with Select Neighbouring Countries', New Delhi, 1996.

Saikia, Anup and Debabrata Das, 'Trade Possibilities: Where Does Arunachal Pradesh Stand?', paper presented in the national seminar on 'Cross Border Trade of Arunachal Pradesh: Retrospect and Prospect', Department of History, Arunachal Pradesh, Doimukh, 28–29 September 2001.

Sebastian, K.O., 'Trade Route of Pangsu Pass: Retrospect and Prospects', paper presented at the national seminar on 'Cross Border Trade of Arunachal Pradesh: Retrospect and Prospect', Department of History, Arunachal University, Doimukh, 28–29 September 2001.

Tiejun, Cheng, 'Promoting Communications Between China and India Based on Geographical Advantages', paper presented at the International Seminar on 'Regional Economic Development', New Delhi, 19–20 November 1998.

Yumnam, Amar, 'Indo-Myanmar Trade Through Moreh: Time to Sow, Time to Reap, paper presented at the seminar on 'Trans-border Trade in North-East India, organized by Society for Conflict Analysis and Resolution, New Delhi, and OKD Institute of Social Change and Development, held at Guwahati, 28 July 1999.

Zhimin, Che, 'Proposition on Formation of Sub-Regional Co-operation Zone of China, India, Myanmar and Bangladesh', paper presented at the International Seminar on 'Regional Development in India and China', New Delhi, 19–20 November 1998.

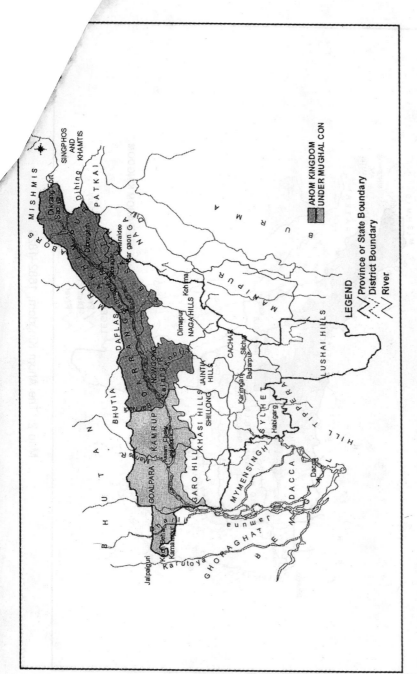

Map 1: The Ahom & The Mughal (Koch)

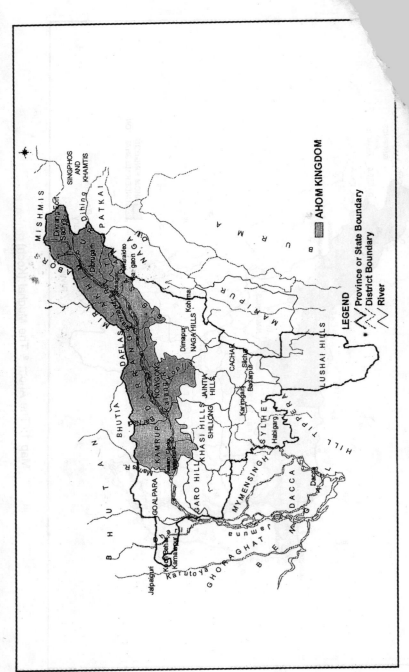

Map 2: The Ahom Kingdom, 1682–1826

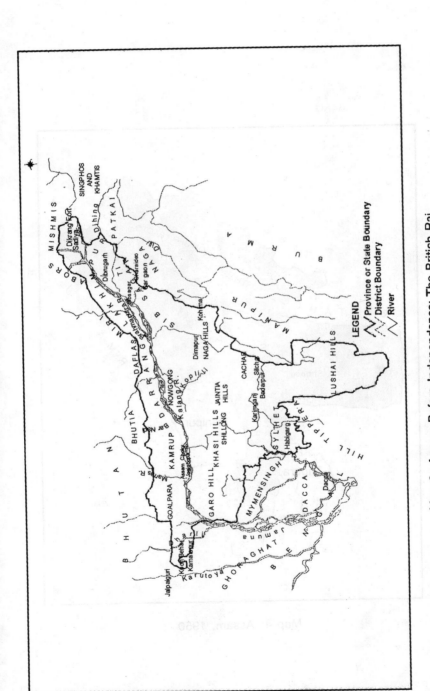

Map 3: Assam Before Independence: The British Raj

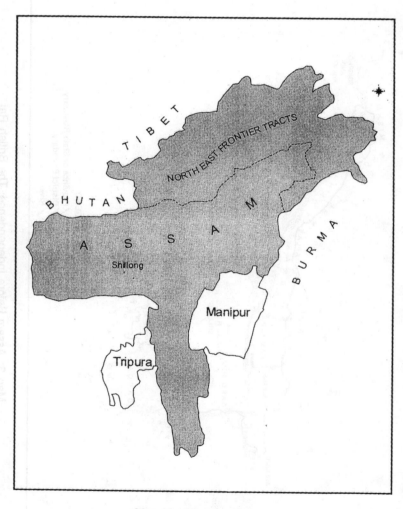

Map 4: Assam, 1950

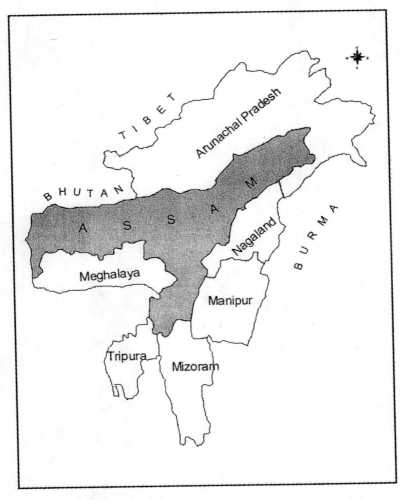

Map 5: Assam, 2005

Contributors

MANMOHAN AGARWAL is Professor of Economics at the International Trade and Development Division, School of International Studies, Jawaharlal Nehru University, New Delhi.

ARINDAM BANDYOPADHAYAY is a Faculty Research Associate at the National Institute of Bank Management, Pune.

BHUBAN CHANDRA BARAH is the principal economist, National Centre for Agricultural Economics and Policy Research, New Delhi.

ALOKESH BARUA, Professor of Economics at the International Trade and Development Division, School of International Studies, Jawaharlal Nehru University, New Delhi.

SANJIB BARUAH is Research Professor at CPR, New Delhi.

SUDIP RANJAN BASU is a Ph.D. candidate, Gradguate Institute of International Studies, University of Geneva, Switzerland. Also, Associate Economic Affairs Officer, UNCTAD, Geneva.

LODEWIJK BERLAGE is Professor of Economics, Catholic University, Leuven, Belgium.

MONICA DAS is a Ph.D. student at the University of California, Riverside, USA.

SANDWIP KUMAR DAS is a Professor of Economics at the International Trade and Development Division, School of International Studies, Jawaharlal Nehru University, New Delhi.

JAYANTA KUMAR GOGOI is Professor of Economics in Dibrugarh University, Dibrugarh, Assam.

HIREN GOHAIN was Professor of English literature in Gauhati University, Guwahati, Assam.

HOMESWAR GOSWAMI is Professor of Economics, Dibrugarh University, Dibrugarh, Assam.

CONTRIBUTORS

AMALENDU GUHA was Professor at the Centre for Studies in Social Sciences, Calcutta.

JAISHREE KONWARH is a Lecturer in Economics at DHSK College, Dibrugarh, Assam.

AJIT KUMAR NEOG is a senior member of Indian Economic Service, New Delhi.

HIRANYA NATH is Assistant Professor of Economics in Sam Houston State University, USA.

HARPRASAD RAY was Professor in the faculty of Chinese Studies at Jawaharlal Nehru University, New Delhi.

SANTANU ROY is Associate Professor of Economics at Southern Methodist University, USA.

GULSHAN SACHDEVA is Associate Professor at the Centre for Russian Studies, Jawaharlal Nehru University, New Delhi.

DIPANKAR SENGUPTA is a Research Fellow in the Center de Sciences Humaines, New Delhi.